The Princeton Review®

Cracking the

ASVAB

Fourth Edition

PrincetonReview.com

DATE DUE

Penguin
Random
House

The Princeton Review
555 W. 18th Street
New York, NY 10011
E-mail: editorialsupport@review.com

Copyright © 2017 by TPR Education IP Holdings, LLC. All rights reserved.

Published in the United States by Penguin Random House LLC, New York, and in Canada by Random House of Canada, a division of Penguin Random House Ltd., Toronto.

ISBN 978-1-101-92072-5
ISSN 1551-6407

Editor: Selena Coppock
Production Editors: Liz Rutzel, Dallin Law
Production Artist: Deborah A. Silvestrini

The Princeton Review is not affiliated with Princeton University.

ASVAB is a registered trademark of the United States Department of Defense, which is not affiliated with The Princeton Review.

Printed in the United States of America on partially recycled paper.

10   9   8   7   6   5   4   3   2   1

Fourth Edition

Editorial

Rob Franek, Editor-in-Chief
Casey Cornelius, VP Content Development
Mary Beth Garrick, Director of Production
Selena Coppock, Managing Editor
Meave Shelton, Senior Editor
Colleen Day, Editor
Sarah Litt, Editor
Aaron Riccio, Editor
Orion McBean, Editorial Assistant

Penguin Random House Publishing Team

Tom Russell, VP, Publisher
Alison Stoltzfus, Publishing Director
Jake Eldred, Associate Managing Editor
Ellen Reed, Production Manager
Suzanne Lee, Designer

Acknowledgments

The editor would like to thank Clarissa Constantine and Derek Humphrey for their hard work and expertise in content development and proofing of the fourth edition of this book.

Contents

Register Your

1 Go to **PrincetonReview.com/cracking**

2 You'll see a welcome page where you can register your book using the following ISBN: 9781101920725

3 After placing this free order, you'll either be asked to log in or to answer a few simple questions in order to set up a new Princeton Review account.

4 Finally, click on the "Student Tools" tab located at the top of the screen. It may take an hour or two for your registration to go through, but after that, you're good to go.

If you have noticed potential content errors, please e-mail EditorialSupport@review.com with the full title of the book, its ISBN number (located above), and the page number of the error.

Experiencing technical issues? Please e-mail TPRStudentTech@review.com with the following information:

- your full name
- e-mail address used to register the book
- full book title and ISBN
- your computer OS (Mac or PC) and Internet browser (Firefox, Safari, Chrome, etc.)
- description of technical issue

Book Online!

Once you've registered, you can...

- Get more practice with assorted drills from different sections of the ASVAB
- Read through lists of Army-Enlisted careers, Navy-Enlisted careers, Army-Officer careers, and more
- Access crucial information about assorted military academies
- Plan out your test preparation with a Study Guide
- Check to see if there have been any corrections or updates to this edition

Look For These Icons Throughout The Book

Proven Techniques

Study Break

Applied Strategies

More Great Books

The **Princeton** Review®

Part I
Orientation

Chapter 1
Introduction

WHAT IS THE ASVAB?

The ASVAB, which stands for Armed Services Vocational Aptitude Battery, is a free test used by the armed services to assess the abilities of recruits and to help place them in the most suitable jobs. The test is given to more than one million people each year, and it's been around since the late 1960s. The ASVAB serves many purposes and is administered in three different forms. There are essentially two versions of the test: a computerized format and a paper and pencil version. The computerized format, the CAT-ASVAB is like a mini-ASVAB (more on that later) and the paper and pencil format is called the MET-site or Student ASVAB. Let's do a quick run down of what to expect from each.

The CAT-ASVAB contains 10 subtests.

Subtests	Minutes	Questions	Description
General Science (GS)	8	16	Measures knowledge of life science, earth and space science, and physical science
Arithmetic Reasoning (AR)	39	16	Measures ability to solve basic math problems
Word Knowledge (WK)	8	16	Measures ability to understand the meaning of words through synonyms
Paragraph Comprehension (PC)	22	11	Measures ability to obtain information from written materials
Mathematics Knowledge (MK)	20	16	Measures knowledge of mathematical concepts and applications
Electronics Information (EI)	8	16	Measures knowledge of electrical current, circuits, devices, and electronic systems
Auto Information (AI)	7	11	Measures knowledge of automotive maintenance and repair
Shop Information (SI)	6	11	Measures knowledge of wood and metal shop practices
Mechanical Comprehension (MC)	20	16	Measures knowledge of the principles of mechanical devices, structural support, and properties of materials
Assembling Objects (AO)	15	16	Measures spatial and problem-solving activities
TOTAL	153	145	

Note: Prospective Navy recruits also take the Coding Speed (CS) test. This test used to be one of the ASVAB subtests. CS is now a special test used only by the Navy for classification into some Navy specialties.

The MET-site ASVAB and the Student ASVAB are administered on paper and contain 8 subtests.

Subtests	Minutes	Questions	Description
General Science (GS)	11	25	Measures knowledge of life science, earth and space science, and physical science
Arithmetic Reasoning (AR)	36	30	Measures ability to solve basic math problems
Word Knowledge (WK)	11	35	Measures ability to understand the meaning of words through synonyms
Paragraph Comprehension (PC)	13	15	Measures ability to obtain information from written materials
Mathematics Knowledge (MK)	24	25	Measures knowledge of mathematical concepts and applications
Electronics Information (EI)	9	20	Measures knowledge of electrical current, circuits, devices, and electronic systems
Auto & Shop Information (AI)	11	25	Measures knowledge of automotive maintenance and repair and wood and metal shop practices
Mechanical Comprehension (MC)	19	25	Measures knowledge of the principles of mechanical devices, structural support, and properties of materials
TOTAL	134	200	

You'll notice that the Assembling Objects section doesn't appear on the MET-site or Student ASVAB. We have an Assembling Objects section in Practice Test 1, but don't worry about that material if you are planning on taking the MET-site or Student ASVAB.

WHY DO YOU NEED THE ASVAB?

The ASVAB is required to enlist in the Armed Forces. Just as college admissions officers use SAT scores to predict student performance, recruiters will use your ASVAB scores to predict where you would best fit within the military. *You can't fail the ASVAB.* However, if you don't score as well as you'd like, you can retake the test. In fact, you can even retake the test once you're already enlisted, should you decide that you'd like to qualify for a different military career.

After taking the ASVAB, you receive several scores, two of which are used by all the service branches: The VE (Verbal Expression) score and the AFQT (Armed Forces Qualification Test) score. Your AFQT score is the most important ASVAB score because it determines if you can enlist in a particular branch of the military. The Armed Forces converts your ASVAB test scores into 10 other composite score areas known as "line scores," which determine what branch of the military an individual may qualify for. Learn more about the specifics of this by visiting www.careersinthemilitary.com. In a few pages we'll discuss this further.

THE MANY FACES OF THE ASVAB

Let's learn more about those three types of ASVAB tests that we just mapped out.

The CAT-ASVAB

This is how most potential recruits take the test and as we mentioned earlier, it's like a mini-ASVAB that isn't a qualifying test, rather it's a recruiting tool. You may have noticed that there are fewer questions on the CAT-ASVAB than on the MET-site or Student. That's because this version of the ASVAB isn't a qualifying test—it's like a mini-ASVAB that is used as a recruiting tool. It's used to get a sense of an applicant's probability of obtaining qualifying ASVAB scores. So you'd be wise to prepare for the MET-site or Student ASVAB and all that those entail. CAT stands for Computer Adaptive Test. This means that the computer picks each question based on how you answered the previous one. In other words, if you keep getting questions right, the computer will throw out harder questions in order to challenge you. If you get a question wrong, however, the computer will adjust the test's difficulty accordingly —and you should note that once you've answered a question, you can't go back and change it. You actually want to reach for those harder questions early on, so you can start at the top; it's more difficult to score high on a CAT if you are only asked easy questions. The CAT-ASVAB is divided into 10 subtests (the Auto & Shop subtest is broken down into two subtests). You can take the CAT-ASVAB at your own pace and, unlike the MET-site ASVAB, you can leave as soon as you're done. However, the CAT-ASVAB does have a time limit, so you will still need to practice good time management.

The MET-site ASVAB

The MET-site ASVAB is given at a Mobile Examination Test site, and you need to be referred by a recruiter to take it. The MET takes a little more than 2 hours and contains 8 subtests (in this one, the Auto and Shop Information tests are combined). The MET-site is a pen and paper test, which means you can change your answers if you need to. But be sure to completely erase all the changes you make—the answer sheet scanner is very sensitive.

The Student ASVAB

The Student ASVAB (often called the Paper & Pencil ASVAB or the P&P ASVAB) is primarily used as a way for high school and college students to explore different career paths and is given in high schools, colleges, and vocational schools. Like the MET-site ASVAB, this is a multiple-choice pen and paper test. Just like the MET-site we discussed in the paragraph above, the Student ASVAB takes a little over 2 hours and is composed of 8 subtests. Although this version is mainly intended as a guide to career exploration, you still receive an AFQT military qualification score, and you can use your test results to enlist if you decide to do so.

THE SUBTESTS

Each subtest is designed to assess different skills. Some of the subtests are very straightforward and simply assess your knowledge level in a particular area. Others are designed to measure how well you perform under time constraints. Let's look at each subtest now.

General Science

General Science tests your ability to answer questions on a variety of science topics drawn from courses taught in most high schools: life science, earth and space science, and physical science. The life science items cover botany, zoology, anatomy, physiology, and ecology. The earth and space science items measure force and motion mechanics, energy, fluids, atomic structure, and chemistry. If you're not familiar with these subjects, be sure to read the review chapter carefully and spend extra time on those areas that seem the most foreign.

Arithmetic Reasoning

Arithmetic Reasoning is one factor that helps characterize mathematics comprehension; it also assesses logical thinking. The Arithmetic Reasoning subtest measures your ability to solve basic arithmetic problems encountered in everyday life. One-step and multi-step word problems require addition, subtraction, multiplication, division, and knowledge of the correct order of operations when more than one step is necessary. The test items include operations with whole numbers, operations with rational numbers, ratio and proportion, interest and percentage, and measurement. If you're weak in any of these areas, you had better practice, since every question on this test requires at least one of these skills and usually more.

Word Knowledge

Word Knowledge tests your ability to understand the meaning of words through synonyms (words that have the same or nearly the same meaning). There shouldn't be too many surprises. But since the CAT-ASVAB gives you 8 minutes to answer 16 questions, the hard part of this test is getting through it all. We'll talk about how to deal with the time pressure later on.

Paragraph Comprehension

Paragraph Comprehension tests your ability to obtain information from written material. You'll read different types of passages of varying lengths and respond to questions based on information presented in each passage. You should know how to identify stated and reworded facts, determine a sequence of events, draw conclusions, identify main ideas, determine the author's purpose and tone, and identify style and technique. As with Word Knowledge, the challenge will be to manage your time in this section: the MET-site and Student ASVABs only give you 13 minutes to answer 15 questions, and that includes time for reading the passages. Later on, we'll discuss techniques that will help you save time and improve your accuracy on this section.

Mathematics Knowledge

The Mathematics Knowledge subtest measures your ability to solve problems by applying your knowledge of mathematical concepts and applications. The problems focus on concepts and algorithms, including number theory, numeration, and probability. Luckily, there is no trigonometry or calculus on this test. You are given 18 minutes to solve 16 questions (24 minutes to solve 25 problems on the MET-site and Student ASVAB tests), which is difficult for many test takers. Don't worry, though—we will talk about time-saving techniques later.

Electronics Information

Electronics Information tests your understanding of electrical current, circuits, devices, and systems. The topics on the test include electrical current and circuits, tools, symbols, devices, and materials. If you're familiar with these subjects, the questions shouldn't be too challenging.

Auto and Shop Information

The Auto and Shop Information subtest measures your aptitude for automotive maintenance and repair and wood and metal shop practices. (In the CAT-ASVAB this section is split into two parts, one for automotive knowledge and one for wood and metal shop knowledge.) The test covers areas commonly included in most high school auto and shop courses, such as automotive components, automotive systems and tools, troubleshooting and repair, building materials, and building and construction procedures.

Mechanical Comprehension

The Mechanical Comprehension subtest assesses your knowledge of principles of mechanical devices, structural support, and properties of materials. Topics include simple machines, compound machines, mechanical motion, and fluid dynamics. If you're familiar with these subjects, the test shouldn't be too difficult for you. If you're not, you may have a hard time with it, so be sure to carefully review the chapter in this book on Mechanical Comprehension.

Assembling Objects

This section is only found on the CAT-ASVAB, and the purpose of this subtest is to assess your ability to visualize three-dimensional objects that have been broken down into their component pieces. This subtest is typically used to see if a person would be a good fit for mechanic, electronic, or similarly skilled jobs. Each question presents a drawing of a disassembled three-dimensional object and four pictures. Your job is to choose the picture that depicts what the object looks like when all the parts are properly assembled. Assembling Objects has 16 questions, and you are given 15 minutes to answer them.

YOUR SCORE

The ASVAB is used as a qualification test for the armed services. It is designed to measure general abilities in various subjects. You'll receive a separate score for each subtest, as well as three academic composite scores. The three composite scores measure your academic achievement and assess your ability to learn more through further training. These three scores are generated as follows:

The Verbal Ability Composite adds the scores from the Word Knowledge and Paragraph Comprehension tests. It is intended to measure the student's capacity for verbal activities.

The Math Ability Composite adds the scores from the Arithmetic Reasoning and Mathematics Knowledge tests. It is intended to measure the student's capacity for mathematical activities.

The Academic Ability Composite adds the scores from the Verbal Ability Composite and Math Ability Composite. It is intended to indicate the student's potential for further education.

Recruiters use these composites to help identify areas in which the potential enlistee may be successful.

The AFQT

On the ASVAB the minimum score you must receive to enlist in the armed services is called the Armed Forces Qualifying Test (AFQT) score. That score is the one that matters the most when you're enlisting, and it differs for each branch of the military. While the minimum score may be different, how the score is generated is the same for all branches. The scores from the Arithmetic Reasoning, Word Knowledge, Paragraph Comprehension, and Mathematics Knowledge tests are combined to generate a raw score.

(Word Knowledge score × 2) + (Paragraph Comprehension score × 2) + (Arithmetic Reasoning score) + (Mathematics Knowledge score) = your raw score.

That raw score is then converted into a percentile score from 1 to 99. Your percentile score tells you how well you did on the ASVAB compared to other people. For example, if you score in the 50th percentile, that means you scored higher than 49% of the people who take the test. Each branch of the military has a minimum percentile score they require of new recruits. Here's the breakdown.

Military Branch	Minimum Score: GED	Required AFQT Score
Air Force	65	36
Army	50	31
Coast Guard	50	40
Marines	50	32
National Guard	50	31
Navy	50	35

Please Note: These scores are subject to change without notice. This list is up-to-date as of January 2017, but you may wish to do some research online to see if these have changed. See page 12 for specific URLs.

Note that if you have a GED instead of a high school degree, you will need a *much* higher minimum score than the score required for high school graduates. On extremely rare occasions, a recruiter may accept a slightly lower score if the potential enlistee has other qualifications.

Tip: Your test score is based on the number of items you have answered correctly in the allotted time; you are not penalized for wrong answers. That's why you should guess if you do not know the answer or if you start to run out of time.

Military Careers Score

Your AFQT score determines your eligibility to join a certain branch of the military. Composite scores from individual subtests are also used to determine specific job qualifications.

You also receive a Military Careers score when you take the ASVAB. This score is used to help recruits determine their chances of qualifying for various occupations within the military. It is a combination of the scores from the Academic Ability Composite and the Mechanical Comprehension and Electronics Information tests. The score range is 140 to 240, with an average of 200. When receiving their test results, recruits receive a copy of the book *Military Careers*. *Military Careers* describes most of the positions available in the armed services, along with the requirements for the job, the training provided, civilian counterparts, and a graph showing chances of acceptance based on the Military Careers score. For example, a recruit with a Military Careers score of 215 stands a 90% chance of qualifying for a job as a diver, whereas someone with a 175 has less than a 10% chance of qualifying. In addition, you can find a number of charts detailing career paths based on Military Careers score at www.military.com.

The test scores from the General Science and Auto and Shop Information subtests are not used to derive the percentile score or the Military Careers score. Rather, they are used by recruiters to help identify other areas in which the recruit may be successful. It's important to note that the recruiter only looks at these scores if the recruit has scored above the minimum percentile score required by that branch. If you don't achieve a high enough score on the Arithmetic Reasoning, Word Knowledge, Paragraph Comprehension, and Mathematics Knowledge subtests, you won't be able to enlist.

Retesting

Each branch of the military has its own policy for retesting. In general, a retest is not allowed for the sole purpose of improving your score unless the initial score was below the minimum requirement. The Air Force, Army, and Marine Corps allow a person who has scored above the minimum requirement to retake the test if something unusual happened during the test and there is evidence that the score does not accurately represent that person's true ability. The Navy only allows a retest if there is evidence of improvement in education or language ability, such as graduating from high school, and if there is a reason for the retest, such as a test taker's desire to qualify for a particular job.

If the recruiter determines that a retest is appropriate, the potential enlistee must wait at least 30 days after taking the first test to take the test again. If the potential enlistee needs to take the test for a third time, that individual must wait at least six months before taking the ASVAB again. All of these scores stay on a potential enlistee's record for two years. When determining eligibility, the military looks at the most recent score.

FOR MORE INFORMATION

For more information on the ASVAB, the enlistment process, the qualifying scores for particular jobs, or the details of careers in the military, contact your local recruiter or check out the websites below.

Air Force:	www.airforce.com
Army:	www.goarmy.com
Marine Corps:	www.marines.com
Navy:	www.navy.com

TAKING CONTROL OF THE ASVAB

By buying this book, you've taken an important first step toward doing well on the ASVAB. Here's how to get the most out of your purchase.

How to Use This Book

- **Subject Review Chapters**: We've reviewed the most important concepts that you may see on the ASVAB and arranged these concepts in order of importance on the test. As you read through the chapters, take notes on the main points. Many people find that they remember things better if they write them down. You may also find it helpful to underline or highlight important concepts in the book.

- **Pre-Quizzes and Quick Quizzes**: To reinforce the important concepts, we've included Pre-Quizzes and Quick Quizzes in the review chapters. Use these quizzes to get a sense of where you are as you launch into subject review and as you complete content review in order to test your understanding of the material you've just studied. If you miss several questions, you know you will need to spend a little more time studying before you move on.

- **Practice ASVAB Tests**: At the back of the book you'll find three full-length practice ASVABs. (Since it's a little hard to fit a whole computer into this book, we can't really simulate a CAT-ASVAB for you.) The practice tests we've included follow the MET-ASVAB and Student ASVAB versions insofar as the number of questions and sections are concerned. We've made these tests as similar to real ASVABs as possible. We suggest you use one test as an assessment of your strengths and weaknesses *before* you begin to study. This will give you an idea of what you really need to focus on during your preparation. Use the second as a full, timed practice test to get an idea of what taking the real test will be like once you've completed your subject review. Then use the third practice test in the days leading up to your actual test date so that you're completely comfortable with the test, the order of sections, and the timing.

- **Answer Explanations**: We have provided an explanation for every question in the practice tests and all the Quick Quizzes. Use these to review questions you answered incorrectly and for tips on how to get them right the next time.

- **Key Terms**: Chapter 4 contains a list of words that every ASVAB taker should know. While we can't guarantee that you will see these words on the test, we wouldn't be surprised if at least a few of them popped up. In addition, they serve as a good assessment of your vocabulary. If you know most of the words on this list, you're probably in pretty good shape. If a lot of them look unfamiliar to you, you better start studying!

Developing Your Study Strategy

The first thing you should do to start preparing for the ASVAB is to develop a strategy. Set up a realistic schedule for studying and stick to it. But before you decide how to allocate your time, take a full-length practice test. This will help you identify what you need to focus on. If you're interested in a particular job opportunity, ask your recruiter which tests are important for that job. You may be able to ignore complete sections of the test if they're not needed for what you want to do.

Here are some more study strategies we recommend you follow as you prepare to take the ASVAB exam.

1. Establish a realistic timeline for taking the ASVAB exam. Pick a date (2–3 months down the road) to take the ASVAB exam and develop a realistic study plan. Develop a schedule that allows you to study at a steady pace. Make a plan that you feel comfortable with, but don't put off studying until the last minute. In your study plan you should set aside time every day to study. You must discipline yourself to study during your study time.

2. Tip: Set aside 1–2 hours a day, study for 20 minutes at a time and take a 5-minute break after every 20 minutes. Get up and move around during your break to get your blood flowing. Blood flow sends oxygen to the brain and makes you more alert.

3. Practice taking the ASVAB test. The saying "practice makes perfect" is really true. In addition to the tests in *Cracking the ASVAB*, you can take full-length practice ASVAB tests for free at **www.military.com**. Take as many practice exams as you can.

4. Set aside a place for study and study only! Find a specific place that you can use for studying (for example, a library, vacant classrooms, quiet areas in your home, etc.). You are trying to build a habit of studying when you are in this place, so it is important that you do not use your study space for social conversations, playing on the Internet, talking or texting family/friends on the telephone, daydreaming, etc. Make sure your study area has good lighting, ventilation, a comfortable chair (but not too comfortable), and a desk large enough to spread out your materials. Also, ensure that your study area does not have a distracting view of other activities that you want to be involved in: a telephone, a loud stereo, a TV, or a family or friends who want to talk a lot.

5. Divide your work into small, short-range goals. It is important that you don't set a goal that's too vague and/or too large. For example, don't say: "I am going to spend all weekend studying!" You'll only set yourself up for failure.

Tip for Setting Realistic Goals
Take a block of time that you have set aside for study and set an attainable study goal for that time period. For example

From 3:00 P.M.–5:00 P.M. on Sunday, I will read chapters 4–6 of Cracking the ASVAB *and take notes in my own words.*

Set your goal when you sit down to study but before you begin to work. Set a goal that you can reach. You may, in fact, do more than your goal, but set a reasonable goal even if it seems too easy.

6. Make flashcards. Flashcards are perfect for use as a learning drill to aid memorization by way of repetition. Flashcards can be a great help to learn simple and complex concepts for a variety of subjects, such as science, math, and vocabulary. Copy words from our Key Terms List onto index cards and write the definitions on the back. Use them to help you memorize formulas for algebra and geometry and to remember unfamiliar science vocabulary. Carry these cards with you and practice with them while you're waiting for the bus or the train, or in line at the post office—anywhere you can't take a book with you!

7. When taking the practice tests, make sure you're in a quiet area where you won't be disturbed. If you're taking a full, timed test or a timed drill, make sure to use a clock, watch, or timer. Try to take the second and third practice tests all in one sitting—just as if you were taking the real thing. You won't be given any breaks between the sections, so try not to take any on the practice tests either. In other words, make them as much like the real ASVAB as possible.

Give Me A Break!
Be careful that you don't burn yourself out with studying for too many hours in a row. Give yourself a break every so often—go for a walk, get a snack, listen to some music.

Test-Day Strategies
Here are some tips to keep in mind for the big test day.

- Stay relaxed and confident. Remember that you've worked hard to prepare for this test and are going to do well. If you feel you're getting nervous, close your eyes and take a few slow, deep breaths to relax. Do this at least several times. Try not to talk to other students before a test; anxiety can become contagious.
- Answer every question. Any questions that you leave blank will be graded as incorrect, so your best bet is to simply take a guess and fill in an answer even if you have no idea. If you can't figure out an answer, take a guess.
- Be careful when you answer questions. Make sure you're marking the answer for the right question. Most incorrect answers are due to sloppiness.

- The day of the test make sure you get a good night's sleep and have a healthy breakfast. Dress comfortably, and make sure you have your ID card with you. Arrive at the testing site early.

HOW TO CRACK THE ASVAB

In addition to providing a thorough review of the material on the ASVAB, we've developed some test-taking techniques that will help you boost your score and make the test easier. Some techniques work great for the entire test, while others work just for a particular section or type of question. Below are some techniques that will help throughout the entire test. Techniques specific to a particular section or question type will be covered in the respective review chapter.

Pace Yourself

While you want to work at a pace that ensures you answer as many questions as possible, you don't want to work too fast. Working too fast causes you to make careless mistakes. This is especially important with the early questions in each section. Questions on the CAT-ASVAB are weighted. When a question is answered correctly, the computer chooses a harder question worth more points. But when a question is answered incorrectly, the computer chooses an easier question worth fewer points.

If you rush and answer a lot of the early questions incorrectly, the computer will choose only easy questions worth fewer points. So try to work at a pace that allows you to answer as many questions as possible without affecting your accuracy, and then use our Process of Elimination technique, detailed below, to guess on the remaining questions if you are running out of time.

Process of Elimination

The ASVAB is a multiple-choice test. That means you get to see the correct answer for every question on the test—it's one of the four choices you're given. You also get to see three incorrect answers. Your job is to pick out the correct answer from among the incorrect answers. If you don't know the answer right away, your best option is to use a technique called Process of Elimination (POE for short). Process of Elimination is the single most important tool you can use on any standardized test.

Since the CAT-ASVAB requires you to choose an answer to each question before moving on, you may have to guess on some questions. POE is useful because it helps you get rid of the answers that you know are wrong, thereby increasing your chances of finding the right answer. Every time you can eliminate an answer choice, your chances of choosing the correct answer increases.

Applied Strategies
Process of Elimination—what we call POE—is a classic strategy that can make even the toughest of questions a bit easier.

Try the following question:

1. What is the capital of Malawi?

If you happen to be from Malawi, this question will be easy for you. If not, then probably all you can do is guess, but you might be able to improve your chances of guessing correctly by using POE. Let's look at the answer choices:

    A.   Washington, D.C.
    B.   Paris
    C.   London
    D.   Lilongwe

You may not know the answer, but three of the choices are obviously wrong. This leaves you with only one answer—(D)—the correct one!

Even when POE doesn't get rid of all of the wrong answers, it can still help you. Let's look at another example:

2. What is the capital of Qatar?

    A.   Paris
    B.   Doha
    C.   Tokyo
    D.   Dukham

This time you can probably eliminate only two obvious wrong choices. That leaves you with two to choose from. But that's still much better than where you started from—you're much more likely to choose the correct answer—(B)—when you have only two choices, instead of four.

As you work through this book, keep some scrap paper handy. When you answer a question, write A, B, C, and D on the paper. As you work through the answer choices, use your pencil to cross off answers that you can eliminate. The paper test doesn't allow you to write in the test booklet, and obviously you can't write on the computer test either, so it's a good idea to get used to using scrap paper. If you practice this now, it will be second nature when you take the real thing!

Your Scrap Paper

You will be given scrap paper on which to do your work. Use it! It is much easier to work out problems on paper than in your head. Using scrap paper also helps you avoid careless mistakes. This is particularly important on the Arithmetic Reasoning and Mathematics Knowledge subtests. Many of the questions in these two tests require several steps to solve. Trying to solve them in your head will only lead to mistakes and slow you down. In addition, you can use your scrap paper to help you with POE, as we discussed earlier.

In Conclusion

As you work through the book, pay attention to different techniques as we discuss them. There are some great tricks that will help you with particular questions. Some of the hardest questions on the test become much easier once you know how to handle them.

Part II
How to Crack
the ASVAB

Chapter 2
Arithmetic
Reasoning

INTRODUCTION TO THE ARITHMETIC REASONING SECTION

The Arithmetic Reasoning subtest measures your understanding of basic arithmetic, including concepts such as fractions, exponents, square roots, and percents. The Met-ASVAB and Student ASVAB version consists of 30 questions, and you are given 36 minutes to complete it. The CAT-ASVAB has 16 questions, and you have 39 minutes to complete it. In this chapter we will review everything you need to know to do well; the key to improving in math, however, is practice. Make sure to learn the concepts and then do the Quick Quizzes and practice tests.

Study Tips for the Math Sections

- Learn the definitions to all of the terms we introduce; you will need them!
- When you're taking the test, use the scrap paper provided. Trying to solve problems in your head only leads to mistakes.
- Draw pictures to help clarify the problem.
- Break the question up into bite-size pieces.
- After you get an answer, double-check your work.
- Ballpark when appropriate.

MATH TERMINOLOGY

Before we begin our review, it is important that you know the definitions to some math terms that you will see.

Term	Definition	Example
Average (or "Mean")	The midway point in a series of numbers	The average of 10 and 20 is 15
Denominator	The bottom number in a fraction	In the fraction $\frac{1}{3}$, the 3 is the denominator
Difference	The result of subtraction	The difference of 5 – 3 is 2
Dividend	The number being divided	The dividend in 10 ÷ 5 is 10
Divisor	The number you are dividing by	The divisor in 10 ÷ 5 is 5
Even	Any integer that is divisible by 2	2, 4, 6, 14, 20, 34, 100...
Exponent	A small raised number next to a big number that indicates how many times to multiply the big number by	The 2 is the exponent in 3^2
Improper Fraction	A fraction with a larger numerator than denominator	$\frac{10}{4}$
Integer	A number that doesn't contain a fraction or a decimal	–5, –4, 0, 4, 5...
Mixed Number	A number that contains both an integer and a fraction	$6\frac{1}{4}$
Negative Number	Any number less than zero	–7, –0.25...
Numerator	The top number in a fraction	In the fraction $\frac{1}{3}$, the 1 is the numerator
Odd	A number not divisible by 2	–3, –1, 1, 3, 5, 11...
Positive Number	Any number greater than zero	1, 4, 0.25...
Prime Number	A number divisible only by 1 and itself 1 is not considered a prime number. All prime numbers are odd except for 2.	2, 3, 5, 7, 11, 13...
Product	The result of multiplication	The product of 2 × 2 is 4
Quotient	The result of division	The quotient of 10 ÷ 5 is 2
Ratio	A relationship between two quantities	1:2, 4:5, 9:10
Sum	The result of addition	The sum of 5 + 5 is 10
Square Root	A factor of a number that, when squared, equals that number	$\sqrt{9} = 3$
Whole Number	All the positive integers and zero	0, 1, 2, 3, 4, 12, 400...

PRE-QUIZ 1

1. $7 + 6 =$ _____

2. $12 - 5 =$ _____

3. $15 + -8 =$ _____

4. $-3 + 4 =$ _____

5. $6 \times 4 =$ _____

6. $-5 \times 8 =$ _____

7. $42 \div 6 =$ _____

8. $75 \div 15 =$ _____

THE NUMBER LINE

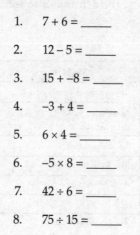

A number line allows you to see the relationship between numbers.

- Zero is a neutral number. It is neither positive nor negative.
- Positive numbers are numbers greater than zero. They lie to the right of zero on the number line.
- Negative numbers are numbers less than zero. They lie to the left of zero on the number line.

Number lines can be useful when adding and subtracting negative numbers.

1. $-5 + 4 = ?$

When you are adding a positive number, go right on the number line.

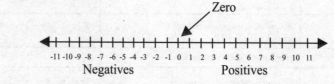

Start at -5 and count 4 to the right. That takes you to -1. That's the answer!

2. $-2 + -3 = ?$

When you are adding a negative number, go left on the number line.

Start at –2 and count 3 to the left. That takes you to –5. That's the answer!

3. 5 – 4 = ?

When you are subtracting a positive number, go left on the number line.

Start at 5 and count to the left 4. That takes you to 1. That's the answer!

4. 5 – –1 = ?

Subtracting a negative number is just like adding a positive number. Change both negative signs to one positive sign.

5. 5 + 1 = ?

Start at 5 and move 1 to the right, since you are now adding. That takes you to 6. That's the answer!

Quick Tip!

Whenever you see two negative signs next to each other, like this: 5 – –3 = , automatically turn the negative signs into an addition sign and simply add the numbers: 5 + 3 = 8.

MULTIPLICATION AND DIVISION
You need to know your multiplication table for the ASVAB.

×	1	2	3	4	5	6	7	8	9	10
1	1	2	3	4	5	6	7	8	9	10
2	2	4	6	8	10	12	14	16	18	20
3	3	6	9	12	15	18	21	24	27	30
4	4	8	12	16	20	24	28	32	36	40
5	5	10	15	20	25	30	35	40	45	50
6	6	12	18	24	30	36	42	48	54	60
7	7	14	21	28	35	42	49	56	63	70
8	8	16	24	32	40	48	56	64	72	80
9	9	18	27	36	45	54	63	72	81	90
10	10	20	30	40	50	60	70	80	90	100

There's no way around it: memorizing this table is essential to doing multiplication problems. But there are a few tricks to help you out. Do you notice any patterns in the table? Look at the 9s column. $9 \times 1 = 9, 9 \times 2 = 18, 9 \times 3 = 27$, and so forth. When you multiply 9 by any number from 1 to 10 you always get an answer whose digits add up to 9. For example, look at $9 \times 4 = 36$. The digits of the product, 36, add up to 9: $3 + 6 = 9$. Or take $9 \times 8 = 72$. The digits of the product, 72, also add up to 9: $7 + 2 = 9$. And so on. Another trick you can use with the 9s is to look at the number you are multiplying the 9 by. The first number in the product will be one less than that number. For example, look at $9 \times 4 = 36$ again. We are multiplying 9 by 4 so the product will start with a 3. This works whenever you are multiplying by a number between 2 and 9.

Another pattern you can use works with the 10s column. Do you see the pattern in the table above? Whenever you multiply 10 by a number, all you have to do is add a zero to that number. For example, $2 \times 10 = 20$ and $9 \times 10 = 90$.

Rules for Multiplying

Here are some more rules to remember when you're multiplying.

- Positive number × Positive number = Positive number

    $2 \times 4 = 8$ [2, 4, and 8 are all positive.]

- Negative number × Negative number = Positive number

    $-2 \times -4 = 8$ [–2 and –4 are negative, and 8 is positive.]

- Positive number × Negative number = Negative number

    $2 \times -4 = 8$ [2 is positive, –4 is negative, and –8 is negative.]

Factorials

When you see the term *factorial*, you're being asked to multiply. You can see factorial questions written in two ways:

5 factorial   or   5!

When you see either of these, do this:

$$1 \times 2 \times 3 \times 4 \times 5 =$$

Then multiply out what you've got:

$$1 \times 2 = 2 \times 3 = 6 \times 4 = 24 \times 5 = 120$$

Division

Division is the opposite of multiplication. Division can be expressed in the following ways:

$$10 \div 5 \quad \text{or} \quad 5\overline{)10} \quad \text{or} \quad 10/5 \text{ (which is the same as } \frac{10}{5} \text{)}$$

- If you see the ÷ sign between two numbers, the number before the ÷ is being divided by the number that comes after the ÷.

- If you see the $\overline{)}$ sign, the number on the outside is being divided into the number on the inside.

- If you see numbers in this form, 10/5 or $\frac{10}{5}$, the number on top is being divided by the number on the bottom.

The number that you are dividing by is called the **divisor,** and the number you are dividing into is the **dividend**. In this example:

$$10 \div 5 = 2$$

10 is the dividend and 5 is the divisor. The result, 2, is called the **quotient**. You can check your division by multiplying the quotient by the divisor. If you've divided correctly, the product of the quotient and the divisor should be equal to the dividend. To check the example above we would multiply the quotient, 2, by the divisor, 5.

$$2 \times 5 = 10$$

We ended up with the dividend, 10, so our division was correct. This is another reason why it's so important you know your multiplication tables well!

Let's look at another example.

$$10 \div 3 =$$

In the example above, the divisor doesn't divide into the dividend an even number of times. So we are going to have a **remainder**. A remainder is what is left over after you divide. In this example, 3 divides into 10 three times for a total of 9, with 1 left over. In other words, the remainder is 1. Let's check our work.

$$3 \times 3 = 9 \text{ plus our remainder of } 1$$
$$9 + 1 = 10$$

<u>Note:</u> The remainder in a division problem will always be smaller than the divisor. Think about it like this: If you divided 25 shirts among 5 friends and gave each friend 4 shirts, then you would have 5 shirts remaining.

$$2\overline{)\,10}^{\,5r5}$$

If you have 5 as a remainder, you have enough to give everybody 1 more shirt. That means you can make the quotient bigger. If you ever have a remainder larger than or equal to the quotient, go back and make the quotient bigger.

QUICK QUIZ 1

This quiz will test you on multiplication and division. You can check your answers at the end of the chapter.

1. $5 + 12 =$ _____

2. $15 - 4 =$ _____

3. $22 + -6 =$ _____

4. $-8 + 14 =$ _____

5. $35 - 11 =$ _____

6. $4 \times 8 =$ _____

7. $5 \times -9 =$ _____

8. $-7 \times -6 =$ _____

9. $81 \div 9 =$ _____

10. $64 \div -8 =$ _____

11. $100 \div 10 =$ _____

12. $-25 \div -5 =$ _____

PRE-QUIZ 2

1. $65 - 3 \times (4 + 5) =$ _____

2. $(4 \times 2 \times 9)(3 + 5) =$ _____

3. $4 \times 2 \times 9 \div 3 + 5 =$ _____

4. $23\overline{)391} =$ _____

Long Division

Sometimes you will be asked to divide large numbers. When this happens, it is best to write your division like this:

$$34\overline{)578}$$

34 is the divisor and 578 is the dividend.

At first glance this looks like a really hard division problem. But you can break it up into smaller, easier-to-handle pieces. First, figure out how many times 34 divides into 57. Well 34 × 2 = 68, so we know that 34 goes into 57 once. Place a 1 above the 7.

$$\begin{array}{r} 1 \\ 34\overline{)578} \end{array}$$

The next step is to multiply the 1 by 34, which gives us 34. Write that below the 57 and subtract the 34 from the 57. You get 23.

Drop the next digit of 578 (the 8) down.

$$\begin{array}{r} 1 \\ 34\overline{)578} \\ -34 \\ \hline 238 \end{array}$$

The next step is to divide 238 by 34. You probably don't know, off the top of your head, how many times 34 divides into 238. That's okay—neither do we. Let's think about this a little. We know that 34 × 10 = 340 because to multiply a number by 10 you only need to add a zero to the end of that number. 340 is greater than 238, so our number will be less than 10. But *how* much less than 10? We also know that there are approximately three 30s in every 100, and there are a little more than two 100s in 238. So our number will be more than 6—for instance, 7. Let's try 7 and see what happens.

$$\begin{array}{r} 17 \\ 34\overline{)578} \\ -34 \\ \hline 238 \\ -238 \\ \hline 0 \end{array}$$

$7 \times 34 = 238$, so there is nothing left over. You also don't have any digits left over to use in 578, so you're done. If you want to check your answer, you can multiply 34 by 17:

$$34 \times 17 = 578$$

Division with Negative Numbers

Dividing with negative numbers is the same as multiplying with negative numbers. Keep these rules in mind:

- Positive number ÷ Positive number = Positive number

$$4 \div 2 = 2$$

- Negative number ÷ Negative number = Positive number

$$-4 \div -2 = 2$$

- Positive number ÷ Negative number = Negative number

$$4 \div -2 = -2$$

ORDER OF OPERATIONS

Sometimes you will see math problems that ask you to perform more than one operation on a series of numbers, such as this: $13 - 2 \times (8 + 4)$. When this happens, you need to know which operations to do first. That order is summarized by the acronym PEMDAS and the mnemonic device **P**lease **E**xcuse **M**y **D**ear **A**unt **S**ally.

Parentheses
Exponents
Multiplication
Division
Addition
Subtraction

Here's an example.

$$10 - (6 - 5) - 2(3 + 3) + 3 =$$

Start by doing the operations in the parenthesis.

$$10 - (1) - 2(6) + 3 =$$

There are no exponents, so next multiply and divide.

$$10 - (1) - 12 + 3 =$$

Finish by adding and subtracting in the order in which the operations are presented, from left to right.

$$10 - 1 - 12 + 3 =$$
$$9 - 12 + 3 =$$
$$-3 + 3 = 0$$

Quick Tip!

Use the following mnemonic to help you remember the order of operations:

Please **E**xcuse **M**y **D**ear **A**unt **S**ally

QUICK QUIZ 2

You can check your answers at the end of the chapter.

1. $18 - 5 \times (2 + 3) =$ _____

2. $(2 \times 3 \times 4) \div (10 - 6) =$ _____

3. $2(2 - 1) + 3(3 - 1) =$ _____

4. $18\overline{)468} =$ _____

PRE-QUIZ 3

Solve.

1. $\dfrac{3}{5} + \dfrac{7}{9} =$ _____

2. $4\dfrac{1}{5} + 6\dfrac{3}{5} =$ _____

3. $\dfrac{3}{8} - \dfrac{5}{6} =$ _____

Compare: Which is bigger?

4. $\dfrac{3}{7}$ or $\dfrac{9}{10}$ _____

5. $\dfrac{12}{17}$ or $\dfrac{15}{23}$ _____

Multiply.

6. $\dfrac{2}{9} \times \dfrac{3}{5} =$ _____

7. $\dfrac{5}{6} \times -\dfrac{2}{15} =$ _____

Divide.

8. $\dfrac{3}{4} \div \dfrac{7}{8} =$ _____

Solve.

9. $\dfrac{\frac{7}{8}}{\frac{3}{16}} =$ _____

FRACTIONS

Fractions are a very important topic for the ASVAB—you'll see many questions that involve them. Fractions are a way of representing numbers that lie between integers on the number line.

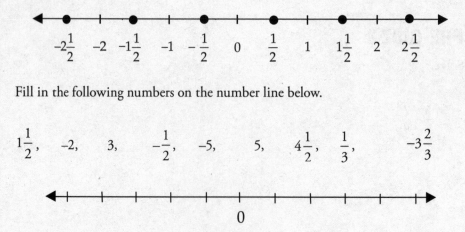

Fill in the following numbers on the number line below.

$$1\tfrac{1}{2}, \quad -2, \quad 3, \quad -\tfrac{1}{2}, \quad -5, \quad 5, \quad 4\tfrac{1}{2}, \quad \tfrac{1}{3}, \quad -3\tfrac{2}{3}$$

By using zero as a starting point, you can determine where all of the numbers should go.

When completed, the number line should look like this:

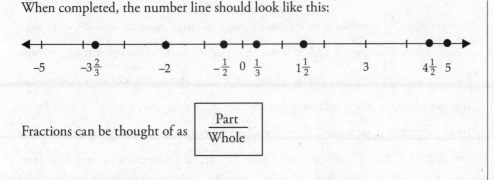

Fractions can be thought of as $\dfrac{\text{Part}}{\text{Whole}}$

Reducing Fractions

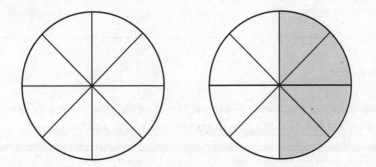

Imagine you had a pizza with 8 slices. You eat 4 pieces of the pizza. What fraction of the pizza did you eat?

You ate $\dfrac{4}{8}$ of the pizza. What is half of 8? It's 4. That means you ate exactly half of the pizza, or $\dfrac{1}{2}$ of the pizza.

Changing the fraction from $\dfrac{4}{8}$ to $\dfrac{1}{2}$ is called *reducing* the fraction. To reduce a fraction to its lowest terms, just divide the numerator and denominator by the same number until you can't divide anymore. Let's reduce $\dfrac{20}{100}$.

$$\frac{20}{1000} \div \frac{2}{2} = \frac{10}{50}$$

We reduced $\dfrac{20}{100}$ to $\dfrac{10}{50}$ by dividing the numerator and denominator by 2. Can the fraction $\dfrac{10}{50}$ be reduced any further? Yes! There is a number that divides evenly into both 10 and 50. That number is 10.

$$\frac{10}{50} \div \frac{10}{10} = \frac{1}{5}$$

The fraction $\frac{1}{5}$ is reduced to its lowest form because there are no numbers that will divide evenly into 1 and 5. Note that, when you're reducing a fraction, you have to use numbers that divide evenly into both the numerator and denominator. For example, when reducing the fraction $\frac{4}{9}$, you cannot divide the two digits by the number 2, because 2 does not divide evenly into 9, though it does divide evenly into 4. $9 \div 2 = 4$ remainder 1, or 4.5. In fact, there are no numbers that divide evenly into both 4 and 9. Therefore, $\frac{4}{9}$ cannot be reduced any further. It has already been reduced to its lowest form.

Quick Tip!

When reducing fractions, always use the same number to reduce both the top and bottom! Try using small numbers like 2, 3, and 5.

Improper Fractions and Mixed Numbers

Improper fractions are fractions in which the top (numerator) is bigger than the bottom (denominator). For example

$$\frac{12}{8}$$

If this improper fraction represented how many slices of pizza we had left, it would indicate that we have more than one whole pizza. To figure out exactly how much pizza we have, we can convert the improper fraction to a mixed number.

$$\frac{12}{8} = 1\frac{4}{8} \text{ or } 1\frac{1}{2}$$

To convert an improper fraction to a mixed number, follow these steps.
1. Divide the denominator into the numerator (8 divides into 12 one time).
2. Put the remainder over the denominator (4 remains, so put it over the 8).
3. Reduce the fraction to lowest terms ($\frac{4}{8}$ reduces to $\frac{1}{2}$).

Adding, Subtracting, and Comparing Fractions

If you want to add, subtract, or compare the sizes of fractions, the denominators of the fractions you're working with **must** be the same.

$$\frac{7}{10} + \frac{2}{10} = \frac{9}{10} \quad \text{YES!}$$

$$\frac{4}{5} + \frac{2}{3} \neq \frac{6}{8} \quad \text{NO!}$$

If you are given two fractions with different denominators and are asked to add, subtract, or compare them, you must first find a common denominator. Here's how:

The Bow Tie

$$\frac{2}{\textcircled{7}} + \frac{3}{\textcircled{4}} = \qquad \text{Different denominators}$$

$$\frac{2}{7} + \frac{3}{4} = \frac{}{28} \qquad \text{Multiply the denominators.}$$

$$\textcircled{8} \qquad \textcircled{21}$$
$$\frac{2}{7} \times \frac{3}{4} = \frac{}{28} \qquad \text{Multiply across the equation.}$$

$$\frac{8}{28} + \frac{21}{28} = \frac{29}{28} \qquad \text{Put your new numerators above the new denominators and add!}$$

Use the same method for subtraction:

$$\textcircled{8} \qquad \textcircled{21}$$
$$\frac{2}{7} \times \frac{3}{4} = \frac{8}{28} - \frac{21}{28} = -\frac{13}{28}$$

If you're asked to compare fractions, use the Bow Tie to see which one is bigger.

$$\frac{2}{5} \quad \text{or} \quad \frac{3}{7}$$

$$\textcircled{14} \qquad \textcircled{15}$$
$$\frac{2}{5} \times \frac{3}{7} = \frac{14}{35} \quad \text{or} \quad \frac{15}{35}$$

Since $\frac{2}{5} = \frac{14}{35}$ and $\frac{3}{7} = \frac{15}{35}$, $\frac{3}{7}$ is bigger.

Adding and Subtracting Mixed Numbers

To add or subtract mixed numbers, you can either change them into improper fractions

$$3\frac{2}{7} + 2\frac{4}{7} = \frac{23}{7} + \frac{18}{7} = \frac{41}{7} = 5\frac{6}{7}$$

or you can work them straight through, starting with the fractions.

$$
\begin{array}{r}
3\dfrac{2}{7} \\
+2\dfrac{4}{7} \\
\hline
\dfrac{6}{7} \\
+5 \\
\hline
5\dfrac{6}{7}
\end{array}
$$

If the fractions do not have the same denominators, you can change them into improper fractions and use the Bow Tie.

$$4\frac{2}{5} + 6\frac{1}{4} = \frac{22}{5} + \frac{25}{4} = \frac{}{20} + \frac{}{20} = \frac{88}{20} + \frac{125}{20} = \frac{213}{20} = 10\frac{13}{20}$$

But sometimes using the Bow Tie produces a very large denominator. For example, if the original denominators are 9 and 12, using the Bow Tie results in a common denominator of 108: $9 \times 12 = 108$. Such a large number may make it difficult to solve the problem. Another way to get a common denominator is to find the lowest common denominator (LCD). For example, if a problem asks you to add $\frac{1}{4} + \frac{5}{6}$, you could use the Bow Tie method and multiply the denominators to get $4 \times 6 = 24$. But 4 and 6 also divide evenly into 12, a smaller number. 12 is the LCD of 4 and 6 because it is the smallest number that they both divide into evenly.

To find the LCD, first see if the smaller number divides evenly into the larger number. Since 4 does not divide evenly into 6, you next should multiply the larger number by 2: $2 \times 6 = 12$. While 6 divides evenly into 12, does 4? Yes, 4 divides into 12 three times: $12 \div 4 = 3$. So 12 is the LCD of 4 and 6. Try finding the LCD for the next problem.

$$5\frac{1}{2} + 4\frac{3}{8} =$$

The original denominators are 2 and 8. First, see if the smaller number divides evenly into the larger number. $8 \div 2 = 4$. 8 is the LCD. Change the fractions to reflect the LCD: $\frac{1}{2} = \frac{4}{8}$ and $\frac{3}{8}$ remains the same. So now the problem looks like this.

$$5\frac{4}{8} + 4\frac{3}{8} = 9\frac{7}{8}$$

Multiplying Fractions

Multiplying fractions is an easier process than adding or subtracting them. Just multiply the numerators and denominators straight across.

$$\frac{4}{5} \times \frac{2}{3} = \frac{8}{15}$$

If you have mixed numbers, be sure to change them to improper fractions before you multiply.

Dividing Fractions

To divide fractions, you multiply by the second fraction's reciprocal. The reciprocal of a number is that number turned upside down. The reciprocal of $\frac{2}{5}$ is $\frac{5}{2}$; the reciprocal of $\frac{1}{2}$ is $\frac{2}{1}$ or 2; the reciprocal of 6 is $\frac{1}{6}$. Once you have the reciprocal of the second fraction, just multiply the two fractions. For example

$$\frac{4}{5} \div \frac{2}{3} = \frac{4}{5} \times \frac{3}{2} = \frac{12}{10} = \frac{6}{5} = 1\frac{1}{5}$$

Complex Fractions

A complex fraction has a fraction as its numerator or denominator. To simplify these, remember that the fraction bar is really a dividing bar:

$$\frac{\frac{2}{3}}{5} = \frac{2}{3} \div 5 = \frac{2}{3} \times \frac{1}{5} = \frac{2}{15}$$

That's all there is to fractions. Try the following drill to test your understanding of fractions before you move on. Fractions are important on the ASVAB. You will see lots of them.

QUICK QUIZ 3

You can check your answers at the end of the chapter.

Solve.

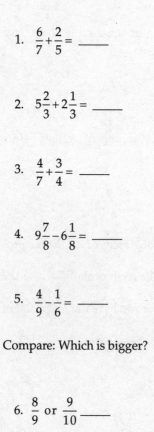

1. $\frac{6}{7} + \frac{2}{5} = $ _____

2. $5\frac{2}{3} + 2\frac{1}{3} = $ _____

3. $\frac{4}{7} + \frac{3}{4} = $ _____

4. $9\frac{7}{8} - 6\frac{1}{8} = $ _____

5. $\frac{4}{9} - \frac{1}{6} = $ _____

Compare: Which is bigger?

6. $\frac{8}{9}$ or $\frac{9}{10}$ _____

7. $\frac{3}{24}$ or $\frac{4}{25}$ _____

8. $-\frac{1}{10}$ or $-\frac{1}{100}$ _____

Multiply.

9. $\frac{2}{3} \times \frac{3}{4} =$ _____

10. $\frac{1}{4} \times \frac{7}{8} =$ _____

11. $\frac{15}{16} \times -\frac{1}{2} =$ _____

Divide.

12. $\frac{1}{2} \div \frac{3}{8} =$ _____

13. $\frac{20}{21} \div \frac{2}{3} =$ _____

Solve.

14. $\dfrac{\frac{2}{5}}{\frac{2}{3}} =$ _____

15. $\dfrac{\frac{10}{9}}{11} =$ _____

16. $23 - 4(12 - 8) - -5 + 9 =$ _____

PRE-QUIZ 4

1. $13.6 + 12.7 =$ _____

2. $31.0112 - 10.436 =$ _____

3. $4.7 \times 3.2 =$ _____

4. $36.6 \div 4.8 =$ _____

5. $\dfrac{3}{9} =$ _____$\% = 0.$_____

DECIMALS

Think back to the pizza example for a moment. Out of 8 pieces of pizza, 4 had been eaten. That left $\dfrac{1}{2}$ a pizza. This can also be written using decimals.

$$\frac{1}{2} = 0.5$$

To find the decimal for a fraction, just remember that a fraction bar is just division in disguise. $\dfrac{1}{2}$ is the same as $1 \div 2$, or $2\overline{)1}$. When you do the division, you get $2\overline{)1.0}$ with 0.5.

You can convert any fraction to a decimal by dividing the numerator by the denominator.

$$\frac{11}{2} = 11 \div 2 = 2\overline{)11.0} \;\; 5.5$$

Where you put the decimal point is very important. Each spot before and after the decimal point has a different meaning.

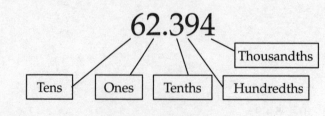

$0.3 = \dfrac{3}{10}$, because the 3 is in the tenths spot.

$5.75 = 5\frac{75}{100}$, because the 5 is in the ones spot, the 7 is in the tenths spot, and the

5 is in the hundredths spot.

Adding and Subtracting Decimals

When you add and subtract decimals, you have to make sure the decimal points are lined up. For example:

$$7.92 + 34.9 + .097 + 6.37 =$$

Line up the numbers like this:

```
  7.92
 34.9
  0.097
+6.37
 49.287
```

Multiplying and Dividing Decimals

You multiply and divide decimals just as you would whole numbers. The important thing to remember is that the number of decimal places in your answer will be equal to the sum of the numbers after the decimals in each of the numbers being multiplied. For example, if you were multiplying 3.283 by .097, it would look like this:

```
    3.283
  × 0.097

   22981
  285470
 0.318451
```

There are six numbers after the decimal in the numbers being multiplied, so there are six numbers after the decimal in the answer.

When you divide a decimal by a whole number, you treat it just like division of whole numbers. The decimal point in the answer should be in the same place as the decimal point in the dividend (the number you're dividing into). For example, if you were dividing 16.1 by 35, it would look like this:

```
        0.46
   35)16.1
       14.0
        210
        210
          0
```

When dividing a decimal by a decimal, you have to eliminate the decimal in the divisor by shifting it to the right of the divisor's last digit—but when you do that, you also have to compensate by shifting the decimal in the dividend the same number of places to the right. For example, if you were dividing 15.5 by .31, it would look like this:

$$0.31\overline{)15.5} = 31\overline{)1550}$$

$$31\overline{)1550} \atop \begin{array}{r} 50 \\ \underline{155} \\ 0 \end{array}$$

Percents

Percents, like fractions and decimals, are another way of describing a part-to-whole relationship. For example, think back to the pizza example again. In that example, four of the eight pieces of pizza had been eaten. That left $\frac{1}{2}$ a pizza, or, using decimals, 0.5 pizzas. You can also express this by using percentages. If a whole pizza is 100%, then half of the pizza is 50% because 50 is half of 100. To do well on the ASVAB, you will want to know how to convert a decimal or fraction into a percent and vice-versa.

To convert a percent into a fraction, just put the percent over 100:

$$3\% = \frac{3}{100} \quad 30\% = \frac{30}{100}$$

To convert a fraction into a percent, remember that a fraction is expressing a $\frac{part}{whole}$ and a percent is just the part. For example

In the fraction $\frac{3}{100}$, the 3 is the part so the percent is 3%.

If the fraction already has a denominator of 100, all you need to do is take the numerator (the top number in the fraction) and add a percent sign. If the denominator is not 100, you need to convert the fraction into a decimal first.

$$\frac{3}{100} = 100\overline{)3.00} \atop 0.03$$

To convert the decimal into a percent, move the decimal point two places to the right and add a percent sign.

$$0.03 = 3\% \quad 0.25 = 25\%$$

To convert a percent into a decimal, just do the opposite. Drop the percent sign and move the decimal point two places to the left.

$$75\% = 0.75 \quad 6\% = 0.06$$

To find the percent of a number, you can convert the percent into either a decimal or fraction and then solve.

For example

What is 20% of 85?

To answer this question using decimals, convert 20% into a decimal, 0.20, and multiply it by 85.

$$20\% = 0.20$$
$$0.20 \times 85 = 17$$
$$20\% \text{ of } 85 \text{ is } 17$$

To use fractions, convert 20% into a fraction and multiply.

$$20\% = \frac{20}{100}$$

$$\frac{20}{100} \times 85 = 17$$

20% of 85 is 17.

QUICK QUIZ 4

Think you got all that? Take this short quiz and find out! You can check your answers at the end of the chapter.

1. $25.3 + 14.7 =$ _____

2. $122.5307 - 36.753 =$ _____

3. $5.2 \times 10.3 =$ _____

4. $2.5 \times 2.5 =$ _____

5. $110.4 \div 9.2 =$ _____

6. $69.2 \div 17.3 =$ _____

7. $7.74 \div .43 =$ _____

8. $\dfrac{4}{16} =$ _____ $\% = 0$_____

9. $0.33 =$ _____ $\% = \dfrac{?}{?}$

10. $50\% = \dfrac{?}{2} = 0$_____

PRE-QUIZ 5

1. $2.6 \times 100 =$ _____

2. $39.45 \div 10 =$ _____

3. Round 3.74 to the nearest tenth. _____

4. $3^3 \times 3^6 =$ _____

5. $4^3 \div 4 =$ _____

6. $\sqrt{12}\sqrt{3} =$ _____

7. Identify the next four terms in the following sequence: 2, 4, 8, _____, _____, _____, _____.

Multiplying and Dividing by Powers of Ten

In this case, a "power of ten" is simply a multiple of 10—10, 100, 1000, 10,000, etc. To multiply decimals by powers of 10, just move the decimal point to the right as many spaces as there are zeros in the power of 10. In other words, if you're multiplying a decimal by 10, you move the decimal point to the right one space. If you're multiplying a decimal by 100, you move the decimal point to the right two spaces.

For example

$$24.7 \times 100 = 2470$$
$$0.385 \times 100 = 38.5$$

Here are some more examples.

$$24.7 \div 100 = .247$$
$$.953 \div 100 = .00953$$

Rounding Numbers

Sometimes you may be asked to round off numbers. The general rule for rounding numbers is this.

If the last digit of the number is less than 5, **round down** (14.4 is rounded off to 14).

If the last digit is greater than or equal to 5, **round up** (14.6 is rounded off to 15).

For example:

24.3 rounded to the nearest whole number is 24.
0.76 rounded to the nearest tenth is 0.8.
−0.22 rounded to the nearest tenth is −0.2.

EXPONENTS AND SQUARE ROOTS

An exponent tells you how many times to multiply a number by itself. For example

$$3^2 = 3 \times 3 = 9$$
$$2^3 = 2 \times 2 \times 2 = 8$$

The number that an exponent is "attached" to is called a base.

Rules for Exponents with the Same Base
- To **multiply**, add the exponents: $x^2 \times x^5 = x^{2+5} = x^7$
- To **divide**, subtract the exponents: $x^6 \div x^3 = x^{6-3} = x^3$
- To **raise the power**, multiply the exponents: $(x^4)^3 = x^{4 \times 3} = x^{12}$

You cannot add or subtract different exponents, so $x^6 + x^3$ is just $x^6 + x^3$. You can't reduce $x^6 + x^3$ any further.

Rules for Exponents with Different Bases

You can't do anything. Don't try to add, subtract, multiply, divide, or cancel.

Exponents and Parentheses

Exponents carry over all parts within the parentheses.

$$2(3a^3)^2 = 2(9a^6)$$

In the problem above, everything inside of the parentheses, $3a^3$, must be multiplied by the exponent outside of the parentheses. $3^2 = 9$ and $(a^3)^2 = a^6$.

Square Roots

The sign $\sqrt{}$ indicates the positive square root of a number. The square root of x, or $\sqrt{x}$, is the number that, when multiplied by itself, equals x. For example, the square root of 25 is 5, or $\sqrt{25} = 5$. That's because $5 \times 5 = 25$. The square root of 9 is 3, and the square root of 36 is 6.

There are two rules you need to know regarding square roots.

1) $\sqrt{x}\,\sqrt{y} = \sqrt{xy}$

   For example, $\sqrt{3}\sqrt{12} = \sqrt{36} = 6$

2) $\sqrt{\dfrac{x}{y}} = \dfrac{\sqrt{x}}{\sqrt{y}}$

   For example, $\sqrt{\dfrac{5}{4}} = \dfrac{\sqrt{5}}{\sqrt{4}} = \dfrac{\sqrt{5}}{2}$

Note that Rule 1 also works in reverse.

$$\sqrt{50} = \sqrt{25} \times \sqrt{2} = 5\sqrt{2}$$

SEQUENCES

A sequence is a list of numbers in a certain order. Each number in a sequence is called a **term**.

When the difference between any two consecutive terms in a sequence is the same, the sequence is called an **arithmetic sequence**. The difference is called the **common difference.**

2, 4, 6, 8, 10 … is an arithmetic sequence with a common difference of 2.

If the consecutive terms of a sequence are formed by multiplying by a constant factor, it's a **geometric sequence**, and the factor is called a **common ratio**.

2, 4, 8, 16, 32 … is a geometric sequence with a common ratio of 2.

If the sequence is neither arithmetic or geometric, it is a **miscellaneous sequence**. There can still be a pattern, just not a common difference or ratio.

If the terms in a sequence get bigger, they are **ascending**; if they get smaller, they are **descending**.

To find missing terms in a sequence, first determine what type of sequence you're dealing with: Subtract the first term from the second, and the second from the third (or vice versa, if the sequence is descending). If the results are the same, it's an arithmetic sequence. If not, try dividing the second term by the first and the third by the second (or vice versa, if the sequence is descending). If the results are the same, it's a geometric sequence. If the sequence is miscellaneous, look for a pattern.

For example, let's look at the sequence 1, 2, 5, 10, 17. The terms here are getting bigger, so the sequence is ascending. This means we want to subtract the first term from the second and the second from the third. The difference between the first and second terms is one; the difference between the second and third terms is 3. The results are also different if we try dividing 2 by 1 (which equals 2) and 5 by 2 (which equals 2.5). So the sequence is miscellaneous, and therefore we need to find the pattern. If we keep subtracting the terms from each other, we will see that the difference between the terms follows the first positive odd numbers in the number line: 1, 3, 5, and 7. Since we've identified the pattern, we can now predict that the next number in the sequence will be 26, because 17 (the last number given in the sequence) + 9 (the next odd number) = 26.

QUICK QUIZ 5

Take this short quiz before moving on. You can check your answers at the end of the chapter.

1. $135.7 \times 10 =$ _____

2. $0.314 \times 100 =$ _____

3. $58.47 \div 100 =$ _____

4. $1.76 \div 10 =$ _____

5. Round 99.6 to the nearest whole number. _____

6. Round 12.12 to the nearest tenth. _____

7. $5^2 =$ _____

8. $3^3 =$ _____

9. $2^2 \times 2^3 =$ _____

10. $7^4 \div 7^2 =$ _____

11. $\sqrt{2}\sqrt{32} =$ _____

12. $\sqrt{\dfrac{81}{9}} =$ _____

13. Identify the next three terms in the following sequence: 24, 21, 18, 15, 12, _____, _____, _____.

PRE-QUIZ 6

1. Bob runs 3 miles per day, except for Saturdays, when he runs 10 miles, and Sundays, which he takes off. What is the daily average distance he runs in one week?

   A.   2.6 miles

   B.   3 miles

   C.   3.6 miles

   D.   4 miles

2. In a bowl, there are 3 peaches, 2 apples, 6 lemons, and 4 plums. If 1 piece of fruit is to be selected at random, what is the probability it will be a lemon?

   A. $\dfrac{2}{15}$

   B. $\dfrac{3}{15}$

   C. $\dfrac{4}{15}$

   D. $\dfrac{6}{15}$

MISCELLANEOUS ARITHMETIC QUESTIONS

Units of Measure

In addition to the math skills being tested, the ASVAB also tests your knowledge of basic units of measurement. Make sure you know all the measurements listed below.

- 1 foot = 12 inches
- 1 yard = 3 feet
- 1 hour = 60 minutes
- 1 day = 24 hours
- 1 year = 365 days
- 1 year = 52 weeks
- 1 dollar = 100 cents = 10 dimes = 4 quarters
- 1 gallon = 8 pints
- 1 gallon = 4 quarts
- 1 pound = 16 ounces

Quick Break?
This arithmetic chapter has covered a lot of ground. Before you dive into the next section, why not take a quick break to clear your head?

Calculating Changes in Percentage

A common type of question on the ASVAB asks you to figure out the percent change in the price of something.

For example:

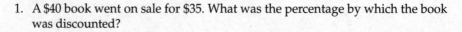

1. A $40 book went on sale for $35. What was the percentage by which the book was discounted?

   A.   5%
   B.   10%
   C.   12.5%
   D.   15%

Here's How to Crack It

To calculate the percent change, use the following formula:

$$\text{percent increase or decrease} = \frac{\text{difference}}{\text{original amount}}$$

So, for this question, we would just plug in the numbers to find the change.

$$\text{percent decrease} = \frac{5}{40} = .125 \text{ or } 12.5\%$$

The answer is (C).

Ratios

A ratio gives information about the relative amounts of things. For example, a banana split may be made up of 1 part banana, 3 parts ice cream, 2 parts toppings, and 1 part whipped cream. Therefore, the ratio of banana to ice cream to toppings to whipped cream is 1 : 3 : 2 : 1. This means that for every one part of banana there are three parts ice cream. For every two parts of toppings there is one part of whipped cream and so on. Let's look at a ratio question.

2. The ratio of red to blue marbles in a bowl is 7 : 8. There are 30 marbles total. How many red and blue marbles are there?

   A.   7 red and 8 blue
   B.   8 red and 7 blue
   C.   10 red and 12 blue
   D.   14 red and 16 blue

Here's How to Crack It

Whenever you see a ratio question, plug the information into a **Ratio Box**.

Red	Blue	Total
7	8	
		30

Put the information about the ratio in the top line and the total number in the bottom line. Then add the numbers from the original ratio and put the sum on the top line in the "Total" category.

Red	Blue	Total
7	8	15
		30

Let's look at the "Total" category. What number multiplied by 15 equals 30? Multiply 15 by 2 and you get 30. So, write "2" in the second row. Your ratio table now looks like this.

Red	Blue	Total
7	8	15
× 2	× 2	× 2
		30

Now all you need to do is multiply the 7 and the 8 by 2 to find the answer. Therefore, there are 14 red marbles and 16 blue marbles. The answer is (D).

Proportions

A proportion is a way of comparing ratios with equal values. Proportions are usually used to figure out how big or small something will be in comparable circumstances. For example, if a 3-foot-high flagpole casts a shadow of 2 feet, then a 6-foot-high flagpole will cast a shadow of 4 feet.

$$\frac{\text{flagpole}}{\text{shadow}} = \frac{3}{2} = \frac{6}{4}$$

Another way to write this proportion is 3 : 2 :: 6 : 4. The four dots in the middle are the proportion sign. The numbers on the outside, 3 and 4, are called the extremes. The numbers on the inside are called the means. The product of the extremes will equal the product of the means. Let's multiply them out and see for ourselves.

$$3 \times 4 = 12 \text{ and } 2 \times 6 = 12$$

How does this help you? It provides you with a way to figure out a missing number in a proportion. For example

If 10 nails cost 4 cents, how much do 50 nails cost?

The question is giving the proportion 10 : 4 :: 50 : ?. You need to complete the proportion 50 : ?. It's simple using what you just learned.

$$4 \times 50 = 200 \text{ so } 10 \times ? = 200$$

Remember that multiplication is the opposite of division, so you can find the missing value by division.

$$200 \div 10 = 20$$

50 nails cost 20 cents.

This method also works if you write the proportion the other way. Just make sure you keep the categories the same on the top and bottom.

$$\frac{\text{nails}}{\text{cents}} = \frac{10}{4} = \frac{50}{?}$$

In this case, the extremes are diagonal from each other, so you need to cross-multiply—in other words, multiply the top number from the first fraction times the bottom number in the other fraction and the top number in the second fraction times the bottom number in the first fraction.

$$\frac{10}{4} = \frac{50}{?}$$

$$4 \times 50 = 200 \text{ and } 10 \times ? = 200, \text{ so } ? = 20 \text{ cents}$$

Probability

Sometimes you may be asked to find the probability of a certain event. For example

———————————◯———————————

3. A pet store has 14 kittens. Three of the kittens are black, 3 are calico, 4 are white, and 4 are black and white. If 1 kitten is selected at random, what is the probability that it will be a calico kitten?

A. $\dfrac{3}{14}$

B. $\dfrac{3}{10}$

C. $\dfrac{11}{14}$

D. $\dfrac{1}{5}$

Here's How to Crack It

In this case, you need to figure out how likely it is that you'd get a calico kitten if you picked one randomly out of the bunch. There are 14 different kittens, which gives fourteen different possible choices. Out of all 14 kittens, 3 of them are calico. Therefore, you would have a 3 out of 14 chance, or a $\dfrac{3}{14}$ chance, of choosing a calico kitten if you chose one at random.

———————————◯———————————

Averages

To find the average of a set of numbers, just add up the numbers and divide the sum by the number of numbers in the set.

What is the average of 3, 5, and 10?

$$3 + 5 + 10 = 18$$

Since there are three numbers in the set, we next divide 18 by 3.

$$18 \div 3 = 6$$

The average of 3, 5, and 10 is 6.

Sometimes the ASVAB will make things trickier by not giving you a list of numbers. But you can still do the problem. To find any average, all you need are two out of three things: the sum of the numbers, the number of things in the set, and the average. To find any one of these things, you need to know the other two. The ASVAB will always give you two of these things and then ask you to find the third. The easiest way to solve average problems is to use the **Average Pie.**

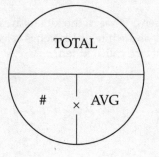

Look at an example.

4. The average of 3 numbers is 22, and the smallest of these numbers is 2. The other two numbers are equal. What are they?

   A. 22
   B. 32
   C. 40
   D. 64

Here's How to Crack It
In this problem, you have the average (22) and the number of items in the set (3). Plug those numbers into the Average Pie. It will look like this:

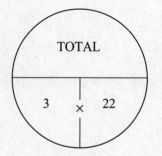

Now you need to find the total. It's $3 \times 22 = 66$. You know that one of the numbers in the set is 2. Subtract 2 from 66 and you are left with 64. The remaining two numbers must be equal to each other, so just divide 64 by 2. That gives 32. The answer is (B).

Weighted Averages

Sometimes one item in a set may be more important than another. In this case, we say the items are "weighted" differently. When this happens, you need to take the weight of each item into consideration when finding the average. For example

---

5. Winnie received a 92 in Math, a 78 in English, and an 85 in Science. Suppose the subjects have the following weights: Math 3, English 4, and Science 3. What is Winnie's average?

    A. 72
    B. 78
    C. 84.3
    D. 93.25

Here's How to Crack It

To find the average, you must first "weigh" the grades accordingly. To do this, just multiply the grade by the weight for that class.

$$\text{Math: } 92 \times 3 = 276$$

$$\text{English: } 78 \times 4 = 312$$

$$\text{Science: } 85 \times 3 = 255$$

Then, add the products together. This is your "Total" for the Average Pie.

$$276 + 312 + 255 = 843$$

You find the number of items in the set by adding the weights together.

$$3 + 4 + 3 = 10$$

You now have two of the spots in the Average Pie filled in and can find the third.

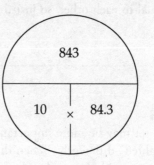

The average is 843 ÷ 10 = 84.3.

The answer is (C).

QUICK QUIZ 6
Try the following problems before moving on. You can check your answers at the end of the chapter.

1. Curtis earns $600 every month except for December and January, when he takes a vacation and earns no income. What is his average monthly income for the entire year?

   A. $500
   B. $484
   C. $300
   D. $275

2. In a bowl there are 5 red sticks, 4 blue sticks, 7 yellow sticks, and 9 white sticks. If 1 stick is to be drawn at random, what is the probability it will be red?

   A. $\dfrac{1}{10}$

   B. $\dfrac{1}{5}$

   C. $\dfrac{5}{10}$

   D. $\dfrac{5}{12}$

3. At a coed camp, the ratio of girls to boys is 5 : 3. If the camp's enrollment is 160, how many of the children are boys?

   A.   20

   B.   60

   C.   100

   D.   120

4. Ken received a 72 in Math, a 64 in Science, and an 80 in Art. If the subjects have the following weights: Math 3, Science 4, and Art 3, what is Ken's average?

   A.   70.5

   B.   71.2

   C.   79.2

   D.   80.0

5. A store owner buys a pound of grapes for 80 cents and sells it for a dollar. What percent of the original price of grapes is the store owner's profit?

   A.   10%

   B.   20%

   C.   25%

   D.   40%

6. Fill in the blanks.

   1 foot = _____ inches

   1 yard = _____ feet

   1 hour = _____ minutes

   1 day = _____ hours

   1 year = _____ days

   1 year = _____ weeks

   1 dollar = _____ cents = _____ dimes = _____ quarters

   1 gallon = _____ pints

   1 gallon = _____ quarts

   1 pound = _____ ounces

MATH TECHNIQUES

We've now covered all the math you need to know for the ASVAB. The next thing we are going to talk about is how to make the questions easier to answer.

Word Problems

The questions in the Arithmetic Reasoning section are usually presented as word problems. For example

○

1. Admission to the zoo costs $8.00 for adults and $5.00 for children. If the Brown family, which consists of two adults and three children, goes to the zoo and pays with two $20.00 bills, how much change will they receive?

   A. $5.00
   B. $9.00
   C. $23.00
   D. $31.00

Here's How to Crack It

All you need to know to answer this question is how to multiply, add, and subtract. Sound easy enough? The tricky part is being able to figure out what to multiply, add, and subtract. That is where Bite-Size Pieces comes into play.

Bite-Size Pieces

Bite-Size Pieces is a technique that helps you take a long, complicated word problem and break it into smaller, easier to handle pieces. Let's take the above example step by step.

Step 1: The first thing to do is to identify what you're being asked to do. In this question, you need to figure out how much change the Brown family will receive from two $20.00 bills, or $40.00.

Step 2: The next thing is to break the problem into smaller parts. First, figure out how much it's going to cost for the two adults to get into the zoo.

$8.00 per adult × 2 adults = $16.00

Next, figure out how much it's going to cost for the children to get in.

$5.00 per child × 3 children = $15.00

Now figure out the total cost for the Brown family to get in.

$$\$16.00 + \$15.00 = \$31.00$$

Step 3: Remember, the question is asking how much change the family will receive from $40.00. So for the last step, subtract the cost of admission from the $40.00.

$$\$40.00 - \$31.00 = \$9.00$$

And that's the answer, (B)!

Try another example.

2. Greg works 30 hours a week at the gas station for $6.45 an hour and 15 hours a week at the coffee shop for $8.00 an hour. Helen works 35 hours a week at the stationery store for $7.50 an hour. What is the difference in the amount of money Helen and Greg make in two weeks?

A. $51.00
B. $102.00
C. $238.00
D. $576.00

Here's How to Crack It
Step 1: Identify what the problem is asking. This word problem is asking you to figure out the difference between what Greg makes in two weeks and what Helen makes in two weeks.

Step 2: Break the problem into Bite-Size Pieces. Since you need to figure out the difference in their incomes, the first thing you need to do is figure out how much each one makes. The problem told you how many hours they work each week and how much they are paid per hour, so start there.

Greg
Greg has two jobs, so you need to figure out how much he makes each week at both jobs.

Gas station: 30 hours per week × $6.45 an hour = $193.50 per week
Coffee shop: 15 hours per week × $8.00 an hour = $120.00 per week

Then add the two numbers together to figure out how much money he makes in total each week.

$$\$193.50 + \$120.00 = \$313.50$$

Then multiply that sum by 2 to figure out how much he makes in two weeks.

$$\$313.50 \times 2 = \$627.00$$

Helen
Helen works only one job, so figuring out her pay will be easier.

Stationery store: 35 hours per week × $7.50 an hour = $262.50 per week
Multiply by 2 to find out how much Helen makes in two weeks.

$$\$262.50 \times 2 = \$525.00$$

Step 3: Refer back to the problem to make sure you're answering the right question. The question is asking what the difference is between Greg and Helen's pay. To figure this out, you just subtract

$$\$627.00 - \$525.00 = \$102.00$$

That's (B).

---○---

Ballparking

Ballparking is a technique that helps you eliminate bad answer choices before you've even worked the problem. For example

---○---

3. On a test of 50 questions, Gertrude answered 47 correctly. If Gertrude answered every question, what percentage did she answer incorrectly?

   A. 97%
   B. 47%
   C. 6%
   D. 3%

Here's How to Crack It

Without even doing the math involved, you can eliminate two answers. You know that she answered 47 out of 50 correctly, which means she got right almost all of the questions—in other words, she did pretty well on the test. Based on that, you can immediately rule out (A) and (B), because they are way too high. If she got almost all the questions right, it would be impossible for her to have gotten 97% or 47% of the answers *wrong*. That leaves (C) and (D). Even if you didn't know how to answer this problem, you could still guess and have a 50/50 shot of getting it right. But you can do the math just to be sure:

$$\frac{47}{50} = 50\overline{)47}^{\,0.94}$$

$$100\% - 94\% = 6\%$$

So the answer is (C).

○

Look at another example.

○

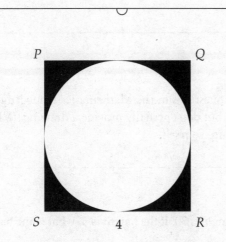

4. The circle above is inscribed in square *PQRS*. What is the area of the shaded region?

    A. $16 - 6\pi$
    B. $16 - 4\pi$
    C. $16 - 2\pi$
    D. 16π

Here's How to Crack It
This is a really tough question, but by Ballparking you can make it easier. Start by looking at the picture. How much of the square do you think is shaded? Half? Three-quarters? Less than half? In fact, about one-quarter of the square is shaded.

Next, do a little math. The length of one side of the square is 4, so the area of the square is 4×4 or 16. The area is 16 and the amount of the shaded area is about one-fourth of the square. One-fourth of the square is $\frac{16}{4}$, or 4. So you need an answer choice that is about 4.

Now look at the answers: π is about 3. Plug 3 into the answers and see what you end up with.

A. $16 - 6\pi$ $16 - 6(3) = 16 - 18 = -2$
B. $16 - 4\pi$ $16 - 4(3) = 16 - 12 = 4$
C. $16 - 2\pi$ $16 - 2(3) = 16 - 6 = 10$
D. 16π $16 \times 3 = 48$

Based on the work you've done, the answer is (B). That is the correct answer.

Draw It!

A lot of the geometry questions in the Mathematics Knowledge section give you a description of a figure but don't actually provide a drawing. When this happens, it helps to draw the picture yourself.

5. The area of a triangle is 30. If the height is 5, what is the base?

A. 10
B. 12
C. 30
D. 40

Here's How to Crack It

It might help if we drew the triangle described in the problem.

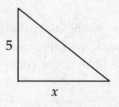

Don't worry too much about what the triangle looks like. All that matters is that the height is 5. We have labeled the base x just to keep track of it. Now let's plug everything into the equation for the area of a triangle and solve for x.

$$\text{Area} = \frac{1}{2} \text{ base} \times \text{height}$$

$$30 = \frac{1}{2} (x)(5)$$

$$30 = \frac{1}{2} 5x$$

$$60 = 5x$$

$$x = 12$$

The base of the triangle is 12, so the answer is (B).

The last example was pretty straightforward. Take a look at a tougher one to see how drawing the picture can really help.

6. A small street is intersected by a highway. The southwest corner of the intersection is an angle of 65 degrees. What is the size of the angle of the northwest corner?

   A.   65 degrees
   B.   90 degrees
   C.   115 degrees
   D.   180 degrees

Here's How to Crack It

Draw the intersection described in the problem to make things a little clearer.

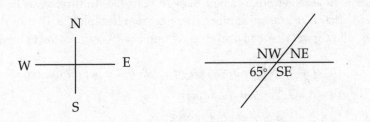

By looking at the diagram, you can see that there are four angles, or corners of the street, that you can label. The problem gives you the size of the southwest angle, which is 65 degrees. Recall from our geometry review that adjacent angles add up to 180 degrees. Based on that, you know that the adjacent angle, the southeast corner, is 115 degrees. Also recall that opposite angles are equal. So, you know that the northwest corner, which is opposite the southeast corner, also equals 115 degrees. The answer is (C).

Plugging In

Plugging In is a problem-solving technique that works when the answers contain variables. When Plugging In, use numbers that will be easy to work with, like 2, 4, or 10. Do not plug in 0 or 1, or numbers that appear in the question. If you have two variables, use two different numbers. Here's an example.

---

7. Clare is C years old and is six years younger than Alan. In terms of C, how many years old will Alan be in 3 years?

    A. $C - 6$

    B. $C - 3$

    C. $C + 3$

    D. $C + 9$

Here's How to Crack It

What did you think when you read this problem? If you're like most people, you probably didn't know what to think. At first glance this problem looks really hard. But if you know how to handle it, this problem is actually quite simple.

Whenever a problem has a variable like C in the answers, you should Plug In to find the answer. To plug in for the example above, you just want to pick a number that you can substitute for C. It's best to choose a number that's easy to work with. Try using 10.

If Claire is 10 years old, that makes Alan 16 years old. In three years he will be 19 years old. That is the target number. The next step is to plug in 10 into the answer choices. The answer that equals the target number 19 is the correct answer.

    (A) $10 - 6 = 4$. *No, we are looking for 19. This is not the answer.*

    (B) $10 - 3 = 7$. *No, not the answer.*

    (C) $10 + 3 = 13$. *Still not the answer.*

    (D) $10 + 9 = 19$. *Yes, this is the answer.*

Plugging In the Answers

Plugging In can even work with questions that do not have variables in the answers. Sometimes the ASVAB will give you answers with actual values, but leave an important piece of information out of the question. Your job is to find the missing piece of information. Luckily, it's one of the answer choices. The easiest way to solve these questions is to plug the answer choices back into the question.

For example

⎯⎯⎯⎯⎯⎯⎯⎯⎯⎯⎯⎯⎯⎯⎯○⎯⎯⎯⎯⎯⎯⎯⎯⎯⎯⎯⎯⎯⎯⎯

9. A mechanic buys a set of tools. He gives half of the tools to one coworker and five of them to another coworker. If the mechanic now has nine tools left, how many tools did he buy originally?

    A. 14
    B. 20
    C. 28
    D. 36

Here's How to Crack It

The missing piece of information in this question is the number of tools the mechanic originally bought. You know that he now has 9 tools left, so that's the target number. To solve this problem, plug the answers into the question and follow the directions. The answer choice that gives you the target number of 9 is the correct answer.

Start with (B): 20 tools. If you plug 20 into the question and follow the directions let's see what you get. He started with 20 tools, gave half to one coworker, leaving him with 10. He then gave five tools to another coworker. That leaves him with 5 tools. That's not the target number, and it's too small, so try a larger number. Plug in (C) now. If he started with 28 tools and gave half to a coworker, he would have 14 tools left. Next he gave 5 tools to another coworker, leaving him with 9 tools. That's the target number. Choice (C) is the answer!

You may be wondering why we started with (B) instead of with (A). We started with (B) because the answer, 20, was a number in the middle. Our answers ranged in value from 14 to 36. By starting with a middle value, we were able to quickly figure out whether we needed a larger or smaller number. Choice (B) turned out to be too small, so we knew that we needed a larger number and tried (C). If we had started with (A), we would have soon figured out that we needed a larger number, but then we would have had three answers left rather than two. When Plugging In the Answers, start with an answer in the middle to save time.

⎯⎯⎯⎯⎯⎯⎯⎯⎯⎯⎯⎯⎯⎯⎯○⎯⎯⎯⎯⎯⎯⎯⎯⎯⎯⎯⎯⎯⎯⎯

ANSWERS TO PRE-QUIZZES, QUICK QUIZZES

Pre-Quiz 1
Page 24

1. $7 + 6 = 13$
2. $12 - 5 = 7$
3. $15 + -8 = 7$
4. $-3 + 4 = 1$
5. $6 \times 4 = 24$
6. $-5 \times 8 = -40$
7. $42 \div 6 = 7$
8. $75 \div 15 = 5$

Quick Quiz 1
Page 28

1. $5 + 12 = 17$
2. $15 - 4 = 11$
3. $22 + -6 = 16$
4. $-8 + 14 = 6$
5. $35 - 11 = 24$
6. $4 \times 8 = 32$
7. $5 \times -9 = -45$
8. $-7 \times -6 = 42$
9. $81 \div 9 = 9$
10. $64 \div -8 = -8$
11. $100 \div 10 = 10$
12. $-25 \div -5 = 5$

Pre-Quiz 2
Page 28

1. $65 - 3 \times (4 + 5) = 38$
2. $(4 \times 2 \times 9) \div (3 + 5) = 9$
3. $4 \times 2 \times 9 \div 3 + 5 = 29$
4. $23\overline{)391} = 17$

Quick Quiz 2
Page 31

1. -7
2. 6
3. 8
4. 26

Pre-Quiz 3
Page 31

1. $\dfrac{3}{5} + \dfrac{7}{9} = \dfrac{62}{45}$ or $1\dfrac{17}{45}$

2. $4\dfrac{1}{5} + 6\dfrac{3}{5} = 10\dfrac{4}{5}$

3. $\dfrac{3}{8} - \dfrac{5}{6} = -\dfrac{22}{48}$ or $-\dfrac{11}{24}$

Compare: Which is bigger?

4. $\dfrac{9}{10}$

5. $\dfrac{12}{17}$

Multiply.

6. $\dfrac{2}{9} \times \dfrac{3}{5} = \dfrac{6}{45}$ or $\dfrac{2}{15}$

7. $\dfrac{5}{6} \times -\dfrac{2}{15} = -\dfrac{10}{90}$ or $-\dfrac{1}{9}$

Divide.

8. $\dfrac{3}{4} \div \dfrac{7}{8} = \dfrac{6}{7}$

Solve.

9. $\dfrac{\frac{7}{8}}{\frac{3}{16}} = \dfrac{14}{3}$

Quick Quiz 3

Page 38

1. $\dfrac{6}{7} + \dfrac{2}{5} = \dfrac{30}{35} + \dfrac{14}{35} = \dfrac{44}{35} = 1\dfrac{9}{35}$

2. $5\dfrac{2}{3} + 2\dfrac{1}{3} = \dfrac{17}{3} + \dfrac{7}{3} = \dfrac{24}{3} = 8$

3. $\dfrac{4}{7} + \dfrac{3}{4} = \dfrac{16}{28} + \dfrac{21}{28} = \dfrac{37}{28} = 1\dfrac{9}{28}$

4. $9\dfrac{7}{8} - 6\dfrac{1}{8} = 3\dfrac{6}{8} = 3\dfrac{3}{4}$

5. $\dfrac{4}{9} - \dfrac{1}{6} = \dfrac{24}{54} - \dfrac{9}{54} = \dfrac{15}{54} = \dfrac{5}{18}$

6. $\dfrac{9}{10}$

7. $\dfrac{4}{25}$

8. $-\dfrac{1}{100}$

9. $\dfrac{2}{3} \times \dfrac{3}{4} = \dfrac{6}{12} = \dfrac{1}{2}$

10. $\dfrac{1}{4} \times \dfrac{7}{8} = \dfrac{7}{32}$

11. $\dfrac{15}{16} \times -\dfrac{1}{2} = -\dfrac{15}{32}$

12. $\dfrac{1}{2} \div \dfrac{3}{8} = \dfrac{1}{2} \times \dfrac{8}{3} = \dfrac{8}{6} = 1\dfrac{2}{6} = 1\dfrac{1}{3}$

13. $\dfrac{20}{21} \div \dfrac{2}{3} = \dfrac{20}{21} \times \dfrac{3}{2} = \dfrac{60}{42} = 1\dfrac{18}{42} = 1\dfrac{3}{7}$

14. $\dfrac{\frac{2}{5}}{\frac{2}{3}} = \dfrac{2}{5} \div \dfrac{2}{3} = \dfrac{2}{5} \times \dfrac{3}{2} = \dfrac{6}{10} = \dfrac{3}{5}$

15. $\dfrac{\dfrac{10}{9}}{\dfrac{11}{}} = \dfrac{10}{1} \div \dfrac{9}{11} = \dfrac{10}{1} \times \dfrac{11}{9} = \dfrac{110}{9}$

16. $23 - 4(12 - 8) - -5 + 9 = 23 - 4(4) + 5 + 9 = 23 - 16 + 5 + 9 = 21$

Pre-Quiz 4
Page 40

1. $13.6 + 12.7 = 26.3$
2. $31.0112 - 10.436 = 20.5752$
3. $4.7 \times 3.2 = 15.04$
4. $36.6 \div 4.8 = 7.625$
5. $\dfrac{3}{9} = 33\dfrac{1}{3}\% = 0.\bar{3}$

Quick Quiz 4
Page 43

1. 40
2. 85.7777
3. 53.56
4. 6.25
5. 12
6. 4
7. 18
8. $\dfrac{4}{16} = 25\% = 0.25$
9. $0.33 = 33\% = \dfrac{1}{3}$
10. $50\% = \dfrac{1}{2} = 0.50$

Pre-Quiz 5
Page 44

1. $2.6 \times 100 = 26$
2. $39.45 \div 10 = 3.945$
3. 3.7
4. $3^3 \times 3^6 = 3^9 = 19{,}683$
5. $4^3 \div 4 = 4^2 = 16$
6. $\sqrt{12}\sqrt{3} = \sqrt{6}$
7. $16, 32, 64, 128$

Quick Quiz 5

Page 48

1. 1357
2. 31.4
3. 0.5847
4. 0.176
5. 100
6. 12.1
7. 25
8. 27
9. $4 \times 8 = 32$
10. $2401 \div 49 = 49$

11. $\sqrt{64} = 8$

12. $\dfrac{\sqrt{81}}{\sqrt{9}} = \dfrac{9}{3} = 3$

13. 9, 6, 3

Pre-Quiz 6

Page 49

1. **C**
2. **A**

Quick Quiz 6

Page 56

1. **A**
2. **B**
3. **B**
4. **B**
5. **C**
6. 12 inches
   3 feet
   60 minutes
   24 hours
   365 days
   52 weeks
   100 cents = 10 dimes = 4 quarters
   8 pints
   4 quarts
   16 ounces

Chapter 3
Mathematics
Knowledge

INTRODUCTION TO THE MATHEMATICS KNOWLEDGE SECTION

The Mathematics Knowledge test covers more advanced mathematics concepts than the Arithmetic Reasoning test. You will see questions on algebra, geometry, and factoring, among others. The CAT-ASVAB has 16 questions that you will have 18 minutes to answer, while the MET-ASVAB and Student ASVAB have 25 questions that you will have 24 minutes to answer.

PRE-QUIZ 1

1. What does FOIL mean?

2. Solve for x: $3x + 9 = x + 21$

3. Factor: $x^2 - 2x - 35$

4. If $2x + 5y = 1$ and $x + 3y = 4$, what is the value of y?

ALGEBRA

Most of the algebra questions on the ASVAB test your ability to solve for a variable or factor. Before we begin our review, let's define a few terms you should know.

Algebra Terminology

Algebra: The mathematics of working with variables.

Coefficient: The number multiplied by a variable or variables in a term. For example, 123 is the coefficient in the term $123x^2y$.

Expression: A mathematical calculation in which numbers and/or variables are added, subtracted, multiplied, divided, raised to a power, or have any other mathematical operation performed on them. An expression does *not* contain the equal sign or any inequality sign. For example

$$(x - 2)^2 + (y + 1)^3$$

Equation: Two expressions set equal to each other.

Factor: The factors of a number are the numbers that, when multiplied together, equal that number. For example, 3 and 2 are factors of 6, because $3 \times 2 = 6$.

Formula: An expression used to calculate a desired result, such as the formula for the area of a circle ($A = \pi r^2$, remember?).

Inequality: An expression where one side is set greater than, or both greater than or equal to, the other side.

Simultaneous equations: Separate equations in which each term has the same variable or variables. For example

$$x^2 + y^2 = 4$$
$$x - y = 2$$

Term: A number or variable that is part of an expression.

Expression	Term
$5a^3 - 2xy + 3$	$5a^3, 2xy$, and 3

Variable: A letter used to represent a number.

Solving for *x*

One of the most common types of algebra questions on the ASVAB is one where you are asked to solve for a variable (usually *x*). You will be given an equation like this.

1. $8x - 4 = 12 + x$

Your job is to figure out what *x* equals. To do this, you must first **isolate the variable** (*x*) on one side of the equation.

$$8x - 4 = 12 + x$$
$$\underline{-x = -x} \qquad \text{Subtract } x \text{ from both sides.}$$
$$7x - 4 = 12$$
$$\underline{+4 = +4} \qquad \text{Add 4 to both sides.}$$
$$7x = 16$$

$$\frac{7x}{7} = \frac{16}{7} \qquad \text{Divide both sides by 7.}$$

$$x = \frac{16}{7}$$

Isolating the Variable

To isolate a variable, you must do the opposite of what the equation does *on both sides* of the equation. For example, if the equation subtracts 4 from one side, you must add 4 to both sides. If it multiplies by 7 on one side, you must divide by 7 on both sides. The cardinal rule is this: **Whatever you do to one side, you must do to the other side**. Take a look at an example.

2. $3x = 27$

To isolate the variable, the coefficient 3 needs to be moved. To move something from one side of the equation to the other you need to perform the opposite operation on both sides of the equation. In this example, the 3 is being multiplied by x, so you need to divide by 3. Again, the most important thing to remember is that whatever you do to one side of the equation you must do to the other side.

$$\frac{3x}{3} = \frac{27}{3}$$

The 3s on the left side divide out, and on the right side, $27 \div 3 = 9$.

$$x = 9$$

Look at another example.

3. $t - 5 = 20$

To isolate the variable t, you need to perform the opposite operation on both sides. The coefficient 5 is being subtracted, so add 5 to both sides.

$$t - 5 + 5 = 20 + 5$$
$$t = 25$$

Another way you might see algebra on the ASVAB is when they provide you with the values of the variables. For example

Solve the equation below if $x = 3$ and $z = -2$.

$$x^2 + 4z + 15 =$$

To answer this question, just plug in the values provided and solve.

$$3^2 + 4(-2) + 15 =$$
$$9 + (-8) + 15 =$$
$$1 + 15 = 16$$

Factoring

The factors of a number are the numbers that when multiplied together equal that number. For example, the factors of 6 are (1, 6) and (2, 3). The factors of 12 are (1, 12), (2, 6), and (3, 4).

You can also identify the factors of algebraic expressions. To factor expressions find a common factor of all the terms in the expression. For example

   4. $6x^2y + 3xy^2$

The first thing you want to look at are the coefficients, 6 and 3. Do they have any common factors? Yes, 3 is a common factor of both of them. Divide the 3 out of each and put the remaining terms in parentheses.

$$3(2x^2y + xy^2)$$

Now you want to factor out the variables. Look at them one at a time. First, factor out the x's. You get x^2 and x. You can also factor an x out of both terms. Move it out of the parentheses.

$$3x(2xy + y^2)$$

Now look at the y's. You have y and y^2. You can factor a y out of both terms. Move it out of the parentheses.

$$3xy(2x + y)$$

The expression is completely factored now. If you multiply it out again, you will see that you end up with the same expression you started with.

$$3xy(2x + y) = 6x^2y + 3xy^2$$

You may also be asked to factor an equation that looks like this.

$$x^2 + 2x = 15$$

To factor this equation, the first thing you need to do is move the 15 to the other side. To do this, just subtract 15 from both sides.

$$x^2 + 2x - 15 = 0$$

Want More Books?
We've got a ton more math books to help you review these topics. Check out some of our greatest hits:
Math Smart
High School Algebra I Unlocked
High School Algebra II Unlocked

Next, figure out what the factors of the last term (15) are. They are

$$(1, 15) \text{ and } (3, 5)$$

Which pair of factors when either added or subtracted will give you the middle term from the equation (2)? The pair (1, 15) definitely won't. If you add them you get 16. If you subtract, you get 14 or –14. What about (3, 5)? If you add them you get 8. If you subtract, you end up with 2 or –2. That's what you're looking for. So you know the factors for this equation are 3 and 5. Since the middle term is 2 and not –2, you need a positive 5 and a negative 3, because 5 – 3 = 2. The factored form of the equation looks like this.

$$(x + 5)(x - 3)$$

To check your work, you can use FOIL. FOIL gives you the order in which to multiply the terms of the factors.

First
Outer
Inner
Last

First, multiply the first terms in the factors together: $x \times x = x^2$.

Next, multiply the outer terms together: $x \times -3 = -3x$.

Then, multiply the inner terms together: $5 \times x = 5x$.

Finally, multiply the last terms together: $5 \times -3 = -15$.

$$(x + 5)(x - 3) = x^2 - 3x + 5x - 15 = x^2 + 2x - 15$$

Look at another example. Pay attention to where the minus sign appears.

5. $r^2 - 9r + 20$

First, identify the factors of the third term: (1, 20), (2, 10), and (4, 5). Which of these pairs combines to form –9? (4, 5) do. But you need them both to be negative, so the factors will look like this.

$$(r - 4)(r - 5)$$

Multiply to check your work. Remember, when you multiply two negative numbers, the result is a positive number.

$$(r - 4)(r - 5) = r^2 - 9r + 20$$

It's important to pay attention to the sign in the expression being factored. Here are some helpful generalizations.

- When the second term of the expression is being subtracted and the third term is being added, both factors will be negative.

$$r^2 - 9r + 20 = (r - 4)(r - 5)$$

- When the second term is being added and the third term is being subtracted, one of the factors will be positive, and one will be negative.

$$x^2 + 2x - 15 = (x + 5)(x - 3)$$

- When both the second and third terms of the expression are being added, both factors are positive.

$$x^2 + 8x + 16 = (x + 4)(x + 4)$$

Simultaneous Equations

Sometimes you will be given two equations and asked to solve for a variable. For example

6. If $2x + 3y = 12$ and $3x - 3y = -2$, what is the value of x?

When given simultaneous equations, stack them up and either add or subtract. The goal is to get rid of the extra variable. Here it's the y. By adding these two equations together, you can eliminate the y. Then, solve for x.

$$
\begin{array}{rcl}
2x + 3y &=& 12 \\
+\ 3x - 3y &=& -2 \\
\hline
5x + 0y &=& 10 \\
5x &=& 10 \\
x &=& 2
\end{array}
$$

If you had subtracted, you'd have gotten $-x + 6y = 14$, which wouldn't help you out at all. If you choose the wrong operation, no big deal. Just try the other one.

Look at a slightly harder example now.

7. If $2x + 3y = 7$ and $3x + 2y = 8$, what is the value of x?

At first glance this problem may not seem any harder. But when you look more closely you'll see that neither of the variables cancels out by adding or subtracting. That is because the coefficients of the terms are different. To solve this problem, make the coefficients of one of the variables equal. Do it with the y terms.

To make the coefficients of the y terms equal, you need to multiply one or both of the equations. It's sort of like finding a common factor.

$$2(2x + 3y = 7)$$
$$3(3x + 2y = 8)$$

By multiplying the equations by 2 and 3, respectively, you will end up with $6y$ in each equation. That will allow you to eliminate the ys and solve for x.

$$4x + 6y = 14$$
$$9x + 6y = 24$$

Now subtract the equations to eliminate the y terms.

$$
\begin{array}{r}
4x + 6y = \ \ 14 \\
- \ (9x + 6y = \ \ 24) \\
\hline
-5x + 0y = -10 \\
-5x = -10 \\
-x = -2
\end{array}
$$

Sometimes the ASVAB likes to be a little tricky. Instead of giving you the two equations you need to add or subtract with, the test gives you one of them and the result. For example

8. If you add $4a - 6b + 2c$ to a polynomial, you get $12a + 3b - 8c$. What is the polynomial?

The question is giving you the sum (result of addition). To find the answer, do the opposite. In this case, that means subtract, which is the same as changing the signs and adding.

$$
\begin{array}{r}
12a + 3b - \ \ 8c \\
+ \ -4a + 6b - \ \ 2c \\
\hline
8a + 9b - 10c
\end{array}
$$

The answer to the question will be $8a + 9b - 10c$. You can check your answer by doing what the question says. In other words, add the polynomial they give you to the polynomial you found.

$$
\begin{array}{r}
8a + 9b - 10c \\
+\ 4a - 6b + \ 2c \\
\hline
12a + 3b - 8c
\end{array}
$$

If you end up with the right result, you have the right answer.

Another way the ASVAB likes to test you is with questions like this.

9. Given the formulas $t = \dfrac{r}{s}$ and $p = tr - s$, which formula expresses the value of p without using r?

The key to solving this problem is in the words *without using r*. What do you think you should do? If you said solve for r, you're right! Solve for r by isolating it and then plugging the value of it into the equation for p.

$$t = \frac{r}{s} \text{ so } r = ts$$

Now you can replace the r in the equation $p = tr - s$ with its value ts.

$p = t(ts) - s$ or $p = t^2 \times ts - s$. So, $p = t^2 \times ts - s$, and that's the answer!

QUICK QUIZ 1

Practice factoring and solving simultaneous equations below. You can check your answers at the end of the chapter.

1. $11x + 4 = -x + 16$

2. $3(x + 2) = 4(2 + x)$

3. Factor: $x^2 - 4x - 21$

4. $a^2 + 10a + 25 = 0$

5. If $3x + 3y = 4$ and $2x - 3y = 1$, what is the value of x?

6. If $2v + w = 13$ and $v + 3w = 19$, what is the value of w?

PRE-QUIZ 2

1. If $7 - 3p < 25$, what is the value of p?

2. What is the formula for interest?

3. What is the formula for rate?

Inequalities

Inequalities are just like equations, with one special exception. If you multiply or divide by a negative number, you must flip the inequality sign.

10. $2x > 16$

Divide both sides by 2. This gives you

$$x > 8$$

What if the equation looked like this?

$$-2x > 16$$

You would divide both sides by -2 and flip the inequality sign around.

$$x < -8$$

What if an inequality looked like the one below?

11. $x - 5 > 3x + 1$

You are solving for x, so you need to isolate it on one side. First, move the x over by subtracting x on both sides.

$$x - x - 5 > 3x + 1 - x$$
$$-5 > 2x + 1$$

Now move the 1 over by subtracting 1 from both sides.

$$-5 - 1 > 2x + 1 - 1$$
$$-6 > 2x$$

Move the 2 by dividing both sides by 2.

$$\frac{-6}{2} > \frac{2x}{2}$$

$$-3 > x \text{ or } x < -3$$

Special Formulas

There are a couple of special formulas the ASVAB likes to test. For both of the formulas, it is simply a matter of plugging in the information the question provides and solving for the missing variable.

Motion

The formula for motion is Distance = rate × time.

———————————○———————————

12. Jackson drove 200 miles in 4 hours. What was his rate of travel?

   A.   50
   B.   80
   C.   204
   D.   800

Here's How to Crack It

The distance in this problem is 200. The time is 4 hours, and the problem asks you to find the rate. Just plug in the numbers and solve!

$$200 = \text{rate} \times 4$$

$$\frac{200}{4} = \text{rate}$$

$$\text{rate} = 50$$

The answer is (A).

———————————○———————————

Interest

The formula used on the ASVAB to determine interest is

I = prt
I = interest
p = amount of money invested (principal)
r = annual interest rate
t = time

―――――――――○―――――――――

13. How long must Cherie invest $500 at 7% to earn $350 in interest?

   A.   5 years
   B.   10 years
   C.   12 years
   D.   15 years

Here's How to Crack It

The problem gives you the principal, interest rate, and interest. You need to find the time. Plug everything in and solve.

$$350 = 500 \times .07 \times t$$

$$\frac{350}{500} = .07t$$

$$\frac{0.7}{0.07} = t$$

$$t = 10$$

The answer is (B).

―――――――――○―――――――――

QUICK QUIZ 2

Try the following problems on your own. You can check your answers at the end of the chapter.

1. $-9m - 12 > 11 - 3m$

2. $10 + x < 14 - 3x$

3. $4x - 5 > 2x + 1$

4. If Bonzo rode his bicycle 30 miles in 5 hours, how long would it take him to ride 12 miles at the same rate?

   A.   2 hours

   B.   2.5 hours

   C.   5 hours

   D.   12 hours

5. If Jen puts $1,000 in a savings account with an annual interest rate of 5%, how much interest will she earn in two years?

   A. $50

   B. $75

   C. $100

   D. $150

6. Rob drove for 6.5 hours at a speed of 45 miles per hour. How far did he travel?

   A.   153 miles

   B.   292.5 miles

   C.   300 miles

   D.   450 miles

PRE-QUIZ 3

1. What is the formula for area of a triangle?

2. What is the formula for area of a parallelogram?

3. What is the Pythagorean Theorem?

4. What does the Pythagorean Theorem allow you to solve?

5. Match the following terms to their definitions:

Column A	Column B
Surface Area	Distance around the outside of a figure
Volume	The amount of matter a container can hold
Perimeter	Sum of the areas of all sides

GEOMETRY

For the ASVAB, you will only need to know a few geometric definitions and equations. Let's start with a terminology review.

Geometry Terminology

π: Also known as "pi," and pronounced "pie." π is a number approximately equal to 3.14. It is the ratio of the circumference of a circle to the circle's diameter and is used in formulas involving circles and spheres.

Area: the space covered within the outline of a figure

Circumference: the perimeter of a circle

Cube: a three-dimensional box in which all edges and faces are equal

Decagon: a ten-sided polygon

Diameter: any line from one side of a circle to the other side through the center of the circle

Equilateral triangle: a triangle in which all sides are the same length and all angles are the same degree

Face: a side of a three-dimensional shape

Hypotenuse: the side that is opposite the right angle in a right triangle

Octagon: an eight-sided polygon

Parallel lines: lines that run infinitely, never meet, and are always the same distance apart; the symbol for this is $\parallel$.

Pentagon: a five-sided polygon

Perimeter: the outline measurement of a figure

Polygon: a closed plane (two-dimensional) figure of three or more sides (such as a triangle, rectangle, or hexagon)

Radius: any line from the center of a circle to any point on the edge of the circle, or the line whose endpoints are any point on the surface of a sphere and its center; symbolized by r

Right triangle: a triangle in which one of the angles measures 90 degrees

Pythagorean Theorem: $a^2 + b^2 = c^2$, where *a*, *b*, and *c* are the lengths of the three sides of a right triangle. In other words, the sum of the squares of the lengths of the two smaller legs of a right triangle will add up to the square of the length of the hypotenuse.

Supplementary angles: two or more angles that together add up to 180 degrees

Triangle: a three-sided polygon

Vertical angles: opposite angles formed by the intersection of two lines

Volume: the amount of space a three-dimensional object occupies or can hold

Geometry: Lines and Angles

There are 360 degrees in a circle.

There are 180 degrees in a straight line.

A right angle (or quarter circle) has 90 degrees.

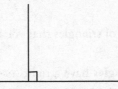

Two angles that form a straight line add up to 180 degrees.

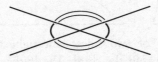

When two lines cross, the vertical angles are equal.

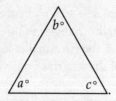

There are 180 degrees in a triangle: $a° + b° + c° = 180°$.

Fred's Theorem

Fred's Theorem is just a name we made up for some rules you need to remember. These three things are always true when a line crosses two parallel lines.

- Two kinds of angles are created: big ones and small ones.
- All the big angles are equal to each other; all the small angles are equal to each other.
- Any big angle plus any small angle equals 180 degrees.

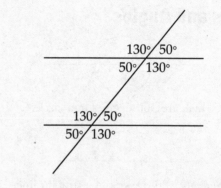

Triangles

There are a few different types of triangles that you need to know about.

Right triangles have a right (or 90°) angle.

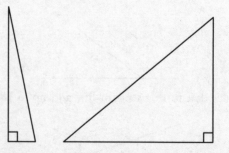

If you know the lengths of two sides of a right triangle, you can use the **Pythagorean Theorem** to find the third. The Pythagorean Theorem states that $a^2 + b^2 = c^2$, where a, b, and c are the lengths of the three sides of a right triangle. In other words, the sum of the squares of the lengths of the two smaller legs of a right triangle will add up to the square of the length of the hypotenuse.

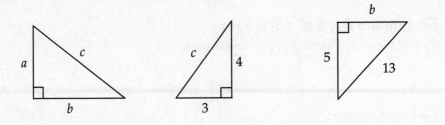

In the formula, *a* and *b* always denote the length of the legs of the triangle, and *c*, the length of the hypotenuse.

If $a = 4$ and $b = 3$, then $4^2 + 3^2 = 25$. Therefore, $c^2 = 25$ and $c = 5$.

If $a = 5$ and $c = 13$, then $5^2 + b^2 = 13^2$. So $25 + b^2 = 169$ and therefore $b^2 = 144$ and $b = 12$.

Isosceles triangles have 2 equal sides and 2 equal angles.

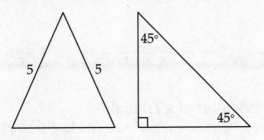

Equilateral triangles have 3 equal sides and 3 equal angles.

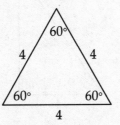

Similar triangles have equal angles and proportional sides.

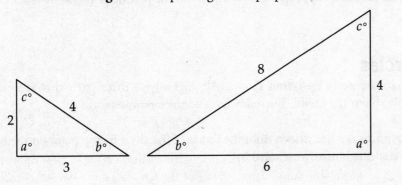

Finding the Area of a Triangle

To find the area of a triangle, use the equation

$$\text{Area} = \frac{1}{2}\,\text{base} \times \text{height}$$

Look at an example.

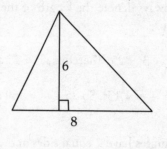

$$A = \underline{\hspace{1cm}}$$

The base = 8 and height = 6, so the equation is Area = $\frac{1}{2}(8)(6) = \frac{1}{2}48 = 24$.

Finding the Perimeter of a Triangle

To find the perimeter of a triangle, just add up the lengths of all the sides.

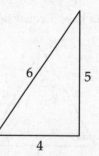

In this example, the sides are 4, 5, and 6. So the perimeter is 4 + 5 + 6 = 15.

Circles

Circles are perfectly round shapes. All circles have three parts that you need to know about: the radius, the diameter, and the circumference.

The **radius** is a line drawn from the center of the circle to any point on the edge of the circle. It is usually denoted by r.

The **diameter** is a line drawn from one side of the circle to the other side, which crosses through the center of the circle. It is equal to two times the radius and can be found with the formula: diameter = $2r$.

The **circumference** of a circle is the perimeter of the circle. You can find the circumference of a circle using this formula: circumference = $2\pi r$.

Remember that π stands for pi. π is the ratio of a circle's circumference to its diameter. π is the same for all circles—it's a number approximately equal to 3.14. When solving problems that use π, the ASVAB will tell you what value to use. Sometimes you can just leave the π as it is. In other words, you don't always have to plug in a numerical value for π, because the answer will be something like 9π or 12π.

You also need to know how to find the area of a circle. The formula for that is Area = r^2.

Now that you know the basics, take a look at some circles!

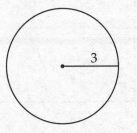

In the above circle, the radius r has been provided. $r = 3$. Therefore,

- Diameter = $2r = 2(3) = 6$
- Area = $\pi r^2 = \pi 3^2 = 9\pi$
- Circumference = $2\pi r = 2\pi 3 = 6\pi$

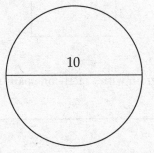

The diameter of the circle is 10. What is the radius and circumference?

Start with the radius, since you need to know that to find the circumference. The diameter is two times the length of the radius, so the radius is $\frac{10}{2} = 5$. Now find the circumference: Circumference = $2\pi r = 2\pi 5 = 10\pi$.

Quadrilaterals

A quadrilateral is a four-sided figure. The measures of its four angles always add up to 360 degrees. There are a few different quadrilaterals you may be asked about.

Parallelograms are quadrilaterals with two pairs of opposite sides that are parallel and two pairs of opposite angles that are equal.

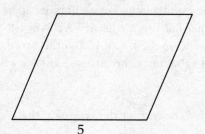

A **rectangle** is a parallelogram with four right angles and equal opposite sides.

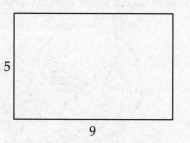

A **square** is a parallelogram with all equal sides and four right angles.

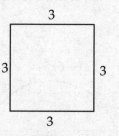

A **trapezoid** is a parallelogram with exactly one pair of parallel opposite sides.

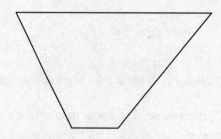

Finding the Area of a Quadrilateral

The formula for finding the area enclosed by a quadrilateral depends on the type of quadrilateral you are working with.

For a rectangle, use: Area = length × width

For a square, use: Area = side × side, or side^2

For a parallelogram or trapezoid use: Area = $\dfrac{\text{base 1 + base 2}}{2}h$

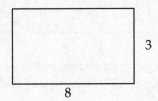

The first quadrilateral above is a square, so use the formula Area = side^2. Area = 4^2 = 16.

The second quadrilateral is a rectangle, so use the formula Area = length × width. Area = 10 × 15 = 150.

The third quadrilateral is a parallelogram, so use the formula Area = base × height. Area = 6 × 4 = 24.

Finding the Perimeter of a Quadrilateral

To find the perimeter of a quadrilateral, just add up all the sides.

The quadrilateral shown above is a rectangle with a length of 8 and a height of 3. To find the perimeter, add up all the sides of the rectangle.

Perimeter = 8 + 8 + 3 + 3 = 22

Remember, although the drawing only gave you two sides, you need to add all four sides.

Finding the Volume of a Box

To find the volume of a box, which is a three-dimensional rectangle, use this formula.

$$\text{Volume} = \text{length} \times \text{width} \times \text{height}$$

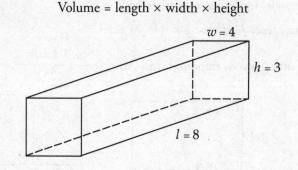

In the figure above, length = 8, width = 4, and height = 3. Using the formula,

$$\text{Volume} = 8 \times 4 \times 3 = 96.$$

Finding the Surface Area of a Box

The surface area of a box is the sum of the areas of all its sides.

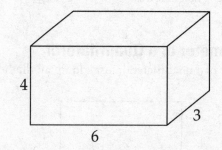

In the figure above, you are given the length, width, and height of the box. To find the surface area, find the area of each side and then add them together.

Front side = 4 × 6 = 24
Back side = 4 × 6 = 24
Top side = 6 × 3 = 18
Bottom side = 6 × 3 = 18
Left side = 4 × 3 = 12
Right side = 4 × 3 = 12
The surface area is 24 + 24 + 18 + 18 + 12 + 12 = 108

QUICK QUIZ 3

That's all the geometry you need to know. Memorize the formulas and then take the Quick Quiz. You can check your answers at the end of the chapter.

1. A circular swimming pool has a circumference of 12π. What is the radius of the pool?

   A.   3

   B.   6

   C.   24

   D.   30

2. If one of the angles in a right triangle measures 20 degrees, what are the measurements of the other two angles?

   A.   20 degrees, 140 degrees

   B.   40 degrees, 120 degrees

   C.   70 degrees, 90 degrees

   D.   80 degrees, 90 degrees

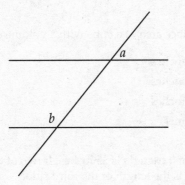

3. A line crosses two parallel lines, creating angle *a*, which measures 50 degrees. How many degrees does angle *b* have?

   A.   50 degrees

   B.   90 degrees

   C.   130 degrees

   D.   180 degrees

4. Mrs. Stewart baked two apple pies. One had a radius of 4 inches, the other a radius of 5 inches. Find the difference in the areas of the two pies.

   A.   1 square inch

   B.   9 square inches

   C. 9π square inches

   D. 41π square inches

5. If a triangle has an area of 21 and a base of 7, what is its height?

    A.   4

    B.   6

    C.   7

    D.   8

6. The length of a rectangle is 2 less than 3 times the width. If the perimeter is 20 mm, what is the length?

    A.   3 mm

    B.   7 mm

    C.   9 mm

    D.   10 mm

7. A box has a length of 5 inches, a width of 3 inches, and a height of 4 inches. What is the volume of the box?

    A.   12 cubic inches

    B.   60 cubic inches

    C.   120 cubic inches

    D.   600 cubic inches

8. What is the surface area of a cube with a volume of 27 cubic inches?

    A.   18 square inches

    B.   27 square inches

    C.   54 square inches

    D.   81 square inches

9. The perimeter of a triangle is 25 inches. If two of the sides are 8 inches and 10 inches, what is the length of the third side?

    A.   5 inches

    B.   7 inches

    C.   12 inches

    D.   18 inches

ANSWERS TO PRE-QUIZZES, QUICK QUIZZES

Pre-Quiz 1
Page 72

1. FOIL represents the process of multiplying two binomials.
   First **O**uter **I**nner **L**ast
2. $x = 6$
3. $x = -7, 5$
4. $y = 7$

Quick Quiz 1
Page 79

1. $12x = 12$
   $x = 1$
2. $3x + 6 = 8 + 4x$
   $x = -2$
3. $(x - 7)(x + 3)$
4. $(a + 5)(a + 5)$
5. $3x + 3y = 4$
   $\underline{+2x - 3y = 1}$
   $5x = 5$
   $x = 1$
6. $2(v + 3w = 19) = 2v + 6w = 38$
   $2v + 6w = 38$
   $\underline{-2v + w = 13}$
   $5w = 25$
   $w = 5$

Pre-Quiz 2
Page 80

1. $p > -6$
2. $I = prt$
   I = interest
   p = amount of money invested (principal)
   r = annual interest rate
   t = time

3. $r = \dfrac{D}{t}$

   r = rate
   D = distance
   t = time

Quick Quiz 2
Page 82

1. $-6m > 23$

   $m < -\dfrac{23}{6}$

2. $4x < 4$
   $x < 1$
3. $2x > 6$
   $x > 3$
4. **A**
5. **C**
6. **B**

Pre-Quiz 3
Page 83

1. $A = \dfrac{1}{2}bh$

2. $A = bh$
3. $a^2 + b^2 = c^2$
4. Given two sides of a right triangle, the Pythagorean Theorem allows you to solve for the third side of a right triangle.
5. Surface Area is the sum of the areas of all sides.
   Volume is the amount of matter a container can hold.
   Perimeter is the distance around the outside of a figure.

Quick Quiz 3

Pages 93

1. **B**
2. **C**
3. **C**
4. **C**
5. **B**
6. **B**
7. **B**
8. **C**
9. **B**

Chapter 4
Word Knowledge

INTRODUCTION TO THE WORD KNOWLEDGE TEST

The MET-ASVAB and Student ASVAB versions of the Word Knowledge test consist of 35 questions designed to test your vocabulary. But since you're given only 11 minutes to complete the section, it's more like a speed-reading test than a vocabulary test. The CAT-ASVAB has 16 questions and only 8 minutes! Luckily, most of the words being tested aren't too difficult. In fact, you probably know most of them already. And those you don't know, we will help you learn. You should try to learn every word in our Key Terms List at the end of the chapter.

IMPROVING YOUR VOCABULARY

There are several techniques you can use to learn new words, so let's get started!

Flash Cards

One of the best ways to learn new words is to use flash cards. You can make your own flash cards out of index cards. On one side of the card, write down the word you're trying to learn. On the other side of the card, write the definition. Then you can quiz yourself on the words or practice with a friend. You can even carry the cards around with you and practice when you have spare time.

The Image Approach

The image approach involves letting each new word suggest a wild image to you and then using that image to help you remember the word. For example, the word *enfranchise* means "to give the right to vote." First, let's use the word in a sentence.

"Women did not become enfranchised in the United States until 1920, when the Nineteenth Amendment to the Constitution guaranteed them the right to vote in state and federal elections."

Now you need to come up with an image that will help you remember the definition. *Franchise* might suggest to you a McDonald's franchise. You could remember the new word by imagining people lined up to vote at a McDonald's. If you remember the image, chances are you'll remember the word. The weirder and more vivid the image you create, the more memorable it will be.

Mnemonics

A mnemonic is a verbal trick that helps you remember something. Once again, the funnier or the stranger you make your mnemonic, the more likely you are to remember it. Here's an example.

Swarm means a large crowd, often of insects. Our mnemonic for this word might be "Swinging ARMs." Think about it—if a swarm of bees were chasing you, you'd probably be swinging your arms. By remembering that image, and the phrase "Swinging ARMs," you can easily remember the definition of the word *swarm*.

Here's another example: *cower* means to hide in fear. Our mnemonic will be "COW fEaR." Picture someone scared of cows and cowering in the corner to avoid them.

As you make up your own mnemonics, write them down. (Flash cards are great for these.) Although you may not be able to think of a clever mnemonic for every Hit Parade word, sometimes you'll end up learning the word just by spending enough time trying to make up a mnemonic.

Look It Up

Well-written general-interest publications—newspapers and news magazines, for example—are good sources for new vocabulary words. You should start to read them on a regular basis. When you come across a new word, write it down, look it up in the dictionary, and make a new flash card for it. And most important, you need to...

Use It

It's not enough to just look up a word in the dictionary. Make that word a part of your life. Use it whenever you can in everyday life. A powerful vocabulary requires lots of exercise.

QUICK QUIZ

You can check your answers at the end of the chapter.

1. What are five ways to improve your vocabulary?

   _____

   _____

   _____

   _____

   _____

2. Try coming up with mnemonics for the following words.

   Chaos: noun; complete confusion

   _____

   Provoke: verb; to cause a feeling or reaction; to push into action

   _____

   Jeer: verb; to taunt or ridicule

   _____

   Aloof: adjective; keeping apart from others

   _____

   Abundance: noun; a great amount

   _____

THE QUESTIONS

Now that you are on your way to a better vocabulary, it's time to discuss the types of questions you will see on the ASVAB. The questions come in two forms. The first form gives you a sentence with a word underlined. Your job is to choose the answer choice that could replace the underlined word in the sentence without changing the meaning of the sentence. For example

1. He was <u>inconsolable</u> when his team lost.

   A. happy
   B. freezing
   C. sad
   D. rushed

Here's How to Crack It

We call these Vocabulary in Context questions, because the word being tested is given in the context of a sentence. Usually the sentence provides valuable clues that can help you find the answer. Look at the example above. You know that the team lost, which is a bad thing. So inconsolable probably means something negative. You can get rid of (A). Of the remaining answers, (C)—sad, makes the most sense in the context of the sentence.

Look at another example.

---

2. He was very upset over the unexpected death of his <u>benefactor</u>.

    A.   dictator

    B.   supervisor

    C.   sponsor

    D.   partner

Here's How to Crack It

The sentence tells you that he was very upset over the benefactor's death. So the benefactor is probably someone he likes. If you didn't know the definition of *benefactor*, you could use this information to eliminate at least a couple of the answers. You could safely eliminate (A) and (B), which would leave you with (C) and (D). At this point, if you guessed, you'd have a 50-50 chance—and that's without even knowing the definition. The correct answer is (C), sponsor. If you didn't know this, make a flash card for *benefactor*.

The second form of question is a straightforward definition question. It gives you a word and asks you to choose the answer choice that is most similar in meaning. For example

3. <u>Chuckle</u> most nearly means

    A.   throw

    B.   laugh

    C.   consider

    D.   change

Unfortunately, these types of questions don't provide any clues. But there are a couple of techniques you can use to make finding the answer easier.

Process of Elimination

Process of Elimination is a very important tool on the Word Knowledge test. It helps you avoid careless mistakes and improves your chances of choosing the correct answer. Always write the answer choices out on your scrap paper and cross them off as you eliminate answers.

Which Side of the Fence?

This is another useful technique. Imagine you are taking the Word Knowledge test. You are moving through the questions quickly and confidently because you know every word on the test. Then, suddenly, you come to a word you can't define. You've heard the word before, but you just can't remember the definition. Don't panic! "Which side of the fence?" is designed for exactly this situation. First, try to recall where you heard the word before. That may help you remember its meaning. Next, try to determine whether the word has a positive or negative connotation. If you know it means something positive, eliminate all negative answer choices. If it's negative, eliminate all the positive choices. Once you've eliminated everything you can, guess from the remaining answers and move on.

The Three Categories

With both types of questions, the first thing you need to do is identify what type of word is being tested. By this we mean assign it into one of three categories: Words You Know, Words You Sort of Know, and Words You Don't Know. The strategy is a little different for each type of word.

Words You Know

These are words you can define accurately. If you can't give a definition of a word that's pretty close to what a dictionary would say, then it's not a word you know.

Strategy: When a question asks you about a Word You Know, define the word in your head. Then look through the answer choices carefully, crossing off answers you know are wrong. If you don't know a word in the answers, don't eliminate it—it could still be the right choice. Choose the one closest in meaning to your definition.

Words You Sort of Know

These are words you've seen before, or heard, or maybe even used yourself, but can't define accurately.

Strategy: Check the answer choices to see if there's any choice you can eliminate based on your sort of knowledge. If you know the word is positive, eliminate any negative words in the answer choices. If you know the word is negative, eliminate any positive words in the answer choices. Again, if you don't know a word in the answers, don't eliminate it. Use context, if available, and guess from the remaining answers.

Note: Whenever you're practicing and you encounter a Word You Sort of Know, look it up in the dictionary and make a flash card for it. Turn it into a Word You Know!

Words You Don't Know

You probably won't see too many words on the test that look totally foreign to you. But if you do...

Strategy: Eliminate any answer choices you can based on context. Then guess from the remaining answers. Never leave a question blank!

KEY TERMS LIST

Obviously, you want as many words as possible to fall into the Words You Know category. But you're probably wondering, what words do I need to know? Well, we can't tell you exactly which words will be tested on the ASVAB, but we can give you a good idea of the types of words that will be there by providing you with a list. The words here are similar to the vocabulary the ASVAB tests. In fact, some of them may even appear on the ASVAB. If you're wondering how you will do on the Word Knowledge test, take a look at this Key Term List. If you know most of the words on the list, you're in pretty good shape. If you don't know a lot of the words, then start studying!

abandon	To forsake or desert
abase	To lower in rank, prestige, or esteem
abolish *shunt*	To do away with /put an end/overthrow
abstruse	Difficult to understand
absurd	Ridiculously unreasonable
abundant	Marked by great plenty (as of resources)
accessible	Able to be reached or used
accidental	Happening by chance or unexpectedly
accurate	Conforming exactly to truth or to a standard
accuse	To charge with a fault; to blame
acumen	Quickness, accuracy, and keenness of judgment or insight
adapt	To adjust or make usable
address	To make a spoken or written communication to

admire	To regard with approval, respect, or satisfaction
admission	Permission to enter
adore	To regard with the utmost esteem and affection
adroit *adept*	Dexterous; deft *skilled*
aesthetic	Having to do with the appreciation of beauty
affable	Easygoing; friendly
alacrity	Cheerful willingness; eagerness
alleviate	To ease a pain or a burden
altruism	Unselfish concern for the welfare of others; selflessness
amalgam	A combination of diverse elements; a mixture
ambiguous	Open to more than one interpretation
ambivalent	Simultaneously feeling opposing feelings; uncertain
amiable	Friendly and agreeable in disposition; good-natured and likable
analysis	The process of looking at something carefully and methodically
anticipate	To feel or realize beforehand; to look forward to
anxious	Mentally upset over possible misfortune or danger, etc.; worried
apathetic	Feeling or showing little emotion
apologize	To express regret, acknowledge faults, or make excuses for
apparel	Clothing; something that covers or adorns
application	Something that is being used or applied
arboreal *wooden coach-built*	Relating to or resembling *similar* a tree
arcane *esoteric*	Known or understood by only a few
archaic	Characteristic of an earlier period; old-fashioned
ascertain	To discover with certainty, as through examination or experimentation
assimilate *reconcile adapt*	Incorporated and absorbed into the mind; made similar; caused to resemble
assume *deem*	To take for granted as true
astute	Shrewd; clever
augment *add*	To make (something already developed or well under way) greater, as in size

aural	Of, relating to, or perceived by the ear
austere	Without decoration; strict
authority	Power to influence or command thought, opinion, or behavior
autonomy	Independence; self-determination; self-government or the right of
averse	Strongly disinclined
awe	An emotion combining fear and wonder
banal	Drearily commonplace and often predictable; trite
basic	Of or relating to essential structure, function, or facts
behavior	The manner of conducting oneself
belie	To picture falsely; misrepresent
belligerent	Inclined or eager to fight; hostile or aggressive
benefactor	Someone who takes care of or gives money to another person
beneficial	Producing or promoting a favorable result; advantageous
benign	Kind and gentle
bias	A preference or inclination; prejudice
bizarre	Very strange; unusual
boast	To speak of or assert with excessive pride
bolster	To buoy up or hearten; to support or prop up
bombastic	Given to pompous speech or writing
brevity	The quality or state of being brief in duration
brilliant	Distinguished by unusual mental keenness or alertness
budget	A sum of money allocated for a particular purpose
burgeon	To grow and flourish; to put forth new buds, leaves, or greenery; to sprout
cacophony	Jarring, discordant sound; dissonance
cajole	To urge with gentle and repeated appeals, teasing, or flattery
callous	Emotionally hardened; unfeeling
candid	Characterized by openness and sincerity of expression; unreservedly straightforward
cantankerous	Ill-tempered and quarrelsome; disagreeable

capricious	Impulsive and unpredictable
castigate	To inflict severe punishment on
cathartic	Causing relaxation after an emotional outburst
censure	To criticize severely; to blame
chaos	Disorder
characterize	To describe the qualities of
chicanery	A trick; deception by trickery
circumscribe	To draw a circle around; to restrict
circumspect	Heedful of circumstances and potential consequences; prudent
cite	To quote or refer to a person's speech or writing
clandestine	Done secretly, especially to deceive; surreptitious
cling	To hold or hold on tightly or tenaciously
colleague	A co-worker
command	To give orders to; to have at your disposal
commodity	Something bought or sold
compel	To force
competition	A contest between opponents
complement	Something that completes, makes up a whole, or brings to perfection
compromise	An agreement that partially satisfies each side
conceive	To imagine
conciliatory	Appeasing; soothing; pleasant
conclusive	Putting an end to any uncertainty or doubt; final
concord	Agreement (antonym: discord)
concur	To agree; to be of the same opinion
conform	To act in accordance with prevailing standards or customs
conjecture	Inference or judgment based on inconclusive or incomplete evidence
conquer	To defeat an opponent
consciousness	The state of being aware and awake
consequence	A result
consideration	Careful thought

conspicuous	Easy to notice; obvious (antonym: inconspicuous)
contentious	Quarrelsome
contiguous	Sharing an edge or boundary; touching
contradiction	A situation in which two things do not make sense together
contrary	Opposite; disagreeing
controversial	Causing debate or argument
conventional	Following accepted customs; normal
convey	To express
convoluted	Intricate; complex
copious	Plentiful; having a large quantity
cordial	Hearty; sincere; warm; affectionate
corruption	Dishonesty; immoral behavior
cosmopolitan	So sophisticated as to be at home in all parts of the world or conversant with
credible	Capable of being believed; plausible
crisis	An unstable or crucial time or state of affairs in which a decisive change is impending
critical	Tending to call attention to flaws
crude	Raw; rude
cult	A religion considered to be extreme
cultivate	To help something grow
curative	Something that cures; a remedy
curiosity	Desire to know
current	Up-to-date; at the moment
cynical	Distrustful of people's motives
dearth	A scarce supply; a lack
debacle	A sudden, disastrous collapse, downfall, or defeat; a rout
debilitate	To sap the strength or energy of; to enervate
debunk	To expose or ridicule falseness, shams, or exaggerated claims
deceive	To cause someone to believe an untruth
deduction	Something that is inferred from something else; something removed or taken away

defunct	Having ceased to exist or live
deleterious	Having a harmful effect
deliberate	To think deeply about
demolish	To throw or pull down; to raze; to destroy the fabric of; to pull to pieces; to ruin
demure	Modest and reserved in manner or behavior
denounce	To condemn openly as being evil or reprehensible
deny	To disclaim connection with or responsibility for
depict	To represent by, or as if by, a picture; to describe
deride	To speak of or treat with contemptuous mirth
derivative	A by-product
derogatory	Tending or intending to belittle
despair	Utter loss of hope
detached	Set apart from others
determined	Committed; certain
devastated	Made uninhabitable; ravaged; ruined; wasted
devious	Characterized by insincerity or deceit; evasive; deviating from a straight course
devise	To imagine or create
didactic	Intended to instruct
diffidence	Timidity or shyness
dilatory	Habitually late
diligent	Careful and steady in application to one's work or duties
diminish	To decrease in size, extent, or range; to lessen the authority, dignity, or reputation of
dirge	A funeral hymn or lament
disaffected	Having lost faith or loyalty; discontent
discouraged	Made less hopeful or enthusiastic
dismiss	To reject serious consideration of
disparage	To speak of in a slighting way or negatively; to belittle
disprove	To overthrow by argument, evidence, or proof
disrupt	To throw into disorder
disseminate	To scatter widely, as in sowing seed

distant	Separated in space or by time
distaste	A feeling of intense dislike
distend	To swell out or expand from or as if from internal pressure
distinguish	To perceive a difference in
disturb	To interfere with
docile	Ready and willing to be taught; teachable
dogmatic	Stubbornly adhering to insufficiently proved beliefs
dominant	Most powerful
draft	A version of a letter or essay
dubious	Doubtful; of unlikely authenticity
duplicitous	Given to or marked by deliberate deceptiveness in behavior or speech
ebullience	Intense enthusiasm
eclectic	Made up of a variety of sources or styles
effect	An outward sign
effective	Producing a decided, decisive, or desired effect
effrontery	Brazen boldness; presumptuousness
effusive	Showing excessive emotion; overflowing
embellish	To make beautiful by ornamenting; to decorate
eminent	Distinguished; prominent
empathetic	Identification with and understanding of another's situation or feelings
enact	To order by virtue of superior authority
enclosed	Closed in or surrounded or included within
encounter	A meeting, especially between hostile parties
encourage	To inspire with courage, spirit, or hope
endurance	The power to withstand hardship or stress; a state of surviving; remaining alive
endure	To undergo (as a hardship), especially without giving in
enhance	To make better or stronger
enigma	One that is puzzling, ambiguous, or inexplicable; a riddle
enthusiasm	A feeling of excitement

ephemeral	Lasting for only a brief time
epitome	A representative or example of a class or type
equivocal	Open to two or more interpretations and often intended to mislead
eradicate	To get rid of as if by tearing it up by the roots; to abolish
erratic	Having no fixed or regular course; wandering
erudition	Deep, extensive learning
esoteric	Intended for or understood by only a particular group especially in mental aptitude
essential	Of the utmost importance; necessary
establish	To bring into existence
esteem	Respect or admiration
euphemism	The act or an example of substituting a mild, indirect, or vague term for one
evident	Obvious; easily seen or understood
exacerbate	To increase the severity, violence, or bitterness of; to aggravate
exasperation	The state of being annoyed or irritated
excavation	Digging
exhibit	To show publicly
exonerate	To free from blame
exorbitant	Exceeding all bounds, as of custom or fairness
expedient	Appropriate to a purpose; speedy
extent	The range over which something extends; scope
extol	To praise highly
extraneous	Irrelevant
extraordinary	Going beyond what is usual, regular, or customary
extrapolate	To infer or estimate by extending or projecting known information
exuberant	Full of unrestrained enthusiasm or joy
fabricate	To make in order to deceive
faculty	Teachers at a school; members of a learned profession
fallacy	A false notion
fascinating	Extremely interesting or charming

fastidious	Possessing careful attention to detail; difficult to please
fatigue	Temporary loss of strength and energy resulting from hard physical or mental work
feasible	Capable of being accomplished; possible
felicitous	Admirably suited; apt
fine	A sum imposed as punishment for an offense
flag	(v.) To decline in vigor or strength; to hang limply; to droop
flagrant	Extremely or deliberately shocking or noticeable
flaw	An imperfection or fault
flippant	Marked by disrespectful levity or casualness; pert
force	Strength or energy exerted or brought to bear; cause of motion or change
forge	To make or imitate falsely, especially with intent to defraud
fragile	Easily broken
fraud	Intentional deception resulting in injury to another person; deliberate trickery intended to gain an advantage
frustration	A feeling of annoyance at being hindered or criticized
fundamental	A leading or primary principle, rule, law, or article, which serves as the groundwork of a system; essential part
funding	Financial resources provided to make some project possible
gaffe	A clumsy social error; a faux pas
generalization	A statement or judgment about a group based on a few examples
generate	To create
generous	Willing to give and share unstintingly
graceful	Characterized by beauty of movement, style, form, etc.; suggesting taste, ease, and wealth; elegant
gracious	Doing or producing good; exhibiting courtesy and politeness
grandiose	Characterized by greatness of scope or intent; grand
gratuitous	Given freely; unearned; unwarranted
hackneyed	Worn-out through overuse; trite
harmony	Compatibility in opinion and action

harsh	Very strict; unkind or cruel
hazardous	Involving risk or danger
headstrong	Bold; stubborn
hesitate	To pause or hold back in uncertainty or unwillingness
hilarious	Marked by or causing boisterous merriment or convulsive laughter
honor	To regard or treat with esteem or respect; to revere
humanity	The quality of being humane; kindness
ideal	A standard of perfection, beauty, or excellence
idiosyncrasy	A structural or behavioral characteristic peculiar to an individual or group
ignominy	Great personal dishonor or humiliation
ignorance	Lack of knowledge or education
ignorant	Lacking knowledge or comprehension
illumination	Lighting
immediate	Direct; without anything in between
impetuous	Characterized by sudden and forceful energy or emotion
impetus	An impelling force; an impulse
implement	Tool
imply	To lead someone to believe something without directly stating it
impolite	Not polite; not of polished manners; wanting in good manners; discourteous; uncivil; rude
impractical	Not usable or effective
impugn	To attack as false or questionable
impulse	Force or urge
inaccurate	Not according to truth; inexact; incorrect; erroneous
inadvisable	Not recommended
incoherent	Lacking cohesion, connection, or harmony
incongruous	Lacking in harmony; incompatible
inconsequential	Unimportant
inconsistency	Discordance in respect to sentiment or action
inconsistent	Not agreeing with another fact or claim

incontrovertible	Indisputable; not open to question
independent	Free; not subject to control by others; not relying on others
indict	To accuse of wrongdoing; to charge
indignation	Moral outrage
infer	To conclude or figure out
influence	Ability to persuade or affect
influential	Having influence or power
ingenuous	Lacking in cunning, guile, or worldliness; artless (antonym: disingenuous)
inhibit	To check; to hold back; to restrain; to hinder; to discourage from free or spontaneous activity
innocent	Free from evil or guilt; lacking intent or capacity to injure
innocuous	Having no adverse effect; harmless
inscrutable	Difficult to fathom or understand; impenetrable
insecure	Not firm or firmly fixed; lacking self-confidence or assurance
insightful	Exhibiting clear and deep perception
insinuate	To introduce or otherwise convey gradually and insidiously
insipid	Uninteresting; unchallenging
insolent	Insulting in manner or speech
insular	Suggestive of the isolated life of an island; narrow or provincial
interpretation	A particular adaptation or version of a work, method, or style; an explanation of something not immediately obvious
intransigence	Refusing to moderate a position, especially an extreme position
inundate	To overwhelm as if with a flood; to swamp
invocation	To call on (a higher power) for assistance, support, or inspiration
irrelevant	Having no connection to a subject
irresponsible	Showing lack of care for consequences
jaded	Worn out; wearied
jocular	Characterized by or given to joking

juxtapose	To place side by side, especially for comparison or contrast
labor	Work; effort
lack	To be deficient in or missing something
laudatory	Giving praise
lavish	Characterized by or produced with extravagance and abundance
legend	A story about mythical or supernatural beings or events; a brief description accompanying an illustration
litigious	Tending to engage in lawsuits
loquacious	Very talkative
loyalty	The quality of being unswerving in allegiance
lucid	Easily understood; clear
lugubrious	Mournful, dismal, or gloomy, especially to an exaggerated or ludicrous degree
magnanimous	Courageously noble in mind and heart
majority	The quality or state of being greater
mass	A large quantity, amount, or number
maverick	One who is independent and resists adherence to a group
mendacious	Lying; untruthful
mercenary	(adj.) Motivated solely by a desire for monetary or material gain; (n.) a professional
mercy	Kindness; forgiveness
mere	Only; nothing more than
meticulous	Extremely careful and precise
misleading	Deceptive
modest	Marked by simplicity
modicum	A small, moderate, or token amount
modify	To make partial changes in; to make different
moral	Relating to principles of right and wrong in behavior
morose	Sad and dreary
multifarious	Having great variety; diverse
multiplicity	The state of being various or manifold
mythical	Fictional; unreal

narcissistic	Having an inflated idea of one's own importance
narrate	To give a detailed account of
nefarious	Infamous by way of being extremely wicked
nostalgic	Longing for familiar things or persons, or for a period of time or an occurrence that has passed
novel	A book that tells a fictional story
obedience	Compliance with that which is required by authority; subjection to rightful restraint or control
obscure	Not clearly understood or expressed
obsequious	Full of or exhibiting servile compliance; fawning
obsessive	Characterized by obsession; excessive, often to an unreasonable degree
obstacle	Something that stands in the way and must be circumvented or surmounted
obstinate	Stubbornly adhering to an opinion or a course of action of development
onerous	Troublesome or oppressive; burdensome
opponent	One that takes an opposite position
optimistic	Anticipating the best possible outcome
opulent	Exhibiting a display of great wealth
organic	Derived from living organisms
origin	The first existence or beginning of anything; the point at which something begins or from which it derives
original	Preceding all others in time or being as first made or performed
ornate	Elaborately decorated
orthodox	Adhering to the accepted or traditional and established faith
outcast	A person who is rejected (from society or home)
outcome	Something that follows as a result or consequence
outdated	Old-fashioned
overdue	Delayed beyond the proper time of arrival or payment
overlook	To fail to see
overthrow	To cause the downfall of

overwhelm	To overcome by superior force or numbers
overwhelming	Tending to overpower in thought or feeling
palliative	Relieving or soothing the symptoms of a disease or disorder without dealing with the underlying cause
parity	Equality, as in amount, status, or value (antonym: disparity)
partisan	Devoted to or biased in support of a party, group, or cause
passion	Extreme feeling or emotion; an irrational but irresistible motive for a belief or action
passive	Not active
patience	Calm endurance of hardship, provocation, pain, delay, etc.
patron	One who uses wealth or influence to help a cause
paucity	Smallness of number; fewness
pedantic	Characterized by a narrow, often ostentatious concern for book learning
pejorative	Describing words or phrases that belittle or speak negatively of someone
penalize	To inflict a penalty or punishment on
penchant	A definite liking; a strong inclination
perceive	To attain awareness or understanding of; to become aware of through the senses
perceptive	Having the ability to understand; keen in discernment
pernicious	Tending to cause death or serious injury; deadly
perseverance	The act of not quitting
persist	To continue
perspicacious	Having or showing penetrating mental discernment; clear-sighted
persuasive	Able to move people to act or believe
pessimist	One who emphasizes adverse aspects, conditions, and possibilities
phenomenon	An observable fact or event
philanthropic	Humanitarian; benevolent
pictorial	Consisting of pictures
pilfer	To steal (a small amount)
pitiful	Eliciting compassion

pity	To feel pity or compassion for; to have sympathy with
placid	Calm or quiet; undisturbed by tumult or disorder
plastic	Easily bendable
playwright	Someone who writes plays
pledge	A binding commitment to do or give or refrain from something
poll	A survey of people's opinions
ponder	To consider carefully; think deeply
portent	An indication of something important or calamitous about to occur
portrait	A picture or painting of a person
potentate	One who has the power and position to rule over others; a monarchy
potential	Ability
practical	Concerned with actual use or practice
pragmatic	Practical
precious	Highly esteemed or cherished
precisely	In a manner or measure or to a degree or number that strictly conforms to a fact or condition
precocious	Manifesting or characterized by unusually early development or maturity
predict	To declare or indicate in advance
predictable	Possible to foretell
predominant	Having superior numbers, strength, or importance
prescience	Knowledge of actions or events before they occur; foresight
primarily	Most importantly
principle	A rule or guide
prodigious	Enormous
profundity	Great depth of intellect, feeling, or meaning
prohibit	To forbid by authority
proliferate	To grow or increase rapidly
prolific	Very productive; producing great quantities
prominence	The state of being noticeable
prosaic	Unimaginative; dull

prose	Words in sentences and paragraphs, as opposed to poetry
prospectus	A formal summary of a proposed venture or project
prosperity	The state of being successful; economic well-being
quarrel	A usually verbal conflict between antagonists
quell	To put down forcibly; to suppress
quest	A long search
quiescent	Being quiet, still, or at rest; inactive
radiant	Filled with happiness; emitting light or heat
rancorous	Hateful; marked by deep seated ill-will
raze	To level to the ground; to demolish
reaction	The act or process or an instance of responding; a response
reciprocate	To mutually take or give
reclusive	Seeking or preferring seclusion or isolation
rectitude	Moral uprightness; righteousness
redolent	Having or emitting fragrance; aromatic; suggestive, reminiscent
redouble	To become twice as great
redundant	Needlessly wordy or repetitive in expression
refute	To disprove
relatively	In comparison to something else
relinquish	To retire from; to give up or abandon
remiss	Lax in attending to duty; negligent
renounce	To give up (a title, for example), especially by formal announcement
repudiate	To reject the validity or authority of
repugnant	Arousing disgust or aversion; offensive or repulsive
repulsive	Tending to repel or drive off; disgusting
resentment	Deep hatred
resolution	Something settled or resolved; the outcome of a decision
reticent	Inclined to keep one's thoughts, feelings, and personal affairs to oneself
revolution	A political overthrow
rhetoric	The art of using language effectively and persuasively

rile	To irritate or stir up
rudimentary	Of or relating to basic facts or principles; elementary; being in the earliest stages
sanctimonious	Feigning piety or righteousness
sanguine	Of a healthy reddish color; ruddy; cheerfully confident; optimistic
scintillating	Brilliant
scrupulous	Principled, having a strong sense of right and wrong; conscientious and exacting self-government
skeptical	Doubtful; disbelieving
solicitous	Anxious or concerned
sonorous	Producing a deep or full sound
soporific	Inducing or tending to induce sleep
specious	Having the ring of truth or plausibility but actually not true
sporadic	Occurring at irregular intervals; having no pattern or order in time
squander	To spend wastefully or extravagantly; to dissipate
squelch	To crush by or as if by trampling; to squash
staid	Unemotional; serious
standard	Common or ordinary
stratify	To form, arrange, or deposit in layers
strident	Loud, harsh, grating, or shrill; discordant
strive	To try very hard
stupor	Mental confusion; daze
stymie	To thwart; to stump
substantiate	To support with proof or evidence; to verify
subterfuge	A deceptive stratagem or device
subtle	Hard to detect; not obvious
sufficient	Enough
supercilious	Disdainful; haughty; arrogant
superfluous	Extra; unnecessary

supplant	To usurp the place of, especially through intrigue or under-handed tactics
surreptitious	Done by secretive means
sycophant	A servile self-seeker who attempts to win favor by flattering influential people
sympathy	Compassion
synergy	The interaction of two or more agents or forces so that their combined effect is greater than the sum of their separate effects
tangential	Merely touching or slightly connected; only superficially relevant
temperate	Moderate in degree or quality; restrained (antonym: intemperate)
temporal	Of, relating to, or limited by time
tenacity	Persistence
tenuous	Having little substance or strength; shaky
terminate	To bring to an end or stop
therapeutic	Having or exhibiting healing powers
tolerance	Ability to endure pain or hardship; respecting the beliefs or practices of others
transient	Passing away with time; passing from one place to another
transparent	Clear; see-through
tumultuous	Noisy and disorderly
turmoil	A state or condition of extreme confusion, agitation, or commotion
ubiquitous	Being or seeming to be everywhere at the same time; omnipresent
undermine	To remove support from; to weaken
unscrupulous	Without honor or morals
vacillate	To sway from one side to the other; to oscillate
validity	Truth; correctness
values	Beliefs of a person or social group
vapid	Lacking liveliness, animation, or interest; dull
variegated	Having streaks, marks, or patches of a different color or colors; varicolored

vend	To sell; to offer (an idea)
veracity	Adherence to the truth; truthfulness
verdant	Green with vegetation; covered with green growth
verify	To test the truth of
vex	To annoy or bother; to perplex
vicarious	Felt or undergone as if one were taking part in the experience or feelings of another
vigilant	On the alert; watchful
vignette	A short scene or incident, as from a movie
vindicate	To free from blame
vindictive	Disposed to seek revenge; revengeful; spiteful
vital	Important, necessary
vituperative	Using, containing, or marked by harshly abusive censure
vivid	Bright or lively
whimsical	Subject to erratic behavior; unpredictable

WORD PARTS

Suffixes

The suffix (the end part of a word) can often tell you what part of speech a word is. Let's quickly review the most basic parts of speech, or you can look them up in a good dictionary.

What is a noun?_____

What is a verb?_____

What is an adjective? _____

What is an adverb? _____

Look at the following suffixes and examples, and add some words of your own that end in each suffix. Then look at all the words that end in that suffix. Which parts of speech are they? Check your answers in the Word Parts Index at the end of this chapter.

-*ness:* happiness, friendliness _____
-*able:* perishable, amiable _____
-*ous:* androgynous, fibrous _____
-*ity:* animosity, charity _____
-*ology:* psychology, sociology _____
-*ical:* tyrannical, hypothetical_____
-*archy*: monarchy, anarchy, matriarchy _____
-*less*: fearless, artless _____

Prefixes and Roots

Prefixes come at the beginnings of words, and roots can be anywhere in words. Both types of word parts are very helpful in trying to remember words that are new to you. For example, say you come upon the word *vociferous* (voh-SIF-uh-rus). You make a card for it, and then you try to think of other words that have that same root, *voc*. *Vocal* is a word you know has to do with speaking, and so now, when you see *vociferous* again, you'll remember it has to do with speaking. If you always imagine *vociferous* being shouted, you'll remember the rest of its meaning: "*loud and insistent* in speaking."

Notice that the sound of *voc* is not the same in *vociferous* as it is in *vocal*. Word parts change their sound over time, and most of the words you'll be learning have been around for hundreds of years. Not only do the sounds change, but the meanings also mutate over time, so today's meaning of a word is sometimes far different from the sum of its word parts. Thus, these word parts are to be used to help you remember and group new vocabulary (there's that *voc* again, in a word that has to do with speaking), and not as a substitute for looking up words.

The word parts on each page of this section can be linked together by the meanings of the words that contain them. This is a great way to think about words in general—they're linked by their word parts, and the many links that crisscross build a web.

How About A Break?
Before you start the Word Web exercises on the next page, how about a quick break to get some fresh air and noodle on what you just covered?

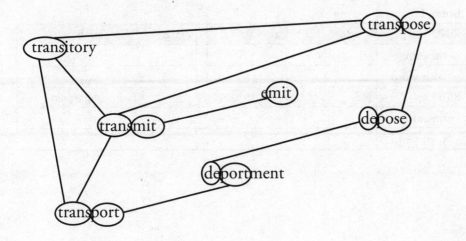

And that's only seven words!

Using the Word Web Pages

On each page in this section, you'll find word parts on the top and words on the bottom.

Here's how to use the pages.

1. Start with one of the words from the bottoms of the pages. Write it in the center. Circle the word parts it contains.

2. Now choose another word from the list that contains a matching word part. Write that word out, circling any word parts it contains, and draw a line between the parts that match in each word.

3. Repeat this step until you have linked all the words that were at the bottom of the page, making a web like the one above.

4. As you come across a word you don't know, look it up and make a flash card for it. There will be many words you don't know on these pages. When you look up these words, remember that the word parts and their meanings are at the beginning of the dictionary entries.

5. Now look at the word parts at the tops of the pages. On the first line under each word part, write down what you think it means, from the context of the words you've seen. Check this in the Master Root List on pages 139–141. The index has abbreviated versions of what each root means. Don't be discouraged if you don't guess correctly the meaning every time; you may be closer than you think because some word parts have wider meanings than just those we've included.

6. On the second line under each word part, write a word of your own that contains that word part. You may also want to add your word to the web you drew.

Dive In!

Let's get going! Build your
own word webs on these
next few pages. This may
seem silly, but trust us,
it will help with
understanding and
memorization.

Group 1

ROOT	chron	a	morph	path
meaning				
your word				
ROOT	**anti**	**par**	**dis**	**dign/dain**
meaning				
your word				

synchronize	chronicle	anachronism	amoral
apathy	apartheid	amorphous	metamorphosis
sympathy	empathy	pathos	antipathy
parity	disparate	dissociate	disparity
disperse	dissuade	dissipate	dignify
deign		disdain	

Group 2

ROOT	mis	gyn	phobe
meaning			
your word			
ROOT	phil	techn	anthr/andr
meaning			
your word			

miscreant	misanthrope	mistake	anthropology
philanthropy	androgynous	misogyny	philosophy
technophile	technophobe	technology	technique

Group 3

ROOT	sub	terr	vers/vert
meaning			
your word			
ROOT	extr	super	anthr/andr
meaning			
your word			

substantiate	subterranean	subordinate	terrestrial
terrarium	subvert	advertise	extrovert
traverse	extraterrestrial	extrapolate	supervise
superimpose	supersede	sediment	sedate
subside	subservient	introvert	

Group 4

ROOT	vor	carn	in/en/im/em	tract
meaning				
your word				
ROOT	ante	bell	am	nat/nas/nai
meaning				
your word				
ROOT	omni	pot	sci	pre
meaning				
your word				

voracious	devour	carnivorous	carnage
incarnation	infiltrate	input	inject
ingratiate	incarnate	intractable	protract
tractor	antecedent	antebellum	rebel
belligerent	bellicose	enamored	amorous
amity	amicable	innate	nascent
naive	natal	native	renaissance
omnivorous	omniscient	omnipotent	potential
potent	potentate	prescience	preface
prefix		predestine	

Group 5

ROOT	amb	re	spec	post
meaning				
your word				
ROOT	circ/circum	ven/vent	scrib/script	man
meaning				
your word				

ambitious   amble   circumambulate   circumscribe

circumvent   circumspect   redo   repudiate

recirculate   convene   intervene   inspect

auspicious   transcribe   manuscript   postpone

postscript   manual   manufacture   manifest

Group 6

ROOT	uni	anim	equi/equ	ad/at
meaning				
your word				
ROOT	voc	magna	loc/loq/log	neo/nov
meaning				
your word				

Are You Loving Word Knowledge?
If you want some more, then check out The Princeton Review's other top notch vocabulary and word knowledge books:
Word Smart
More Word Smart
Grammar Smart

unified	unanimous	animosity	magnanimous
equitable	equilibrium	iniquity	equanimity
equivocate	attract	adhere	advocate
vociferous	vocal	convoke	magnificent
magniloquent	eloquent	loquacious	circumlocution
neologism	novice	innovate	neophyte

Group 7

ROOT	epi	hyper	hypo	derm
meaning				
your word				
ROOT	dem	tens/ten	pan	
meaning				
your word				

epilogue   epithet   hypertension   hypodermic

epidermis   dermatologist   tensile   tenuous

epidemic   democracy   demographics   pandemic

panorama

Group 8

ROOT	eu	phon	dys	bene
meaning				
your word				
ROOT	dic	mal	fac	fic/fig
meaning				
your word				

euphoria	euphemism	eulogy	euphony
utopia	megaphone	cacophony	dystopia
dyslexia	benefit	beneficent	benevolent
benediction	benign	dictionary	dictation
contradict	malediction	malevolent	malicious
malign	maleficent	malodorous	facile
factory	malefactor	manufacture	deficient
proficient	prolific	effigy	soporific

Group 9

ROOT	ex/ej	clu/clo/cla	cis
meaning			
your word			
ROOT	**culp**	**ten**	**ac/acr**
meaning			
your word			

exit	eject	exculpate	excise
exclusive	preclude	cloister	foreclose
recluse	scissors	incisive	concise
culprit	culpable	extenuate	tenable
tentative	tenacious	acrid	acerbic
acumen	exacerbate	acrimonious	

Group 10

ROOT	co/com/con	cur/cour	her/hes	sequ/secru
meaning				
your word				
ROOT	tact	gen	homo	norm/nym
meaning				
your word				
ROOT	hetero	fid	vi/viv	vid/vis
meaning				
your word				

confide   convivial   cogent   concurrent

convoke   cursory   current   precursor

incur   coherent   cohesive   inherent

consequently   consecutive   tactile   contact

genesis   congenial   progeny   homogenous

homonym   synonym   anonymous   pseudonym

misnomer   ignominy   heterogenous   heterdox

fidelity   infidel   bona fide   diffident

perfidy   fiduciary   vivacious   viable

vivid   vivisection   vista   evident

video   visage   supervise

Group 11

ROOT	bi	di	ab/abs
meaning			
your word			
ROOT	ad/at	us/ut	ob
meaning			
your word			

bipartisan   bicycle   bisect   dichotomy
digress   diaphanous   divide   dissect
abhor   abdicate   abscond   abstain
attract   adjacent   advocate   abuse
utilitarian   utilize   obstinate   obviate
obscure

Group 12

ROOT	in/il/im/ir	un/non	cred	mut
meaning				
your word				

ROOT	pun/pen	apt/ept	plac	
meaning				
your word				

illegible	incredible	irresponsible	improper
unusual	nonsense	credible	credence
immutable	permutation	impunity	penalty
punitive	penance	adapt	apt
inept	adept	implacable	placid
placate			

Group 13

ROOT	pro	cli	inter	intra
meaning				
your word				
ROOT	pon/pos	de	port	trans
meaning				
your word				
ROOT	mit/mis	luc/lum/lus	esce	
meaning				
your word				

propose   produce   recline   proclivity
disinclination   interject   interpose   interlude
intervene   intravenous   transpose   deposit
depose   deport   decipher   defame
deportment   purport   portfolio   transitory
transport   translucent   transmit   emissary
missive   remission   demise   emit
luminescent   illustrious   lucid   lackluster
elucidate   obsolescent   coalesce   quiescent
acquiescent

MASTER ROOT LIST

Now that you've learned to look for root words and you can recognize the ones you used for the Word Webs, here is an even bigger list of root words to learn!

a	negative prefix		**dign/dain**	worth
ab	away from/		**digt**	finger, digit
	negative prefix		**dis**	apart from, not
ac/acr	sharp		**domi**	rule over
ad/at	to, toward		**dorm**	sleep
amb	go/walk		**duc/dul**	lead
ambi	both/mixed		**dys**	faulty, bad
ami/amo	love		**e/ex/ej**	out, outward
an/anti	against		**en/em**	into
andr	human, male		**epi**	upon
anim	life, spirit		**equ/equi**	equal
ante	before		**esce**	becoming
anthr	human		**eu**	good, pleasant
apt/ept	skill, ability		**extr**	outside, beyond,
arbo	tree			additional
arch	rule, over		**fac/fic/fig**	do, make
aud	sound		**fer/ferr**	strong, iron-like
auto	self		**fid**	faithful
bell/belli	war		**fort**	strong
ben/bono	good		**fract**	break, split
bi	two		**frat**	brother
bio/bios	life		**fren**	highly energetic
bra	arm		**gen**	birth, creation, kind,
carn	meat, flesh			type
cent	hundred		**geo**	earth
chron	time		**gno/kno**	know
circ/circu	around		**grand**	big
cis/cise	cut		**graph**	write
clu/clo/cla	close, shut		**grat**	grateful
co/com/con	with, together		**gress**	step
contr	against		**gust**	taste
cred	believe		**gyn**	female
culp	blame		**hemi**	half, split part
cur/cour	run (a course)		**her/hes**	stick (on)
de	away from/		**herb**	plant
	opposite, of		**hetero**	different, mixed
dec/deci	ten		**hex/sex**	six
dent	teeth		**homo**	same
derm	skin		**hyd/hydr**	water
desc	down		**hyper**	over, beyond
dext	dexterity, ability		**hypo**	under, insufficient
di	two, apart, split		**il**	not
dic/dict	say, tell		**im**	not, into

in	not, into	**patr**	father
inter	between	**pen/pend**	weight
intra	within	**pent**	five
itis	inflammation, infection	**peri**	around
		pet/pec	small
ium	place, building of	**phil**	love, high regard
jeu/ju	play, youthful	**phob**	fear
jaun	yellow	**phon**	sound
lab/labo	work	**pod/ped**	foot
laud	praise	**pon/pos**	place, put
lav	wash	**port**	carry
lev	rise	**post**	after
log/loqui	to speak	**poten**	power, influence
lu/luc/lum	light	**pre**	before
mag/magna	great	**pro**	for
mal	bad	**prox**	near
man/manu	hand	**pseudo**	false
mar/mer	sea	**pug**	fighting
matr	mother	**quad**	four
met/meter	measure	**qui**	quiet
meta	more, beyond	**quint**	five
mic/micro	tiny	**re**	again
mill	thousand	**schi**	split
mis	wrong, bad	**sci/scien**	knowledge
mit	send	**scop**	see
mob/mobi	moving	**scrib/scrip**	write
mor/mort	death	**sec/sequ**	follow, come after
morph	change (shape)	**sed/sid**	sit, be still
mut	change, alter	**solo**	alone
nat/natu	natural, birth	**son/soni**	sound
neg	negative	**soro**	sister
neo/nov	new	**spec/spic**	see, look
noct	night	**sta/sti**	still, unmoving
nom/nym	name	**sua**	smooth
non/not	negative prefix	**sub**	under
nounce	call	**super**	beyond, greater than
nox/nec	harmful	**syn/sym**	bring together
ob	against	**tact**	touch
olfac	smell	**tech/techn**	tools
ology	study of	**tele**	at a distance
omni	all, every	**temp**	time
ory	place of	**ten/tend**	hold
pac/pax/plac	peace, pleasing	**terr**	earth, ground
pan	all, everywhere	**tox**	harmful, poisonous
par	equal	**tract**	pull
para	beyond	**trans**	across
path	feeling, emotion	**trep**	fear, anxiety

tri	three	**verge**	boundary, together
un	not	**verse**	turn
uni/uno	one	**vete**	experienced
us/ut	use	**vi/vit/viv**	alive
val/vale	value, feel	**vid/vis**	see
vend	sell	**voc**	call, talk
ver/vera/very	true	**vor**	eat, consume
verd	green		

ANSWERS TO QUICK QUIZ

Quick Quiz
Page 102

1. Flash cards, the image approach, mnemonics, look it up, and use it.
2. *Chaos* means complete confusion. Your mnemonic might be anything that helps you remember the definition. Here's ours: Stay lost.

   Provoke means to cause a feeling or reaction; to push into action. Our mnemonic: Poke.

   Jeer means to taunt or ridicule. Our mnemonic: Jerks.

   Aloof means keeping apart from others. Our mnemonic: ALone on the rOOF.

   Abundance means a great amount. Our mnemonic: A BUNch in attenDANCE.

Chapter 5
Paragraph
Comprehension

INTRODUCTION TO THE PARAGRAPH COMPREHENSION TEST

On the CAT-ASVAB, the Paragraph Comprehension test has 11 questions that you must answer in 22 minutes. The Paragraph Comprehension test on the MET- and Student-ASVABs has 15 questions that you must answer in 13 minutes. The questions are intended to test your ability to comprehend written material. The answer to every question can be found in the passages. You will never need any outside information to answer a question on this test.

THE PASSAGES

The passages vary in length from a couple of sentences to several paragraphs. The length of the passage tends to correspond to the number of questions that accompany it. Shorter passages usually have only one question, while longer passages can have several questions. The passages cover a wide variety of topics. You could see anything from art to business to science to history.

The passages differ from the reading most people are used to, in that they're specifically designed to relay information in a small amount of text. So if you read the ASVAB passages like you read a book or newspaper, you are going to have a hard time on this section. That's because you normally read with the goal of remembering everything. On the ASVAB, trying to remember everything is not necessary and can actually hurt your score.

If this advice seems strange, think about it this way: Your goal in the test is to answer the questions correctly. You won't get any points for reading the passage thoroughly if you don't answer the questions correctly. So the majority of your time should be spent on the questions and answers, not on reading the passages. Slow down and make sure you check each answer choice carefully. When you choose an answer, you should be able to point to the place in the passage that supports your answer. Use the passage to help you find the correct answer, but don't get caught up in it and waste time memorizing things you won't need. Remember, you can always go back to the passage later if you need to.

Think of the ASVAB as an open-book test. In a way it is—the questions and the passages are right in front of you. All you need to do is find the answers in the passages. The hard part is the time limit. We've devised a system to help you improve your accuracy while saving time. The best part of our system is that it will work for every question and every passage you see.

THE THREE-STEP SYSTEM

If you're taking the MET-site or Student ASVAB, you'll be given only 13 minutes for the whole section, which is less than one minute per question. The CAT-ASVAB gives you a little more time, but you'll still be racing the clock. That's why you need a system in place to tackle every question and passage on this test. Our system has three simple steps.

1. Read the Questions
2. Skim the Passage
3. Use Process of Elimination

Step 1: Read the Questions

The first thing you should always do is read all the questions for a particular passage. By reading the questions *before* you read the passage, you'll know what to be on the lookout for when you do read the passage.

You will see a variety of questions on this test. All questions can be assigned to one of two categories: specific or general.

Specific Questions

Specific questions ask you about a detail from the passage. You don't need to understand the entire passage to answer this question, just the part of the passage to which the question refers. There are four main types of specific questions. Here are the types, with some examples of each.

1. Fact
   - According to the author/passage…
   - The author states that…
   - Which of the following questions is answered by the passage?
   - All of the following are mentioned EXCEPT…
2. Definition in context
   - What does the passage mean by X?
   - X probably represents/means…
3. Specific interpretation
   - It can be inferred from paragraph X…
   - The most likely interpretation of X is…
4. Purpose
   - The author uses X in order to…
   - Why does the author say X?

The questions above range from flat-out requests for information found in the passage to questions that require some interpretation of what you find in the passage.

When you encounter specific questions, recognize and jot down any words that will help you find the answer in the passage. We call these **lead words**. They include names, places, and phrases that will be easy to find in the passage. If the passage asks for a detail from the passage, write down something to remind you of the detail. For example, if the question states, "The word *lunar* most nearly means," write down the word *lunar*. This will help you remember what's important as you work through the passage. Take a look at a few questions with the lead words underlined.

- According to the passage, people suffering from <u>high cholesterol</u> are more at risk for…
- In the author's view, the phrase "<u>modern art</u>" means art that…
- The passage best supports the statement that <u>underage drinking</u> is…

When looking for the lead words in a question, keep in mind that you want them to be specific to the question at hand. Look at the first question above. You wouldn't want to choose *people* because that's a common word that might appear in several parts of a passage. *High cholesterol* is a good choice because it's much more specific.

Some specific questions don't have lead words. You will have to find the relevant part of the passage without their help. That's one reason why reading the questions first is so helpful. If you read the questions first, you will recognize relevant parts of the passage as you skim through the passage later. That makes it easier to find the answers.

QUICK QUIZ 1

Practice finding the lead words in specific questions. Underline the lead words in the following questions. Answers can be found at the end of the chapter.

1. The stars are considered luminous because

2. According to the passage, an opaque object

3. The passage best supports the idea that elementary schools

4. The planet Jupiter differs from all other planets in the solar system in that it

5. According to the passage, Pygmy Marmosets are commonly found in

6. According to the passage, anthropologists study

General Questions

The other type of question you will see asks you about a large part of the passage or the whole passage. We call these **general questions.** There are four types.

1. Main idea
   - Which of the following best expresses the main point?
   - The passage is primarily about…
   - The main idea of the passage is…
   - The best title for this passage would be…
2. Tone/attitude
   - The author's tone is…
   - The attitude of the author is one of…
3. General interpretation
   - The author would most likely agree with…
   - This passage deals with X by…
   - The passage implies that…
   - Which of the following words best describes the passage?
   - It can be inferred from the passage that…
   - The style of the passage is most like…
   - What is the author's opinion of X?
4. Purpose
   - The purpose of the passage is…
   - The author wrote this passage in order to…

All of these questions require that you know the main idea of the passage, but the ones at the beginning of the list are more straightforward. The ones at the end of the list require you to interpret a little more.

When reading these general questions, use your scrap paper to jot down what you're on the lookout for. For example, if the question asks for the main point of the passage, write down "main point" or "m.p." for short.

QUICK QUIZ 2

Identify each of the following questions as specific or general. The answers can be found at the end of the chapter. Then, identify what type of specific or general question it is. For example

The woman probably mentions "blizzards" in order to…

This is a specific purpose question.

1. The passage primarily concerns:

2. The last sentence of paragraph 1 implies that:

_____

3. According to the passage, television has become a medium whose main goal is:

_____

4. The author's reference to "talking hair-dos" is a reference to:

_____

5. According to the passage, which of the following was an artist?
   I. Brancusi
   II. Cox
   III. Hughes

_____

6. The author of the passage can most reasonably be described as:

_____

Step 2: Skim the Passage

After you've read the questions for a passage, skim through the passage. Note that you should *skim* the passage and not read it. As we've already stated, you don't get any points for good, thorough reading. The purpose of skimming the passage is to get a general idea of what the passage is about, not to memorize it. Remember, the majority of the passage will have nothing to do with the questions. As you skim, keep on the lookout for the lead words that you've already jotted down. When you find them, read carefully a few lines above and a few lines below. The answer to a question should be close by.

If the passage is long or particularly difficult, it may help to take some short and simple notes on your scrap paper. Don't write a book report about the passage, just a few words to help you remember.

Step 3: Process of Elimination (POE)

This is where you should spend the majority of your time. Write the letters A, B, C, and D on your scrap paper and cross them off as you eliminate each answer choice. Always refer back to the passage when crossing off an answer. When you settle on one answer, you should be able to support that answer with something in the passage.

Answering a Specific Question

To answer a specific question, you should always reread the relevant part of the passage. Remember, this is an open-book test. Use that to your advantage! You don't want to reread the entire passage, of course, just the part the question is focusing on.

Answering a General Question

To answer a general question, you need to know the main point of the passage. Before you look at the answer choices, spend a few seconds trying to state the passage's main point in your own words. Then use Process of Elimination to get rid of answers that either don't answer the question or answer it incorrectly.

> For **main idea** questions, eliminate answers that are too narrow or too broad. The correct answer will cover the entire passage without claiming more than the passage actually says.

> For a **tone/attitude** question, first determine if the author was for, against, or neutral on the subject. Use that information to eliminate as many answers as you can. For example, if the author was in favor of the subject he or she was discussing, eliminate any negative answers. Then, determine the degree of the author's tone. Was the tone mild or strong? Be wary of answers that go further than the passage does.

> For **general interpretation** questions, choose the answer that comes closest to what the passage says. For questions asking for an "inference," look for an answer that paraphrases the passage.

> For **general purpose** questions, ask yourself why the author wrote the passage. Keep in mind the tone of the passage as you answer this question.

Eliminating Answer Choices

Process of Elimination is one of the most important tools you can use throughout any standardized test. You should train yourself to automatically eliminate any answer that you know is wrong. Sometimes you can find the correct answer to a question just by eliminating answers that you know are wrong. Remember, it doesn't matter how you get to the correct answer, as long as you get there!

In order to effectively use POE in the Paragraph Comprehension test, you must be able to recognize incorrect answers. Luckily, there are a few types of wrong answer choices that you will see over and over again. Let's look at them, so you will be able to recognize and eliminate them!

Extremes: Be on the lookout for extreme statements in the answer choices. The passages on the ASVAB are rarely extreme in tone, so the answers shouldn't be either. If you see extreme words—such as "all," "none," "every," and "must"—in an answer, be suspicious. It's probably wrong. Of course, if the passage is extreme in tone, the answer might be extreme too.

Correct But Irrelevant; True But Not Stated: Some incorrect answers are, in a sense, absolutely true. They just don't answer the question that's being asked. Make sure the answer you choose is not only correct, but also answers the question.

Direct Opposite: Sometimes you will be given the exact opposite of what you're looking for. If you're not careful, you might choose that answer instead of the correct one. When you see two answer choices that directly contradict each other, it is very likely that one of them is the correct answer.

Out of Scope: You need to be particularly careful with general questions to avoid answers that are out of scope. You don't want an answer that is too broad or too narrow. Keep in mind that the correct answer choice must be limited to what's in the passage, but must cover all of it.

I, II, III Questions

Questions with Roman numerals are time-consuming and more difficult than other questions. But though they take more work than other questions, with careful use of POE, they can be answered. Here's an example.

---

8. According to the passage, which of the following is true?

    I. The sky is blue.
    II. Nothing rhymes with "orange."
    III. Smoking cigarettes increases lung capacity.

    A. I only
    B. I and II only
    C. I and III only
    D. II and III only

Here's How to Crack It

The best way to tackle these questions is with careful POE. First, determine whether the first statement was stated in the passage. If it was, eliminate every answer that doesn't include statement I. If it wasn't, eliminate every answer that *does* include statement I. If you still have more than one answer remaining, do the same for the next statement. Let's try this with the question above.

Let's assume the passage says that the sky is blue and nothing rhymes with orange. Therefore, eliminate answers that don't include statement I. That gets rid of (D). You also want to eliminate any answers that don't include statement II, which gets rid of (C) and (A). That leaves (B).

EXCEPT/LEAST/NOT Questions

This is another type of confusing question. The test writers are asking you to look for the answer that is false. Again, with careful POE, this question type is doable. For example

---

9. All of the following can be inferred from the passage EXCEPT:

   A.   Americans are patriotic.
   B.   Americans have great ingenuity.
   C.   Americans love war.
   D.   Americans are brave in times of war.

Here's How to Crack It

Let's assume that the passage says every one of these statements except for C. Now read through the answers, writing "T" for true on your scrap paper next to the answer choices that are stated in the passage and "F" for false next to the one that isn't. Your answer is the one with the "F" next to it.

What Do I Keep?

In general, correct answers are likely to be

- paraphrases of the words in the passage
- traditional and conservative in their outlook
- moderate, using words like *may, can,* and *often*

One Last Tip

If you've eliminated all but two answer choices, don't get stuck and waste time. Keep the main idea in the back of your mind and step back.

- Reread the question.
- Look at what makes the two answers different.

- Go back to the passage.
- Which answer is worse? Eliminate it.

Staring at the answers won't make the correct one jump out at you; it will only waste time!

Putting It All Together

Let's work through the following passage. Remember to use the three-step technique.

Step 1: Read the Questions: Read all seven questions and jot down on scrap paper a list of the things you need to look out for in the passage.

Step 2: Skim the Passage: Skim the passage, looking for the things you listed on your scrap paper. As you work through the passage, jot down notes. If you find the answer to a question, you can even write down where you found it to save time later.

Step 3: POE: Refer back to the passage as you cross off incorrect answer choices. When you've chosen your answer, make sure the passage supports it.

Questions 1–7 are based on the following passage.

Contrary to popular belief, the first European known to lay eyes on America was not Christopher Columbus or Amerigo Vespucci but a little-known Viking by the name of Bjarni Herjolfsson. In the summer of 986, Bjarni sailed from Norway to Iceland, heading for the Viking settlement where his father resided.

When he arrived in Iceland, Bjarni discovered that his father had already sold his land and estates and set out for the latest Viking settlement on the subarctic island called Greenland. Discovered by a notorious murderer and criminal named Eric the Red, Greenland lay at the limit of the known world. Dismayed, Bjarni set out for this new colony.

Because the Vikings traveled without chart or compass, it was not uncommon for them to lose their way in the unpredictable northern seas. Beset by fog, the crew lost their bearings. When the fog finally cleared, they found themselves before a land that was level and covered with woods.

They traveled farther up the coast, finding more flat, wooded country. Further north, the landscape revealed glaciers and rocky mountains. Though Bjarni realized this was an unknown land, he was no intrepid explorer. Rather, he was a practical man who had simply set out to find his father. Refusing his crew's request to go ashore, he promptly turned his bow back out to sea. After four days' sailing, Bjarni landed at Herjolfsnes on the southwestern tip of Greenland, the exact place he had been seeking all along.

1. This passage is primarily about

    A. the Vikings and their civilization
    B. the waves of Viking immigration
    C. the sailing techniques of Bjarni Herjolfsson
    D. one Viking's glimpse of the new world

2. It can be inferred from the passage that prior to Bjarni Herjolfsson's voyage, Greenland

    A. was covered in grass and shrubs
    B. was overrun with Vikings
    C. was populated by criminals
    D. was as far west as the Vikings had traveled

3. What was the author's purpose in writing this passage?

    A. To turn the reader against Italian adventurers
    B. To show his disdain for Eric the Red
    C. To demonstrate the Vikings' nautical skills
    D. To correct a common misconception about the European discovery of America

4. According to the passage, Bjarni Herjolfsson left Norway to

    A. found a new colony
    B. open trading lanes
    C. visit his relations
    D. settle in Greenland

5. Bjarni's reaction upon landing in Iceland can best be described as

    A. disappointed
    B. satisfied
    C. amused
    D. indifferent

6. "The crew lost their bearings," in the third paragraph, probably means that

    A. the ship was damaged beyond repair
    B. the crew became disoriented
    C. the crew decided to mutiny
    D. the crew went insane

7. With which of the following statements about Viking explorers would the author most probably agree?

    A.   Greenland and Iceland were the Vikings' final discoveries.

    B.   Viking explorers were cruel and savage.

    C.   The Vikings' most startling discovery was an accidental one.

    D.   All Viking explorers were fearless.

Here's How to Crack It

During step 1, you should have made a short list of what you're looking for on your scrap paper. That list might look something like this.

> about?
> before voyage
> author's purpose
> Norway
> Iceland
> crew lost bearings…
> author agree?

During step 2 you should have skimmed the passage looking for its main point—in other words, what the passage was about (question 1). While doing this, you may have recognized some of the words from the questions. If you did, that's great! If not, you'll still have the chance to find them in the next step.

Most of your time should be spent in step 3, and that's where we will spend most of our discussion.

1. This passage is primarily about

    A.   the Vikings and their civilization

    B.   the waves of Viking immigration

    C.   sailing techniques of Bjarni Herjolfsson

    D.   one Viking's glimpse of the new world

This is a general purpose question, so think about why the author wrote the passage. Use POE to answer the question. You can get rid of (A) because the passage doesn't really talk about Viking civilization. It also never mentions Viking immigration, (B), or Bjarni's sailing techniques, (C), so that leaves (D).

2. It can be inferred from the passage that prior to Bjarni Herjolfsson's voyage, Greenland

    A.   was covered in grass and shrubs

    B.   was overrun with Vikings

    C.   was populated by criminals

    D.   was as far west as the Vikings had traveled

This is a specific question, so you should have referred back to the part of the passage that discusses Bjarni right before he left for his voyage. This part is located at the end of paragraph one. By reading a few lines before and a few lines after, you can see that (A), (B), and (C) are never stated. What you do know is that "Greenland lay at the limit of the known world," which (D) paraphrases.

3. What was the author's purpose in writing this passage?

    A. To turn the reader against Italian adventurers

    B. To show his disdain for Eric the Red

    C. To demonstrate the Vikings' nautical skills

    D. To correct a common misconception about the European discovery of America

Before trying to find the answer to this question, think about the tone of the passage. Did the author exhibit an opinion at any time? Not really, so it's unlikely that (A) and (B) could be correct. The passage doesn't really talk about their nautical skills either, so the answer is (D).

4. According to the passage, Bjarni Herjolfsson left Norway to

    A. found a new colony

    B. open trading lanes

    C. visit his relations

    D. settle in Greenland

This is a specific question, and the lead word is Norway. So, find the place in the passage that discusses Norway. It's in the first paragraph. By reading a few lines before and after, you see that he went to Norway to visit his father. Thus, the answer is (C).

5. Bjarni's reaction upon landing in Iceland can best be described as

    A. disappointed

    B. satisfied

    C. amused

    D. indifferent

This is another specific question, and the lead word is Iceland. The paragraph in the passage that mentions Iceland, states that Bjarni was "dismayed." The best answer is (A), disappointed.

6. "The crew lost their bearings," in the third paragraph, probably means that

    A.   the ship was damaged beyond repair

    B.   the crew became disoriented

    C.   the crew decided to mutiny

    D.   the crew went insane

This specific question tells you exactly where to go for the answer. By referring back to paragraph 3, you see that the passage is describing how common it was for the Vikings to get lost. Choice (B) goes best with this.

7. With which of the following statements about Viking explorers would the author most probably agree?

    A.   Greenland and Iceland were the Vikings' final discoveries.

    B.   Viking explorers were cruel and savage.

    C.   The Vikings' most startling discovery was an accidental one.

    D.   All Viking explorers were fearless.

This is a general interpretation question, so you are looking for the answer that comes closest to saying something that the passage says. The passage never says whether Greenland and Iceland were the Vikings' final discoveries, so you can cross off (A). Choice (B) is extreme and never stated, so you can cross that off too. Choice (C) sounds reasonable, so leave it in. Choice (D) is also extreme and unfounded, so the answer is (C).

QUICK QUIZ 3

Here's a quiz on our techniques. Fill in the blanks, and check your answers at the end of the chapter.

1. What should you do when answering a main idea question?

2. What should you do when answering a tone/attitude question?

3. What should you do when answering a general interpretation question?

4. What should you do when answering a general purpose question?

_____

5. When you're using POE to get rid of answers choices, what types of answers should you keep?

_____

6. What should you do when you've got the answer choices down to two?

_____

PACING IN PARAGRAPH COMPREHENSION

One of the biggest hurdles to overcome in the Paragraph Comprehension test is the time limit. The ASVAB doesn't give you very much time to read all those passages and answer the questions.

So don't spend too much time on one question. The worst thing you can do on this section is get hung up on one question. If you get stuck on a question, use POE to get rid of as many wrong answers as possible and then guess from the remainder and move on.

LETTER OF THE DAY

Don't forget; in the ASVAB there's no penalty for guessing. That means it's always to your benefit to answer every question. That doesn't mean you need to read every passage and work every question. It just means that you should record an answer for every question. Keep track of the time with your own watch. When time is almost up, let's say one minute or so, pick your favorite letter, A, B, C, or D, and choose it for any questions you haven't gotten to.

TECHNIQUES FOR THE PAPER TEST ONLY

If you are taking the ASVAB on paper (that is, if you're not taking the CAT-ASVAB), try to do the questions in an order that works for you. If you see a passage that looks difficult, skip it. You can always come back to it later. Why spend four minutes answering a question worth one point when you can spend two minutes on an easier question worth the same amount?

If you're confronted with a long passage with several questions, answer the specific questions first. Not only are they usually simpler, but by answering them first you learn more about the passage. That makes the general questions easier when you get to them.

Well, that's it—everything you need to know about the Paragraph Comprehension test. Not so bad, was it? Practice everything you've learned on the following questions. Answers can be found at the end of the chapter.

QUICK QUIZ 4

1. The force of lunar activity is not as strong as Earth's own gravitational pull, which keeps our bodies and our homes from being pulled off the ground, through the sky, and into space toward the Moon. The lunar force is strong enough, however, to exert a certain gravitational pull as the Moon passes over the Earth's surface. This pull causes the water level to rise (as the water is literally pulled ever-so-slightly toward the Moon) in those parts of the ocean that are exposed to the Moon and its gravitational forces. When the water level in one part of the ocean rises, it must naturally fall in another, and this is what causes tides to change, dramatically at times, along any given piece of coastline.

    The author's primary purpose in writing this paragraph is to

    A. prove the existence of water on the Moon
    B. refute claims that tides are caused by the Moon
    C. explain the main cause of the ocean's tides
    D. argue that humans should not interfere with the processes of nature

2. Florence Nightingale began a school in London, England, to set the standards for nursing. She was able to do this because she had already established a reputation for her work with soldiers during the Crimean War. She carried a lamp above her head as she walked among the wounded men, thereby earning the nickname "the lady with the lamp." It was this great lady who lit the way for nursing to become the respected profession it is today.

    The primary reason that Florence Nightingale was able to open a school for nursing was that

    A. she was already famous for her work in the war
    B. her family was willing to finance her work
    C. she had cared for many wealthy sick people herself
    D. she worked endless hours every night

3. There are many types of microscopes, from the simple optical microscope to the electron microscope. While a simple, inexpensive optical microscope may magnify an object from about fifty times its size to about one to two thousand times its size, the expensive electron microscope can magnify an object by up to about 250,000 times. The electron microscope works not with glass lenses, but with magnetic lenses as well. These lenses use electrons instead of light to produce an image. Just as a ray of light bends as it passes through a curved lens, streams of electrons bend as they pass by a magnetic lens. Very small objects do not affect light at all, but they do affect electrons. Because of that, an electron microscope can distinguish objects that are very small and very close together.

The passage implies that the greatest advantage of the electron microscope is

A. its expense

B. its versatility

C. its use of magnets

D. its greater ability to magnify

4. A black hole starts out as a star. A star burns hydrogen, and this process, called fusion, releases energy. The energy released outward works against the star's own gravity, pulling inward and preventing the star from collapsing. After millions of years of burning hydrogen, the star eventually runs out of fuel. At this point, the star's own gravity and weight cause it to start contracting. If the star is small and not very heavy, it will shrink a little and become a white dwarf. If the star is bigger and heavier, it will collapse very quickly in an explosion. If the matter that remains is not too much heavier than our sun, it will eventually become a very dense neutron star. However, if the matter that remains is more than 1.7 times the mass of our sun, there will not be enough outward pressure to resist the force of gravity, and the collapse will continue. The result is a black hole.

A collapsing star will become a neutron star if

A. it is less than 1.7 times the mass of our sun

B. it still has fuel to use for fusion

C. it is more than 1.7 times the mass of our sun

D. it shrinks slowly for a short time

5. An Eskimo navigating in polar darkness and whiteouts makes use of many clues to find his way. When traveling on ice in the fog, the Eskimo uses the voices of seabirds against the cliffs and the sound of the surf at the edge of the ice. When he begins to travel over open terrain, he marks the angle of the wind and aligns the fur of his parka with the breeze. He notes the trend of any cracks in the ice as he crosses them. Sea ice cracks can reveal the presence of a cape or headland invisible in the distance, or they may confirm one's arrival at a known area. Constant attention to such details, memories of the way the land looks, and stories told by other travelers are used together with the movements of animals, to keep the traveler on course. The most dependable sources of direction for most Eskimos are the behavior of the wind and ocean currents, and such subtle clues as the flow of a river.

All of the following are mentioned as techniques Eskimos use for navigation EXCEPT:

A. consulting with elders of the Eskimo community

B. examining cracks in the ice along the route

C. learning from the experiences of earlier travelers

D. using the angle of the wind to judge direction

6. As the name implies, the electric eel has the ability to generate a strong electric field. When it comes time to feed, the eel relies on its electrical system for hunting. Because small animals have a different electrical "signature" than do plants or rocks, the electric eel effectively has a kind of radar that allows it to find fish. When the eel finds its prey, it delivers a strong electric current, which can instantly kill smaller animals, such as fish. The force of the charge is often strong enough to kill or stun even larger animals. How does the eel avoid hurting itself? The eel has evolved a kind of insulation that protects its nervous system. This insulation acts as a buffer against the electricity that it generates.

It can be inferred from the paragraph that the electricity is dangerous because it

A. damages the nervous system

B. interferes with breathing

C. deprives animals of food

D. causes animals to bleed

7. Most people know that the ancient Egyptians mummified their dead. But few people know the details of how or why a mummy was made. The point of mummification was to remove all of the parts of the body that could decompose, to ensure that the remaining parts lasted forever. This was important to the Egyptians, who believed that parts of a person's soul needed a body to live in. If the body were to rot and disappear, the soul would be left homeless for eternity. To prevent the body from rotting, all the water had to be removed and all the bacteria had to be killed.

    According to the paragraph, the Egyptians mummified their dead in order to ensure that

    A. the dead person would be protected from wolves
    B. the dead person's soul would have a home
    C. nobody would rob the dead person's grave
    D. the dead person's organs were not lost

8. Julius Caesar was perhaps the most important political leader of all time. It was his military and political genius that created the Roman Empire, a civilization so large and powerful that no other western government could be considered its equal until the 1700s. Caesar's historical influence was so great that the German and Russian words for emperor (Kaiser and Czar) are derived from his name.

    The author gives us the German and Russian words for emperor to demonstrate

    A. the similarities between the German and Russian languages
    B. how words can change over time
    C. the importance of Julius Caesar in western history
    D. that Julius Caesar spoke German and Russian

9. The initial American policy toward both World Wars was to stay out of them. The U.S. remained neutral at the beginning of both wars until certain events (the sinking of the *Lusitania* and the Zimmerman Telegram in World War I, and the bombing of Pearl Harbor in World War II) caused them to get involved.

    Based on the above paragraph, all of the following are true EXCEPT:

    A. Pearl Harbor was bombed during World War II.
    B. Initially, the U.S. did not want to enter either World War.
    C. The U.S. heavily supported the Allies at the beginning of World War II.
    D. The sinking of the *Lusitania* was one reason the U.S. entered World War I.

10. In a preliminary test-tube laboratory study, a scientist found elevated growth rates in cancer cells exposed to low doses of microwave radiation. These results are only preliminary because, first of all, there has been no controlled study of the effects of microwaves on human beings. Second, this study was only of short duration, raising the possibility that the dangers of long-term exposure have not yet been assessed.

According to the information presented, the cancer cells' increased growth in the laboratory experiment is most probably due to

A. the sterile conditions of the laboratory
B. the cancer cells' natural reproductive rate
C. a short-term growth spurt that might mean nothing
D. exposure to microwave radiation

11. When I was eighteen I wanted something to do. I had tried teaching for two years and hated it; I had tried sewing and could not earn my bread that way, at the cost of health; I tried storywriting and got five dollars for stories that now bring a hundred; I had thought seriously of going up on the stage, but certain highly respectable relatives were so shocked at the mere idea that I relinquished my dramatic aspirations.

The author implies that writing is a job that is

A. profitable
B. rewarding
C. miserable
D. unprofitable

12. The first "horseless carriages" of the 1880s may have been worthy of a snicker or two, but not the cars of today. The progress that has been made over the last one hundred years has been phenomenal. In fact, much progress was made even in the first twenty years—in 1903 cars could travel at 70 mph. The major change from the old cars to today is the expense. Whereas cars were once a luxury that only the very wealthy could afford, today, people of all income levels own cars.

The "progress" mentioned in line 2 most likely refers to

A. the ability of a car to move forward
B. technological advancement
C. research
D. the cost of the car

13. Born as Gertrude Margaret Zelle in the Netherlands in 1876, Mata Hari was probably the most famous spy of all time. During World War I, she was a beautiful dancer who worked in Paris. Mata Hari was her stage name.

Many believe that Mata Hari was a double agent, someone who spies for two countries at the same time. It was thought that she spied for Germany by stealing secrets from the French, and for the French by stealing secrets from the Germans. She charmed military men with her great beauty. Mata Hari was arrested and executed by the French in 1917.

What is the primary purpose of the passage?

A. To discuss the moral ramifications of spying

B. To help uncover the reasons Mata Hari turned to spying

C. To discuss the life of Mata Hari

D. To demonstrate Mata Hari's great beauty

14. The native inhabitants of the Americas arrived from Asia more than 20,000 years ago. Many were skilled hunters, farmers, and fishers. They belonged to numerous tribes. Some of the most famous Native American tribes are the Sioux, the Cheyenne, the Iroquois, and the Apache. These tribes settled and developed organized societies. The European settlers who arrived in America many years later often fought the Native Americans for land. Geronimo was the last great Native American chief to organize rebellions against the settlers. He led raids across the southwest and into Mexico. Although he was eventually captured, he later became a celebrity.

The passage names all of the following as skills of the Native Americans EXCEPT:

A. farming

B. hunting

C. fishing

D. gathering

Questions 15–19 are based on the following passage.

Marie Sklodowska was born November 7, 1867, in Warsaw, Poland. She grew up in a family that valued education, and as a young woman she studied at the Sorbonne in Paris, France. There she met Pierre Curie, a physics teacher at the University of Paris. The two quickly married and began conducting research on radioactive substances. Together they discovered two highly radioactive elements, radium and polonium. In 1903 they were awarded the Nobel Prize for physics for their work. They shared the award with another French scientist, Antoine Henri Bacquerel, who had discovered natural radioactivity. In 1906 Pierre was killed when he was run over by a car.

In 1911 Marie won the Nobel Prize for chemistry for her work in isolating radium and studying its chemical properties. In 1914 she helped found the Radium Institute in Paris and was its first director. When World War I broke out, she believed that X-rays would help doctors locate bullets in soldiers. Since it was dangerous to move wounded soldiers, she invented portable x-ray machines and trained 150 women to operate them. On July 4, 1934, Marie Curie died at the age of 67. The cause of death was leukemia. It is believed that exposure to high levels of radiation due to her research caused the cancer. After her death the Radium Institute was renamed the Curie Institute in her honor.

15. What did Pierre and Marie Curie win the Nobel Prize in physics for?

    A. Inventing the X-ray machine
    B. Discovering radium and polonium
    C. Founding the Radium Institute
    D. Training X-ray technicians

16. Why did Marie Curie invent portable x-ray machines?

    A. So she could study radium in its natural environment
    B. In order to win another Nobel Prize
    C. To locate bullets in wounded soldiers without moving the soldiers
    D. Because X-ray machines were very expensive and by making them portable, several laboratories at the Radium Institute could share one machine

17. Why was the Radium Institute renamed the Curie Institute?

    A. As a tribute to Marie Curie for her great advances in the fields of chemistry and physics
    B. In honor of Pierre Curie, who had originally conceived of the idea for the institute
    C. Because Marie Curie left a large sum of money to the institute in her will
    D. Because Pierre Curie was killed on its grounds

18. Who discovered natural radioactivity?

    A. Pierre Curie
    B. Marie Curie
    C. Scientists at the Radium Institute
    D. Antoine Henri Bacquerel

19. The author of this passage probably believes that Marie Curie was

    A. a gifted scientist
    B. given more credit than she deserved
    C. unworthy of the two Nobel prizes she won
    D. uninterested in biology and other life sciences

---

20. On October 22, 1998, Hurricane Mitch formed over the Caribbean. By October 28th the storm had moved over the Central American country of Honduras and wreaked havoc on the country. During the next five days the country was pummeled with immense volumes of rain. In the capital city of Tegucigalpa a large mud slide stopped up the Rio Choluteca in the center of town, causing flooding along the riverfront. By the time the storm left, 7,007 people were killed and 11,998 were injured.

According to the passage, which of the following are true?

    I.   Hurricane Mitch formed over the Central American country of Honduras.
    II. A large mud slide stopped up the Rio Choluteca.
    III. 7,007 people were killed by the storm in Honduras.

    A. I only
    B. II and III only
    C. III only
    D. I, II, and III

ANSWERS TO QUICK QUIZZES

Quick Quiz 1
Page 146

1. The stars are considered <u>luminous</u> because
2. According to the passage, an <u>opaque</u> object
3. The passage best supports the idea that <u>elementary schools</u>
4. The planet <u>Jupiter</u> differs from all other planets in the solar system in that it
5. According to the passage, <u>Pygmy Marmosets</u> are commonly found in
6. According to the passage, <u>anthropologists</u> study

Quick Quiz 2
Page 147

1. The passage primarily concerns:
   General main idea
2. The last sentence of paragraph 1 implies that:
   Specific interpretation
3. According to the passage, television has become a medium whose main goal is:
   Specific fact
4. The author's reference to "talking hair-do's" is a reference to:
   Specific interpretation
5. According to the passage, which of the following was an artist?
   I. Brancusi
   II. Cox
   III. Hughes
   Specific fact
6. The author of the passage can most reasonably be described as:
   General interpretation

Quick Quiz 3
Page 156

1. Eliminate answers that are too broad or too narrow. The correct answer should cover the entire passage without claiming more than the passage actually says.
2. Determine whether the author was for, against, or neutral on the subject and eliminate any answer choices you can. Then ask yourself about the degree of the author's tone, i.e., whether it was mild or strong.

3. Choose the answer that comes closest to what the passage says. Look for a paraphrase.

4. First ask why the author wrote the passage. Keep the author's tone in mind.

5. Paraphrases of the passage, and answers that use moderate wording like *can*, *may*, and *often*.

6. Reread the question, look at what makes the two answers different, refer back to the passage, and eliminate the worse answer. Whatever you do, don't just sit and stare at the answers!

Quick Quiz 4
Page 158

1. **C** The passage never mentions water on the moon, so eliminate (A). Choice (B) is the exact opposite of what the passage says, so eliminate it. Choice (D) is never mentioned, so the answer is (C).

2. **A** The answer to this specific question is located in lines 2–3, "she had already established a reputation for her work with soldiers during the Crimean War." Choice (A) paraphrases that.

3. **D** Choice (A) isn't an advantage of the electron microscope, (B) isn't stated, (C) is true but not an advantage, and so the answer is (D).

4. **A** Use the lead words "neutron star" to find the answer. By reading a few lines before and a few lines after, you can see that (A) is the answer.

5. **A** Use POE to eliminate answers that are stated in the passage. That gets rid of (B), (C), and (D).

6. **A** The passage states, "The eel has evolved a kind of insulation that protects its nervous system." Based on this you can infer that electricity is dangerous to the nervous system.

7. **B** The passage states that if the body was not preserved, "the soul would be left homeless for eternity." Also, the passage never mentions (A), (C), or (D).

8. **C** The passage is describing what an important political figure Caesar was, and (C) goes best with that.

9. **C** Use POE to get rid of answers that are mentioned in the passage. That gets rid of (A), (B), and (D).

10. **D** The answer to this question is stated plainly in the first sentence. If you read the question first it should have been obvious. The rest of the passage is there to waste time and confuse you.

11. **D** The passage says "I tried storywriting and got five dollars for stories that now bring a hundred," implying that the author didn't make much money.

12. **B** The sentence is discussing the technological advancement from the first "horseless carriages" to the cars of today.

13. **C** The passage never discusses the morality of spying or the reasons why Mata Hari spied, so eliminate (A) and (B). Though the passage does mention her great beauty, this is not the main purpose of the passage, so eliminate (D). The answer is (C).

14. **D** This is an EXCEPT question. By crossing off the answers that are mentioned in the passage, you are left with (D).

15. **B** The answer can be found in lines 4–5 of the passage. The other choices can be eliminated: The passage never says who invented the X-ray machine, (A), Pierre was dead before the Radium Institute was founded, (C), and (D) occurred after they won the Nobel prize.

16. **C** The passage states "Since it was dangerous to move wounded soldiers, she invented portable X-ray machines."

17. **A** The answer can be found in the last sentence of the passage.

18. **D** The lead words "natural radioactivity" take you right to the answer, Antoine Henri Bacquerel.

19. **A** The entire passage describes Marie Curie's achievements, so it's unlikely that the author would think she was given more credit than she deserved, (B), or unworthy of the two Nobel prizes, (C). Choice (D) is never mentioned, so the answer is (A).

20. **B** Statement I is false, so use POE to get rid of (A) and (D). Statement II is true. Choice (C) does not include statement II, so the answer is (B).

Chapter 6
General Science

INTRODUCTION TO THE GENERAL SCIENCE TEST

The ASVAB General Science test covers basic concepts taught in most high school science courses. It's a broad survey of important topics from the life sciences, earth and space sciences, and physical sciences. More specifically, the following areas are covered:

- Life Sciences: biology, ecology, human anatomy, nutrition, botany, and zoology
- Earth and Space Sciences: geology, astronomy, meteorology, and oceanography
- Physical Sciences: chemistry, units of measurement, and physics

While the test covers a broad range of topics, the Met-ASVAB and Student ASVAB are only 25 questions long; the CAT-ASVAB has 16 questions. Most of those questions will focus on the life and physical sciences, with just a few about the earth sciences. The questions tend to be short and relatively straightforward. Here's an example.

---

1. Which organelle is considered the "control center" of the cell?

   A. Ribosome
   B. Cytoplasm
   C. Lysosome
   D. Nucleus

Here's How to Crack It

The answer is (D), the nucleus. You'll have only 11 minutes to answer all 25 questions (and 8 minutes to answer the 16 questions on the CAT-ASVAB), so you'll need to move quickly. That's why it's important that you feel comfortable with the concepts being tested. Since science is such a broad field, it's impossible for us to review everything here. Don't worry, though—we'll cover all the important concepts and terms you need to know!

Study Tips for the General Science Section

- Don't try to learn everything in one or two "cram" sessions. Plan ahead and study a little bit at a time.
- Make flashcards to help you remember key concepts and definitions.
- Have friends or family members quiz you on the topics after you have studied them.

- Pay close attention to topics you didn't cover in school. You may need to study those a little more.
- Use the quiz at the end of each section to make sure you didn't miss anything important.
- Review any topics that you missed in the quizzes.

PRE-QUIZ 1

1. What does a Punnett Square help to determine?

    A. Gender of a fetus
    B. Probability of traits in offspring
    C. Whether an organism is a producer or consumer
    D. Number of chromosomes a cell contains

2. In an ecosystem, grass plays which of the following roles?

    A. Producer
    B. Consumer
    C. Decomposer
    D. None of the above

3. Which of the following describes the process by which plants make food?

    A. Fertilization
    B. Respiration
    C. Photosynthesis
    D. Meiosis

4. Which of the following is NOT necessary for the body to produce energy?

    A. Vitamins
    B. Protein
    C. Carbohydrates
    D. Fat

5. Which type of blood is considered a universal donor?

    A. Type A
    B. Type B
    C. Type AB
    D. Type O

THE LIFE SCIENCES

The life sciences include biology, ecology, human anatomy, nutrition, botany, and zoology. That's a lot of information to know, but the ASVAB only tests certain concepts from each field of study. We will review all of the most important concepts. Pay close attention to the words in bold, because you'll need to know what they mean. After the review, we'll test your knowledge with a quiz. So let's get started…

Biology

Classification of Living Things

Since the beginning of human civilization, scientists have worked to understand how living organisms are related to each other. To do this, they need a system of classification that assigns plants and animals to groups based on shared traits. Species are first classified into large groups that have fewer traits in common and then smaller groups with more traits in common.

Those groups are

Less Related ⟵——————————⟶ More Related

Kingdom, Phylum, Class, Order, Family, Genus, and Species

To help remember the order of classification, use the following mnemonic:

King	(Kingdom)
Philip	(Phylum)
Came	(Class)
Over	(Order)
From	(Family)
Germany	(Genus)
Soaked	(Species)

Here's how the classification system works.

- Each kingdom is made up of many phyla.
- Each phylum (the plural is "phyla") is made up of many classes.
- Each class is made up of many orders.
- Each order is made up of many families.
- Each family is made up of many genuses.
- Each genus is made up of many species.

The 6 Kingdoms	Characteristics	Examples
Archaebacteria	Unicellular; can survive in extreme conditions	Thermophiles (live in extreme heat), halophiles (live in salty environments)
Eubacteria	Unicellular; lack nuclei and organelles	*E. coli,* blue-green algae
Protista	Unicellular or colonial; have nucleus and organelles	Protozoa, algae (except blue-green algae)
Fungi	Mainly multicellular; plant-like, but cannot carry out photosynthesis	Mushrooms, yeast
Plantae	Multicellular; carry out photosynthesis	Trees
Animalia	Multicellular; possess complex organ system	Humans

Humans belong to the Animalia Kingdom. Therefore, it's important that you know the characteristics of the phyla in the Animalia Kingdom.

CLASSIFICATION OF ANIMALS

Phylum	Characteristics	Examples	
1. Porifera	Two layers of cells with pores	Sponge	
2. Cnidaria	Two layers of cells; hollow digestive cavity with tentacles	Hydra, jellyfish	
3. Platyhelminthes (Flatworms)	Three layers of cells; flat; bilateral symmetry	Tapeworm, planaria, fluke	
4. Nematoda (Roundworms)	Digestive system with a mouth and anus; round	Hookworm	
5. Rotifera	Digestive system	Rotifer	
6. Annelida (Segmented worms)	Long, segmented body; digestive system; closed circulatory system	Earthworm	
7. Mollusca	Soft bodies; hard shell	Clam, snail	
8. Arthropoda	Segmented body; jointed legs; exoskeleton		
Class Crustacea	Gills for breathing; jointed legs	Crab, lobster	
Insecta	Three body parts; one pair of antennae; six legs; tracheal breathing system	Bee, grasshopper	
Arachnida	Two body parts; eight legs	Spider	
Chilopoda	One pair of legs per segment	Centipede	
Diplopoda	Two pairs of legs per segment	Millipede	
9. Echinodermata (Spiny-skinned)	Spiny exoskeleton; complete digestive system	Star fish, sea urchin, sea cucumber	
10. Chordata	Bilateral symmetry; segmented body; endoskeleton		
Class Agnatha	Jawless fish	Lamprey eel	
Chondrichthyes	Cartilaginous fish; internal fertilization	Shark, ray	
Osteichthyes	Bony fish; live in fresh and salt water; external fertilization	Trout	
Amphibia	Reproduce in water	Frog, toad	
Reptilia	Internal fertilization; dry skin with scales	Turtle, lizard, snake	
Aves	Feathers; wings; hollow bones	Bird	
Mammalia	Hair; mammary glands; different types of teeth	Human, kangaroo, bear, cat	

The Human Body

The human body is made up of several complex systems that work together to obtain and distribute nutrients throughout the body, remove wastes, adapt to the environment, and reproduce. We will review each system separately.

The Musculoskeletal System

The musculoskeletal system is responsible for holding the body together. Without a skeleton, humans would be just a pile of skin and organs. Humans wear their skeletons on the inside, which is called an **endoskeleton.** Organisms who wear their skeleton on the outside, such as insects, have **exoskeletons**. Both endoskeletons and exoskeletons provide support and protection for the organism.

The human skeleton is made up of **cartilage** and **bone.** Cartilage is found at the end of all bones, at the joints, in the nose, and in the ear. It is more flexible than bone and is used as a buffer between bones and as a support in the ear and nose. Bones provide the primary support for the body. They also protect the organs, produce blood cells, and store minerals, such as calcium.

Muscles work with the skeleton to support, protect, and move the body. There are three types of muscle in the body: **cardiac, skeletal,** and **smooth.** Cardiac muscles are found in the heart. Their movements are what you feel when you say your heart is pounding. Skeletal muscles are attached to the skeleton and move your body around. They are responsible for all voluntary movements you make. Smooth muscles are found in the stomach, intestines, and bladder. They are involuntary, meaning that you have no control over their movements.

The Digestive System

The digestive system is responsible for breaking down the food you eat into molecules that the body can absorb. It consists of the mouth, esophagus, stomach, small intestine, large intestine, rectum, and anus.

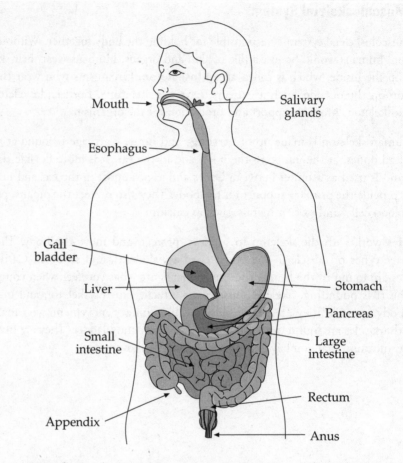

Mouth: Food enters the mouth, and the tongue and teeth begin the process of breaking food down by chewing.

Esophagus: The chewed food moves from the mouth into the esophagus. Contractions push the food through the esophagus and into the stomach.

Stomach: The food is mixed with gastric acids and **pepsin,** which break the food down further.

Small Intestine: The food moves from the stomach to the small intestine. The small intestine is very long, about 23 feet long on average. The food is broken down completely by enzymes produced in the walls of the small intestine and the pancreas. Bile, which is produced by the liver, breaks down fats. The broken-down food is absorbed into the bloodstream from the small intestine and carried throughout the body.

Large Intestine: The remaining matter moves into the large intestine where water and minerals are absorbed into the body.

Rectum: The solid waste matter is stored here.

Anus: Solid waste matter is periodically released through the anus. Liquid waste (urine) is sent to the bladder and released through the urethra.

The Excretory System

The organ that regulates excretion is the **kidney.** The kidneys are made up of millions of tiny structures called **nephrons.** The function of the nephrons is to filter the blood. The fluid filtered out of the blood is called filtrate. The filtrate travels through the nephron to the ureter and then into the bladder, where it is stored. The filtrate, now called urine, remains in the bladder until it is excreted out of the body through the **urethra.**

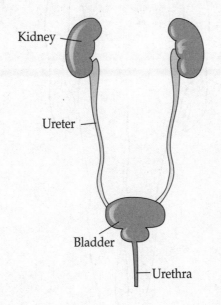

More Great Books

For more in-depth coverage of anatomy and biology, plus a chance to do some serious coloring, check out these titles from your pals at The Princeton Review:
Biology Coloring Workbook
Anatomy Coloring Workbook

The Respiratory System

You need oxygen to survive. The job of the respiratory system is to collect air from the environment, filter out oxygen from the air, and deliver the oxygen to the circulatory system.

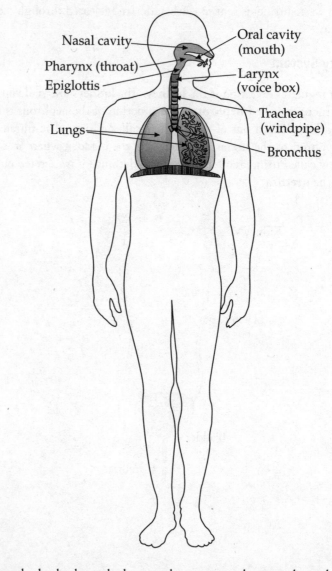

Nasal cavity
Oral cavity (mouth)
Pharynx (throat)
Epiglottis
Larynx (voice box)
Lungs
Trachea (windpipe)
Bronchus

Air enters the body through the mouth or nose and passes through the **pharynx** and **larynx.** It then enters the **trachea,** which is covered by the **epiglottis.** The epiglottis prevents food from going down the wrong pipe. The trachea branches into the **left and right bronchi,** collectively known as the **bronchus.** These two tubes break down into smaller tubes called **bronchioles.** Each bronchiole ends in a small sac called an **alveolus.** In the alveolus, the oxygen crosses from the lungs into the blood stream.

The Circulatory System

The purpose of the **circulatory system** is to transport nutrients and oxygen throughout the body and to get rid of wastes. The main organ in the circulatory system is the **heart.** The heart pumps blood through the body. It is divided into four chambers, two on the left and two on the right. Once in the blood stream, oxygen is moved throughout the body by the circulatory system. The circulatory system also brings carbon dioxide back to the alveolus so the respiratory system can get rid of it when you exhale.

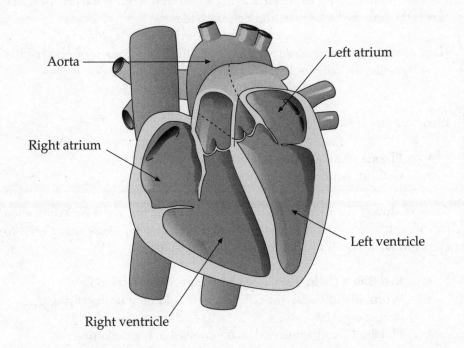

Blood flows through the body in a circuit. Blood leaves the heart to travel through the body from the left ventricle. It flows through a large blood vessel called the **aorta,** which then branches into smaller **arteries.** Arteries always carry blood *away* from the heart. Arteries branch off into smaller **arterioles,** which branch off into **capillaries.**

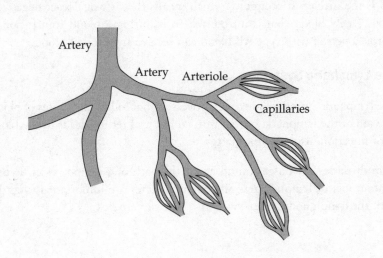

You have thousands of capillaries in your body. Capillaries exchange oxygen, nutrients, and wastes with the tissues of your body.

Once the blood has been through the tissues and returned to the capillaries it has very little oxygen left. It moves from the capillaries to vessels called **venules.** The venules meet up with larger vessels called **veins.** The veins carry the blood *into* the heart through the right atrium and then the right ventricle. The blood is sent from the right ventricle directly to the lungs for more oxygen. Once the blood has become **oxygenated** it moves back into the heart through the left atrium. From the left atrium it is sent into the left ventricle, which is where it started. To review, here is the path the blood takes through the body.

Left Ventricle → Artery → Arterioles → Capillaries → Tissue → Capillaries → Venules → Veins → Right Atrium → Right Ventricle → Lungs → Left Atrium → Left Ventricle

Blood consists of two things.

- **Plasma** (the liquid part of blood)
- **Cells** (the stuff suspended in the liquid)

As we've already discussed, blood carries oxygen, nutrients, and wastes throughout the body. It also carries three types of cells: red blood cells (also called erythrocytes), white blood cells (called leukocytes), and platelets.

- **Red Blood Cells:** The oxygen-carrying cells of the blood
- **White Blood Cells:** The cells that fight infections by destroying foreign organisms
- **Platelets:** Cell fragments that are involved in blood clotting

All blood cells are made in the bone marrow, which is located in the center of the bones.

Blood comes in four different types: A, B, AB, and O. Type O is the **universal donor,** which means that it can be given to anyone in a blood transfusion. Type AB is the **universal recipient,** which means that it won't react negatively to any type of new blood that is introduced to it during a blood transfusion. In other words, a person with type AB blood can receive any kind of blood.

The Lymphatic System

The lymphatic system is a network of vessels that follow the routes of blood vessels. The job of the lymphatic system is to collect and return fluids to the blood and to fight infection, using **lymphocytes.**

Lymph nodes are bulges found along the path of a lymph vessel. Lymph nodes contain lots of lymphocytes. Since lymphocytes are important in fighting infection, the lymph nodes often swell up when you are sick.

The Nervous System

The nervous system consists of the brain, spinal cord, and billions of nerve cells called **neurons.** The nervous system serves two primary purposes: to control the functions of the body and to receive stimuli from the environment.

There are two parts to the nervous system, the **central nervous system** and the **peripheral nervous system.** The central nervous system includes the neurons in the brain and the spinal cord. The peripheral nervous system is made up of all other neurons, including neurons in the skin, organs, and blood vessels. It can be broken down further into the **somatic nervous system** and the **autonomic nervous system.** The somatic nervous system controls voluntary actions, such as waving your hand or dancing. The autonomic nervous system controls involuntary actions, such as your heartbeat and your digestive system. The autonomic nervous system can be broken down into the **sympathetic** and **parasympathetic** nervous systems. Both of these systems are responsible for preparing the body to defend itself, also known as the "fight or flight" response. The sympathetic nervous system raises your heart and respiration rates, causes your blood vessels to constrict, increases glucose levels, and produces "goosebumps" when you feel threatened. The job of the parasympathetic nervous system is to return the body to normal when the danger is over. To remember the divisions of the nervous system, take a look at the flow chart on the next page.

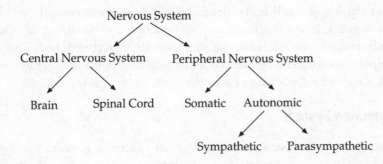

The **brain** is made up of the cerebrum, cerebellum, hypothalamus, and medulla.

Divisions Within the Brain	
Parts of the Brain	**Function**
Cerebrum	Controls all voluntary activities; receives and interprets sensory information
Cerebellum	Coordinates muscle activity
Hypothalamus	Regulates homeostasis and secretes hormones
Medulla	Controls involuntary actions such as breathing and swallowing

The brain is called the "control center" of the body, because information from every part of the body and the surrounding environment is sent to the brain for processing. The brain responds to this information by sending out messages through neurons.

Neurons are specialized cells found in the nervous system. Their job is to send impulses between body parts. Here is what a typical neuron looks like.

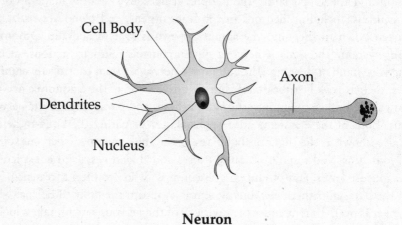

Neuron

A neuron consists of a **cell body, dendrites, nucleus,** and **axon.** The cell body contains the nucleus and other objects. The nucleus is the "brain" of the neuron. The dendrites receive impulses and transmit them through the cell body and axon. If the impulse is strong enough, the axon will send it on to the next neuron, which will pick it up via its dendrites and start the process over again.

The Endocrine System

We've seen how the nervous system controls body functions. It works very quickly and its results last only a short time. The **endocrine system** also works to control the body, but it works slower and the results last longer. It works through the release of **hormones.** Hormones are chemical messengers that are made by endocrine glands and secreted into the blood stream. Once in the blood stream, they go everywhere in the body, but only affect organs that have receptors for that particular hormone. These organs are called target organs. Here is a summary of the hormones and their effects on the body.

Organ	Hormone(s)	Effect
Anterior Pituitary	FSH	Stimulates activity in ovaries and testes
	LH	Stimulates activity in ovary (release of ovum) and production of testosterone
	ACTH	Stimulates the adrenal cortex
	TSH	Stimulates thyroid gland
	Growth Hormone	Stimulates bone and muscle growth
	Prolactin	Causes milk secretion
Posterior Pituitary	Oxytocin	Causes uterus to contract
	Vasopressin	Causes kideny to reabsorb water
Thyroid	Thyroid Hormone	Regulates metabolic rate
	Calcitonin	Lowers blood calcium levels
Parathyroid	Parathyroid Hormone	Increases blood calcium concentration
Adrenal Cortex	Aldosterone	Increases Na^+ and H_2O reabsorption in kidney
Adrenal Medulla	Epinephrine Norepinephrine	Increases blood glucose level and heart rate
Pancreas	Insulin	Decreases blood sugar concentration
	Glucagon	Increases blood sugar concentration
Ovaries	Estrogen	Promotes female secondary sex characteristics
	Progesterone	Thickens endometrial lining
Testes	Testosterone	Promotes male secondary sex characteristics

While both the nervous system and endocrine system work to control the body, there are important differences between the two that you should know.

- The nervous system sends impulses using neurons, whereas the endocrine system secretes hormones.
- Nerve impulses act quickly and control short-lived events such as muscle contractions, whereas hormones are slower acting but can last much longer—for example, the testosterone produced during puberty is a hormone.

The Reproductive System

Reproduction involves two sets of organs, the male reproductive organs and the female reproductive organs. During reproduction, the male sperm fuses with the female ovum, creating a **zygote.** The zygote eventually develops into a fetus.

The **male reproductive system** produces **sperm** in the testes in small tubes called the **seminiferous tubules.** These tiny tubules merge to form a large duct called the **vas deferens.** The vas deferens connects with the urethra, which then carries the sperm out of the body. The sperm is carried out in a fluid called semen. Semen is secreted by several glands and provides nutrients for the sperm.

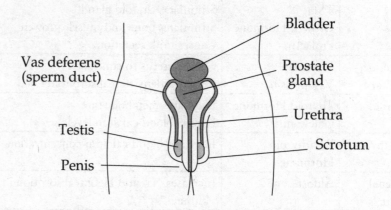

The main organs involved in the **female reproductive system** are the **ovaries** and the **uterus.** The ovaries store the ova and release one ovum every menstrual cycle. The ovum travels through the fallopian tube to the uterus. If the ovum is fertilized by a sperm, the fertilized ovum implants itself in the lining of the uterus, and pregnancy follows. If the ovum is not fertilized, the lining of the uterus breaks down and is eventually passed out of the body through the vagina in a process called **menstruation,** and then a new cycle begins.

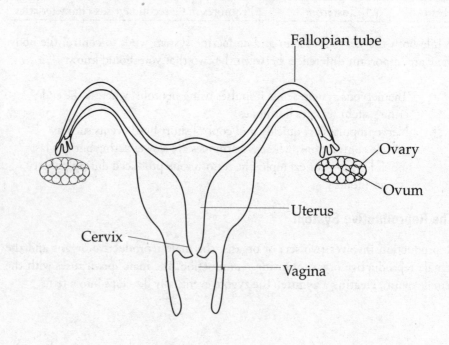

Nutrition

A healthy diet requires protein, carbohydrates, fat, fiber, minerals, and vitamins. Protein, carbohydrates, and fat are necessary for your body to produce energy. Fiber, vitamins, and minerals are necessary for your body to function properly.

Protein: Protein is necessary for the body's growth and repair. It can be found in meat, fish, eggs, cheese, peas, legumes, and grains.

Carbohydrates: There are two types of carbohydrates—sugars and starches. These are the main energy sources necessary for the body's metabolism. Starches are found in bread, cereal, and pasta. Sugars come from fruit, cane sugar, and beets.

Fats: Fats also provide energy for metabolism. There are three types of fats: saturated, monosaturated, and polyunsaturated. Saturated fats tend to increase the levels of bad cholesterol in the blood, while monosaturated and polyunsaturated fats tend to decrease levels of bad cholesterol. Fats can be found in meat, dairy products, fish, and oil.

Fiber: Fiber passes through the body unchanged but is necessary for a healthy diet. It provides bulk, which allows the large intestine to carry away waste matter.

Minerals: Small amounts of minerals are needed for a balanced diet. Most people get enough. Some necessary minerals are iron, zinc, calcium, magnesium, and sodium chloride (salt).

Vitamins: Vitamins help regulate the metabolism. Below is a table of vitamins necessary for good health.

Vitamin	Sources	Result of Deficiency
A	Eggs, fruit, butter, liver, vegetables	Night blindness, skin infections, loss of appetite, diarrhea
B_1	Wheat germ, bran, grains, poultry, eggs, pasta, beans	Loss of appetite, beriberi
B_2	Liver, dairy, whole grains, green vegetables	Weakness, skin infections
B_{12}	Meat, dairy, eggs, fish	Anemia, nerve degeneration
C	Citrus fruit, tomatoes, vegetables, strawberries	Scurvy
D	Milk, eggs, dairy, fish	Rickets, tooth decay
E	Vegetable oils, nuts, meat, cereals, egg yolk	Anemia
K	Green vegetables, egg yolk, cheese, pork, liver	Excessive bleeding

The Cell

Every living organism—plants, animals, and others—is made up of cells. The smallest organisms, like bacteria, are called **unicellular,** because they are made up of only one cell. Larger organisms, like humans, are made up of billions of cells and are called **multicellular.** Inside all cells are small structures called **organelles.** There are several different organelles, each with their own distinct functions. Here is what a typical cell looks like.

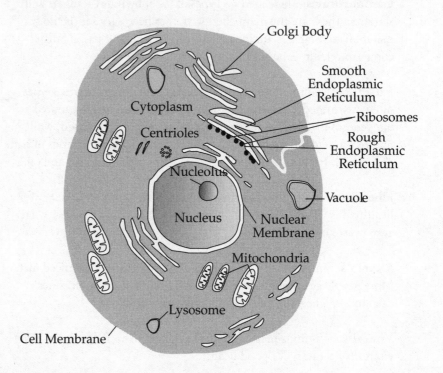

Organelle	Function
Cell membrane	Outer membrane of the cell; controls what enters and leaves the cell
Centrioles	Form spindle fibers during cellular division
Golgi Body	Sorts and packages proteins
Lysosomes	Digest old organelles and foreign substances
Mitochondria	Produce energy for the cell
Nucleolus	Part of the nucleus; makes ribosomes
Nucleus	Control center of the cell; contains the chromosomes
Ribosomes	Site of protein synthesis
Rough endoplasmic reticulum (ER)	Makes proteins to be exported out of cell; studded with ribosomes.
Smooth endoplasmic reticulum	Makes lipids and detoxifies enzymes
Vacuole	Stores wastes and other materials

The cells of plants and animals are similar, with just a few differences. Those differences are the following:

- Both plant and animal cells have a cell membrane that surrounds the cell. Plant cells, however, also have a rigid, protective outer covering, called the **cell wall,** which surrounds the cell membrane.
- Plant cells possess **chloroplasts,** while animal cells do not. Chloroplasts are involved in photosynthesis (the process through which plants make their own food).
- The vacuoles in a plant cell are much larger than the vacuoles in animal cells, and they tend to crowd the other organelles.

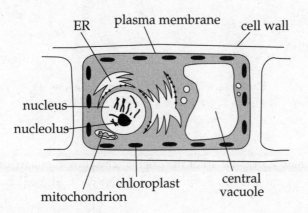

A Quick Word about Chromosomes

Chromosomes are located in the nucleus of cells. They contain **DNA**—the hereditary blueprint of the cell. DNA determines the genetic makeup of organisms. It tells the cell how to function, when to reproduce, and when to die. Things like eye color, hair color, height, weight, and even some diseases are controlled by DNA. That's why people who are related look alike—they share similar DNA! Every human cell, except for the sex cells, has 46 chromosomes. A human cell with 46 chromosomes is **diploid.** That means it has two sets of 23 chromosomes each. Sex cells, which have only 23 chromosomes, are called **haploid.** We will talk more about this later. For now all you need to remember is that most human cells have 46 chromosomes.

The Cell Cycle

Thousands of cells are dying in your body right now. Cells have only a limited life span and die when that life span is over. But don't worry—your body is making new cells as quickly as the old ones die out. In fact, your skin cells die off so fast that you have an entirely new skin every few weeks. The body produces all these new cells through a process called **cell division.**

Cell division, also called **mitosis,** is a process that allows our body to replace the aging cells with fresh new ones. There are two periods in a cell's life span: interphase and mitosis.

Interphase

Interphase is the period after the cell's birth, and before it undergoes mitosis, when it copies itself. During interphase the cell is carrying out its normal functions. Before interphase ends the cell makes a copy of all its chromosomes. The duplicated chromosome is connected to the original chromosome by the centromere. Each individual chromosome is called a **chromatid.**

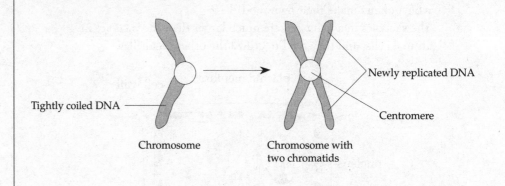

Tightly coiled DNA

Chromosome

Newly replicated DNA

Centromere

Chromosome with two chromatids

When interphase is over, all 46 of the original chromosomes have duplicated. The cell now has 46 chromosomes with 2 chromatids each. The cell is now ready for mitosis.

Mitosis

Mitosis is the process a cell goes through when it divides. There are four stages to mitosis, with the end result being a new cell.

Stage 1: Prophase. During prophase the nuclear membrane begins to break up. The chromosomes thicken and form coils. The centrioles move away from each other and form a system of microtubules called **spindle fibers.** The spindle fibers attach to the chromosomes and help them move around.

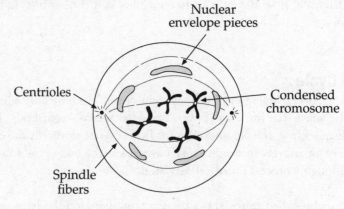

Nuclear envelope pieces

Centrioles

Condensed chromosome

Spindle fibers

Note: In the drawing above, only 4 chromosomes are shown. This is only to keep the drawing simple. Remember, in a real cell there are 46 chromosomes, all doing exactly the same thing.

Stage 2: Metaphase. Now that the spindle fibers are attached to the chromosomes, they help them line up in the middle of the cell. That area of the cell is called the **metaphase plate.**

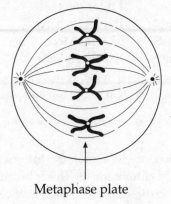

Metaphase plate

Stage 3: Anaphase. During this stage, the spindle fibers pull the chromatids apart. The separated chromatids are pulled to opposite poles.

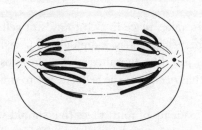

Stage 4: Telophase. The last stage is telophase. During this stage, a nuclear membrane forms around each set of chromosomes. Then the cytoplasm splits in a process called **cytokinesis.** The cell membrane forms around each new cell, and two daughter cells are formed, each with 46 chromosomes.

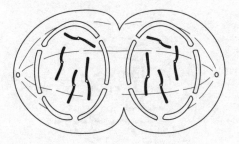

Once the daughter cells are formed, they enter interphase, and the whole process starts up again.

Here is a mnemonic device you can use to help you remember all that

I've Probably Mixed All This Up!

I've	Interphase	I is for Interlude
Probably	Prophase	P is for Prepare
Mixed	Metaphase	M is for Meet
All	Anaphase	A is for Apart
This	Telophase	T is for Tear
Up!	Up	Up to the top and start over again

Meiosis

Recall from our discussion of chromosomes that sex cells are **haploid,** which means they contain only 23 chromosomes. This is because the sex cells, the sperm, and ova combine during fertilization to create a new cell, called a zygote. If they both had 46 chromosomes, then the new zygote would have 92 chromosomes, twice the number it should have. Therefore, sex cells are made differently from all other cells. The process by which sex cells are made is called **meiosis.** Meiosis occurs only in sex organs called gonads. In males, the sex organs are the **testes;** in females they're the **ovaries.**

Meiosis, unlike mitosis, takes place in two rounds of cell division, called meiosis 1 and meiosis 2. Before meiosis starts, a diploid cell (a cell with 46 chromosomes) undergoes interphase. Just like in mitosis, the chromosomes replicate into 46 paired sets. Once this has occurred, the cell is ready to undergo meiosis 1.

Meiosis 1: is made up of four stages that should sound familiar: prophase 1, metaphase 1, anaphase 1, and telophase 1.

Prophase 1: During prophase 1, the nuclear membrane disappears, and the centrioles move to opposite poles of the nucleus, just like in mitosis.

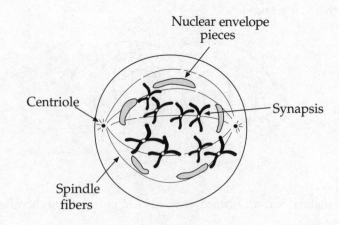

Unlike in mitosis, however, the chromosomes do not split up. Instead, they undergo **synapsis.** Synapsis occurs when two sets of chromosomes combine, forming a tetrad. The tetrad consists of four chromatids. Once synapsis has occurred, the four chromatids exchange segments in a process called **crossing over.**

Crossing over
at two sites

In the picture above, the white chromosome is swapping segments with the black chromosome. When crossing over is complete, each chromosome will consist of white segments and black segments. This creates new combinations of DNA in the chromosome. New combinations of DNA guarantee that each organism is unique.

Metaphase 1: The tetrads line up at the metaphase plate just like in mitosis. The only difference is that the chromosomes are lined up in pairs (tetrads) during meiosis. Recall that during mitosis, the chromosomes are lined up individually.

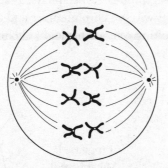

Anaphase 1: The tetrads separate and move to opposite poles. Compare this to mitosis, where the chromatids separated.

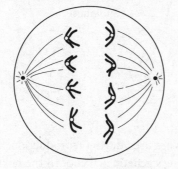

Telophase 1: The nuclear membrane forms around each set of chromosomes. The cells undergo cytokinesis, and two daughter cells are the result. Notice that the cells are still diploid.

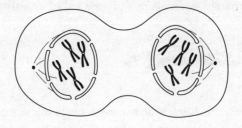

Earlier in our discussion we said that sex cells are haploid. At this point there are two diploid daughter cells. That means that meiosis isn't finished yet. It still needs to go through the second stage of meiosis.

Meiosis 2 is almost identical to mitosis. The only difference is that at the beginning of mitosis there are two sets of chromosomes in the nucleus. In meiosis 2, there is only one set. The cell undergoes all of the stages of mitosis: prophase, metaphase, anaphase, and telophase. Since the cell starts with 46 chromosomes and divides in half during meiosis 2, the resulting cells are haploid (23 chromosomes).

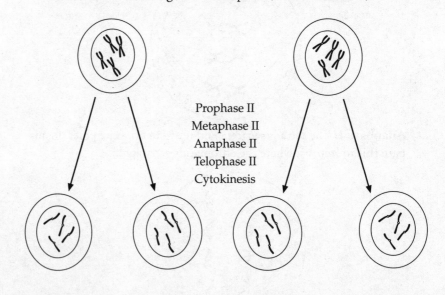

Prophase II
Metaphase II
Anaphase II
Telophase II
Cytokinesis

The resulting haploid cells are used during reproduction. The chromosomes in the cells determine the offspring's genetic makeup. In the next section, we will discuss how those chromosomes combine to create unique individuals with their own genetic characteristics.

Genetics

Genetics is the study of heredity. Heredity is the process by which traits are passed from parents to children. Let's start by covering some basic definitions.

A **trait,** or characteristic, is produced through heredity by **genes.**

Genes, which are located in the chromosomes of cells, tell the cells how to behave. Genes consist of a pair of hereditary factors called **alleles.** Each organism carries two alleles for a trait.

An allele can be **dominant** or **recessive.** If an individual has two identical alleles for a trait—either two dominant alleles or two recessive alleles—then the individual is **homozygous.** If an individual has two different alleles for a trait, then he or she is **heterozygous.**

We indicate dominant alleles by using uppercase letters such as *B*. When denoting recessive alleles, use lowercase letters such as *b*.

A recessive allele is one that will produce its effect only in a homozygous individual. A dominant allele will produce its effect in either a homozygous or heterozygous individual. For example

- *Bb* is heterozygous. It contains a dominant (*B*) and recessive (*b*) allele. Thus, it will express the dominant trait.
- *bb* is homozygous. It contains two recessive (*b*) alleles. Since recessive alleles are only expressed in individuals homozygous for the recessive trait, the recessive trait will be expressed here.
- *BB* is also homozygous, but for the dominant (*B*) allele. Since it includes the dominant allele, the dominant trait must be expressed.

When discussing the physical characteristics of a person, we refer to his or her **phenotype.** When discussing genetic makeup, we are talking about **genotype.**

One way the ASVAB may test you about genetics is by asking you to predict phenotypes and genotypes. This might sound difficult, but it's actually quite simple if you use Punnett Squares.

A Punnett Square is just a four-chambered box like the one below.

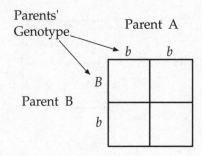

On the sides of the Punnett Square you list the genotypes of the two parents. Then you fill in the box according to what you wrote on the outside. This gives you the probability of each genotype in the offspring. Look at an example using eye color.

Suppose the allele for blue eyes is recessive and the allele for brown eyes is dominant. You would express this using *B* for the dominant allele brown, and *b* for the recessive allele blue. Assume you have two parents with the following genotypes:

Parent A   Parent B
bb   *Bb*

You can fill in the Punnett Square using this information.

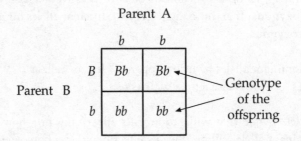

By looking at the genotypes of the parents, you can see that Parent A is homozygous with a genotype of *bb* and Parent B is heterozygous with a genotype of *Bb*. Now look at the offspring.

Two of the offspring have the heterozygous genotype *Bb*, which means they have brown eyes, and the other two have the homozygous genotype *bb*, which means they have blue eyes. This means that 50% of the offspring will have the brown phenotype and 50% will have the blue phenotype.

Try one more problem. Suppose that a plant produces flowers that are either white or pink. White is the dominant trait, and pink is recessive. Take a look at a cross between two plants with these genotypes.

Parent A   Parent B
Ww   *Ww*

Here is what the Punnett Square looks like.

Parent A

	W	w
W	WW	Ww
w	Ww	ww

Parent B

Both parents have the genotype *Ww*, which means that both parents have white flowers, because *W* denotes the dominant gene. However, both parents also carry the recessive gene for pink flowers, *w*. The parents in this example are both heterozygous. Now let's discuss the offspring.

Our four results in the Punnett Square are *WW*, *Ww*, *Ww*, and *ww*. What do each of these mean?

- *WW* means the plant is homozygous for the white trait and has a white phenotype.
- *Ww* means the plant is heterozygous for the white trait and has a white phenotype.
- *ww* means the plant is homozygous for the pink trait and has a pink phenotype.

Therefore, 75% of the plants will have the white phenotype, and 25% will have the pink phenotype.

Sex Determination

The sex of offspring is determined by genes located in the sex chromosomes. Females carry the homozygous genotype *XX*, and males the heterozygous genotype *XY*. As you will recall, conception occurs when a sperm fertilizes an egg. At this time, each parent contributes one sex chromosome to the offspring. The mother always contributes an *X* chromosome. The sperm that fertilizes the egg determines the sex of the offspring. If the sperm carries another *X* chromosome, the offspring will be female (*XX*). If it contributes a *Y* chromosome, the offspring will be male (*XY*).

Plants

So far, most of our review has focused on animals, humans in particular. You may see some questions, however, asking you about plants.

Plants, like humans, are multicellular. As we mentioned above, plant cells differ from animal cells in that they possess a cell wall. The purpose of the cell wall is to provide support for the plant and to help prevent it from drying out. Another difference that we mentioned before is that plant cells possess **chloroplasts.** Chloroplasts are essential for photosynthesis.

Photosynthesis

As you have probably noticed, plants do not need to search for food—they don't hunt, cook, or shop for groceries. But like all living things, they do need nutrients to survive. What makes plants special is that they produce their own food. The process by which nearly all plants make food is called **photosynthesis.**

Photosynthesis is a process by which plants turn energy from the sun into chemical energy. The chemical reaction for photosynthesis is

$$6CO_2 + 12H_2O \xrightarrow{\text{sunlight}} C_6H_{12}O_6 + 6O_2 + 6H_2O$$

The plant uses carbon dioxide (CO_2), water (H_2O), and sunlight to make the simple sugars that the plant uses for energy ($C_6H_{12}O_6$), in addition to byproducts of oxygen and water. Photosynthesis occurs in the chloroplasts of the plant.

Classification of Plants

Just as we classified the animal kingdom earlier, we can also classify the plant kingdom.

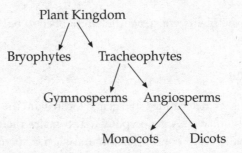

As you can see from the flow chart, all plants fall into one of two categories: **bryophytes** and **tracheophytes.** Bryophytes are more primitive plants, lacking true stems and leaves. Some bryophytes you may be familiar with are mosses and liverworts. Tracheophytes are what you probably think of when you think of plants. They have stems, leaves, and roots. All trees, flowers, shrubs, and ferns are tracheophytes.

Fungi

Fungi are often mistaken for plants, but are a separate kingdom completely. They are multicellular like plants, but differ in that they do not carry on photosynthesis. They live on decomposing matter. Some common fungi are mushrooms, yeasts, and molds.

Ecology

Ecology is the study of the interactions between living things and their environments. Just as biologists classify living organisms, ecologists have a system of classification.

> **Biosphere:** This is the area of the earth where all living things exist. It is made up of the soil, water, and air. It can be divided up into regions called biomes.

Biome: A large region of the earth, biomes are areas that are grouped together because of similar climate, vegetation, and animal life.

Ecosystem: The interaction of living and nonliving things

Community: The area in which a group of populations live

Population: A group of individuals that belong to the same species

The Biome

The biosphere is divided into several large regions called biomes. You may need to know the various biomes and the plant and animal life they contain for the ASVAB.

Biome 1: The Tundra. Tundra climates are found in the northern parts of Alaska, Europe, and Asia. The soil in a tundra is permanently frozen, so it is difficult for plants to grow roots. Therefore, very few trees can be found in the tundra. Common vegetation includes short shrubs, grasses, and mosses. There aren't many animals living in this rugged environment, but reindeer, caribou, wolves, and bears manage to survive here, as well as several types of insects.

Biome 2: The Taiga. Taiga is found a little south of the tundra. (Note that neither the taiga nor the tundra are found in the southern hemisphere.) It's known as coniferous forest, because it contains many conifers (evergreen trees). Taigas have long, severe winters. Animals that can be found here include bears, wolves, elk, beavers, deer, squirrels, rabbits, and moose.

Biome 3: The Deciduous Forests. Deciduous forests are found south of the taiga and include eastern North America, central and southern Europe, Japan, and New Zealand. The climate here has distinct hot and cold seasons and a lot of rain. A wide variety of plants and animals can be found in these forests. Trees here, unlike coniferous trees, lose their leaves in the winter and regrow them in the spring. Some animals you might find include deer, beavers, raccoons, squirrels, foxes, bears, and rabbits.

Biome 4: The Grasslands (Savanna). Characterized by grasses and a few trees, grasslands can be found in the American Midwest, Africa, Eurasia, and South America. Summers here are hot, winters cold, and rainfall is unpredictable. Animals found in the grasslands include antelope, kangaroo, zebra, giraffe, elephants, ferrets, snakes, and lizards.

Biome 5: Tropical Rain Forests. Tropical rain forests are characterized by the heaviest rainfall anywhere on earth and the largest variety of plants and animals. They are found in South America, Africa, and Southeast Asia. The trees here tend to grow very tall, forming a canopy of leaves that prevents sunlight from reaching the ground. Animals found here include monkeys, birds, lizards, snakes, tapirs, and insects.

Biome 6: The Desert. Deserts are the driest places on earth. They are found in the American Southwest, Africa, Asia, and the Middle East. People often associate heat with deserts, but deserts can be hot or cold. Plant and animal life is scarce and must be adapted to the arid environment. Plants consist primarily of cactuses. Animals include jackrabbits, owls, snakes, lizards, kangaroo, and small rodents.

The Community

All biomes can be divided into ecosystems, which are further divided into communities. A community is made up of living things that interact with each other. All members of a community fall into one of three roles: producers, consumers, or decomposers.

Producers, also known as autotrophs, make their own food. They don't have to rely upon other species for survival. Plants, which make their own food through photosynthesis, are producers.

Consumers, also know as heterotrophs, can't produce their own food. They are forced to get it from outside sources. Primary consumers are organisms that feed on producers directly. Cows are primary consumers, since they only eat plants (they are called herbivores). Above primary consumers on the food chain are secondary consumers. They eat other primary consumers, usually animals (so they are called carnivores). Some examples are lions, wolves, and sharks. Tertiary consumers eat producers, primary consumers, and secondary consumers. Organisms that eat both plants and animals are called omnivores. Humans are an example of omnivores.

Decomposers are organisms that break down organic matter into simple products. Examples are fungi and bacteria. Eventually everything in the food chain will succumb to decomposers.

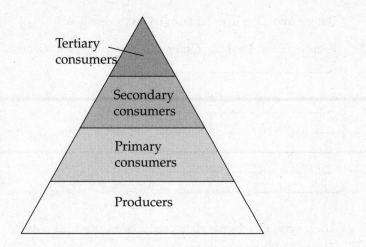

As you can see, decomposers have been left off the diagram. They are usually not considered a part of the food chain. Just remember that they decompose all living matter.

QUICK QUIZ 1

Test your knowledge of life sciences with the quiz below. You can check your answers at the end of the chapter. If you miss any questions, be sure to go back and review. Good luck!

1. Match the organelle on the left with its function/description on the right.

    _____ Cell Membrane   A. control center of the cell, contains DNA

    _____ Centrioles   B. synthesizes proteins to be exported out of the cell

    _____ Golgi Body   C. site of protein synthesis

    _____ Lysosomes   D. site of energy production

    _____ Rough ER   E. makes lipids and detoxifies enzymes

    _____ Ribosomes   F. stores waste and other substances

    _____ Nucleolus   G. sorts and packages proteins

    _____ Vacuole   H. related to the formation of spindle during mitosis

    _____ Smooth ER   I. site of ribosome synthesis in the nucleus

    _____ Mitochondria   J. barrier that controls what enters and leaves the cell

    _____ Nucleus   K. digest foreign substances and worn organelles

2. Put the following in order from largest to smallest:

Family Class Phylum Order Kingdom Species Genus

_____

_____

_____

_____

_____

_____

_____

3. The process by which a plant produces its own food is called

_____ .

4. The soil here is permanently frozen. Deep root growth is difficult, so there are very few trees. Animals such as reindeer, wolves, bears, and caribou are found here. Which biome is being described?

    A. Desert
    B. Grasslands
    C. Taiga
    D. Tundra

5. Earlobes can be attached or unattached. Attached earlobes are the dominant trait.

           Parent A   Parent B
             Aa   *Aa*

Fill in the Punnett Square below.

The probability that the parents produce offspring with attached earlobes is _____ %.

The probability that the parents produce offspring with unattached earlobes is _____ %.

6. Match the description on the right with the stage of mitosis on the left.

_____ Interphase   A. nuclear membrane forms, cytokinesis occurs

_____ Prophase   B. chromatids split and chromosomes move to opposite poles

_____ Metaphase   C. chromosomes replicate

_____ Anaphase   D. chromosomes line up

_____ Telophase   E. nuclear membrane breaks up, spindles form, centrioles move to opposite poles

7. Fill in the blanks.

The nervous system can be divided into two parts: _____ and _____. The brain and the spinal cord are parts of the _____.

The peripheral nervous system can be divided into the _____ and _____. The _____ controls voluntary actions. The _____ controls involuntary actions. The autonomic system can be divided into the _____ and _____.

8. Which organism in the food chain is a producer?

A.   Birds

B.   Insects

C.   Plants

D.   Snakes

9. Match the description/deficiency to the vitamin.

_____ Vitamin A   A. a lack of this may cause anemia

_____ Vitamin B_1 B. a lack of this may cause rickets

_____ Vitamin B_2 C. a lack of this may cause night blindness

_____ Vitamin B_{12} D. a lack of this may cause weakness or skin infections

_____ Vitamin C   E. a lack of this may cause appetite loss or beriberi

_____ Vitamin D   F. a lack of this may cause anemia

_____ Vitamin E   G. a lack of this may cause excessive bleeding

_____ Vitamin K   H. a lack of this may cause scurvy

10. True or False: Type O blood is the universal recipient. _____

11. Which of the following is a bryophyte?

A.   Fern

B.   Oak tree

C.   Moss

D.   Mushroom

12. Which of the following are functions of the kidney?

    I. Filtration of blood to remove wastes
    II. Blood pressure regulation
    III. pH regulation

    A. I only
    B. I and II only
    C. I and III only
    D. II and III only

13. All of the following are true about the endocrine system EXCEPT:

    A. it relies on chemical messengers that travel through the bloodstream
    B. it is a control system that has extremely rapid effects on the body
    C. the hormones affect only certain "target" organs
    D. it is involved in maintaining body homeostasis

14. Plants that have true roots, stems, and leaves are classified as
    _____.

15. Which of the following groups have the most in common with one another?

    A. Members of the same kingdom
    B. Members of the same genus
    C. Members of the same phylum
    D. Members of the same class

16. An organism that feeds at several trophic levels is

    A. a carnivore
    B. an omnivore
    C. a primary consumer
    D. a herbivore

17. Which of the following animals would you be most likely to find in a grass-land biome?

    A. Caribou
    B. Beaver
    C. Bear
    D. Zebra

18. The _____ is a large duct that conducts sperm from the testes to the urethra.

19. The three types of muscle are

    1) _____

    2) _____

    3) _____

20. A cell that has just completed meiosis 1

    A. has 23 chromosomes
    B. has 46 chromosomes
    C. is diploid
    D. Both B and C

21. Food moves through the digestive system in which order?

    A. Mouth, esophagus, stomach, small intestine, large intestine, rectum,
        anus

    B. Mouth, stomach, esophagus, large intestine, small intestine, rectum,
        anus

    C. Mouth, stomach, small intestine, large intestine, esophagus, rectum,
        anus

    D. Mouth, esophagus, small intestine, stomach, large intestine, rectum,
        anus

22. Circle the appropriate word to complete the sentence.

    Ova travel from the [ovaries/uterus] through the [cervix/fallopian tubes]
    to the [ovaries/uterus].

23. Two parents are homozygous for the dominant trait X. Their child's genotype
    will be

    A. Xx
    B. XX
    C. XY
    D. Not enough information to determine

24. The area of the lungs where oxygen and carbon dioxide cross into and out of
    the blood stream is called the

    A. bronchioles
    B. trachea
    C. alveolus
    D. capillary

PRE-QUIZ 2

1. Name two types of eclipses: _____ ,
   _____ .

2. Which of the following is a Jovian planet?

   A. Mercury

   B. Venus

   C. Earth

   D. Jupiter

3. What is the earliest recognized geologic era?

   A. Precambrian

   B. Paleozoic

   C. Mesozoic

   D. Cenozoic

4. Meteorology is the study of

   A. Earth's atmosphere

   B. Earth's oceans

   C. Earth's lands

   D. other planets

EARTH AND SPACE SCIENCE

Earth science is the study of the earth and the universe around it. It encompasses geology, oceanography, meteorology, and astronomy. A few questions on the ASVAB will test your knowledge of earth science. Let's start by looking back in time...

Geology

Geology is the study of the origin, history, and structure of the Earth. Geologists look inside the Earth for clues about what it was like thousands and even millions of years ago. The surface of the Earth is always changing, due to erosion, volcanic eruptions, earthquakes, and the weather. These changes are recorded in the Earth's layers, and geologists have created a geologic time scale to track them.

Geologic Time Periods

There are four geologic time periods, also called **eras.**

Precambrian Era: This era began at the formation of the Earth, approximately 4.6 billion years ago, and ended about 570 million years ago. It is by far the longest era. There are very few fossils from this time period. Those found tend to be bacteria and algae, but a few fossils of primitive sponges, worms, and corals from the end of the era have also been found.

Paleozoic Era: The next era, the Paleozoic, lasted about 325 million years. A wide variety of fossils of plants and animals have been found from this era.

Mesozoic Era: This era started about 245 million years ago and ended about 65 million years ago. Fossils from this time period show a variety of lizards, turtles, snakes, and dinosaurs. Toward the end of this era, the mass extinction of numerous species occurred, including all dinosaurs.

Cenozoic Era: This era started 65 million years ago and continues today. During this period, a wide range of mammals have flourished, including humans.

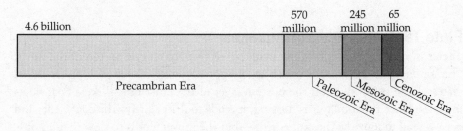

Layers of the Earth

The Earth is made up of three major layers. The outermost layer, the **crust,** makes up only about 1% of the Earth's total mass. Directly below that is the **mantle.** The mantle is a thick layer of rock that makes up about two-thirds of the Earth's mass. The center of the Earth is the **core.** The core has a dense liquid outer layer and a solid inner layer of iron. It makes up almost one-third of the Earth's mass.

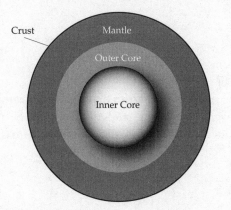

Types of Rocks

There are three major types of rocks.

> **Igneous Rock:** rocks formed when magma, which is called lava when it reaches the Earth's surface, cools

> **Sedimentary Rock:** small pieces of rock, minerals, and organic matter that are cemented together under immense pressure

> **Metamorphic Rock:** existing rock that is changed by certain forces and processes, such as extreme heat, pressure, and chemical reactions

Rocks gradually change on the Earth's surface through **weathering.** Weathering that occurs as a result of temperature changes, ice, plants, water, wind, and other physical causes is called **mechanical weathering.** Weathering that is the result of chemical reactions that alter the internal structure of the rock is called **chemical weathering.** A common type of chemical weathering is oxidation. Oxidation occurs when metallic elements in the rock combine with oxygen. The reddish tint of soil in the southern United States is due to oxidation.

Weathered rocks are sometimes moved by a process called erosion. Water, gravity, glaciers, and wind all cause rocks to erode.

Plate Tectonics and Earthquakes

The crust of the Earth is actually made up of two layers, one on top of the other. The top layer of the crust is made up of approximately 30 separate pieces called plates. These plates float on the bottom layer of the crust much like a boat floats in water. Since the top layer is floating, it tends to drift slowly. The continents and oceans tend to move as the crust drifts—but the movement is so slow that it's only noticeable after millions of years.

The area where one plate ends and another plate begins is called a **fault line.** When two or more fault lines move against each other, the ground vibrates and an earthquake results. The reason there are so many earthquakes along the west coast of the United States is because a long fault line runs up the coast. When an earthquake occurs, scientists use the Richter scale to measure its magnitude. This scale uses a 1 to 10 system, with 1 being for the smallest earthquake and 10 for the largest earthquake.

Oceanography

Oceanography is the study of the earth's oceans. Since nearly three-fourths of the Earth's surface is covered by oceans, studying them can be a big job. Oceanographers study waves, tides, currents, plants, and marine animals.

Marine Biomes

Recall from our discussion of ecology that the Earth is divided into biomes. The ocean is also divided into biomes. There are three that you need to know.

Biome 1: The Intertidal Zone. This is where the land and water meet. This zone alternates between total submersion in water and dryness as the tides rise and fall. Organisms found here include crabs, mussels, clams, snails, starfish, and sponges.

Biome 2: The Neritic Zone. This zone starts where the intertidal zone ends and extends to the edge of the continental shelf. Organisms found here include starfish, sea urchins, seaweed, and many species of fish.

Biome 3: The Oceanic Zone. This zone includes all of the open ocean. Due to the depth of the water there is very little vegetation, as the seawater filters out all light before it can reach the ocean floor. Organisms living here tend to be very large and carnivorous. This includes marine mammals such as dolphins and whales, sharks, large squids, and sea turtles.

Two other zones to remember are the photopic and the aphotic. The **photopic zone** begins at the water's surface and extends down as far as light will penetrate. The **aphotic zone** is the area that no light reaches.

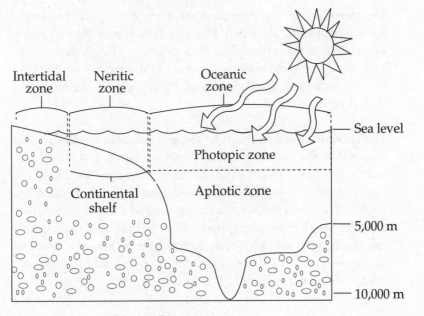

Marine Biomes

Meteorology

Meteorology is the study of the Earth's atmosphere, including the atmospheric conditions that cause weather.

Layers of the Atmosphere

The atmosphere is divided into four large layers that lie on top of each other, extending out from the surface of the Earth.

The Troposphere: The layer closest to the Earth is the troposphere. Depending on the latitude and the season, the troposphere can range from 6 km to 17 km thick. The majority of the water vapor and carbon dioxide in the atmosphere is found here. As you travel away from the Earth's surface, the temperature of the air drops, until you reach the upper boundary of the troposphere. This area is called the tropopause. An interesting fact about the tropopause is that the temperature remains almost constant here.

The Stratosphere: The stratosphere starts at the tropopause and extends about 50 km above the Earth. This layer is home to the ozone layer. The temperature as you enter the stratosphere is about −60°C. As you approach the upper boundary of the stratosphere, called the stratopause, the temperature begins to rise, as a result of direct solar energy.

The Mesosphere: This layer starts above the stratosphere and extends about 80 km above the Earth. Here, the temperature begins to drop again as you move further away from the Earth. This is the coldest layer of the atmosphere—temperatures can drop as low as −90°C. As you approach the upper boundary of the mesosphere, the mesopause, the temperature stabilizes.

The Thermosphere: In this layer, the highest in the atmosphere, the temperature rises as you get farther from the Earth, and nitrogen and oxygen atoms absorb more solar energy from the Sun. Temperatures as high as 2,000°C have been recorded here. The thermosphere is divided into two regions, the ionosphere and the exosphere. The lower region, the ionosphere, starts about 80 km above the Earth and continues to about 550 km. The exosphere is almost a complete vacuum—it contains almost no matter. It extends for thousands of kilometers above the Earth.

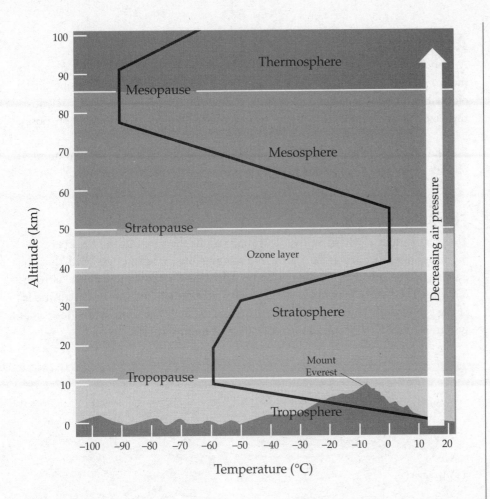

Humidity

Humidity is the measure of the water vapor in the air. As water evaporates into the air, humidity rises. The amount of water vapor the air can hold increases as the temperature rises and decreases as the temperature drops. When the air holds the maximum amount of water vapor that it can, it is saturated.

Fronts

You've probably heard meteorologists talking about warm fronts and cold fronts on your local news. A front is just a boundary between two unlike air masses. When a warm air mass overtakes colder air, you have a warm front. When a cold air mass overtakes warmer air, you have a cold front. Sometimes two air masses meet and neither is displaced. This is called a stationary front. When cold air overtakes warm air very quickly, it sometimes pushes the warm air up high into the atmosphere. This is called an occluded front.

Astronomy

Astronomy is the study of the universe beyond the Earth. Astronomers study the moon, planets, solar system, galaxy, and everything farther away. It is one of the oldest branches of science, dating back to ancient times. In fact, some scientists theorize that the pyramids in Egypt were actually used for astronomical purposes.

For the purposes of the ASVAB, you only need to know about a few astronomical objects. All of them are in our part of the universe, the solar system.

The Solar System

The solar system is where we live. It is made up of the sun and the objects revolving around it, including the Earth. For a long time, scientists believed that the Earth was the center of the solar system. Nicolaus Copernicus, a Polish astronomer, was the first to introduce the idea of a heliocentric, or sun-centered, model of the solar system in the sixteenth century. It has since been proven that our solar system is indeed heliocentric. Our solar system looks like this.

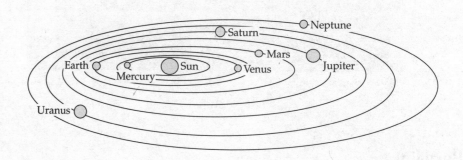

Terrestrial Planets

The four planets closest to the sun—Mercury, Venus, Earth, and Mars—are called the terrestrial planets, or inner planets. They consist mainly of rock with metal cores. They do not have rings, but some, such as the earth, have moons.

Jovian Planets

The four planets farthest from the sun—Jupiter, Saturn, Uranus, and Neptune—are called the outer planets. They are also sometimes called the Jovian planets because their structure is similar to that of Jupiter. The Jovian planets are the largest in the solar system. They all have numerous moons, ranging from 8 to approximately 20. They also all have rings.

Remember Pluto?

Pluto, a planet that was once considered the outermost major body in our solar system, has been controversial since its discovery in 1930. Once considered the smallest of the planets, in 2006 the International Astronomical Union (IAU) formally downgraded Pluto to a dwarf planet. It has a moon almost half its size, and its elliptical orbit sometimes brings it closer to the sun than Neptune. Some scientists speculate that Pluto is the largest of the Kuiper Belt Objects (see below).

Asteroids, Comets, and Meteoroids

The solar system also contains millions of smaller objects. Asteroids are large pieces of rock that orbit the Sun, just as the planets do. Most asteroids are located between Mars and Jupiter in an area that is called the asteroid belt. Meteoroids are small pieces of rock and metal. Sometimes meteoroids enter the Earth's atmosphere. When that happens, they are called meteors. Usually the meteor will burn up when passing through the atmosphere. However, on rare occasions they hit the Earth and are then called meteorites. Comets are made up of rock, dust, methane, and ice. Like asteroids, they also orbit the Sun. The Kuiper Belt is a disk-shaped region past the orbit of Neptune that is thought to be the source of the short-period comets.

The Earth's Orbit

At this very moment the Earth is traveling around the Sun at an average speed of about 106,000 km per hour. It takes the Earth about 365 days (one year) to make one trip—or revolution—around the Sun. As the Earth revolves around the Sun, it is also spinning on its axis. This spinning is called rotation. It takes the Earth 24 hours (one day) to make one complete rotation.

Structure of the Sun

The Sun is made up of two main regions.

> **The Core:** The core, the center of the Sun, is extremely hot, about 15,000,000 degrees Celsius. At that temperature the only matter that can exist is gas. Because of this intense heat, nuclear reactions are constantly occurring in the core.

> **The Inner Zones:** The area surrounding the core is called the radiative zone. In this zone, the energy from the core is turned into radiation. Beyond the radiative zone is the convective zone. This zone carries the radiation to the surface of the Sun.

> **The Atmosphere:** The innermost layer of the Sun's atmosphere is the photosphere, which is made up of gases from the convection zone. These gases give off visible light; this is the light that we see on Earth. Above the photosphere is the chromosphere, a thin layer of gases that move back and forth. The outermost layer of the sun is the corona. The corona keeps most of the Sun's atomic particles from escaping into space.

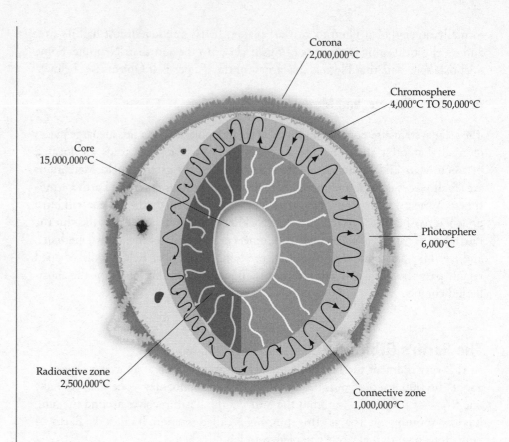

Corona
2,000,000°C

Chromosphere
4,000°C TO 50,000°C

Core
15,000,000°C

Photosphere
6,000°C

Radioactive zone
2,500,000°C

Connective zone
1,000,000°C

Eclipses

Eclipses occur when a planet or moon passes through the shadow of another. There are two types of eclipses: solar and lunar.

> **Solar Eclipse:** A solar eclipse occurs when the Moon moves between the Sun and the Earth. The Moon blocks the light of the Sun, casting a shadow over a certain part of the Earth. During a total eclipse, all of the Sun's light is blocked. During a partial eclipse, only part of the Sun is blocked.

> **Lunar Eclipse:** A lunar eclipse occurs when the Earth moves between the Sun and the Moon. When this happens, the Earth blocks the sunlight, casting a shadow over the Moon. A total eclipse occurs when the Earth's shadow obscures all of the Moon, and a partial eclipse occurs when the Earth's shadow obscures only part of the Moon.

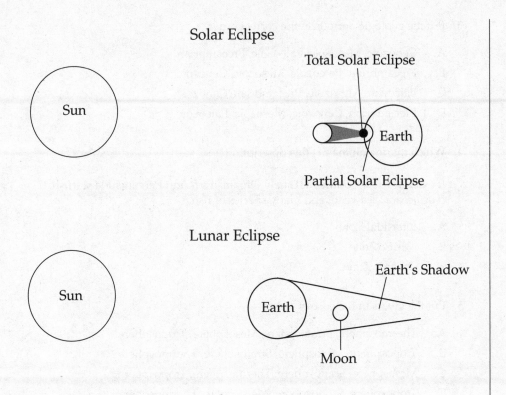

Solar Eclipse

Sun

Total Solar Eclipse

Earth

Partial Solar Eclipse

Lunar Eclipse

Sun

Earth's Shadow

Earth

Moon

QUICK QUIZ 2

The following quiz will test you on earth sciences and astronomy. You can check your answers at the end of the chapter. If you miss any questions, be sure to go back and review.

1. Match the type of rock on the left to the description on the right.

_____ Igneous

_____ Sedimentary

_____ Metamorphic

A. small pieces of rock, minerals, and organic matter that have been compressed and cemented together

B. starts as magma and then cools and hardens

C. changes from one type of rock into another due to extreme heat, pressure, or chemical processes

2. Name the front.

A. A cold air mass overcomes a warm air mass.

_____

B. Cold and warm air masses meet but neither is displaced.

_____

C. A cold air mass rushes in and pushes up a warm air mass.

_____

3. Put the geologic periods in the correct order.

    A.   Cenozoic, Mesozoic, Paleozoic, Precambrian
    B.   Precambrian, Paleozoic, Mesozoic, Cenozoic
    C.   Paleozoic, Mesozoic, Precambrian, Cenozoic
    D.   Precambrian, Cenozoic, Mesozoic, Paleozoic

4. Which marine biome fits this description?

    It extends to the continental shelf. Organisms found here include starfish, crustaceans, seaweed, and many species of fish.

    A.   Intertidal Zone
    B.   Neritic Zone
    C.   Oceanic Zone

5. Put the layers in the correct order.

    A.   Thermosphere, Stratosphere, Mesosphere, Troposphere
    B.   Troposphere, Mesosphere, Stratosphere, Thermosphere
    C.   Mesosphere, Stratosphere, Thermosphere, Troposphere
    D.   Troposphere, Stratosphere, Mesosphere, Thermosphere

6. It takes the Earth _____ to revolve around the Sun. It takes the Earth _____ to rotate once.

7. The weathering of rocks occurs as a result of

    I. Wind
    II. Water
    III. Ice
    IV. Plants and animals

    A.   I and II
    B.   I, II, and III
    C.   II and III
    D.   I, II, III, and IV

8. A _____ occurs when the Earth moves between the Sun and the Moon, casting a shadow over the Moon. A _____ occurs when the Moon moves between the Sun and the Earth, casting a shadow over the Earth.

9. True or False: A meteoroid is a large rock that orbits the Sun, usually somewhere between the planets Mars and Jupiter. _____

10. Fill in the diagram below with the layers of the earth.

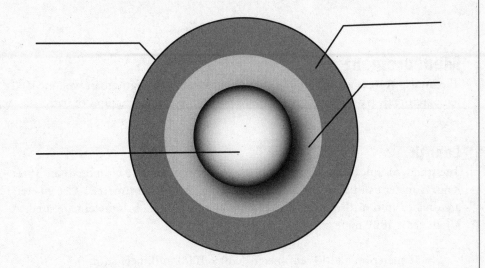

PRE-QUIZ 3

1. 1 meter = _____centimeters = _____millimeters

   1 kilometers = _____meters

   1 kilogram = _____grams

   1 liter = _____milliliters

2. An atom is

   A.   a combination of molecules

   B.   a positive component of a nucleus

   C.   a substance that can't be broken down any further

   D.   the smallest component of an element that retains qualities of that
        element

3. A concave lens is caved _____ and a convex lens is curved _____.

PHYSICAL SCIENCE

Measurement

The **metric system** is used around the world to measure length, mass, volume, and temperature. It is a decimal system based on multiples and fractions of ten.

Length

The standard unit of measurement is the meter. A meter is a bit more than 3 feet long. A meter can be broken into smaller units, called **centimeters.** Centimeters are divided into **millimeters.** To measure long distances, **kilometers** are used. A kilometer is 1000 meters.

> 1 meter (m) = 100 centimeters (cm) = 1000 millimeters (mm)
> 1000 meters = 1 kilometer (km)

Mass

Grams (g), **kilograms** (kg), and **milligrams** (mg) are used to measure mass. A kilogram is about 2.2 pounds.

> 1 kg = 1000 g = 1,000,000 mg

Volume

Volume is the amount of space an object occupies. You can obtain the volume of an object by multiplying its length × its width × its height. In the metric system, volumes are measured in **milliliters** (ml), **cubic centimeters** (cm³), or **liters** (L).

> $1 cm^3$ = 1 ml
> 1 liter (L) = 1000 milliliters (ml)

Temperature

Temperature can be measured on the **Celsius** (C) scale or the **Fahrenheit** (F) scale. In the United States, we usually use the Fahrenheit scale. On this scale, water freezes at 32 degrees F (or "F°") and boils at 212 degrees F. On the Celsius scale, water freezes at 0 degrees C and boils at 100 degrees C. Use the equations below to convert from Fahrenheit to Celsius, or from Celsius to Fahrenheit.

$$F° = \frac{9}{5} C° + 32$$

$$C° = \frac{5}{9} (F° - 32)$$

Another temperature scale, one that's commonly used by scientists, is the **Kelvin** scale, or absolute zero scale. This scale starts at absolute zero (–273 degrees Celsius). Water freezes at 273 degrees Kelvin and boils at 373 degrees Kelvin.

	Water Freezes	Water Boils
Celsius	0	100
Fahrenheit	32	212
Kelvin	273.15	373.15

States of Matter

As a substance gives off or absorbs heat, two things can happen: The substance's temperature can change, and the substance can change states. All matter can exist in three states: solid, liquid, or gas. Water, for example, is a solid (ice) until it reaches 32 degrees Fahrenheit or 0 degrees Celsius, at which point it becomes a liquid. When it reaches 212 degrees Fahrenheit or 100 degrees Celsius, it changes to a gas (water vapor, or steam). All types of matter can change properties, but they do so at different temperatures.

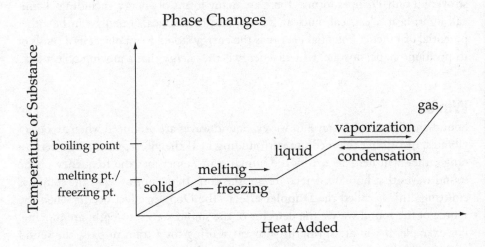

Phase Changes

Physics

Important Formulas

Memorize these important terms and formulas; you may need them on the test.

> **Momentum:** The tendency for an object to continue moving in the same direction.
>
> $$\text{Momentum} = \text{mass} \times \text{speed}$$

> **Power:** The rate at which work is done. Power is measured in watts. Work is energy expended, measured in joules (J).
>
> $$\text{Power} = \text{work} \div \text{time}$$

> **Speed (or Velocity):** The distance traveled by an object over a certain amount of time.
>
> $$\text{Speed} = \text{distance} \div \text{time}$$

Forms of Energy

Energy can be defined as the capacity to do work. It can never be created or destroyed; it only changes forms. There are many forms of energy, including chemical, light, heat, electrical, nuclear, sound, and mechanical. Energy can be either potential or kinetic. Potential energy is the energy stored in an object as a result of its position, shape, or state. Kinetic energy is the energy that a moving object has.

Waves

Sound and light energy travel in waves. Sound waves are produced when an object vibrates, disturbing the medium surrounding it. If the vibrations are in a certain range, they will be detected by the human ear. Sometimes the frequency of the sound waves that humans detect are not the same frequency as what the source is emitting. This is called the **Doppler effect.** The Doppler effect occurs when the source of the sound waves, the detector of the sound waves, or both, are moving. For example, if you are sitting in your car waiting for a train to pass, the sound of the train changes as it moves closer to you and then past you. The sound waves being emitted from the train are not changing, just your position in relation to the train, and therefore the sound waves that your ear perceives are different.

Light waves are subject to the Doppler effect. For example, when you look up at the night sky, what you see is light coming from the stars and planets. That light can be measured in wavelengths. If you measure the wavelengths on the star or planet and compare them to a measurement taken on the Earth, you would see that they are different. This difference occurs because the stars, planets, and the Earth are in constant motion.

Electromagnetic Spectrum

The light that you see only makes up a small part of the electromagnetic spectrum. This spectrum is composed of radiowaves, microwaves, infrared, visible light, ultraviolet, X-rays, and gamma rays. Visible light waves are in the middle of the spectrum. Different frequencies of light waves are perceived as different colors. Red, for example, has the lowest frequency, and violet, the highest. When light waves enter your eye, they strike rods and cones in the back of your eyeball. The rods and cones send neural impulses to the brain. The brain determines what color you're seeing based on the frequency of the wavelengths that entered your eye. When you look at a red apple, the light waves that are entering your eye are in the range on the electromagnetic spectrum for red light. This is because the apple is absorbing all of the waves except for the red light waves. Those are being reflected by the apple. A green object, like a leaf, is absorbing all light except for green light waves.

Electromagnetic Spectrum

Frequency (Hz)

10^{22}	
10^{21}	Gamma rays or γ rays
10^{20}	
10^{19}	
10^{18}	X-rays
10^{17}	
10^{16}	
10^{15}	Ultraviolet
10^{14}	Visible light
10^{13}	Infrared
10^{12}	
10^{11}	
10^{10}	Microwaves
10^{9}	
10^{8}	
10^{7}	Radiowaves
10^{6}	
10^{5}	

Wavelength (m)

10^{-14}
10^{-13}
10^{-12}
10^{-11}
10^{-10}
10^{-9}
10^{-8}
10^{-7}
10^{-6}
10^{-5}
10^{-4}
10^{-3}
10^{-2}
10^{-1}
1
10^{1}
10^{2}
10^{3}

Violet: $3.90 - 4.55 \times 10^{-7}$ m
Blue: $4.55 - 4.92 \times 10^{-7}$ m
Green: $4.92 - 5.77 \times 10^{-7}$ m
Yellow: $5.77 - 5.97 \times 10^{-7}$ m
Orange: $5.97 - 6.22 \times 10^{-7}$ m
Red: $6.22 - 7.70 \times 10^{-7}$ m

Refraction

Refraction is the bending of light. For example, when sunlight enters a prism, the light refracts, or bends, and all of its different frequencies separate, creating a rainbow. White light (like sunlight) is a combination of all of the colors in the visible spectrum.

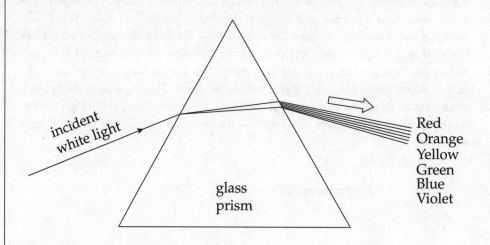

Convex and Concave

A mirror or lens can either be concave or convex. A concave lens is caved in, and a convex lens is curved out.

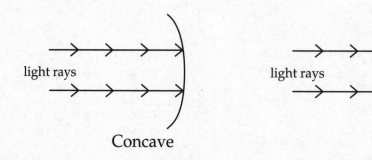

Heat

Heat energy is transferred by conduction, convection, or radiation. **Conduction** occurs when heat is transferred from a source with a high temperature to something with a lower temperature. For example, when you cook on a stove you're transferring heat from the stove to the food. **Convection** occurs when a gas or liquid changes density due to higher heat. For example, a hot air balloon rises in the air because of convection. The air inside the balloon is heated up, causing it to rise and taking the balloon with it. **Radiation** occurs when electromagnetic waves transmit heat. For example, the Sun heats up a sidewalk because the Sun is sending out electromagnetic waves, which are absorbed by the cement.

Magnetism

Have you ever heard the saying "opposites attract"? Well, in the case of magnets, it's true. Magnets have a north pole and a south pole. The north poles of two magnets will repel each other, and the south poles of two magnets will repel each other. But, if you bring the north pole of one magnet close to the south pole of another magnet, they will attract each other.

Chemistry

Let's start with some basic terms you should know.

> **Element:** An element is a substance that can't be broken down any further by a chemical reaction. Some examples of elements are hydrogen, carbon, and oxygen. All of the elements are listed in the **periodic table.**

> **Atom:** An atom is the smallest component of an element that still retains the properties of that element. Atoms are often known as the building blocks of matter. Atoms are made up of protons, neutrons, and electrons.

> **Proton:** A proton is a component of an atomic nucleus with a mass of 1 and a charge of +1 (a positive charge of 1).

> **Neutron:** A neutron is another component of an atom's nucleus. A neutron does not have a charge. It is neutral, so its mass is 1 and its charge is 0.

> **Electron:** Electrons are atomic elements outside of and surrounding the nucleus. They have a negative charge (−1) and a very small mass.

More Great Books
To dive even deeper into science topics, check out some of these books from The Princeton Review: *High School Chemistry Unlocked* *High School Physics Unlocked* *High School Biology Unlocked*

Periodic Table of the Elements

1 H 1.0																	2 He 4.0
3 Li 6.9	4 Be 9.0											5 B 10.8	6 C 12.0	7 N 14.0	8 O 16.0	9 F 19.0	10 Ne 20.2
11 Na 23.0	12 Mg 24.3											13 Al 27.0	14 Si 28.1	15 P 31.0	16 S 32.1	17 Cl 35.5	18 Ar 39.9
19 K 39.1	20 Ca 40.1	21 Sc 45.0	22 Ti 47.9	23 V 50.9	24 Cr 52.0	25 Mn 54.9	26 Fe 55.8	27 Co 58.9	28 Ni 58.7	29 Cu 63.5	30 Zn 65.4	31 Ga 69.7	32 Ge 72.6	33 As 74.9	34 Se 79.0	35 Br 79.9	36 Kr 83.8
37 Rb 85.5	38 Sr 87.6	39 Y 88.9	40 Zr 91.2	41 Nb 92.9	42 Mo 95.9	43 Tc (98)	44 Ru 101.1	45 Rh 102.9	46 Pd 106.4	47 Ag 107.9	48 Cd 112.4	49 In 114.8	50 Sn 118.7	51 Sb 121.8	52 Te 127.6	53 I 126.9	54 Xe 131.3
55 Cs 132.9	56 Ba 137.3	57 *La 138.9	72 Hf 178.5	73 Ta 180.9	74 W 183.9	75 Re 186.2	76 Os 190.2	77 Ir 192.2	78 Pt 195.1	79 Au 197.0	80 Hg 200.6	81 Tl 204.4	82 Pb 207.2	83 Bi 209.0	84 Po (209)	85 At (210)	86 Rn (222)
87 Fr (223)	88 Ra 226.0	89 †Ac 227.0	104 Rf (261)	105 Db (262)	106 Sg (266)	107 Bh (264)	108 Hs (277)	109 Mt (268)	110 Ds (281)	111 Rg (272)	112 Cn (285)	113 Uut (286)	114 Fl (289)	115 Uup (288)	116 Lv (293)	117 Uus (294)	118 Uuo (294)

*Lanthanide Series:	58 Ce 140.1	59 Pr 140.9	60 Nd 144.2	61 Pm (145)	62 Sm 150.4	63 Eu 152.0	64 Gd 157.3	65 Tb 158.9	66 Dy 162.5	67 Ho 164.9	68 Er 167.3	69 Tm 168.9	70 Yb 173.0	71 Lu 175.0
†Actinide Series:	90 Th 232.0	91 Pa (231)	92 U 238.0	93 Np (237)	94 Pu (244)	95 Am (243)	96 Cm (247)	97 Bk (247)	98 Cf (251)	99 Es (252)	100 Fm (257)	101 Md (258)	102 No (259)	103 Lr (260)

As you can see from the periodic table, every element has a number above it. That number is called the atomic number. The atomic number tells you how many protons are in the nucleus of one atom of that element. The number of protons in the nucleus determines which element the atom is. For example, the element hydrogen has an atomic number of 1. That means it has 1 proton in its nucleus.

Oxygen has 8 protons in its nucleus. Its atomic number is 8. The atomic number for potassium (K) is 19. It has 19 protons.

Ions

When an atom has the same number of protons and electrons, it is neutral. Sometimes, however, an atom loses or gains an electron. When this happens the number of protons and electrons is not equal, and the atom is no longer neutral. If it gains an electron the atom is negatively charged, and if it loses one it is positively charged. When an atom isn't electrically neutral anymore it is called an ion.

Mass Number

Atoms have two things in their nuclei: protons and neutrons. Each proton and neutron has a mass that is approximately equal to 1 atomic mass unit (amu). Electrons have practically no mass, so an atom's mass is determined by the number of protons and neutrons it has. For example, if a carbon atom has 6 protons and 6 neutrons, its mass is 12.

Isotopes

In the carbon example above, the number of protons and the number of neutrons were equal. But that isn't always the case. Atoms can have an unequal number of protons and neutrons. When two atoms of the same element have different numbers of neutrons in their nuclei, they are called isotopes. For example, a carbon atom with 8 neutrons and a carbon atom with 6 neutrons are isotopes.

Molecules

As you may know, an atom is the smallest possible part of an element. Atoms often have a strong attraction to each other, however, and can attach to each other. When different atoms bind together they are called molecules. The chemical formula for water, H_2O, indicates that one molecule of water is made up of 2 hydrogen atoms and 1 oxygen atom. The smallest unit of water is one molecule.

Compounds and Mixtures

A substance made up of two or more elements is called a compound. Water (H_2O) is a compound of hydrogen (H) and oxygen (O). A mixture is made up of different elements that are not chemically bonded to each other. For example, granite is made up of three different types of matter: quartz, mica, and feldspar. If you look at granite, you can see the separate layers of matter. The three layers are not chemically bonded to each other.

Acids, Bases, and pH

Acids are substances that release hydrogen ions when added to water. Some common acids are vinegar and lemon juice. They taste sour. Bases are substances that take up hydrogen ions. Some common bases are soap and ammonia. They feel slippery and taste bitter. The concentration of hydrogen ions in a substance is measured on the pH scale. The pH scale ranges from 0 to 14. A pH of 7 means that the substance is neutral. Acids have a pH of less than 7. The lower the number, the stronger the acid is. Bases have a pH greater than 7. The higher the number, the stronger the base.

Solutions, Solvents, and Concentrations

Solutions are mixtures of solutes and solvents. **Solutes** are substances that dissolve into something. **Solvents** are the mediums that the solutes are dissolved into. For example, salt water is a solution made up of salt (the solute) and water (the solvent). The amount of solute in a solvent is called the **concentration.** The concentration tells us how salty the water is. The higher the concentration, the saltier the water.

Metals

Metals are elements that share certain characteristics. Metals tend to be shiny, malleable (capable of being shaped, perhaps by hammering or by pressure), and good conductors of heat and electricity. The most important thing to remember about metals, though, is that they tend to give up electrons when they bond. Approximately 75% of the elements are metals. Nonmetals tend to share or gain electrons when they bond. Some common metals are copper, gold, silver, and iron.

Chemical Reactions

A chemical reaction is a process that changes one or more substances into different substances. There are two types of chemical reactions that you should be familiar with.

> **Combination/synthesis reactions:** When two different substances combine to form a new substance.

> **Decomposition reactions:** When one substance breaks down into two or more separate substances.

QUICK QUIZ 3

That's everything you need to know about physics and chemistry. Think you got it all? Take this little quiz to find out. You can check your answers at the end of the chapter. As always, if you get any question wrong, go back and review the topic. Good luck!

1. Energy that is stored in an object as a result of its position, shape, or state is called _____ energy. Energy that a moving object has is called _____ energy.

2. True or False. Warming up your hands in front of a fire is an example of convection _____.

3. An atom is made up of _____, _____, and _____.

4. Match the definition to the word on the left.

   _____ Isotope   A. found in the nucleus, positively charged

   _____ Molecule   B. the smallest unit of a particular element

   _____ Ion   C. found in the nucleus, not charged

   _____ Atom   D. found outside the nucleus, negatively charged

   _____ Proton   E. two atoms of the same element with an unequal number of neutrons

   _____ Neutron   F. an atom with a charge, either positive or negative

   _____ Electron   G. the smallest unit of a chemical

5. Fill in the blanks.

   1 meter = _____ centimeters = _____ millimeters

   1 kilometers = _____ meters

   1 kilogram = _____ grams

   1 liter = _____ milliliters

6. When water reaches 212 degrees Fahrenheit it

    I.   freezes

   II. boils

  III. has a temperature equivalent to 100 degrees Celsius

  IV. has a temperature equivalent to 273 degrees Kelvin

  A.   II only

  B.   II and III only

  C.   II, III, and IV only

  D.   I, III, and IV only

7. The atomic number for the element sodium (Na) is 11. Based on this, sodium always

    I. has 11 neutrons

   II. has 11 protons

  III. has 11 electrons

  A.   I only

  B.   II only

  C.   III only

  D.   I, II, and III

8. Circle the correct word.

> A substance with a pH of 9 is [an acid/a base/neutral]. A substance with a pH of 7 is [an acid/a base/neutral]. A substance with a pH of 5 is [an acid/a base/neutral].

9. As a train approaches, its sound changes. This can be explained by

  A.   convection

  B.   refraction

  C.   the Doppler effect

  D.   momentum

10. The equation for power is

  A.   power = work + time

  B.   power = work × time

  C.   power = work ÷ time

  D.   power = time ÷ work

ANSWERS TO PRE-QUIZZES, QUICK QUIZZES

Pre-Quiz 1
Page 171

1. **B** A Punnett Square is used to help determine the probability that a child will inherit dominant or recessive traits from its parents.
2. **A** Grass produces its own energy, which is then provided to other animals, so it is a producer.
3. **C** Photosynthesis is the process by which plants create their own energy.
4. **A** Vitamins are necessary for proper function of the body, but not for energy production.
5. **C** Type AB is the universal recipient.

Quick Quiz 1
Page 199

1. **J**	Cell membrane	J.	barrier that controls what enters and leaves the cell
H	Centrioles	H.	related to the formation of spindle during mitosis
G	Golgi Body	G.	sorts and packages proteins
K	Lysosomes	K.	digest foreign substances and worn organelles
B	Rough ER	B.	synthesizes proteins to be exported out of the cell
C	Ribosomes	C.	site of protein synthesis
I	Nucleolus	I.	site of ribosome synthesis in the nucleus
F	Vacuole	F.	stores waste and other substances
E	Smooth ER	E.	makes lipids and detoxifies enzymes
D	Mitochondria	D.	site of energy production
A	Nucleus	A.	control center of the cell, contains DNA

2. The order from largest to smallest is
    Kingdom
    Phylum
    Class
    Order
    Family
    Genus
    Species

3. photosynthesis

4. **D** tundra

5.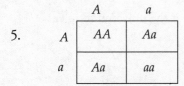

    The probability that the parents produce offspring with attached earlobes is 75%.
    The probability that the parents produce offspring with unattached earlobes is 25%.

6. **C** Interphase   C. chromosomes replicate

    E Prophase   E. nuclear membrane breaks up, spindles form, centrioles move to opposite poles

    D Metaphase   D. chromosomes line up

    B Anaphase   B. chromatids split and chromosomes move to opposite poles

    A Telophase   A. nuclear membrane forms, cytokinesis occurs

7. The nervous system can be divided into two parts: the central nervous system and the peripheral nervous system. The brain and spinal cord are parts of the central nervous system. The peripheral nervous system can be divided into the somatic nervous system and the autonomic nervous system. The somatic nervous system controls voluntary actions. The autonomic nervous system controls involuntary actions. The autonomic system can be divided into the sympathetic and parasympathetic nervous systems.

8. **C** plants

9.

C	Vitamin A	C. a lack of this may cause night blindness
E	Vitamin B$_1$	E. a lack of this may cause appetite loss or beriberi
D	Vitamin B$_2$	D. a lack of this may cause weakness or skin infections
A	Vitamin B$_{12}$	A. a lack of this may cause anemia
H	Vitamin C	H. a lack of this may cause scurvy
B	Vitamin D	B. a lack of this may cause rickets
F	Vitamin E	F. a lack of this may cause anemia
G	Vitamin K	G. a lack of this may cause excessive bleeding

10. False. Type O is the universal donor, not the universal recipient.

11. **C** moss

12. **A** I only

13. **B** The endocrine system works slower than the nervous system, but its results last longer.

14. tracheophytes

15. **B** members of the same genus

16. **B** an omnivore

17. **D** zebra

18. The vas deferens is a large duct that conducts sperm from the testes to the urethra.

19. smooth, skeletal, and cardiac

20. **D** Both B and C

21. **A** mouth, esophagus, stomach, small intestine, large intestine, rectum, anus

22. Ova travel from the ovaries through the fallopian tubes to the uterus.

23. **B** *XX*

24. **C** alveolus

Pre-Quiz 2
Page 204

1. Lunar, solar
2. **D** Jupiter is the only Jovian planet listed.
3. **A** The Precambrian Era is the first of the four geologic time periods known to man.
4. **A** Meteorology is the study of Earth's atmosphere.

Quick Quiz 2
Page 213

1. **B**   Igneous   B. starts as magma and then cools and hardens

   A   Sedimentary   A. small pieces of rock, minerals, and organic material that have been compressed and cemented together

   C   Metamorphic   C. changes from one type of rock into another, due to extreme heat, pressure, or chemical processes

2. **A** cold front
   B stationary front
   C occluded front

3. **B** Precambrian, Paleozoic, Mesozoic, Cenozoic

4. **B** Neritic Zone

5. **D** Troposphere, Stratosphere, Mesosphere, Thermosphere

6. It takes the Earth <u>365 days/1 year</u> to revolve around the Sun. It takes the Earth <u>24 hours/1 day</u> to rotate once.

7. **D** I, II, III, and IV

8. A <u>lunar eclipse</u> occurs when the Earth casts a shadow on the Moon. A <u>solar eclipse</u> occurs when the Moon casts a shadow on the Earth.

9. False (This statement describes an asteroid, not a meteoroid.)

10.

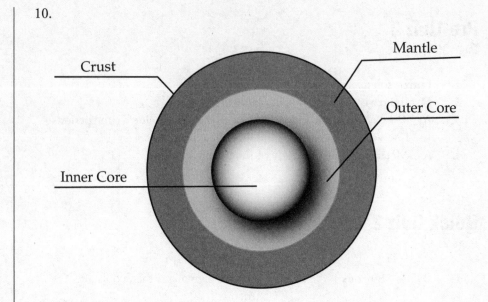

Crust

Mantle

Outer Core

Inner Core

Pre-Quiz 3
Page 215

1. 1 meter = <u>100</u> centimeters = <u>1,000</u> millimeters
    1 kilometers = <u>1,000</u> meters
    1 kilogram = <u>1,000</u> grams
    1 liter = <u>1,000</u> milliliters

2. **D** An atom is the smallest component of an element that retains qualities of that element

3. A concave lens is caved <u>in</u> and a convex lens is curved <u>out</u>.

Quick Quiz 3
Page 224

1. Energy that is stored in an object as a result of its position, shape, or state is called <u>potential</u> energy. Energy that a moving object has is called <u>kinetic</u> energy.

2. False (This is an example of conduction.)

3. An atom is made up of: <u>protons</u>, <u>neutrons</u>, and <u>electrons</u>.

4. **E**   Isotope   E.   two atoms of the same element with an unequal number of neutrons

     G   Molecule   G.   the smallest unit of a chemical

     F   Ion   F.   an atom with a charge, either positive or negative

     B   Atom   B.   the smallest unit of a particular element

     A   Proton   A.   found in the nucleus, positively charged

     C   Neutron   C.   found in the nucleus, not charged

     D   Electron   D.   found outside the nucleus, negatively charged

5. 1 meter = <u>100</u> centimeters = <u>1000</u> millimeters
    1 kilometer = <u>1000</u> meters
    1 kilogram = <u>1000</u> grams
    1 liter = <u>1000</u> milliliters

6. **B**   II and III only

7. **B**   II only

8. A substance with a pH of 9 is a base. A substance with a pH of 7 is neutral. A substance with a pH of 5 is an acid.

9. **C**   the Doppler effect

10. **C**   power = work ÷ time

Chapter 7
Auto and Shop
Information

INTRODUCTION TO AUTO AND SHOP INFORMATION

You won't need detailed knowledge and years working as a mechanic to do well on the Auto and Shop section of the ASVAB. This section gives you 11 minutes to answer 25 questions, half of which are related to automobile systems (mainly simple problem diagnosis) and the other half to identifying and choosing the right shop tool for a particular job. The questions range in difficulty throughout the section, so if you are taking the paper version of the test, it is best to simply start at the beginning of the section you do best on and work straight through without spending too much time on any one question. Of course, you will have the opportunity to see what kinds of questions you do better on later in this chapter. But first we need to go into a brief review of the concepts you'll need to know.

Note: On the CAT-ASVAB the Auto and Shop sections are separate. You have 11 questions in each section, but 6 minutes to take the Shop section and 7 minutes to take the Auto section.

SHOP SECTION

There are three basic types of questions that you will find in the Shop section. The first kind is Tool Identification. Tool Identification questions will ask you to identify a tool either from its picture or from its purpose. For example

1. The tool shown above is a

   A. flathead screwdriver
   B. Phillips screwdriver
   C. chisel
   D. Allen wrench

The second type of question is called Tool Part Definition. This type will either give you a term and ask you to choose the correct definition from a list of four, or give you the definition of a term referring to a part of a tool and ask you to select the proper term. Take a look at the following example:

2. The end of the saw that is located the farthest from the handle is called the

   A. heel
   B. knee
   C. toe
   D. bight

The third type of question, Shop Methods, will ask about proper methods and processes used in the shop. For example, you might be asked about how to cut wood, how to harden metals, and why some bolts have to be tightened down with a certain amount of torque.

Basic Tool Review

Everyone can recognize a saw or a hammer, but the ASVAB, as in the first example above, is also going to ask you to differentiate between various types of similar tools. When reviewing this section, be sure to pay attention to the differences between the individual tools within each type and how they are each used.

Measuring Tools

Tape Measure

The ability to measure objects is essential in order to be able to construct anything. To complete quick measurements that do not require a high degree of accuracy, a rule or **tape measure** is often used. Measuring tapes and rules are both marked off in regular intervals, normally feet and inches or meters and centimeters. Rules are designed to give accurate measurements quickly. They are generally marked down to 1/64th of an inch, indicating that they are accurate to about 1/32nd of an inch, or about one millimeter. Rules are shorter and thicker than measuring tapes. Their rigidity prevents them from shrinking and expanding as the temperature changes and allows a more accurate measurement over shorter distances. Measuring tape generally expands or contracts a little bit in extreme temperatures.

Measuring tape is normally calibrated to measure exactly as its markings indicate when the temperature of the tape is 70 degrees Fahrenheit.

However, measuring tapes are preferred for measuring long distances, as they generally come in lengths from five feet to several hundred feet. The tape is usually made out of a thin steel strip that is curved slightly upward to give it support when extended. Many tape measures designed to give more precise measurements at longer distances include a table that shows how far the tape will stretch on a hot day or shrink on a cold day.

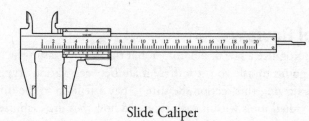

Slide Caliper

Calipers are measuring tools used to measure diameters of pipes and tubes. All calipers have points that are set an adjustable distance from each other. The two points are set inside of a pipe or hole or outside of a rod and secured so that they touch the object being measured. There are several variations on this basic idea.

Simple calipers look a little like a pair of legs. If the points, or the feet, are turned outward, then the calipers are used to measure the inside diameter of pipes and holes. If the points are turned inward, then the calipers are used to measure the outer diameter of the pipe or rod. After the calipers have been secured at the set distance, they are taken out, and the distance between the points is measured with a rule.

A **slide caliper** has a rule built into the caliper. One of the points is fixed to the rule and the other one slides along the rule. The distance between the two points is then measured directly off of the rule or from a gauge that is connected directly to the rule. If a special type of scale called a vernier scale is used, then the caliper is called a **vernier caliper.** This type of caliper is accurate down to as little as 0.001 inch.

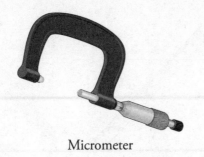

Micrometer

If accuracy in small measurements is important, a **micrometer** can be used. This tool has two small surfaces connected to a sliding rule, similar to a slide caliper. The moveable surface is connected to an arm that allows the surface to go around an object. The rule is normally connected to a vernier scale or a digital gauge and has excellent resolution.

There are several other types of measurement tools that you should be familiar with. At times, it is important to know what direction is straight down from a hook or other object and what point lies directly beneath it. The **plumb line** uses the effects of gravity to determine where this point is. A plumb line is a string attached to a round weight, called a plumb bob. The plumb bob has a ring to which you can attach a string at one end and a pointer at the other end. The plumb bob is dangled from the hook (or other object) above by the string. Gravity will pull the plumb bob straight down and the pointer on the plumb bob will point to the spot directly underneath the hook. This system is not very technically advanced, but it works well.

Carpenter's Level

A **carpenter's level** is used to tell when a surface, such as a table, is level to the ground or a wall is standing straight up and down. A level uses the idea that a bubble will always rise to the highest point of a liquid. Therefore, within the level, a bubble is set in a transparent tube of liquid, and the tube is marked so that when the level is completely horizontal, the bubble rests between the two marks on the tube. If one side is too high, the bubble will rest to the other side of the tube. Levels can also tell you whether an object's edge is straight up and down or not. Some levels feature digital readouts that show the grade of the tilt of a surface.

Thickness gauges are used to determine how much space there is between two surfaces that are close together. Thickness gauges are normally found in a set that consists of several thin calibrated plates or wires. The plates are slid into the gap between the two objects until one of the plates fits snugly. The thickness of that particular plate is the same as the gap between the two objects. One example of a thickness gauge is the wire gauge used to check the separation between the two points of a spark plug.

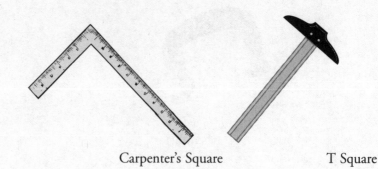

Carpenter's Square   T Square

Squares look like a giant, metal letter "L" and help carpenters and machinists know when two objects or surfaces are at right angles to each other.

Hammers

Hammers are one of the most well-known tools. Several types of hammers are shown below.

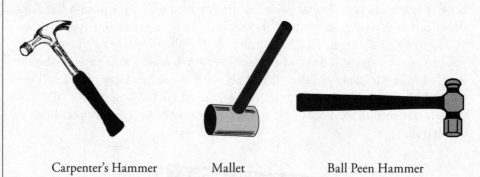

Carpenter's Hammer   Mallet   Ball Peen Hammer

The main differences in the hammers above are in their parts. Parts of tools are generally named either for what the tool does or for a body part. For hammers, we refer to the "head," "neck," and "face." The **head** of the hammer is always the heavy part of the hammer, and the **face** is the flat part, used for striking something. The head is connected to the handle at the **neck.** The only part of the hammer that is not considered part of the head is the **claw,** which, not surprisingly, looks like a claw.

The first hammer shown above is a **carpenter's hammer.** It is used for driving nails into wood with the head or for pulling them out with the claw. The claw on this type of hammer is generally two pronged.

The second hammer is a **mallet.** Mallets generally have a soft double-sided head, made of rubber or plastic, and no claw. The soft head of the mallet will not leave a mark or a dent in what it strikes, so a mallet is used for shaping metal or striking something that a hard-headed hammer would damage. Mallets are also used to hit the back of chisels, punches, or other tools, so as not to damage the tool. Whenever a tool must be struck as part of a process, a mallet should be used.

The third hammer above is a **ball peen hammer,** used mainly by machinists and metalworkers. These hammers have a peen in place of a claw. The peen can be shaped in many different ways; its purpose is to allow the machinist to flatten metal. Most peen hammers are named after the shape of the peen. Machinists' hammers can also have soft heads, so as not to mar the surface that is to be struck.

Screwdrivers

A screwdriver is a device designed to either tighten or loosen screws in both wood and metal objects. A screwdriver works by increasing the amount of **torque** applied to a screw so that you can turn it far more easily than if you simply used your fingers. You'll need to be able to distinguish between the basic types of screwdrivers and to understand why each type is used. The screwdriver has three parts: the **handle,** which you hold; the **blade,** which fits into the top of the screw; and the **shank,** which connects the handle and the blade. The only difference between the two types of screwdrivers is the shape of the blade of the screwdriver.

Flathead Screwdriver

Phillips Head Screwdriver

Flathead Screw

Phillips Head Screw

The first picture above is a **standard** or **flathead** screwdriver. These screwdrivers come in a wide variety of lengths, widths, and blade thicknesses. They are to be used to drive simple slotted screws only, usually into wood, and not as a chisel or pry bar.

In order to allow the screwdriver to stay in the slot easier and to transfer more torque to the screw to prevent slipping, a **Phillips head** screw and screwdriver was developed. The Phillips head screw looks like it has an imprinted "plus" sign on the top of the screw instead of a simple slot. The Phillips head screwdriver fits into this plus sign snugly. This type of screw is found in many applications, because it is easy to work with.

Wrenches

Wrenches are used to turn nuts, bolts, pipes, and other types of fasteners. They work in the same fundamental way that screwdrivers work, by using torque or mechanical advantage to turn the fastener. All wrenches are in some way able to "grip" a fastener and turn it. There are many types of wrenches and each one has its own particular use. Outlined here are the 10 most common types and their uses.

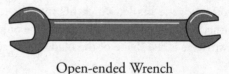

Open-ended Wrench

Open-ended wrenches have jaws that cannot be adjusted. They come in different sizes to be used for different-sized bolts or fasteners. Generally, you slip the wrench around the sides of the bolt head and then turn the bolt. This is the simplest type of wrench. However, if a wrench is the wrong size, then it can't be used.

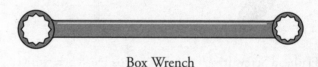

Box Wrench

Box wrenches are similar to open-ended wrenches in that you have to choose one of the correct size to be used on a particular bolt. What's different about a box wrench is that the jaws are completely closed, in order to fit snugly around the head of the bolt. This wrench can't slip sideways off a bolt, making it easy to affix to the bolt head. Box wrenches, like open-ended wrenches, come in a wide array of sizes.

Socket wrenches are similar to box wrenches in that the socket completely surrounds the nut or bolt head. The socket comes in an array of specific sizes and can be attached to a handle or ratchet unit easily. One end of the socket looks like the jaws of a box wrench, and the other end has a square hole that attaches to one of three sizes of drives on the handles. The handles come in a wide variety of shapes, lengths, and sizes, allowing access to hard-to-reach places. This wrench is relatively cheap, is easy to use, and versatile.

Crescent Wrench

The shape of the jaws of the wrench will help you to remember its name.

A **crescent wrench** allows you to adjust the gap between the wrench's open jaws by turning a screw adjuster located in the handle. This wrench can be used with many sizes of bolts, as opposed to open-ended and box wrenches, which cannot be adjusted. The top jaw on crescent wrenches is fixed to the handle, while the lower jaw can be moved to match the size of the nut or bolt.

Monkey Wrench

Another type of adjustable wrench, the **monkey wrench,** is a close relative of the crescent wrench. The monkey wrench, like the crescent wrench, has a fixed top jaw and an adjustable lower jaw. But monkey wrenches are generally a little stronger, with bigger jaws, and are used for more heavy-duty jobs.

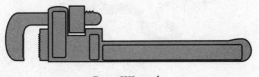

Pipe Wrench

The purpose of the **pipe wrench** is to turn pipes in order to attach them to other pipes. The pipe wrench is also an adjustable open-jaw wrench. This wrench has the lower jaw fixed to the handle and a movable upper jaw. The jaws are set at a slight angle to each other, to allow better gripping of pipes and tubes. This is generally a heavy wrench, larger than the other kinds of wrenches.

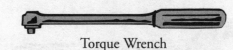

Torque Wrench

It is often important to know how tight a bolt is when you're tightening it down. If the bolt or nut is tightened too much, the bolt can strip, or lose its shape. If it's not tightened enough, it can sometimes loosen even more and fall off. To avoid this, a wrench was developed to measure how hard you're turning the bolt in terms of the amount of torque placed on the bolt. A **torque wrench** is generally a long bar or handle attached to a pointer and a scale. As you tighten a bolt, the wrench will bend slightly and the pointer will point to a number on a scale signifying the amount of torque that you are exerting on the bolt. These wrenches often fit sockets, so that they can be interchanged with the right wrench size.

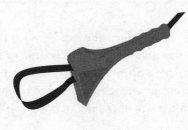

Strap Wrench

A different type of wrench is used to turn large-diameter pipes and other shafts. The **strap wrench** uses a webbing strap, much like a seatbelt, that wraps tightly around the pipe. You can then turn the pipe by applying a force to the handle of the wrench. The friction between the strap and the shaft keeps the handle fixed to the shaft so that they will turn together. It is often difficult to use this type of wrench on a wet or lubricated shaft.

Chain Wrench

Chain wrenches are similar to strap wrenches but feature a chain instead of a strap. This type of wrench is used when a strap wrench will slip or when the surface of the shaft does not need to be smooth. The chain wrench will mark the surface on which it is used.

Allen Wrench

Allen wrenches are hexagon-shaped bars bent about one third of the way down the shaft. These wrenches fit into machine screws that have a hexagonal hole in the head. Allen wrenches and Allen screws are used for many of the same applications that screws and screwdrivers are used for, but provide even more force to turn the screw without stripping the head.

Pliers

  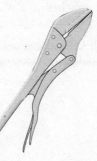

Slip Joint Pliers   Needle Nose Pliers   Vise Grips

Pliers are great tools to use to hold objects that would otherwise be difficult to grip. Pliers come in many different types but all have the same basic shape. They have **jaws** (like a wrench), a **handle,** a **joint** or **pivot point,** and a **nose,** located at the end of the jaws. Different types of pliers have different noses. The nose can be either straight or curved. It can also be either stubby and short or long and thin, in which case the pliers are called **needle nose pliers.** Most pliers have a fixed pivot, limiting the size of the material that can be held. Some pliers have adjustable jaws so that the tool can be used on objects of many different sizes. This special type of pliers is called **slip joint pliers,** because the joint can "slip" into different sizes.

Another type of pliers, called **vise grips,** allow the user to clamp down onto something and lock the jaws. Vise grips are great for holding onto something very tightly. A special lever in the tool allows it to release.

Vises and Clamps

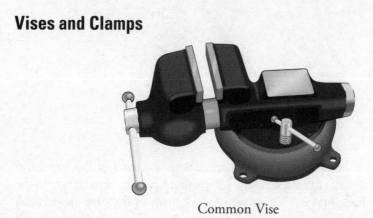

Common Vise

Many shops also contain tools called vises that help to hold materials that are being cut, drilled, or glued. A **vise** is a heavy, solid iron or steel tool. One end of the vise is fixed and bolted to a table. The other end can be adjusted by tightening a lever attached to a worm gear; in this way, the jaws close upon an object. Vises must be heavy to be able to hold onto materials and keep them from moving even when they're under heavy pressure. The main jaws of a vise must be kept free from nicks and gouges, so that the objects can be held as tightly and evenly as possible.

C Clamp

Often times, an object can't fit into a vise because it is too big or awkward, so a clamp is used instead. The most common type of clamp is a **C clamp,** so called because it's shaped like the letter "C." The clamp has one side attached to the C and the other fixed to an adjustable screw. It's then simply put in place and tightened to hold an object. There are other types of clamps, but all have only two flat jaws connected by some type of screw to tighten them down.

Cutting Tools—Saws

There are dozens of types of tools used to cut materials in a shop. Each one has its own specialized use. We will start with the most widely known cutting tools and then discuss the ones used for shaping.

The most recognizable type of cutting tool is the **saw.** Most saws have a similar set of parts. The part of the saw that you hold on to is called the **handle.** The handle is connected in some way to the **blade.** The blade is the part of the saw that contains the **teeth,** which are responsible for actually cutting through the material. The end of the saw is called the **toe** and the part next to the handle is called the **heel.** Some or all of these parts will be different for each type of saw. One major difference is in the blade.

The blade on a saw has several major components. The cutting portion on a saw blade normally cuts only when the saw is pulled back or pushed forward—in other words, only in one direction. The teeth on the saw are bent slightly outward so that the slot being cut is slightly wider than the saw blade. The distance that the teeth are bent from the edge of the saw blade is called the **set** of the saw. The bigger the set, the more clearance there will be between the saw blade and the side of the cut slot. The total width of the slot that is cut is the same as the total width of the teeth, called the **kerf.** It is important to know the kerf of the saw when cutting something. If a thin material is being cut, a saw blade with teeth that are close together must be used.

Handsaw

For cutting wood, two major types of blades are used. **Ripsaws** are for cutting along the grain of the wood, and **crosscut saws** are for cutting across the grain of the wood. The difference between the saws is in the shape of their teeth. It's easy to remember that *cross*cut saws cut *across* the grain.

The saw shown above is a **handsaw.** The teeth on this saw can be arranged for ripping or for cross cutting. This is the saw most commonly used for cutting wood.

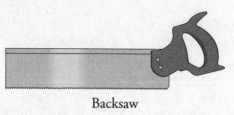

Backsaw

Backsaw and **dovetail** saws are used for cutting a straight line across the grain of the wood. The backsaw is reinforced with a strong metal back, so that the blade will not bend. Its teeth are for ripping. The handle is like that of the handsaw above. The dovetail saw is similar to the backsaw in that it has a strong backing, but its handle is shaped more like a file and the blade is much thinner. Sometimes, with these saws, a block of wood called a miter box is used to help keep the blade and the direction of the cut in a straight line.

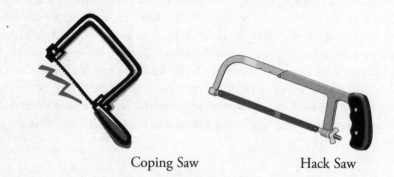

Coping Saw   Hack Saw

The **coping saw** is used for cutting curves in wood. Its thin blade allows it to twist slightly in thin pieces of wood. The **compass saw** is used to cut intricate shapes in thicker pieces of wood. Its thicker blade gives it more support.

The **hack saw** looks similar to the coping saw except that its blade is much thicker and the arm that holds the blade is much stronger. The hacksaw is used for cutting metal. The arm of the saw extends and stretches the blade. The tension put on the blade helps it to remain stable when cutting. Various hack saw blades can be fit to the same saw; these blades come in a wide variety of teeth depths, number of teeth per inch along the blade, and kerfs.

Other Cutting Tools

Shears

Shears or **snips** look like scissors with a long handle and a short blade. They are used primarily for cutting very thin sheet metal. Cutting sheet metal with a saw is similar to trying to cut paper with a saw. It is much easier to use a scissor-like cutting tool on thin metal.

What do you use when you want to cut a pipe or piece of tubing? One option is a hacksaw. But a **pipe cutter** is a much better choice. A pipe cutter looks like a C-clamp with several circular blades. The cutter is affixed around the pipe and then tightened. The pipe or tube is then rotated, and the circular blades cut into the pipe. This method leaves a much cleaner and smoother surface than cutting with a hacksaw would.

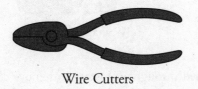

Wire Cutters

It is generally not advisable to use snips, shears, or scissors to cut electrical or other types of wire. This will damage the blades and wear down the tools. **Wire cutters** have a thicker and stronger blade, so they do not get damaged.

Bolt cutters are reinforced snips designed to cut through thicker pieces of hard metals, bolts, and rods. The handles on bolt cutters are very long and the cutting jaws very short, so that more leverage can be applied to cut thick bolts. These cutters generally also have a mechanism of levers near the jaws that help to transfer more force to the bolt. Bolt cutters should not be used as wire cutters.

Shaping Tools

Many times it is necessary to shape material after it has been cut to allow it to fit snugly with other parts. The tools discussed below are used to shape material in specific ways.

Grader

Graders, or planes, are used to give wood a smooth surface and to remove small layers of wood. Graders are devices that allow the user to hold the tool and put pressure on the material, to shave part of it away. They can cut either with or across the grain of stock. Jackplanes, the most common type, have a slight convex curve to the blade.

Scraper

Scrapers have been used throughout history to remove chips and pieces of wood and other material in order to make planks and other shapes. They're also used to help make and clean out grooves in wood. A scraper has a straight handle and a flat, smooth blade. You hold the handle of the scraper in your hand and then strike the handle with a rubber mallet (not with a hammer). This process removes little chips of wood.

Chisel

A **chisel** is used to remove layers of metal. The face of the chisel is covered with teeth, which can be cut diagonally in either one or two directions, making either single-cut or double-cut chisels. Chisels that have more cuts per inch will leave a smoother surface on the material. The faces of chisels come in a variety of shapes, including square, flat, round, and triangular. At the heel of the chisel is a tang that's inserted into a universal handle. Chisels should never be struck with a hammer.

Grinder

Another type of tool used to remove material from a metal part is a grinder. A **grinder** is an abrasive wheel that spins at a high speed on an axle. Before operating a grinder, you should check the wheel to make sure it does not have cracks. If there are cracks, the wheel might explode while spinning. The metal part of the grinder is pressed into the wheel with medium force and moved slightly over the center of the wheel. The part to be ground should always be in contact with the lower part of the wheel, just above the wheel guard, so that if you lose control of the part it will be thrown to the ground instead of into the air.

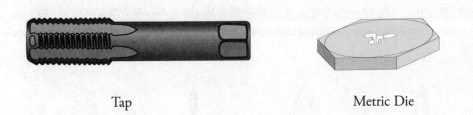

Tap   Metric Die

Taps and **dies** are two special types of shaping tools used to make threads on objects. Taps are tools that look like a screw with the corners cut out and a handle at one end. They are used for making threads in metal holes so that a screw may be used in the hole. The tap is inserted into the hole, twisted about five times, and then pulled out to allow the shavings to be taken out of the hole; then it's inserted and twisted again an additional five times further than the previous time. This cycle repeats until the threads go far enough into the hole for the screw. A die is a block with what appears to be four connected holes going through it. The middle hole is threaded, and the outer holes are smooth. The die is used for making threads on the outside of a tube or rod. It is placed over the rod and twisted so that the threads are cut just as with the tap.

Drills, Braces, and Bits

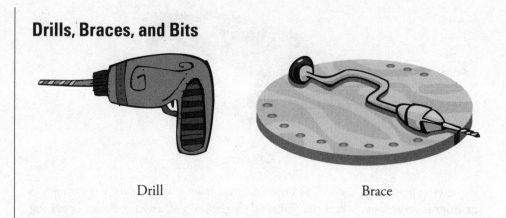

Drill   Brace

The best way to make a hole in a material using a hand tool is with a **bit** and a **drill** or **brace.** A drill is a device that turns a cutting tool at a very high rate of speed. Drills that use a manual crank are called braces. Braces are generally long enough to fit two hands on the shaft. The shaft is bent in several places to accommodate a handle that is offset from the main shaft and allows the user to turn the brace. Drills have a chuck that attaches to any one of a number of drill bits, which are the parts that actually come into contact with the material being drilled into.

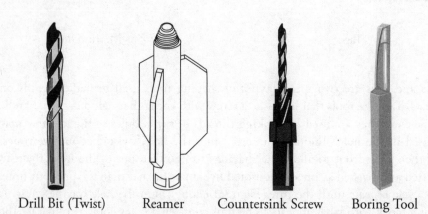

Drill Bit (Twist)   Reamer   Countersink Screw   Boring Tool

The drill bit that we are used to seeing is called a standard **twist drill bit.** It is used for drilling holes into metals and wood stock. The twist bit has two blades that are located inside the body of the bit. The cutting edges are straight and are separated by a portion of the tip of the drill bit that does not cut called the dead center. Consequently, if a large hole is being drilled, the dead center can sometimes be too large, and the drill can't cut into the material. To avoid these problems, a smaller hole is first drilled into the material. Then the larger bit is used. The small hole removes the material that would have been encountered by the dead center so that the larger bit can enter the material. The twisted portion of the drill bit does not cut the hole. It is used to help to pull material out of the hole.

A **reamer** is a drill bit that is used to make an existing hole bigger. The cutting edges on a reamer are located on the outside edge of the body and not at the end. This allows the bit to cut out a hole of larger diameter than what already exists.

Sometimes a surface will need to be flat after it is screwed or bolted into place. In order to accomplish this, a **countersink screw** must be used. The hole that the screw goes into must be drilled with a countersink drill bit to accommodate the screw. The countersink drill bit is a cone-shaped bit that cuts out a cone at the top of a drilled hole to allow a screw to tighten so that its head is below the surface of the material.

Boring tools are often used to drill holes in wood. The boring tool has several parts that make it different from a twist drill. The tip of the boring tool is a threaded screw that grabs and pulls the bit into the material. The next part of the bit to come in contact with the material consists of two points that score the circumference of the circle that is to be cut. The blades on a boring tool are found between the points and the threaded tip and are shaped like half moons. The cutting edges chip out the material within the scored circle. As the threaded tip pulls the boring tool further into the material, the twist moves material from the blades to the top of the hole.

Punch

Sometimes, before you start to drill in metals, you need to make a small indentation to allow the bit to drill in the right place. Without this indentation, the bit can jump and spin all over the surface of the metal and fail to drill the hole at the correct point. To make this small indentation, you can use a **punch,** which is a metal shaft that's flat on one end and sharp on the other. The punch point is placed on the center of the hole to be drilled and gently hit on the flat part with a rubber or plastic mallet. You then drill the hole at the spot by placing the center of the drill bit into the punch mark and starting the hole.

Punches can also be used to knock a pin out of a hole or to line up holes when assembling an object.

Welding

Welding is a method of bonding two pieces of metal or parts together permanently by melting the metal in a specific place on the pieces to be joined. The small area of melted metal is spongy and forms a bead. The welder uses a tool to push the bead of molten metal along the joint, adding a small amount of metal as needed to keep the joint strong. The parts are then normally cooled in oil or water, recrystalizing the metal and hardening it into one part.

Welding Torch

The tool that welders use is called a **welding torch.** One of the most common types of torches is the **acetylene torch.** A pressurized tank feeds the gas to the end of the torch. The valves are opened and the torch lit with a spark. The welder then uses the flame to melt the metal and push the bead along the joint.

Another common type of welding is **arc welding,** which requires a tool connected to a voltage source. When the tool comes into contact with a metal object, it will conduct electricity. If the tool is pulled a small distance away from the metal object, an arc of electricity will form, heating up the metal and melting it at the arc point. The welder then joins the two pieces as with the acetylene torch. In some types of welding, the lead of the tool supplies the additional metal needed for the joint. This metal is then consumed by the welding process and incorporated into the joint.

Using Process of Elimination

POE is the most powerful tool that you have to answer the questions on the exam. Even if you're unsure of the answer to a question on the Auto and Shop section, you can still use POE to give you a good chance of getting it right.

Sometimes you will be given a picture of a tool that you do not recognize or even have never seen before. Don't give up! Chances are that you are going to know some of the tools that are listed below the picture in the answer choices. From your knowledge of what those tools look like, you can eliminate incorrect answers, and then you can guess from the answers you have left. This will greatly improve your odds of getting the question right.

AUTO SECTION

Now that we have reviewed the basic tools and shop procedures, we are going to discuss automobiles. About half of the auto questions on the ASVAB will be related to engine and automotive systems components, like carburetors, struts, and valves. The other half will involve the basic diagnosis of some given problem or condition in an automobile. Before we can diagnose problems, we need to understand the underlying principles and basic components of the automobile.

Automobiles can be broken down into several integrated systems that all work together but perform different functions. Many of the components from these systems overlap. But without each one of these systems working properly, it will not be long before the car is on the side of the road. Auto systems that you will need to know are

> **Engine and exhaust:** processes the fuel and turns the wheels

> **Cooling:** keeps the engine from overheating

> **Drive train:** transports energy from the engine to the wheels

> **Steering:** allows the car to be turned from side to side

> **Braking:** allows the car to be stopped

> **Electrical:** ties into most of the other systems on the vehicle and allows the car to continue running

Automobile Systems Review

The Engine

The basic idea behind an engine is that it harnesses the energy from burning fuels. An engine is a device that contains combustion and uses the energy to turn a shaft. Where does combustion come from? The explosion comes from igniting a mixture of fuel and air. The fuel is the benzene-based gasoline or diesel that you normally fill your car's gas tank with at the station. In order for anything to burn, it needs oxygen. In automobiles, oxygen is supplied from the air and mixed with the gasoline. The mixture is then ignited with a spark and explodes, releasing energy. When something burns or combusts, it does not disintegrate into oblivion; it leaves behind residues and gasses that must be removed. In the case of the automobile, this waste removal is done by the exhaust system.

The heart of the car is the engine, and the heart of the engine lies in the **cylinders.** A cylinder is basically a tube that is open at one end and closed off on the other, with the exception of two small holes to allow fuel and air to enter and exhaust gasses to exit. The closed side of the cylinder also has one end of the spark plug in it.

The open side of the cylinder is "plugged" by another cylindrical object called the **piston.** The piston has a slightly smaller diameter than the cylinder to allow it to move up and down inside the cylinder easily. Two metal rings, called **piston rings,** wrap around the piston head and seal off the inside of the cylinder. The piston rings fit into small grooves in the piston and expand, so they always brush along the walls of the cylinder and create a tight seal. This seal helps to contain the combustion in the cylinder and use more of its energy. The piston is connected to the **piston rod,** a bar that extends out of the cylinder and attaches to the crankshaft. The piston rod is not connected to the center of the crankshaft; it is connected a little offset. In fact, no part of the crankshaft has a rod that passes all the way through the center. As the piston moves up and down, the **crankshaft** turns in a complete circle. This is much like watching someone pedaling a bicycle: The legs and knees are traveling up and down, but because the pedals are offset from the bicycle's crankshaft, the pedals and the person's feet will turn around in a circle. This motion is extremely important, because the turning of the crankshaft ultimately turns the wheels.

If the piston were the only thing attached to the crankshaft, the shaft would not turn smoothly but would jerk around in its circle. A heavy wheel, called the **flywheel,** is attached to the end of the crankshaft. Once it has started rotating, the flywheel is difficult to stop and helps the crankshaft and piston to move smoothly.

Cars do not run with a single cylinder and piston. Most cars have four-cylinder, six-cylinder, or eight-cylinder engines. Most of the four-cylinder engines are built with all of the cylinders lined up with the pistons entering from the bottom. This is called a "straight four" or "in-line" four-cylinder engine. However, most six- and eight-cylinder engines have the cylinders and pistons oriented to look like a letter "V" and are consequently called "V-6" or "V-8" engines.

So where does the initial up-and-down motion of the piston come from? Let's follow the fuel as it moves through the engine.

The Exhaust System

On older automobiles, the gasoline starts in the gas tank and is pumped by the fuel pump into the **carburetor,** which is responsible for mixing air and fuel together. The carburetor consists of a float tank to store fuel, an air intake valve, an air filter, and a series of tubing. The air enters through the filter, which removes dust and other impurities that could leave residue on the engine, ignite early in the combustion chamber, and decrease the life of the engine. The air then travels through a special tube called a venturi that looks like a pipe constricted in the middle. A tube coming from the fuel reservoir intersects the venturi at the smallest part. The air traveling by the small tube does two things: First, it sucks fuel into the air through the small tube; second, it mixes the fuel instantly and completely with the air. If the air and fuel do not mix completely, not all of the fuel will burn in the combustion chamber, leading to wasted fuel and increased pollutants. If there is too much fuel, the air/fuel mixture is said to be too rich, and the vehicle will not burn all of the fuel completely. If there is too little fuel, the mixture is called lean, and the engine will not get enough power. In order to get the mix just right, the carburetor uses about 15 pounds of air for every 1 pound of fuel.

A special valve called the **throttle valve** controls the amount of the fuel/air mixture that is sent to the engine. As the driver presses on the gas pedal, the valve opens and allows more of the mixture to enter the engine, giving a larger explosion and therefore more power.

That's how it's done on older vehicles. New cars—cars made after the mid-1990s—have **fuel injectors,** instead of carburetors, to mix the air and fuel together and then inject this mixture into the engine. Fuel injectors perform basically the same function as the carburetor but allow more control over the exact mixture and the amount of fuel injected into the engine. These devices help reduce exhaust emissions by delivering the exact amount of fuel and air needed and improve the efficiency of the car.

Sometimes gasoline in the fuel line will vaporize, either because it is too hot or because the pressure drops too low. The vapor does not flow the same way as liquid fuel, causing the fuel to get stuck in the line. This situation is called **vapor lock.** This is a fairly rare condition with today's fuel-injected vehicles.

Ignition and Combustion Systems

Now the fuel enters the cylinder. In order for the fuel to ignite and push on the piston, the piston has to go through two complete up-and-down cycles. This type of engine is referred to as a **four-stroke engine.** Here's how it works.

1. The intake valve opens on the top of the cylinder while the piston is brought to the bottom of its stroke by the crankshaft. This motion draws the fuel/air mixture into the cylinder.
2. The intake valve closes tightly. This is called the intake stroke. The crankshaft then pushes up on the piston, compressing all of the air and fuel in the cylinder. The compression ratio is the common way to describe how much this gas is compressed. For example, if the amount of volume that the gas takes up is reduced to a quarter of what it was originally, then the compression ratio will be 4 : 1. Higher compression ratios are desired. This stroke is called the compression stroke.
3. The spark plug ignites the fuel/air mixture. The hot, burning mixture wants to expand and pushes out in all directions from inside the cylinder. The only part of the cylinder that can move is the piston. Consequently, the piston is pushed all the way down to the bottom of the cylinder by this combustion. This part of the cycle—the part that actually turns the crankshaft—is called the power cycle. The power cycle provides all the necessary energy to continue the motion of the crankshaft.
4. The exhaust valve opens, and the cylinder is pushed back up by the crankshaft, pushing all of the leftover gasses out to the exhaust system. This is called the exhaust stroke.

This cycle continues to run in all of the cylinders. The cylinders are timed in such a way that for each one of these strokes, one of the cylinders is on its power cycle and pushing the crankshaft for the other cylinders. At any moment in a four-cylinder vehicle, one of the cylinders is on the intake stroke, one is on compression, one is on power, and one is on exhaust. This keeps the car running smoothly and allows the car to have continuous power. Cars generally run in the range of 600 to 4000 rotations of the crankshaft every minute. The number of revolutions is normally shown to the driver on a gauge on the dash called a **tachometer.** This is not the speed of the car, but only a gauge of how hard the engine is working.

The valves are controlled by a system of components called the **rocker arm** and **camshaft.** The camshaft is driven by the **timing belt,** a special belt with bumps like gear teeth. The camshaft rotates at half the speed of the crankshaft, because the valves need to open and close only one time for each two revolutions of the crankshaft.

The timing belts should be visually inspected every time the oil is changed on the vehicle. If a belt appears to be cracking, or some of the teeth are starting to wear down, it should be replaced. If a timing belt breaks during travel, the engine could be severely damaged. Remember that the timing belt is the link responsible for opening and closing the valves at exactly the right time. If the valves can't open and close, then the fuel can't enter or leave the engine.

A **cam** is a device that attaches to a shaft like a gear, except that, unlike a gear, the cam is not normally connected through the center like a gear and has no teeth. As the **camshaft** turns, the cams push a rod up and down. The rod is connected to a rocker arm that works like a teeter-totter to push the top of the valve down. This allows the valve to open and close when needed. If the valves are not timed to open and close at precisely the right time, then the engine will stop working. The valves are spring-loaded so that they will seal tightly in the closed position.

Exhaust System

After the burned fuel leaves the engine through the exhaust valve, it enters the **exhaust system**. The exhaust system consists of everything necessary to remove the spent fuel from the engine, reduce the pollutants from the gasses, and expel the gasses back into the atmosphere. If we lived in a perfect world, all of the exhaust gases coming from the combustion of the fuel would be carbon dioxide and water vapor. However, three major pollutants—carbon monoxide, nitrogen oxides, and hydrocarbons—are also expelled. Hydrocarbons come from unburned molecules of gasoline. If the fuel/air mixture is rich, then carbon monoxide will be formed instead of carbon dioxide. The nitrogen oxides will form because the source of the oxygen, the atmosphere, is mainly nitrogen and the temperatures at which the hydrocarbons burn is very high. The exhaust gasses leave the cylinders and enter an exhaust manifold, or a chamber, that connects to all of the cylinders. Some of the gasses are then taken back to the air intake and injected back into the fuel air mixture to help bring down the temperature of the explosion and reduce nitrogen oxides. From the manifold, the gases travel through a device called the catalytic converter, which contains very small pellets made of a special material that allows the unused hydrocarbons and the carbon monoxide to continue to oxidize at lower temperatures. Upon leaving the catalytic converter, the gases are almost completely carbon dioxide and water vapor. They then travel through the muffler, which helps deaden the noise of the exhaust, and out of the car.

Another common source of hydrocarbons is from vaporizing fuel in the gas tank or from leftover hydrocarbons in the catalytic converter after the car has been turned off. In order to keep these vapors from escaping into the atmosphere, vent tubes are connected to both devices and to a container filled with charcoal. The charcoal absorbs the hydrocarbon vapors and holds them until the car is started again and they are returned to the engine.

Other materials can also be left behind by the combustion process. It is common to have carbon deposits form in parts of the exhaust system and fuel lines. The carbon deposits can hamper air flow in the exhaust system, but generally, small deposits are not troublesome.

Cooling and Lubrication System

Because of the constant, though controlled, explosions of fuel and air, the temperature inside the engine gets very high—so high that, without a cooling system, the iron or aluminum in the engine would begin to melt! But the heat is reduced by a device that circulates water around the engine. This is similar to putting a cool cloth on the forehead of a fever-stricken child. The water in the cloth absorbs some of the heat, and then the cloth is re-cooled and placed back on the child. The system in the car is a little more complicated, though. Here's how it works.

The turning crankshaft turns a belt called the **fan belt** that connects to the fan and water pump. The **water pump** moves the water from the radiator at the front of the car and into channels, called water jackets, in the engine block. The channels go around the cylinders and the oil reservoir and then out the other side of the engine block. All of the water traveling around the cylinders picks up heat from the hot cylinders and carries it to a special **manifold** on top of the engine. When the coolant in the manifold reaches a certain temperature, a valve called the **thermostat** opens and allows the water to enter the top of the radiator. The **radiator** is simply a network of tubes that have air flowing around them. The fan that is connected to the fan belt helps draw cool air from the environment over the radiator to take heat from the water and carry it back into the atmosphere. When the water in the engine reaches a certain temperature, the thermostat will open again and the now-cooled water will be pushed back into the engine to be heated again.

Sometimes the thermostat will stick and not open, so that the hot water is not permitted to cool in the radiator. The water pump also tends to wear out and will sometimes fail. Both of these situations will result in the car overheating. The car actually becomes so hot that the coolant trapped in the water jackets and manifold vaporizes and can blow through the tubes it is traveling through. The best thing to do when the car overheats is to pull over and allow it to cool. Consequently, if the fan belt breaks, the cooling system and the electrical generation system will also fail.

The **oil** that you put into the car is also part of the cooling and lubrication system. The oil keeps metal parts from rubbing on each other, creating friction and heat, and damaging components. The oil is pumped through a filter to remove impurities and then throughout the crankcase and camshaft to help lubricate the pistons, rods, cams, and bearings by forming a thin film on the metal surfaces. The oil is then circulated back to the oil pan on the bottom of the car.

Oil can seep through various parts of the engine and into the combustion chamber. When this occurs, the engine is said to "burn oil." This often results in a blue cloud of smoke from the tailpipe and the need to refill the oil reservoir often. Oil can enter the combustion areas through the head gasket (which seals the engine head with the valves to the engine block) or through the piston rings.

Drive Train

The drive train is the portion of the car that takes the spinning crankshaft and uses it to spin the wheels. The drive train consists of the clutch, transmission, differential gear, axles, wheel bearings, rims, and tires. With the engine running, the flywheel is spinning at a constant rate. If you want to speed up the flywheel, you can depress the gas pedal and open the throttle valve to let more fuel and air into the cylinders. But just connecting the wheels to the crankshaft would allow the vehicle to move at only a small range of speeds. To give the car more speed and power variability, a **transmission** is inserted between the wheels and the engine. There are two main types of transmissions: manual and automatic. We will discuss manual transmissions first.

The **manual transmission** consists of a variety of gears that can be slid back and forth along several shafts and allow several possible arrangements and gear ratios. The gears and shafts convert the revolution rate of the incoming shaft to a new rate at the drive shaft. As we said previously, car engines work best under a limited range of rotation speeds. To keep the car engine working in this range and yet allow the wheels to travel at slower and faster ranges, you need to change the drive-shaft revolution rate.

When two **gears** mesh together, it is important to keep track of the number of teeth on each gear. (See the Mechanical Comprehension chapter for more on this.) Let's say that you have a gear with 36 teeth that's spinning in a complete circle one time every second. If you then connect another gear with 18 teeth, how much faster will the second gear be turning? Since the second gear has half as many teeth, it will be turning exactly twice as fast. Using this same idea, you can slide into different gears to allow a different gear ratio and therefore different speeds for the drive shaft.

But, if you were to simply take the car out of one gear and put it in another, you would get a loud noise as the gears traveling at different speeds try to connect and grind into each other. The manual clutch provides a way to connect the two shafts turning at different speeds.

The manual clutch consists of three plates, all aligned with the drive shaft. The plate that is connected to the crankshaft is the **flywheel.** A separate shaft is lined up with the crankshaft and acts as the incoming shaft for the transmission. This shaft has a plate called the **pressure plate** mounted to it. A spring-loaded plate called the **clutch plate** is in between the two. The spring holds the clutch plate tightly between the pressure plate and the flywheel so that all three plates turn together. When the clutch pedal is depressed in the car, the clutch plate is pulled away from the flywheel, disengaging the pressure plate and the drive shaft. This then allows the operator to shift the transmission into a new gear. After the gears have been changed, the operator lifts his or her foot off the clutch pedal, bringing the spinning flywheel and the stationary pressure plate back into contact. By bringing the plates slowly together, the pressure plate can speed up until it is traveling the same speed as the flywheel and the car is in the next gear.

The **automatic transmission** and **torque converter** operate the same way, with slightly different components. The automatic transmission uses a system of planetary gears, which mesh on the inside of the gears as well as the outside. By holding some of the gears or gear housings stationary and allowing others to turn, the car can achieve several different gear ratios. Instead of three plates, as in the manual clutch, the automatic has what looks like three fans. All three of the fans are housed inside a container of hydraulic fluid, which is necessary for the operation of the torque converter. The fan that is connected to the crankshaft is called the pump. The pump is always spinning at the same rate as the crankshaft. When the car is put into gear, the pump starts to spin the fluid inside the transmission in one direction. The second fan, called the stator, helps the fluid to circulate back to the pump, spinning in the same direction that it left and adding to the torque of the pump. A third fan, the turbine, is spun around by the motion of the fluid. A short while after engaging, the pump, turbine, and stator will all be turning at the same rate, and therefore the two shafts will be turning at the same rate.

After leaving the transmission, the drive shaft enters another grouping of gears called the **differential gear.** The differential gear sits at the junction between the axle and the drive shaft. As a car turns a corner, the wheels on the outside of the corner will have to travel a slightly longer distance than the wheels on the inside. That means that the outside wheel will need to travel a little faster than the inside wheel to keep up around the corner. The differential gear allows one wheel to turn slower than the other one but still maintain the same average rotation speed for both of the axle halves. It is important to note that the total amount of power going to the wheels does not change, just the distribution. During straight travel, the differential gear allows both of the wheels to turn at the same rate.

The differential gear is attached to the **axles** and the axles to the **wheels.** The wheels consist of wheel bearings, a hub, a rim, and a tire. The wheel bearings allow the wheel to attach to the car chassis and still be able to spin. The **rim** and the **tire** form an airtight seal that allows the tires to be filled and maintain air pressure. Note that this is different from how a bike tire is inflated. A bike tire affixes to the rim in much the same manner, but, unlike a car tire, the bike tire has a separate tube to hold the air.

The tires should always be inflated to the proper air pressure to ensure that the car is getting good traction. When inflated properly, the tire should be bulging slightly at the bottom. If the tire is underinflated, the outsides of the tire will wear quicker than the insides. If the tire is overinflated, the middle part of the tire will wear and the tread will still be good on the outsides. In both cases, the tires will have to be replaced.

Brakes

The car needs to move forward, but it's just as important for the car to stop. There are two types of brakes that help cars to slow down and stop: **disc brakes** and **drum brakes.** Normally, automobiles have disc brakes on the front wheels and drum brakes on the back. Disc brakes have a metal disc, or rotor, connected to the wheel. The rotor spins with the wheel in between two small arms called **calipers,** similar to brakes on a bicycle. On the surface of each side of the calipers are the **brake pads.** Drum brakes have a bowl, or **drum,** attached to the wheel. Two half-circle **brake shoes** fit inside the drum and are attached to two springs to keep them from touching the drum.

When a brake pedal is depressed, it causes brake fluid in a device called the master cylinder to build up pressure. This pressurized brake fluid then travels down hoses, or **brake lines,** to the brakes. On disc brakes, the fluid squeezes the calipers together around the rotor, creating friction and slowing the car. On drum brakes, the fluid causes the shoes to push outward against the drum and create the friction to slow the car. Both types of brakes are spring loaded to disengage the rotor or the drum when the pedal is released. As the brake pedal is pushed harder, more pressure builds up in the brake lines, and the wheels stop faster. Over time, the surface of the brake shoes gradually rubs away, and the brakes will need to be replaced.

On occasion, the brake lines fail. A few decades ago, the result would be that the car would have no brakes but the parking brake. But cars today have a dual action piston in the master cylinder. If one of the sides fails, the other will be able to provide the friction to stop the vehicle safely. The system will still need to be repaired or replaced afterwards, but that's certainly better than having the car sail uncontrolled down a hill!

Steering

The car's front wheels are connected to a **steering bar** attached to the axle. The steering bar is connected to a **tie rod** that in turn is attached to a flat gear called the **rack.** The teeth of the rack are designed to fit with the teeth on a round gear called the **pinion.** The pinion is attached to the bar that goes through the center of the steering wheel. The pinion is held in place, and the rack is allowed to move from side to side. When the steering wheel is turned, the pinion begins to turn and shuttles the rack to one side. This action pulls the back part of the inside wheel toward the center of the car and pushes the back of the outside wheel away from the car.

Vehicles with **power steering** usually have a similar setup, except that they use hydraulic fluid pumped into an actuator on the steering rod to help move the bar to the side.

Electrical System

Almost all the systems in a car are in some way connected to the electrical system. In order for anything on the vehicle to operate, it needs electrical power. Initially, a battery supplies the electric power. When a key is turned in the ignition switch, a connection is made in the circuit for the starter. The **starter** is an electric motor mounted to the engine block that provides enough torque to the crankshaft so that it starts to turn. At the same time, the other systems in the car start up and supply the engine with fuel and air to allow the engine to run on its own. After the car is started, the starter is not needed.

In the early 20th century, the starter was a hand crank on the front of the car.

The **spark plugs** in the cylinders need electricity to fire and ignite the gases to move the pistons. Spark plugs are essentially two metal leads that stick into the cylinders. The metal leads are separated by a small gap. If enough electrical charge builds up across the gap, the electricity will arc across the gap. This arc ignites the fuel air mixture in the cylinder.

While the car is running, the battery does not supply the car with the necessary energy it needs to continue to run. Instead, a device called an **alternator** is used. An alternator is basically a motor that runs in reverse; instead of taking in power and using it to turn a shaft, the alternator takes a spinning shaft (turned by the fan belt on the engine) and produces electricity from it. The electricity travels to a device called a **voltage regulator** and is used to recharge the battery and run other systems in the car. Some of the electricity goes into the **distributor,** which is responsible for sending the right amount of electricity to each spark plug at the right time to get the cylinders to fire in the correct sequence. Of course, some of the electricity also goes to the lights, radio, air conditioner, and other systems in the car.

Problem Diagnosis

The auto portion of this section has about 5 to 7 questions asking you to diagnose a vehicle problem by analyzing a few symptoms. Here are some tips to help you answer these questions.

1. Does the question tell you specifically what system is malfunctioning? If so, then you can eliminate all of the answers that have nothing to do with that system.

2. Is the symptom associated with a particular part or system that has not been specified? Once again, you can eliminate the components or answers that are not related to that part or system. Keep in mind that sometimes a malfunction with one part of a system has an impact on another part later in the system or even on another system, so be careful.

3. After you've eliminated answer choices that clearly could not be right, for each answer choice you have left, trace the problem given through the system and try to think what the result might be. Does it match the symptom given in the question? If so, you have found the right answer. You will probably not have time to look at all of the answer choices carefully following this procedure, so be sure to use steps 1 and 2 to eliminate impossible answer choices first.

4. If you feel that you are spending an excessive amount of time and you still can't decide between two or more answer choices, take a guess and move on. Even by eliminating one answer choice, you are improving your chances of answering the question correctly.

Chapter 8
Mechanical
Comprehension

INTRODUCTION TO MECHANICAL COMPREHENSION

The CAT-ASVAB consists of 16 Mechanical Comprehension questions, and you will have 20 minutes to complete them. The MET-ASVAB and Student ASVAB versions consist of 25 questions, and you will have 19 minutes to complete them.

This section contains questions that will test your ability to apply logic to the physical world. The word *mechanical* in the title refers to simple machines such as pulleys and levers, rather than to complex devices such as automobiles. Most of the questions should be familiar to those who have taken high school physics. But if you have never taken a physics course, don't despair; this isn't a heavily weighted part of the ASVAB, and most of the problems in this section are based upon a few general rules that we will cover in this chapter. If you learn these rules and apply them with creativity throughout the section, you should be able to get through this portion of the exam without much worry.

Force

A force is something that changes the motion of an object. In baseball, the pitcher applies a large force to the ball when he throws it toward the plate. After the ball is released, the force of wind resistance will slow the ball down and may cause it to change direction (if the pitcher threw a curveball). Finally, if the batter manages to connect with the ball, then the bat will apply a very large force that will change both the direction and the speed of the ball and send it into the field of play.

The forces in the example above originate from very different sources, and yet they have two things in common: direction and size. Both of these features are crucial. The size of a force determines how much effect it will have on the object to which it is applied. The size of a force is usually measured in pounds. (Your weight is actually the amount of force that gravity exerts upon your body.)

The direction of a force determines the direction in which the motion of the object will change. For example, the brakes of an automobile produce a force that points in the opposite direction of the car's motion. This force slows the car down and brings it to a halt. Direction can be measured in degrees (like an angle), but for the purposes of the ASVAB, you will usually only need to pay attention to the relationship that a force has with other forces in the problem. Are they in the same direction, opposite directions, or perpendicular (at right angles) to each other? When two forces act in the same direction, you should add their sizes together. When forces act in opposite directions, you should subtract the size of the smaller force from the size of the larger. When forces act in perpendicular directions, the resulting force will be diagonal to both of them. Imagine two dogs wrestling over a bone. If both dogs pull on the bone with the same amount of force, but in opposite directions, the bone (and the dogs) will remain stationary. If one of the dogs exerts a larger force than the other, then both the bone (and the other dog) will move toward the stronger canine. Now imagine that their owner is taking them both for a run on their leashes at the same time. If the dogs are both directly in front of the owner, they will exert a force in the same direction along their leashes and will pull her along with twice the force that a single dog would apply.

Take a look at an example force problem to illustrate these ideas.

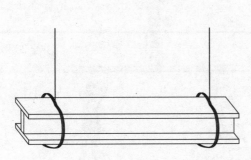

1. The ropes attached to the girder can each support a maximum of 200 lbs. without snapping. What is the largest weight that the girder can be without breaking a rope?

    A.   100 lbs.

    B.   200 lbs.

    C.   400 lbs.

    D.   800 lbs.

Here's How to Crack It

To solve this problem, make a list of the forces that act on the girder. There are two ropes, and they both act in the "up" direction. The only other force that acts on the girder is gravity, and gravity points "down." The girder is not moving, so the up forces should total to the same size as the down force. Each rope can support 200 lbs., so the total up force is 400 lbs. (remember—"lbs." is the abbreviation for "pounds"). The force of gravity (which is the same thing as the weight of the girder) must also be 400 lbs. The answer is (C).

Try another force problem:

180 lbs.

20 lbs.

2. How much weight must the man on the ground support?

    A.   90 lbs.
    B.   100 lbs.
    C.   180 lbs.
    D.   200 lbs.

Here's How to Crack It

Again, make a list of the forces in the problem. This time there are two forces that push downward, the weight of the plank and the weight of the man. We need to add these two weights together, for a total downward force of 180 lbs. + 20 lbs. = 200 lbs. That means that you need to have a total of 200 lbs. pushing upward. There are two up forces in this picture. The stepladder pushes up on the left side of the plank, and the man pushes up on the right side of the plank. The painter stands in the exact center of the plank, so the man and the stepladder must exert the exact same upward force. That means that you need to divide the total up force by 2 in order to figure out how much weight the man on the ground must support: 200 lbs. ÷ 2 = 100 lbs. The answer is (B).

Remember, when you're solving a force problem, follow these steps.

- Make a list of the forces in each direction.
- Add together all the forces that point in the **same** direction.
- Make sure to set the totals of the forces that point in **opposite** directions equal to each other (i.e., be sure to set the total up force equal to the total down force, and the total right force equal to the total left force).
- Use this information to find the missing force. You can also eliminate answer choices using Process of Elimination.

Simple Machines

There are many situations in the modern world where it is difficult or impossible to complete a job with muscle power alone. Imagine a worker who has to lift an 800-pound crate onto a loading dock that's 6 feet above the ground. This crate far exceeds the weight that a normal person can lift. However, the worker can use a simple machine to make the task much easier. He could roll the crate up a ramp or lift it with a system of pulleys. In both cases, the force that the worker must exert in order to complete the job is reduced to a manageable fraction of the total weight of the crate.

It is often possible to solve a problem that involves a simple machine with the techniques that we just learned for force problems. Take a look at a few sample questions.

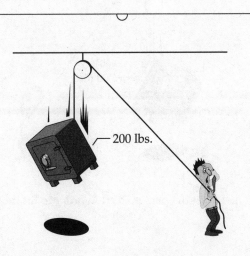

3. How much force must the person exert on the rope in order to lift the safe?

   A.   50 lbs.

   B.   100 lbs.

   C.   150 lbs.

   D.   200 lbs.

Here's How to Crack It

Take a look at the forces that act on the safe. Gravity pulls downward on the safe with 200 lbs. of force. The rope pulls upward on the safe. That's it; there are no other forces that act directly upon the safe. That means that the force of the rope must be 200 lbs., exactly equal to the force of gravity. How does this help us to figure out the force with which the person must yank on the rope? The answer is that the force that is transmitted through a rope must be the same everywhere. If the rope pulls up on the safe with 200 lbs., then it must also pull on the person with 200 lbs. of force. That means that the person must exert a force of 200 lbs. in order to lift the safe. The answer is (D).

You may have noticed that this pulley did not reduce the force needed to lift the safe. When you use a single pulley that does not move (for instance, a pulley that is attached to the ceiling), the force needed to lift the load does not change. The only advantage to be gained from this type of pulley arrangement is that you can change the direction of the force that you must apply. In the above example the pulley allows the person to pull downward on the rope. That means that he can use his own weight to help to lift the safe.

Now look at a pulley arrangement that really *does* reduce the force that is needed to lift a load:

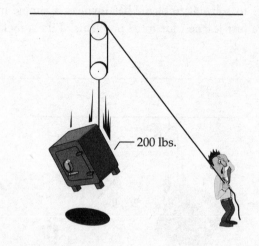

200 lbs.

4. How much force must the person exert in order to lift the safe?

A.   50 lbs.

B.   100 lbs.

C.   150 lbs.

D.   200 lbs.

Here's How to Crack It
Use the same technique to answer this question. There is one downward force in this problem: the 200-pound force of gravity. However, now there are two up forces, because the rope pulls upward on both sides of the pulley. Remember, the force transmitted through a rope is the same everywhere, so it must be the same on each side of the pulley. That means that the force in the rope is 200 lbs. ÷ 2 = 100 lbs. The rope transmits this same force back to the person, so he must pull with 100 lbs. of force in order to lift the safe. The answer is (B).

Mechanical Advantage

In the last problem we discovered that a system of two pulleys can multiply the force that is applied to a load by a factor of two. This multiplication of force is called "mechanical advantage." The mechanical advantage of a simple machine is equal to the amount that the applied force is multiplied by. For example

300 lbs.

5. The lever in the picture above provides a mechanical advantage of three. What is the minimum amount that the person must weigh in order to successfully lift the boulder?

   A. 100 lbs.

   B. 300 lbs.

   C. 900 lbs.

   D. It is impossible to lift the boulder in this fashion.

Here's How to Crack It

In this problem, it is stated that the mechanical advantage is 3. That means that the lever applies to the boulder a force equal to three times the person's weight. Since you would need to apply at least 300 lbs. to the boulder in order to lift it, the person must weigh at least 300 lbs. ÷ 3 = 100 lbs. The answer is (A).

Mechanical Disadvantage

So far you have learned that a simple machine can amplify a person's strength and allow him or her to lift a very heavy load. Alas, nothing in life is free, so along with mechanical advantage there must be a compensating disadvantage. The disadvantage is that the force must be applied over a larger distance. For example, take another look at the pulley arrangement in problem number 4. For every foot that the safe is lifted the rope must also move a foot on *both* sides of the pulley. This means that the person on the other end of the rope must pull two feet of rope for every one foot that the safe is lifted. The disadvantage always multiplies the distance by the same amount that the advantage multiplies the force. Fortunately for test takers, you can turn the mechanical disadvantage into a test-taking strategy...

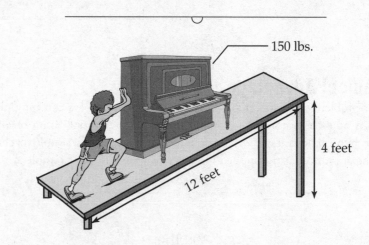

6. How much force is needed to push the piano up the ramp?

   A.   30 lbs.
   B.   50 lbs.
   C.   60 lbs.
   D.   100 lbs.

Here's How to Crack It

For this problem, you may have trouble using the force technique that you learned in the last section because the force that the person applies to the piano is not straight up. Therefore, you can't set it equal to the gravity, the downward force, which is the weight of the piano. It's much easier to look at the mechanical disadvantage instead. The purpose of the ramp is to lift the piano four feet above the ground. In order to travel four feet upward, the person must push the piano along twelve feet of ramp. This means that the mechanical disadvantage is three ($12 \div 4 = 3$). The disadvantage and the advantage are always the same number, so the person only needs to push with one-third of the weight of the piano in order to move it up the ramp. That means that the force needed is 150 lbs. $\div$ 3 = 50 lbs. The answer is (B).

Levers

A lever is a simple machine that utilizes a length of stiff material that is braced against an object that does not move in order to create mechanical advantage. The immovable object is called the "fulcrum." The mechanical advantage is the ratio of the distance from the fulcrum to the applied force over the distance from the fulcrum to the load. (Remember, you learned about ratios in Chapter 2.) If this sounds complicated, don't worry; we will look at several examples to be certain that you understand.

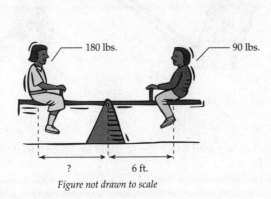

180 lbs.   90 lbs.

?   6 ft.

Figure not drawn to scale

7. At what distance from the fulcrum should the adult sit in order to perfectly balance the seesaw?

   A.   3 feet

   B.   4.5 feet

   C.   6 feet

   D.   9 feet

Here's How to Crack It

The seesaw in this problem acts like a lever. The fulcrum is the triangle that the seesaw is balanced on. The child is one-half the weight of the adult, so the lever needs to supply the child with a mechanical advantage of 2. The mechanical advantage is the distance from the fulcrum to the child (6 feet) divided by the distance from the fulcrum to the adult (unknown). You can write this as an equation: $6 \div ? = 2$. You can rearrange this equation so that the question mark is on the other side of the equal sign: $6 \div 2 = ?$. Six divided by 2 is 3, so the adult must sit three feet from the fulcrum in order to perfectly balance the seesaw. That's (A)!

> **Quick Tip!**
>
> To identify the fulcrum in a lever problem, look for the part of the lever that will never move. That's where the fulcrum is.

Take a look at another problem:

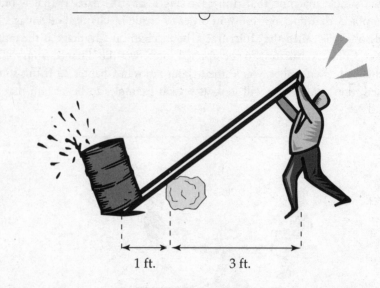

1 ft.   3 ft.

8. 90 lbs. of force is required to tip the barrel. How much force must the worker apply to the lever?

A.   10 lbs.

B.   30 lbs.

C.   45 lbs.

D.   60 lbs.

Here's How to Crack It

The mechanical advantage of this lever is the distance from the fulcrum to the worker (3 feet) divided by the distance from the fulcrum to the barrel (1 foot). Three divided by 1 is 3. The worker needs to apply one-third of 90 lbs. to his end of the lever in order to tip the barrel. One-third of 90 is 30, so the answer is (B).

Sometimes the load and the force are both on the same side of the fulcrum. Look at another problem to see how this works…

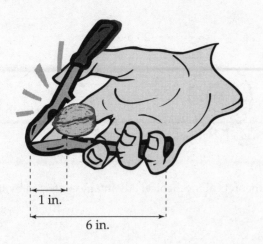

1 in.

6 in.

9. If the force required to crack a walnut without using any tool is 30 lbs., how much force must be applied to the nutcracker in the diagram in order to crack the walnut?

A. 5 lbs.

B. 10 lbs.

C. 30 lbs.

D. It's too tough a nut to crack.

Here's How to Crack It

To solve this problem, you must first locate the fulcrum. Remember, the fulcrum is the place where the lever does not move. In this case, it's at the hinge. The walnut is 1 inch from the hinge and the hand is 6 inches from the hinge. That means that the mechanical advantage is 6 ÷ 1 = 6. Apply one-sixth of 30 lbs. to the nutcracker in order to crack the walnut. Thirty divided by 6 is 5, so the answer is (A).

Gears

A gear is a wheel with "teeth" along its outside. There's a lot of variety in the shapes and sizes of gear teeth, but in the end they all do the same thing: turn other gears. To calculate the mechanical advantage of a set of gears, count the teeth on each gear. Divide the number of teeth on the gear that is being turned by the number of teeth on the gear that is doing the turning. That's the mechanical advantage. Often, the mechanical advantage for a gear is smaller than one.

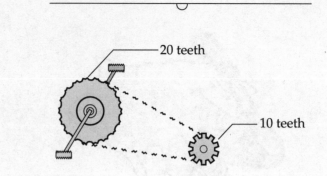

20 teeth

10 teeth

10. What is the theoretical mechanical advantage conferred by the gears of this bicycle?

A. $\frac{1}{2}$

B. 1

C. 2

D. There is no mechanical advantage; the gear system is just a convenient way to transmit muscle power into forward motion.

Here's How to Crack It

In this problem, the big gear is turning the small gear. Put the number of teeth on the small gear into the numerator (the top number) of the ratio and the number of teeth on the big gear into the denominator (the bottom number). That yields $\frac{10}{20}$, which reduces down to $\frac{1}{2}$. The answer is (A).

What is the point of using a gear that *increases* the amount of force that you put into it? Remember the compensating disadvantage that goes with mechanical advantage. A simple machine that increases force also reduces distance. In problem 4 you had to pull the rope 2 feet to lift the safe 1 foot. Well, when the mechanical advantage is less than one, the distance is increased. In the bicycle gear above, the small gear turns twice every time the big gear turns once. It's twice as hard to turn, but it goes twice as fast.

Here's another problem where you will need to count teeth...

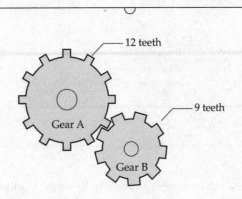

11. How many times will gear A turn if gear B turns 20 times?

    A.   9 times
    B.   12 times
    C.   15 times
    D.   20 times

Here's How to Crack It

The important concept here is that the teeth of gear A move through the teeth of gear B on a one-for-one basis. You can eliminate (D) immediately, because gear B will only move 9 teeth on gear A per rotation, and that is not enough to turn gear A all the way around. All of the other answer choices are smaller than the number of rotations for gear B, so you can't eliminate any of them yet. Twenty rotations of gear B move 20 × 9 = 180 teeth on gear A. Gear A rotates once for every 12 teeth moved, so if you divide 180 by 12, you will find the answer. Twelve goes into 180 15 times, so the answer is (C).

There are a few types of gear problems that don't force you to count teeth. For instance, you may need to figure out which direction a gear rotates in. Usually, you can solve a problem like this with two simple rules: When two gears touch, they rotate in opposite directions; when two gears are connected by a chain or a belt, they rotate in the same direction.

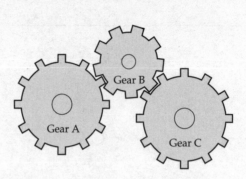

12. If gear A rotates clockwise, what direction does gear C rotate in?

    A. Clockwise
    B. Counterclockwise
    C. Gear C does not rotate.
    D. It is impossible for gear A to rotate clockwise.

Here's How to Crack It

Gear A turns gear B, which in turn will turn gear C, so (C) and (D) are incorrect. Gear A and B rotate in opposite directions, so B turns counterclockwise. B and C also rotate in opposite directions, so gear C has to rotate clockwise. That means that the answer is (A).

There are two more rules that you will need to remember when you tackle a gear problem (Actually, these rules apply to *anything* that rotates).

- Two points on the same gear or disk will always rotate at the same rate.
- A point near the outside of a disk will move with a faster linear speed than a point near the center of a disk.

Be careful here. If the question asks for *rate of rotation*, you need to use the first rule; if it asks use for the *speed of a point*, you need to use the second.

Here are a few examples:

13. Which point on the above bicycle wheel will move at the highest rate of rotation?

A. Point 1

B. Point 2

C. Point 3

D. They all move at the same rate of rotation.

Here's How to Crack It

This is a trick question. All three points are on the same disk, so they all move at the same rate of rotation. The answer is (D).

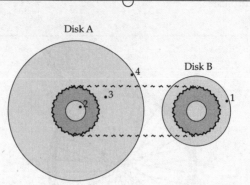

Disk A

Disk B

14. Disk B rotates in the clockwise direction at a constant rate. Which of the following is true?

A. Point 2 rotates in the clockwise direction and has a higher linear speed than point 1.

B. Point 3 rotates in the counterclockwise direction with the same linear speed as point 1.

C. Point 4 rotates in the clockwise direction with a higher linear speed than point 1.

D. Point 4 rotates in the counterclockwise direction with a higher linear speed than point 1.

Here's How to Crack It

There are a lot of details to sift through in this problem, so look for something simple to start with. The two disks—Disk A and Disk B—are connected with a chain, so they both have to rotate in the same direction. That means that all of the points move clockwise. You can immediately eliminate (B) and (D) because they give a counterclockwise rotation. At this point, you could guess and have a 50% chance of success! However, you can do better than that. The gears that turn these disks are the same size, so the two disks have to move at the same rate of rotation. That means that you can use the second of the two rules above to figure out the relationship between the linear speeds of points 1, 2, and 4. Point 2 is closer to the center of its disk than point 1 is, so it has to move more slowly. Point 4 is further away, so it moves more quickly. Choice (A) is incorrect, because it claims that 2 moves faster than 1. That leaves (C). Point 4 does indeed move more quickly than point 1.

Momentum

Momentum is a subject that most people understand without really knowing why. You already know what will happen if a huge truck collides head-on with a compact car: the car will be crushed, and the truck will continue to move straight ahead at almost the same speed that it had before the collision. You also know that if two football players of the same size and speed collide head-on they will both stop at the point of collision. And you know that a small bullet can knock down a large man. These examples all illustrate the concept of momentum.

Momentum is a combination of weight and speed. A bullet can knock a man down, even though it is very light, because it has a very high speed. The two football players had the same weight and speed, so they both stopped at the point of collision. The truck kept moving after the collision because it is much more massive than a compact car.

> **Definition of Momentum:**
>
> Technically, momentum is mass times velocity. For the ASVAB, just multiply the weight of the object by its speed and you'll have momentum. (Note: "weight times speed" is not actually the correct way to calculate momentum, but it will allow you to solve any momentum problem that you might encounter on the ASVAB, and that is all that we really care about here.)

Collision Problems

There are two types of problems where momentum is important. The first involves collisions. When two objects collide head on and stick together, they will both move in the direction that the object with the larger momentum was moving in before the collision. If they both have the same momentum, then they will stop. Here is an example.

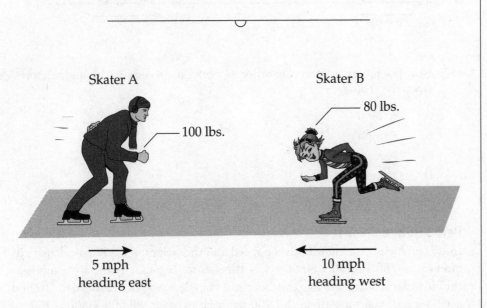

Skater A — 100 lbs.
5 mph
heading east

Skater B — 80 lbs.
10 mph
heading west

16. Skater A and B will collide and stick together. After the collision which of the following is true?

   A.   Both skaters stop at the point of impact.

   B.   The skaters will move to the east at a speed greater than 10 mph.

   C.   The skaters will move to the west at a speed less than 5 mph.

   D.   The skaters will move to the east at a speed less than 10 mph.

Here's How to Crack It

The first thing you need to do here is calculate the momentum of each skater. The momentum of skater A is 100 × 5 = 500. The momentum of skater B is 80 × 10 = 800. That means that skater B has a larger momentum. You can immediately eliminate (A), because the two skaters will only stop if they have the same momentum. You can also eliminate (C), because they will only move to the west if the momentum of skater A is larger than the momentum of skater B. Take a closer look at (B) and (D). You don't know how to calculate the speed of the skaters after the collision, but you *do* know that you need to exert a force on something in order to speed it up. There are no forces acting to the east on skater B, so there is no way that skater B will ever skate faster than 10 mph. That means that (B) is wrong, so the answer must be (D).

Try another one:

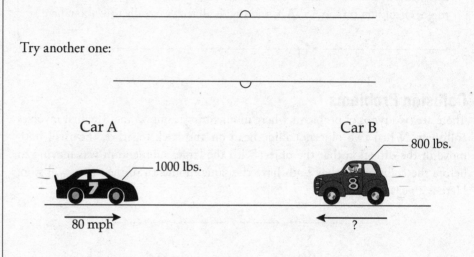

17. How fast must car B travel in order for both cars to come to a complete stop when they collide?

    A.   60 mph

    B.   80 mph

    C.   100 mph

    D.   120 mph

Here's How to Crack It

In this problem, you know both the speed and the weight of car A, so calculate its momentum: 80 × 1000 = 80,000. Car B needs to have exactly the same momentum in order to bring the two cars both to a complete stop in the collision. To find car B's speed, you must divide 80,000 by car B's weight. 80,000 ÷ 800 = 100, so car B has to go 100 mph. That's (C).

"Push Off" Problems

The second type of momentum problem features two objects starting from rest and then pushing off each other. This is the exact opposite of the case in which two objects collide and stop, so both objects need to have the same momentum after they push off. Here is an example:

18. The person dives out of the boat with a speed of 4 feet per second. What is the speed of the boat after the jump?

    A.   3 feet per second

    B.   4 feet per second

    C.   5 feet per second

    D.   8 feet per second

Here's How to Crack It

Both the boat and the person need to have the same momentum after the jump. The person has a speed of 4 and a weight of 150, so his momentum is 600. You know that the weight of the boat is 200, so the speed of the boat is 600 ÷ 200 = 3. That's (A).

Fluids and Pressure

A fluid is a substance that will automatically flow to take the shape of its container. Water and air are two common examples of fluids. Fluids are composed of many molecules that move in random directions and constantly bump into each other, the walls of their container, and any object that happens to be submerged within the fluid. The force that these countless collisions exert is called pressure. Pressure is the key to almost all fluid problems.

The technical definition of pressure is "force per area" or "force divided by area." The ASVAB will usually give you pressure in pounds per square inch (also known as "psi"). If you ever need to translate a pressure into a force, just multiply it by an area. Here is an example.

---

19. The water pressure surrounding a submarine is 100 psi. Its porthole is 10 square inches. What is the force on the porthole?

    A.   10 pounds

    B.   100 pounds

    C.   1000 pounds

    D.   The water exerts no force on the porthole.

Here's How to Crack It

A fluid will exert force on any object that is submerged within it, so get rid of (D). To find the force on the porthole, you need to multiply the pressure of the water by the area of the porthole. That is 100 psi × 10 square inches = 1000 lbs. The answer is (C).

Liquids and Pipes

The **flow rate** of a fluid through a pipe is the volume of liquid that passes through a cross section of the pipe in a certain amount of time. If you need to calculate the flow rate of a fluid, then you should multiply the velocity of the fluid by the cross-sectional area of the pipe. Often you will just need to compare the flow rate in two different pipes. Here are three rules to keep in mind when you compare flow rates.

- If two pipes have the same area, then the pipe carrying liquid with the greatest velocity (or pressure) will have the highest flow rate.
- If two pipes carry liquids with the same velocity, then the pipe with the greatest area will have the highest flow rate.
- A single pipe has the same flow rate from beginning to end, even if the area of the pipe changes.

Here is an example:

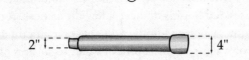

20. Water flows into the pipe from the left at a speed of 8 feet per second. What is the speed of the water as it leaves the pipe from the right?

    A.   1 foot per second

    B.   2 feet per second

    C.   4 feet per second

    D.   8 feet per second

Here's How to Crack It

You have a single pipe here, so the flow going into it must be the same as the flow going out of it. The problem gives you enough information to calculate the flow rate through the pipe, but that's a bit complicated, so use Process of Elimination to get rid of a few answers first. The pipe is bigger on the right side than it is on the left side, so that means that for the flow rate to remain the same, the water *must* slow down. Choice (D) gives the same velocity that the water began with, so eliminate it. The area of a pipe is proportional to the square of its radius. The pipe is twice as big on the right side as it is on the left side, so the area of the right side must be four times the area of the left side. The speed of the water needs to slow down by a factor of four to compensate, so the answer is (B).

The Pressure of a Liquid

Finally, let's talk about how the pressure of a liquid changes as it moves through a pipe. Take another look at the pipe in the last question. How do you think that the water pressure changes as the water moves from the thin part of the pipe to the thick part? Your intuition might tell you that the pressure is higher in the thin part of the pipe, because it is a "tighter squeeze" in there. Actually, that is incorrect; the pressure is lowest in the thin section of the pipe. This is because the speed of the water is high in the thin section of pipe and low in the thick section. Something has to slow the water down as it moves between the sections of pipe, and that something is pressure. Remember, pressure is the force that the molecules inside the fluid exert on everything that they come into contact with, including other parts of the water. As the water flows from the thin part of the pipe to the thick part, it encounters an increase in water pressure that slows it down.

Gases

A gas is a fluid, so it will obey all of the rules for fluids that we've already discussed. However, gases and liquids do have a few differences. A gas will expand to fill any available volume, whereas a liquid will always maintain a constant volume. For instance, a pint of water remains a pint of water regardless of whether it is in a large container or a small container. But a pint of a gas will expand to fill an entire room if you remove the lid of the container that holds it.

The ASVAB may ask you questions about the volume, pressure, or temperature of a gas under many different circumstances. Here is a list of rules that gases follow.

(1) If the volume of a gas increases, then its pressure will decrease (and vice versa).

(2) If the temperature of a gas increases, then its pressure will increase (and vice versa).

(3) If the amount of gas inside a container increases, then the pressure will increase.

(4) If a gas inside a container has a greater pressure than the air outside the container, the gas will apply a force to the inside of the container, causing it to expand (if the container is too weak to withstand the force). Likewise, if the pressure of the air outside the container is greater, the air will apply a force to the outside of the container, causing it to shrink (again, if the container is too weak to withstand the force). If the pressures inside and outside are the same, then the net force on the container is zero.

(5) A gas will flow from a region of high pressure into a region of low pressure. If there is no difference in pressure, then there will be no net movement of gas. That also means that if no gas is moving, then there must be no difference in pressure.

Take a look at a few problems:

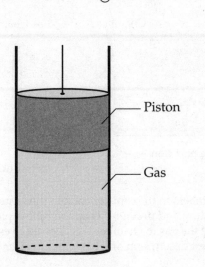

21. A spark ignites the gas within this cylinder. Which of the following is the best explanation of what happens next?

   A. The explosion increases the temperature of the gas. The increase in temperature causes the pressure to drop; and the piston moves inward.

   B. The temperature inside the cylinder is increased dramatically by the ignition of the gas, and this in turn increases the pressure of the gas. The increased pressure forces the piston outward.

   C. A reduction in the air pressure outside the piston causes the piston to move.

   D. The force of the explosion causes the piston to move outward.

Here's How to Crack It

Go through these options one at a time. Choice (A) claims that the pressure of the gas will be reduced after its temperature is increased. This violates rule number 2, so eliminate (A). Choice (B) says that the piston moves because the temperature of the gas increases the pressure inside the chamber. Rule number 2 states that the pressure of a gas will increase when its temperature increases, so this might be the correct answer. Choice (C) claims that the pressure outside the piston drops when the gas inside the piston ignites. This option is unlikely, because the spark inside the piston has no direct impact upon the air outside the piston. Discard (C). Choice (D) claims that the "force" of the explosion causes the piston to move outward. It is certainly true that the explosion creates a force that causes the piston to move, but this is not a very informative answer. Choice (B) provides a much more detailed explanation of what this force is. Since you are looking for the best explanation of what happens inside the cylinder after the ignition, choose (B).

Take a look at another problem.

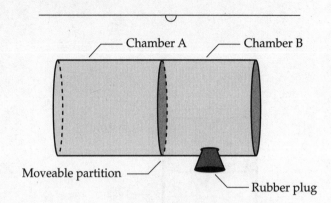

Chamber A   Chamber B

Moveable partition

Rubber plug

22. Initially, both chambers in the canister contain the same amount of gas at the same temperature and pressure. Then the rubber plug is temporarily removed, and half the gas in chamber B is allowed to escape. Which of the following is the best description of what happens after the plug is replaced?

A. The pressure of the gas in chamber B is reduced after the gas escapes. The partition will move to the right until the pressure in the two chambers equalizes.

B. The partition moves a little bit to the right. The pressure in the two chambers will not equalize because they no longer contain the same amount of gas.

C. The pressure drop in chamber B causes the partition to move to the right. As the gas in chamber A expands, both its pressure and its temperature are reduced. The partition will stop moving when the pressure in both chambers is the same.

D. The pressure drop in chamber B causes the partition to move to the right. As the gas in chamber A expands, both its pressure and its temperature are reduced. The partition will stop moving when the temperature in both chambers is the same.

Here's How to Crack It

Refer back to the list of rules for gases to solve this problem. Rule number 3 states that a gas will increase the size of its container as long as the pressure outside of the container is smaller than the pressure inside. This rule also says that there will be no expansion if the pressures are equal. Choice (B) claims that the partition will stop moving before the pressures equalize, so get rid of it. Choice (D) claims that the partition will stop moving when the temperatures in the two chambers are the same. This may or may not happen when the pressures are equal, so it does not have to be true. Eliminate (D). Choices (A) and (C) both state that the partition will move until the pressures in the two chambers are equal. The only difference between these two choices is that (C) claims that the temperature in chamber A will drop as the partition moves. Combine rules 1 and 2 to evaluate this extra information. According to rule 1, the pressure will drop as the gas expands. According to rule 2, the temperature will drop if the pressure drops. This implies that the temperature will drop when the gas expands. That means that (C) is better than (A), because it provides a more detailed and accurate description of what happens inside the chambers.

Chapter 9
Electronics
Information

INTRODUCTION TO ELECTRONICS INFORMATION

The Electronics Information section of the ASVAB asks questions about the construction and maintenance of simple electronic circuits. There is a fairly large variety in the types of questions you may see in this section because electricity is used in a wide array of situations throughout the modern world. In this chapter, we will cover the basic ideas on the subject. The Electronics Information section of the CAT-ASVAB has 16 questions, and you have 8 minutes to complete it. The MET-ASVAB and Student ASVAB have 20 questions, and you have 9 minutes to complete it.

A SIMPLE CIRCUIT: THE LIGHT BULB

One of the most common circuits in use today is the circuit that allows you to turn a light bulb on and off. Below is a simplified version of this circuit. In this section we'll talk about how this circuit works.

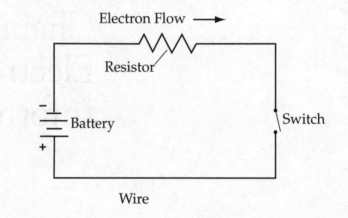

Current

When the switch is in the on position, a countless number of tiny charged particles called electrons flow through the wires of the circuit. This flow of charges is called **current.** Charges flow through a circuit very much like water flows through a river. When people talk about the "size" of a current, they are referring to the amount of charge that flows through a wire during one second. It's possible to have too much current flowing. You have probably had times in your life when you blew a fuse. That happened when the current flowing through a fuse exceeded a certain limit. A fuse is a device that is designed to break in that situation—when the current flowing through it exceeds a certain limit. When the fuse breaks, the current can no longer flow in the circuit. The current is generally measured in **amperes** (abbreviated as "amps" or as "A"). Current also has direction. Current always flows away from the negative terminal of a battery and toward the positive terminal (we'll talk about batteries later in this section). Finally, note that the most common symbol used to represent current in an equation is the letter "I."

Positive and Negative

Technically, electrons are negative particles, so they really flow away from low voltage and toward high voltage. However, circuit designers always pretend that the charged particles in the circuit are positive and that they move away from high voltage and toward low voltage. This practice began in the early days of circuit design when it was believed that the charges in the circuit really were positive. The circuit will work either way, so circuit designers (and ASVAB test writers) have chosen to stick with the accepted practice of pretending that the charges are positive.

AC/DC

Current comes in two different flavors, AC and DC. You need to know the difference between the two. The abbreviation AC means **alternating current.** An alternating current changes direction many times per second. The **frequency** of an AC current refers to the number of times the current changes direction back and forth per second.

DC means **direct current.** A direct current is a steady current that maintains the same direction, from negative to positive, and the same amperage as long as the circuit is operating. DC current is usually produced by a chemical reaction (such as in a battery) or by a special circuit called a **rectifier** that converts AC current into DC current.

Voltage

Electric current does not flow by itself. Something has to force it to flow—**voltage.** Voltage forces current to flow in a circuit similar to the way gravity forces water to flow in a river. Water flows downhill, away from high ground and toward low ground. Electric current flows away from high voltage and toward low voltage. Voltage is measured in units called **volts,** abbreviated simply as V. It is important to remember that volts are always measured as a difference in voltage between two places in a circuit. It makes no sense to say "the voltage at the filament of the bulb is 120 V" unless you specify another point in the circuit that has a voltage that is 120 V lower than the filament of the bulb. A more likely statement would be "the voltage *across* the filament of the bulb is 120 V." This means that the voltage on one side of the filament is 120 V higher than the voltage on the other side. This voltage difference is the force that impels the current to flow through the filament of the bulb. If both sides of the filament had an equal voltage above some other point in the circuit, there would be no voltage difference across the filament, and no current would flow through it. Current and voltage vary in proportion to each other. This means that a large voltage will cause a large current, and a small voltage will cause a small current. We will discuss this further in the next section.

Voltage is sometimes called **electromotive force** (Emf) because it is the force that causes charges to move through a circuit.

Resistance

When the current flows through the light bulb, the electrons bump into the filament of the bulb and lose energy. The electrical energy lost by the electrons becomes the light that is radiated from the bulb and the heat that causes the bulb to be hot. The characteristic of the filament that causes the electrons to lose energy is called "resistance." The current that flows through a circuit varies inversely with the amount of resistance found in the circuit. That means that if you take two circuits with the same voltage, the circuit with the larger resistance will have a smaller current than the circuit with the smaller resistance.

Resistance is measured in **ohms.** The abbreviation for ohms is the capital Greek letter omega (Ω). The letter R is used to represent resistance whenever it appears in an equation. Sometimes the sum of the resistances in all or part of a circuit is called the **load** on the circuit. In a circuit diagram, the symbol for a large resistance is a zigzag line (for instance, the zigzag in the light bulb on page 288).

All parts of a circuit possess some resistance to the flow of current, even the wires that connect the circuit together. However, wires are usually made of material that has a small resistance so that the current can be delivered to the parts of the circuit that need it (such as the filament of the light bulb) without losing any energy on the way. Materials that have a resistance low enough to be used in wires are called **conductors.** In a circuit diagram, conductors are drawn as straight lines.

Most conductors are metals. In the table below, we list several good electrical conductors. The numbers on this chart are not actually the resistance of the metals, because resistance depends on the shape and size of the metal as well as its composition. The details of how we got the numbers in this chart won't help you on the ASVAB, so for now just use them to compare the metals in the chart. A metal with a small number is a better conductor than a metal with a big number. You should try to memorize the order that the metals appear in the chart, but you won't have to memorize the numbers.

Substance	Specific Resistance (in microhms) at 20°C
Silver	1.6
Copper	1.7
Gold	2.4
Aluminum	2.82
Carbon	3.9
Tungston	5.5
Brass	7.0
Nichrome	10
Steel	15

Materials with extremely large resistance are also important in circuits. They are called **insulators.** Insulators are used to prevent currents from entering places where they are not wanted. All of the conductors in a circuit should be insulated from each other so that the currents they carry do not interfere with each other. It is also important to insulate wires so that people can safely handle them while a current flows through them. Plastic makes an excellent insulator because its resistance is high enough to stop all but the largest currents and because it is flexible and resilient enough to coat a wire. Below is a table of insulators. Try to memorize the order in which the insulators appear in the chart.

Good Insulations (starting with the most resistant)
Dry air
Glass
Mica
Ebonite
Guttan percha
Sealing wax
Silk
Dry paper
Porcelain
Oils
Slate

Some materials have a resistance that is too large to be used as a conductor, but too small to be used as an insulator. These materials are called semiconductors. These materials often have other unique characteristics that are very useful in a circuit. For instance, a diode is a device that is constructed from two different types of semiconductors. The properties of the two semiconductors work in such a way that the diode has a very large resistance if current flows in one direction and a very small resistance if current flows in the other direction. We will talk about some important applications of this device later. Many other useful electronic components are also constructed from semiconductors.

CIRCUIT ANALYSIS

Now that you know a bit about the terminology and materials that go into a circuit, you need to learn how to analyze a circuit. In this section we will talk about a few of the theories that circuit designers use to build their circuits (and ASVAB designers use to build their questions).

Ohm's Law

For this section of the ASVAB, you'll need to know the relationship between current, voltage, and resistance. This relationship is called **Ohm's Law.** Here it is.

$$V = IR$$

You can also remember Ohm's Law using this chart.

Remember, the *V* represents voltage, the *I* represents current, and the *R* represents resistance. As always, the voltage in this equation is the voltage difference between two places. In this case, it is the voltage difference across something that has a resistance. Ohm's Law states that the voltage across a resistance is equal to the resistance times the current that flows through it. If the resistance is increased, then the voltage must also increase in order to maintain the same current. Alternatively, if the resistance in a circuit is increased, then the current will be decreased (the more likely scenario). Here is a sample problem to illustrate this point.

1. A fuse rated at 1 amp is used to protect a 6-volt DC voltage supply. Which of the following is the minimum resistance that could be placed in series with the fuse in order to guarantee normal operation of the motor?

   A.   3 ohms
   B.   6 ohms
   C.   9 ohms
   D.   12 ohms

Here's How to Crack It

Use Ohm's Law to find out how much resistance the circuit has when the current is 1 amp. First, start with the equation.

$$V = IR$$

The question asks about resistance, so you need to get *R* alone on one side of the equation. So divide both sides by *I*. This yields

$$R = V/I$$

If *V* is 6 volts and *I* is 1 amp, then *R* must be 6.0 ohms. Does this mean that the answer is (B)? Not at all! Remember that 1 amp is the point at which the fuse will break. If the resistance of this circuit is exactly 6 ohms, then the current will reach 1 amp and the fuse will blow. That means that you need to choose a larger resistance, to get a current of less than 1 amp. The next largest resistance is 9 ohms, so the answer is (C).

Voltage drop

Ohm's Law tells you what the voltage difference is between the two sides of a device, if you know the value of its resistance and the value of the current through the device. This voltage difference is often called the **voltage drop** across the resistance.

POWER

Power is a measure of the amount of work that can be done in a certain amount of time. In an electric circuit, power is measured in **watts** (W). What we mean by "work" really depends upon the type of electric device that we are talking about. A light bulb with a large wattage rating will produce lots of light. A speaker with a large wattage rating can make a loud noise. Basically, more watts means more light, heat, sound, or more of whatever else it is that the device is supposed to produce. More watts also means a larger electric bill.

There are three equations that you can use to measure the power in a circuit.

$$P = IV$$
$$P = I^2R$$
$$P = V^2/R$$

All three of these equations will give the exact same answer, so you should pick the equation that has the variables you're given. Here is a sample question to illustrate the point.

2. How much current will a 60-watt light bulb draw if it is plugged into a 120-volt socket?

    A. 0.25 A
    B. 0.5 A
    C. 0.75 A
    D. 1.0 A

Here's How to Crack It

This problem involves power, voltage, and current, so the first equation is appropriate. Let's solve it for current.

$$I = P/V$$
$$I = 60/120$$
$$I = 0.5$$

The answer is (B).

Kirchoff's Laws

There are two Kirchoff's laws, one for voltage and one for current. We aren't going to go into detail about what these laws are, but we do want you to know what they are used for. Kirchoff's laws allow circuit designers to figure out how much current is going to go through each part of a circuit. Basically, if you know the resistance of each part of a circuit and you know the amount of voltage supplied to the circuit, then you can use Kirchoff's laws together with Ohm's Law to calculate the current in every wire in the circuit.

Note that in a simple circuit all you need is Ohm's Law. Kirchoff's laws are needed when you must analyze a circuit that has lots of complicated wiring. You will still use Ohm's Law in a complicated circuit, but you must supplement it with Kirchoff's laws in order to fully calculate the current in each part of the circuit. Ohm's Law is used in every circuit; Kirchoff's laws are generally just used in complicated circuits. Just knowing that information will help you on the ASVAB.

ELECTRONIC COMPONENTS

In this section we will talk about many of the common devices that are used to build circuits. We are going to tell you a little bit about how each device works and how it's used, and we'll show you the symbol that represents each device in a circuit schematic diagram. You'll need to memorize these symbols.

Ground

In a circuit, the **ground** is the portion of the circuit that is at the lowest voltage. In a safe circuit, the ground is at the same voltage as the outside world, so that no current will flow through a person who touches the container that houses the circuit. Often, the ground level of a circuit is established by connecting a wire to a metal rod that has been driven into the earth (hence the name "ground").

DC Voltage Source

The source of DC (direct current) voltage in a circuit is represented as parallel lines with one line longer than the other. The long line represents the positive terminal of the DC source; the short line represents the negative terminal.

AC Voltage Source

An AC (alternating current) voltage supply is represented as a circle that contains a wavy line. The symbol does not tell you which terminal is positive or negative because the direction of the current (and the voltage) changes several times per second with an AC source.

Resistors

The resistor is the most common device in almost any circuit. A resistor is a device built to have a specific resistance to the flow of current. A resistor looks like a small cylinder with a wire protruding from each end. Generally, the manufacturer will paint colored bands around the resistor in a special code that indicates the level of resistance of the resistor. In a circuit diagram, a resistor is depicted as a zigzag line.

A resistor has so many uses that it would be impossible to list them all here. Resistors can be used to regulate the amount of current in a circuit (remember Ohm's Law). They can also control the amount of voltage that reaches different parts of a circuit (Ohm's Law again). And resistors are commonly used in conjunction with **capacitors** to create timing circuits and bandpass filters (more on these circuits later).

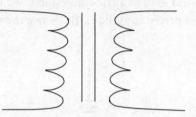

Often, there will be many resistors in a single circuit. The following schematic shows one of the basic ways to connect resistors in a circuit. This is called a **series** circuit. The same current goes through both resistors, so the total resistance that is faced by the current is the sum of the resistances of the two resistors. This relationship works for any number of resistors that are connected in series.

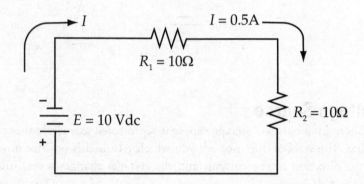

The next drawing shows another very common arrangement, called a **parallel** circuit. The current here has to split into two streams at point 1, so the current through the two resistors is not the same. However, the voltage across both resistors is the same. The current will take the path of least resistance through the circuit, so most of it will flow through the smaller resistor. Some of it will still flow through the larger resistor, however, so the total resistance of the parallel circuit will actually be less than the resistance of the smaller resistor. Below are the equations for adding series and parallel resistors.

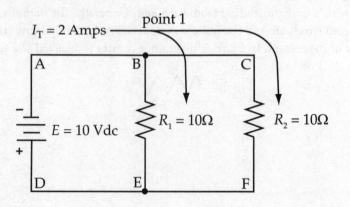

Series and Parallel Resistors

In **series**, add the resistance of each resistor to get the total resistance.

$$R = R_1 + R_2 + \dots R_n$$

In a **parallel** circuit, you take the *inverse* of each figure.

$$\frac{1}{R} = \frac{1}{R_1} + \frac{1}{R_2} + \dots \frac{1}{R_n}$$

You need to memorize both of these equations.

Capacitors

A capacitor is a device that stores charged particles. A capacitor is constructed from two pieces of metal that are placed very close to each other but not allowed to touch. When the two pieces of metal are connected to the positive and negative terminals of a battery, the negative charges are drained from the positive sheet and added to the negative sheet. The charge builds up until the voltage across the gap between the two sheets is the same as the voltage across the terminals of the battery. The amount of charge that the capacitor can store per volt is called its **capacitance.** Capacitance is measured in **farads** (f). The letter C is usually used to represent capacitors in equations. Here's the schematic symbol:

One application of the capacitor is in timing circuits, often called RC timing circuits. When a capacitor is placed in series with a resistor, the current that charges the capacitor must flow through the resistor first. The amount of time that it takes to charge or discharge the capacitor depends upon both the size of the capacitor and the size of the resistor. If the capacitance and resistance are chosen carefully, the time to charge can be tuned to any needed value. Some cars use RC timing circuits instead of a distributor to generate the timing for the spark plugs.

Another application of the capacitor is to block DC signals in an AC circuit. In a DC circuit, the capacitor will simply charge up until the voltage across the capacitor is equal to the voltage of the DC supply. The DC current will cease to flow once the capacitor has fully charged. An AC current switches directions repeatedly, so the capacitor will charge and discharge as the current changes directions. Thus, the AC current can pass through the capacitor, but the DC current cannot. Blocking capacitors of this sort are commonly used in stereos. If the blocking capacitor is connected in series to a resistor, then it will block low-frequency AC signals as well.

Inductors

An inductor is a wire that is coiled about some material. When a current flows through the inductor, a magnetic field is formed through the center of the coil. The magnetic field resists any change in the current through the coil, so the inductor acts like a resistor in an AC circuit, but does absolutely nothing in a DC circuit. The size of the resistance to current change in an inductor is called **inductance,** and it is measured in henrys (h). In an equation, the inductor is represented with an L. The schematic symbol for an inductor looks like a squiggly line.

One important application of the inductor is in the tuner of a radio. Here, an inductor is connected in parallel with a capacitor. The inductor in this circuit blocks high-frequency currents, but allows low-frequency currents to flow to ground. The capacitor, on the other hand, blocks low-frequency currents and allows high-frequency currents to flow to ground. There is a very small range of frequencies that cannot pass either the capacitor or the inductor, and these frequencies are passed through to the rest of the radio. The allowed frequency range depends upon the size of the capacitor and inductor. The inductance of the inductor can be changed to tune the radio.

Diodes

A diode is a device that has a very low resistance to current in one direction and a very high resistance to current in the other direction. Basically, a diode acts like a one-way door in a circuit. One application of this unusual property is in a **rectifier,** a device that transforms AC current into DC current. The diode is at the heart of this device, because it does not allow the AC current to pass when it travels in the wrong direction. The symbol for a diode is a triangle with a line through it. The arrow points in the direction that current is allowed to pass through the diode.

Transistors

The transistor is an odd-looking electronic component, because three wires protrude from it instead of two. This makes the transistor look like a tripod. The three legs are called the base, the collector, and the emitter. Very roughly, if the base is at a higher voltage than the collector, any current that flows into the base and out through the emitter is amplified by a fairly large amount. One of the applications of this property is in the amplifier of a radio. The transistor converts the faint radio waves received by the antenna into the large currents needed to drive loudspeakers.

ELECTRIC MOTORS

You may also come across a few questions that relate to electric motors. Below is a diagram of a basic electric motor that has appeared on the ASVAB before.

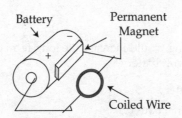

The basic principle illustrated above is that magnetism is used to repel a certain end of a coiled wire. A power source, in this case a battery, generates current through a coiled wire to create an **electromagnet.** Between the battery and coiled wire is a **permanent magnet** that attracts its opposite pole and repels its like pole.

Let's go back a step and review the basic principles of magnetism. Magnets will attract each other based on their polarity. The poles of a magnet are either "north" or "south." Opposite poles of a magnet will attract each other, and similar poles will repel each other as illustrated here:

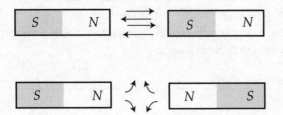

Now, let's turn back to the electric motor. The permanent magnet between the battery and the coiled wire will have one pole facing the coiled wire—let's say "north" for the sake of this example. The coiled wire will become an electromagnet once current is applied, but for it to have the ability to spin on its axis, the opposite pole of the electromagnet must be disabled in some way so that it cannot attract itself to the permanent magnet. If the similar poles of the two magnets are the only ones that are exposed, they will make every effort to repel one another, as you can see in the following illustration:

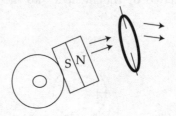

The force against the poles will cause the coil to spin. Once the coil makes a complete spin, the same force is reapplied, continuing the spinning cycle and creating an electric motor.

Take a look at a possible example from the test.

6. Which of the following would increase the long-term efficiency of a motor that operates on a 6-volt battery?

    A. Use a larger battery.
    B. Add an additional battery.
    C. Use a lithium battery instead of an alkaline.
    D. Replace the battery with an AC power supply.

Here's How to Crack It

The correct answer is (D). Choice (A) may not even have a positive effect at all, because a larger battery could have lower voltage which, in turn, could cause an inefficient spinning cycle. A lithium battery is not necessarily better for a motor than an alkaline; it has a different life and consumption cycle. So (C) is incorrect. Choice (B) isn't the best answer because while an additional battery will add short-term benefit, the long-term benefit will be very minimal. Choice (D) is correct because an AC power supply will provide a steady source of uninterruptible current, creating an efficient, long-term motor.

QUICK QUIZ 1

You can check your answers on the following page.

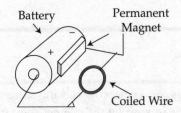

1. In the correctly working electric motor illustrated above, what would happen if the polarity was switched on the electromagnet?

    A. The motor would spin faster.

    B. The motor would spin slower.

    C. The motor would not be able to spin.

    D. The motor would spin in the opposite direction.

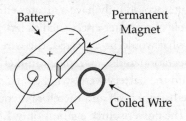

2. What would happen to the electric motor shown above if a stronger, permanent magnet was used?

    A. The motor would spin faster.

    B. The motor would spin slower.

    C. The coiled wire will bend due to the excess force.

    D. Nothing will happen.

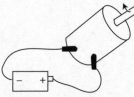

3. The motor shown above is running on a 1.5-volt D-cell battery. What could happen if the lead on the positive terminal is switched with the lead on the negative?

    A. The battery will begin to leak.

    B. The motor will burn up.

    C. The motor will spin in the opposite direction.

    D. None of the above.

ANSWERS TO QUICK QUIZ

Quick Quiz 1
Page 301

1. **C** If the magnet is correctly working as described, the polarity plays a vital role in keeping the magnet spinning. If the polarity were switched, the magnet would no longer help the coil spin but would instead attract it, thus effectively stopping all spinning motion. Therefore, (C) would be the correct answer.

2. **A** Remember that the permanent magnet is the one shown attached to the battery. If the magnet were larger and stronger, it would exert greater forces upon the coiled wire. The purpose of the magnet is to initiate and sustain the spinning motion, so a larger magnet would only have a greater effect. Spinning faster is one example of a greater effect such as (A). Choice (B) is the opposite of what would be expected; the wire bending is not a realistic expectation and is extremely unlikely.

3. **C** If the leads on the battery were switched, this would have no effect on the battery itself and therefore it could not leak, eliminating (A). The power source again is only 1.5 volts and a D-cell battery. This is not nearly enough to cause the motor to burn up, so (B) is incorrect. However, if the leads were switched between positive and negative on a simple motor, the motor will in fact spin in the opposite direction, which means (C) is the correct answer.

Chapter 10
Assembling
Objects

INTRODUCTION TO ASSEMBLING OBJECTS

The Assembling Objects section of the ASVAB is only given on the CAT-ASVAB. It does not appear on the Student version or the MET-site. Assembling Objects tests your ability to visualize and construct basic geometric shapes. The key to this is not to look for the correct answer at all; this will take more time and you are less likely to have success. Instead, look for the wrong answers by finding out key differences in the shapes. Usually you can eliminate one or two answers with just a quick look at the shape. Follow that with some fine tuning, and the Assembling Objects section will be a piece of cake.

The Basics

There are really just two kinds of problems that you will encounter. The first will give you a set of basic geometric figures and lines that are labeled at various points (*A, B, C,* etc.). The idea is to take the points, connect them together at their corresponding letters, and form a larger group of shapes and lines all connected together. The other type will show you a set of geometric shapes in which you must identify which of the correct answers is a single geometric shape composed of all the smaller ones.

Count the Shapes

This first and easiest thing you should do on any of these is count the total number of shapes. If the problem shows five triangles and it wants you to assemble them into a square, look at all of the assembled squares and make sure they contain only five triangles: no more, no less, and definitely no other shapes. This is the easiest way to eliminate a choice or two without really having to look at the figure in too much detail.

Check the Dots

When you are connecting shapes to each other with dots, make sure the correct number of things are connected to the correct number of dots. For example, if a line has 3 dots on it, exactly 3 things must be connected to that line. Don't even bother looking at what is connected to the dots yet. The next thing you need to do is to make sure the shapes connect to the right points on one another. If the problem shows a line with a dot at one end and a triangle with a dot in the middle of one of its sides, make sure the shapes connect at those points. This is probably the most clever and subtle trick the test writers use on the test. Remember, you want to eliminate as much as possible as quickly as possible.

Which Way Does It Go?

Once you have eliminated as many choices as you can, it is time to look at these shapes a little more closely. The most common trick that the test will use is to change the orientation of the shapes. Watch out for shapes that are a mirror image of what they are supposed to be. While the correct answer might be rotated, it will not be mirrored or inverted in any way.

Look at the Big Picture

Finally, don't forget to look at the final shapes as a whole. Remember that the shapes and lines are all drawn to scale. They will not get larger or smaller or change dimensions between the original question and the answer choices. The two-dimensional shapes can only rotate before fitting together. If you do come across a three-dimensional figure, the only other thing it can do in addition to rotating is spin around (any direction of a spin is okay). Don't worry, though; generally you will see nothing more difficult than a simple one-way rotation.

QUICK QUIZ

You can check your answers on the following page.

1.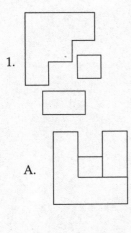

A.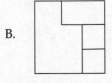

B.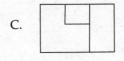

C.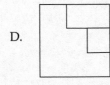

D.

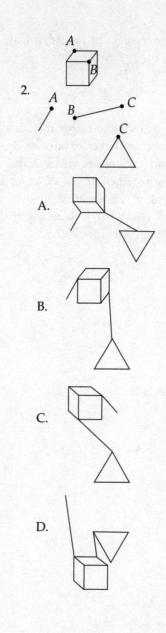

2.

A.

B.

C.

D.

ANSWERS TO QUICK QUIZ

Quick Quiz 1
Page 305

1. **D** Remember, it's all about eliminating. There are three shapes in the problem. Eliminate (B) right away because it has four shapes. From here you can go in any direction. The next one to get rid of could be (A) because it has the square and rectangle in it; it doesn't have the shape that looks like a set of stairs. Toss (C) next because even though it has the shapes, the one like stairs is one step too small. The correct answer is (D); it has the right shapes at the right size.

2. **C** Count the shapes. All the answers look good so far, so check the dots. Everything looks fine here except for (D). The problem shows the small line connecting to the triangle, not the long line. Choice (A) is almost right, but the triangle is connected along the edge, not at the point like it is supposed to be. Choice (B) doesn't work, either, because while all the shapes and lines appear to be oriented correctly, the lines are actually supposed to be on the same face of the cube—but (B) shows them on complete opposite sides of the cube. This leaves (C), which has the correct shapes and the correct placement.

Part III
ASVAB Practice Tests

Chapter 11
Practice Test 1
CAT-ASVAB

PART 1

General Science

Time: 8 Minutes—16 Questions

1. The nervous system of the body is primarily concerned with

   A. respiration
   B. reproduction
   C. communication
   D. circulation

2. Chromosomes play an important role in

   A. genetics
   B. nutrition
   C. energy transformation
   D. ionization

3. Organisms that sustain their life cycles by producing their own food are

   A. decomposers
   B. producers
   C. scavengers
   D. consumers

4. The mass of an atom is determined by its number of

   A. protons and electrons
   B. electrons and neutrons
   C. isotopes
   D. protons and neutrons

5. Heating food on a stove is an example of

   A. conduction
   B. convection
   C. refraction
   D. reflection

6. The current geologic time period is

   A. Paleozoic
   B. Mesozoic
   C. Cenozoic
   D. Precambrian

7. The largest planet in the solar system is

   A. Neptune
   B. Jupiter
   C. Earth
   D. Mars

8. The chromosomes line up in the middle of the cell during which stage of mitosis?

   A. Interphase
   B. Anaphase
   C. Telophase
   D. Metaphase

9. Which is an example of a bryophyte?

   A. Mushroom
   B. Fern
   C. Moss
   D. Tree

10. Which biome is being described here: Distinct hot and cold seasons and lots of rain. Trees lose their leaves in the winter and regrow them in the spring. A large variety of plants and animals are found.

    A. Tundra
    B. Deciduous forest
    C. Taiga
    D. Grassland

11. The outermost layer of the Earth is called the

    A. crust
    B. mantle
    C. core
    D. photosphere

12. A warm air mass overtaking a cold air mass is called a

    A. cold front
    B. stationary front
    C. warm front
    D. occluded front

GO ON TO THE NEXT PAGE.

13. A solar eclipse occurs when the

    A. Earth blocks the Sun's light
    B. Sun blocks the Moon
    C. Moon moves behind the Sun
    D. Moon blocks the Sun's light

14. Pepsin is found in the

    A. muscles
    B. stomach
    C. large intestine
    D. spinal cord

15. A person who can donate blood to anybody has

    A. type O blood
    B. type AB blood
    C. sickle cell anemia
    D. red blood cells

16. A severe deficiency in which of these vitamins can lead to rickets?

    A. Vitamin B_1
    B. Vitamin C
    C. Vitamin D
    D. Vitamin K

STOP!
IF YOU FINISH BEFORE THE TIME IS UP, YOU MAY
CHECK OVER YOUR WORK ON THIS PART ONLY.

PART 2

Arithmetic Reasoning

Time: 39 Minutes—16 Questions

1. Nelly buys a sweater that normally costs $60. It is on sale for 20% off. How much does she end up paying?

    A. $40
    B. $43
    C. $48
    D. $50

2. Mrs. Abbott bought 3 pounds, 8 ounces of hamburger for $3.43. What is the cost of 1 pound of hamburger?

    A. $0.98
    B. $0.99
    C. $1.00
    D. $1.02

3. The town of Orionville loves pets. Every family owns either a dog or a cat. If the ratio of dogs to cats is 4 : 6 and there are 100 pets total in the town, how many dogs and cats are there?

    A. 30 dogs, 70 cats
    B. 40 dogs, 60 cats
    C. 50 dogs, 50 cats
    D. 60 dogs, 40 cats

4. Tommy is selling chocolate bars for $1.00 and bags of jellybeans for $1.25. If he sold 40 bags of jellybeans and collected $70.00 total, how many chocolate bars did he sell?

    A. 24
    B. 28
    C. 31
    D. 32

5. Gladys opened a savings account 10 years ago with $100. The account earned 4% annually on the original $100 only. She has not deposited or withdrawn any money since opening the account. How much money is in the account now?

    A. $100
    B. $140
    C. $148
    D. $400

6. Alice can knit a scarf in 2 hours and 30 minutes. How many scarves can she knit in 17 hours and 30 minutes?

    A. 4
    B. 5
    C. 6
    D. 7

7. If $x = 7$, then $x^2 + 4x - 6 =$

    A. 64
    B. 67
    C. 71
    D. 89

8. James bought a stereo that was priced at $500. He paid 20% up front, and the remaining balance was paid in 8 equal payments of $60 each. How much more than the original price did he pay?

    A. $60
    B. $70
    C. $80
    D. $480

9. $\sqrt{64}$

    A. 5
    B. 9
    C. 7
    D. 8

10. Jack bought a coat for $275. Three days later Rob bought the same coat with a 20% discount. How much more did Jack pay for the coat than Rob?

    A. $40
    B. $55
    C. $120
    D. $220

GO ON TO THE NEXT PAGE.

11. When 120 is divided by a certain number, the result has a remainder of 1. What is that number?

   A. 5
   B. 6
   C. 7
   D. 9

12. A man drove 32 miles of a 47-mile trip with his left turn signal on. On what percentage of the trip did he not have his turn signal on?

   A. 32%
   B. 47%
   C. 50%
   D. 68%

13. Jim mowed 33 lawns this week. If his mower uses 0.8 gallons of gas per lawn, how many gallons of gas did he use this week?

   A. 24.4
   B. 26.4
   C. 32.4
   D. 41.2

14. What is the value of x in this equation: $\frac{x}{4} = 24$?

   A. 64
   B. 72
   C. 88
   D. 96

15. Chris is selling hats for $5 and T-shirts for $8. If he sold 35 T-shirts and collected $355 total, how many hats did he sell?

   A. 13
   B. 15
   C. 17
   D. 19

16. Subtract $4x^3 + 2x^2 + 5$ from $12x^3 + 7x^2 - 9$.

   A. $-8x^3 + 5x^2 - 4$
   B. $-8x^3 + 5x^2 - 14$
   C. $8x^3 - 5x^2 - 14$
   D. $8x^3 + 5x^2 - 14$

STOP!
IF YOU FINISH BEFORE THE TIME IS UP, YOU MAY
CHECK OVER YOUR WORK ON THIS PART ONLY.

PART 3

Word Knowledge

Time: 8 Minutes—16 Questions

1. <u>Accuse</u> most nearly means

   A. invite
   B. blame
   C. endure
   D. embitter

2. The <u>unscrupulous</u> politician won the election to the surprise of many in his political party.

   A. popular
   B. wealthy
   C. unpredictable
   D. immoral

3. <u>Prominent</u> most nearly means

   A. productive
   B. popular
   C. noticeable
   D. powerful

4. <u>Conclusive</u> most nearly means

   A. final
   B. inactive
   C. beginning
   D. secure

5. To <u>endure</u> most nearly means

   A. to forgo
   B. to undergo
   C. to include
   D. to hinder

6. He was filled with <u>overwhelming</u> joy.

   A. delusional
   B. continuous
   C. overpowering
   D. fascinating

7. The harvest was <u>abundant</u>.

   A. late
   B. plentiful
   C. destroyed
   D. healthy

8. <u>Chagrin</u> most nearly means

   A. disappointment
   B. deception
   C. impudent
   D. beneficial

9. <u>Anthology</u> most nearly means

   A. ancient
   B. repentant
   C. collection
   D. format

10. To <u>dilute</u> most nearly means

    A. to strengthen
    B. to prevent
    C. to change
    D. to weaken

11. The <u>wretched</u> woman tried to hide her tears.

    A. poor
    B. miserable
    C. exhausted
    D. terrified

12. The child was very <u>precocious</u> for her age.

    A. precious
    B. skilled
    C. advanced
    D. slow

GO ON TO THE NEXT PAGE.

13. To <u>utilize</u> most nearly means

    A.   to make use of
    B.   to build
    C.   to take apart
    D.   to create

14. To <u>chastise</u> most nearly means

    A.   to donate
    B.   to remove
    C.   to scorn
    D.   to punish

15. The attorney was very <u>cynical</u>.

    A.   distrustful
    B.   argumentative
    C.   expensive
    D.   rude

16. The <u>feud</u> between the two families goes back 200 years.

    A.   arrangement
    B.   dispute
    C.   contract
    D.   competition

STOP!
IF YOU FINISH BEFORE THE TIME IS UP, YOU MAY
CHECK OVER YOUR WORK ON THIS PART ONLY.

PART 4

Paragraph Comprehension

Time: 22 Minutes—11 Questions

1. Franklin is widely regarded as the first person to realize that lightning was made of electrically charged air. As a way of testing his theory, he attempted to discover whether lightning would pass through a metal object. To show this, he used a kite to raise a key into the air on a stormy night. From this experiment, Franklin realized that this electricity could be guided to the ground by a metal wire or rod, thereby protecting houses, people, and ships from being hurt.

One of Franklin's discoveries was

A. how to protect houses from lightning
B. the battery
C. the electric generator
D. a hydroelectric dam

2. One way to measure sound is by its frequency, which is the number of complete cycles of a sound wave within one second. One cycle per second is called 1 hertz. Human ears can detect sounds from about 20 hertz (the lowest sound) to 20,000 hertz (the highest sound). Below 20 hertz, humans feel only the vibration of the sound. Above 20,000 hertz, they can't hear the sound at all.

Which of the following can be inferred about a sound wave of 10 hertz?

A. A human could not hear it, but a dog could.
B. A human could hear it only with a hearing aid.
C. A human could not hear it, but would feel the vibration.
D. A human could not hear it or feel the vibration.

3. Krakatau, an island located in the Sundra Strait, disappeared on August 27, 1883. It was destroyed by a series of powerful volcanic eruptions. The most violent blew upward with an estimated force of 100–150 megatons of TNT. The sound of the explosion traveled around the world, reaching the opposite end of the Earth near Bogota, Colombia, whereupon it bounced back to Krakatau and then back and forth for seven passes over the Earth's surface. The sounds, resembling the distant cannonade of a ship in distress, carried southward across Australia to Perth, northward to Singapore, and westward to Rodriques Island in the Indian Ocean. This was the longest recorded distance traveled by any airborne sound in history.

The author mentions "the distant cannonade of a ship in distress" in order to

A. describe a ship damaged by a volcanic eruption
B. show that sound travels very quickly over water
C. help illustrate the sound made by the Krakatau eruption
D. illustrate the distance traveled by the volcano's heat wave

4. The Roman Empire was an autocracy in which power was held by one man—the emperor. Augustus ruled from 27 B.C. to 14 A.D.; he brought about fairer taxation and a civil service. This so-called Augustan Age was the start of 200 years of stability, peace, and progress called the *Pax Romana*.

According to the passage, the Augustan Age

A. lasted 200 years
B. brought about a civil service
C. was a democracy
D. ended the *Pax Romana*

GO ON TO THE NEXT PAGE.

5. Blood is made up of two main elements: (1) plasma, and (2) the solid components of blood—red blood cells, white cells, and platelets (important for forming blood clots). If a patient has lost a lot of blood, the patient will probably need a transfusion of "whole blood," which induces red blood cells and plasma. However, sometimes the patient only needs an increase in the volume of liquid in the bloodstream, in which case plasma alone can be substituted. A person must be tested for blood type before certain kinds of transfusions because of differences in the way red blood cells react to each other.

When would it be necessary to test a patient for blood type?

A. For whole blood transfusions only
B. For plasma transfusions only
C. For both plasma and whole blood transfusions
D. If the patient requested it

6. Most seeds will germinate when they have moisture, oxygen, and the right temperature, but different seeds need differing proportions of each of these ingredients. Most seeds require a temperature of between 15 degrees and 27 degrees centigrade to germinate, although some seeds, such as the maple, can germinate in far colder climates, and some other seeds, such as corn, require warmer temperatures.

Based on the information above, which of the following is most likely true?

A. Maple seeds can germinate in any temperature.
B. Corn is difficult to grow.
C. Oxygen is not necessary for germination.
D. There are some seeds that do not require a temperature between 15 and 27 degrees for germination.

7. Louis Pasteur, after spending many hours looking through a microscope, discovered that germs could reproduce very rapidly and be very dangerous to humans. This led him to conclude that doctors—who, up until that time, did not always wash their hands or their instruments—were spreading disease and needed to sterilize their equipment and scrub their hands. People began, for the first time, to use antiseptics, and this helped to greatly reduce the number of infections in hospitals.

It can be inferred from the paragraph that an antiseptic is

A. something that kills germs
B. a machine used to heat milk
C. a kind of bacteria
D. a kind of microscope

8. Passive protection is a method by which organisms protect themselves from predators, not by fighting, but by their appearance, smell, or sound. Protective resemblance is one type of passive protection in which an animal's coloring mimics the natural environment, acting as a kind of camouflage. Protective mimicry is another type of passive protection in which a defenseless organism resembles a more powerful organism. Another interesting example of passive protection is the Monarch butterfly, which smells and tastes so bad to other organisms that virtually no other animal or insect will eat it.

The Monarch butterfly is an example of what?

A. An organism that defends itself using protective resemblance
B. An organism that defends itself using protective mimicry
C. An organism that defends itself using passive protection
D. An organism that changes its appearance for protection

GO ON TO THE NEXT PAGE.

9. Coniferous forests grow in colder climates and show little change throughout the year. Rain forests, which tend to grow in tropical climates, get lots of rain and tend to grow year-round. Deciduous forests grow in temperate regions, undergoing seasonal changes each year.

Which of the following statements are true?

   I.   Rain forests tend to grow year-round.
   II. Seasonal changes vary from year to year in deciduous forests.
   III. Coniferous forests are found in colder climates.
   A.   I only
   B.   II only
   C.   II and III only
   D.   I and III only

10. An experiment was undertaken by a scientist to see if men will go bald if exposed to a particular chemical compound. A group of 1000 adult men over the age of 30 were given this compound, and it was found that 60 percent of the men eventually did go bald. From this, the scientist concluded that the compound causes baldness in men.

What can be inferred from the paragraph above?

   A.   The compound does not cause baldness in women.
   B.   Of the 1000 men in the study, more of them eventually went bald than did not.
   C.   Men that are not exposed to this chemical compound probably will not go bald.
   D.   The chemical compound should be studied further to explain why it causes baldness.

11. For years, scientists have debated whether the archaeopteryx, a creature that lived 150 million years ago, was an early species of bird or a dinosaur. Paleontologists argue that the archaeopteryx was a dinosaur that spent most of its time on the ground. Its feathers and wings were of only limited use, they say, and could not sustain flight. Ornithologists, on the other hand, believe that the archaeopteryx was first and foremost a bird. As evidence, they point to fossil remains of the creature that show its claws were curved so that it could perch on tree limbs. Curved claws would have prevented the animal from walking or running quickly on the ground.

Scientists' theories about the archaeopteryx are based on

   A.   studies of the creature in its native habitat
   B.   examinations of fossilized remains
   C.   studies of modern descendants of the archaeopteryx
   D.   old written records

STOP!
IF YOU FINISH BEFORE THE TIME IS UP, YOU MAY
CHECK OVER YOUR WORK ON THIS PART ONLY.

PART 5

Mathematics Knowledge

Time: 20 Minutes—16 Questions

1. What is the value of $x^2 + 4x - 3xy + 2y^2$ if $x = 3$ and $y = -4$?

   A. 17
   B. 89
   C. 121
   D. −121

2. If p pieces of candy cost c cents, 10 pieces of candy will cost

   A. $\dfrac{pc}{10}$ cents

   B. $\dfrac{10c}{p}$ cents

   C. $10pc$ cents

   D. $\dfrac{10p}{c}$ cents

3. If the lengths of the sides of a rectangular plot of land with an area of 12 square feet are doubled, what is the new area of the plot in square feet?

   A. 24
   B. 36
   C. 48
   D. 60

4. A drawing of an orchard has a scale of 1 inch to 25 feet. On the drawing, how far apart are the grape vines from the apple trees if the scale is $2\dfrac{1}{2}$ inches?

   A. 60 feet

   B. $61\dfrac{1}{2}$ feet

   C. $62\dfrac{1}{2}$ feet

   D. 65 feet

5. The formula for converting temperature from Celsius to Fahrenheit is $C = \dfrac{5}{9}(F - 32)$. If the temperature in Celsius is 12 degrees, what is the temperature in Fahrenheit?

   A. 38.7 degrees
   B. 53.6 degrees
   C. 65.4 degrees
   D. 72.1 degrees

6. Vicky, Roger, and Adam want to buy a $90 radio. If Roger agrees to pay twice as much as Adam, and Vicky agrees to pay three times as much as Roger, how much must Roger pay?

   A. $10
   B. $20
   C. $30
   D. $40

7.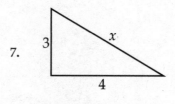

What is the length of x?

   A. 3
   B. 4
   C. 5
   D. 6

GO ON TO THE NEXT PAGE.

8. A statue in the shape of a right triangle has a height of 7 meters, a base of 24 meters, and a hypotenuse of 25 meters. A sculptor is commissioned to make a replica of the statue. If the new hypotenuse is 13 meters long, how long is the new base?

   A. 12
   B. $12\frac{12}{25}$
   C. 13
   D. 30

9. Beth is two years older than Debbie and four years younger than Marnie. If Debbie is d years old, how old is Marnie, in terms of d?

   A. $2d + 4$
   B. $d + 2$
   C. $d + 4$
   D. $d + 6$

10. If rice costs r cents per kilogram, how many kilograms may be bought for $5?

    A. $\dfrac{50}{r}$
    B. $\dfrac{5}{r}$
    C. $\dfrac{r}{500}$
    D. $500r$

11. Two less than a certain number is one-third of that number. What is the number?

    A. 1
    B. 3
    C. 6
    D. 8

12. A carpenter builds a hexagon-shaped table. If he puts a leg at each corner, how many legs does he need?

    A. 3
    B. 4
    C. 5
    D. 6

13. A right triangle has an angle of 25 degrees. How big are the other two angles?

    A. 25 degrees and 25 degrees
    B. 30 degrees and 60 degrees
    C. 45 degrees and 90 degrees
    D. 65 degrees and 90 degrees

14. A circle has a diameter of 7 inches. What is its area?

    A. 49π inches
    B. 25π inches
    C. 12.25π inches
    D. 3.5π inches

15. Solve for y: $11y + (2)^3 = -5y + (2)^4$

    A. $y = 0.5$
    B. $y = -0.5$
    C. $y = 1.2$
    D. $y = 2$

16. Jim has built a larger pool than his neighbor Steve. Steve's pool is 9 feet deep, 15 feet long, and 10 feet wide. Jim's pool is 12 feet deep, 20 feet long, and 12 feet wide. What is the difference in volumes between these two pools?

    A. 10 cubic feet
    B. 1350 cubic feet
    C. 1530 cubic feet
    D. 4230 cubic feet

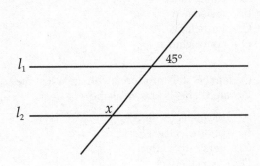

STOP!
IF YOU FINISH BEFORE THE TIME IS UP, YOU MAY
CHECK OVER YOUR WORK ON THIS PART ONLY.

PART 6

Electronics Information

Time: 9 Minutes—16 Questions

1. "Hot" wires may be colored

   A. white
   B. green
   C. gray
   D. black

2. Which of the following is the best insulator?

   A. Porcelain
   B. Sea water
   C. Copper
   D. Silver

3. How many watts of power are delivered by a 120 V generator that supplies 10 A?

   A. 110 W
   B. 130 W
   C. 500 W
   D. 1200 W

4. The ability of a conductor to induce voltage in itself when the current changes is its

   A. capacitance
   B. resistance
   C. inductance
   D. conductance

5. Certain crystals produce a voltage when they are vibrated. This is known as the

   A. piezoelectric effect
   B. photoelectric effect
   C. generative effect
   D. coaxial effect

6. A good substance for conducting electricity is

   A. copper
   B. rubber
   C. iron
   D. plastic

7. A micrometer would be used to measure a wire's

   A. length
   B. conductivity
   C. voltage
   D. diameter

8. Resistance is measured in

   A. ohms
   B. amps
   C. watts
   D. farads

9. How much current will a 30-watt light bulb draw if it is plugged into a 120-volt socket?

   A. 0.25 A
   B. 0.5 A
   C. 0.75 A
   D. 1.0 A

10. The most commonly used law for solving problems involving voltage, current, and resistance is

    A. Kirchoff's Law
    B. Ohm's Law
    C. Henry's Law
    D. Faraday's Law

11. When an accidental connection is made between two hot wires, the result is

    A. a grounded circuit
    B. a short circuit
    C. a hot circuit
    D. a faulty circuit

12. The frequency of current alternations is measured in

    A. farads
    B. watts
    C. hertz
    D. amperes

GO ON TO THE NEXT PAGE.

13. It's important when soldering to

    A. work in a quiet environment
    B. work in a perfectly level environment
    C. work in a cool environment
    D. work in a well-ventilated environment

14. A diode has low resistance to current in one direction and

    A. negative resistance to current in the other direction
    B. no resistance to current in the other direction
    C. low resistance to current in the other direction
    D. high resistance to current in the other direction

15. Power is equal to voltage times

    A. resistance
    B. capacitance
    C. current
    D. frequency

16. A device that provides a visual representation of variations in voltage or current is

    A. an oscilloscope
    B. a frequency counter
    C. a signal generator
    D. a logic probe

STOP!
IF YOU FINISH BEFORE THE TIME IS UP, YOU MAY
CHECK OVER YOUR WORK ON THIS PART ONLY.

PART 7

Auto and Shop Information

Time: 13 Minutes—22 Questions

1. All of the following are parts found in a manual transmission EXCEPT:

   A. the flywheel
   B. the drive shaft
   C. the rotors
   D. the clutch plate

2. The fuel pump moves fuel from the gas tank to

   A. the intake valve
   B. the intake manifold
   C. the catalytic converter
   D. the fuel injector

3. Which of the following could result from a faulty voltage regulator?

   A. The electric polarity can switch
   B. The battery can become overcharged
   C. The distributor will malfunction
   D. The battery will completely discharge

4. The temperature gauge on the dash shows the engine is beginning to overheat. The problem could be

   A. too much oil
   B. a rich fuel/air mixture
   C. a broken water pump belt
   D. a malfunctioning alternator

5. Most automobiles run on which of the following cycles?

   A. The two-stroke cycle
   B. The four-stroke cycle
   C. The diesel cycle
   D. The gasoline cycle

6. The oil pressure indicator in a car operating under normal conditions suddenly drops and blue smoke comes out the tail pipe. The cause of this is probably

   A. debris in the oil
   B. not enough oil
   C. too much oil
   D. a blown head gasket

7. The most likely symptom of the water pump failing is

   A. the engine overheating
   B. water entering the combustion chamber
   C. the alternator failing to charge the battery
   D. vapor lock

8. The torque converter contains all the following except the

   A. rotor
   B. stator
   C. turbine
   D. pump

9. Vehicles can stall for all of the following reasons EXCEPT:

   A. vapor lock
   B. worn clutch plate
   C. timing belt failure
   D. stuck piston

10. None of the following have gear-like teeth except the

    A. timing belt
    B. fan belt
    C. cams
    D. rocker arm

11. Pistons are always made smaller than the cylinder to

    A. allow enough room for the piston rings
    B. allow vapors from the combustion to slip by the piston
    C. give the car more power
    D. allow the piston to expand when heated and not jam in the cylinder

GO ON TO THE NEXT PAGE.

12. To enlarge the diameter of an existing fastener hole,

    A. an expansion bolt should be used
    B. a twist drill should be used
    C. a hacksaw should be used
    D. a reamer should be used

13. The kerf of a saw refers to the

    A. shape of the handle
    B. total width that the teeth will cut
    C. angle the teeth are bent to
    D. number of teeth per inch on the blade

14. The tool shown above is a(n)

    A. monkey wrench
    B. pipe wrench
    C. Allen wrench
    D. crescent wrench

15. The tool shown above is used to

    A. cut the tops off of nails
    B. countersink holes
    C. smooth and flatten wood
    D. clamp down on wood while cutting

16. The tool above is a

    A. hacksaw
    B. backsaw
    C. coping saw
    D. carpenters saw

17. The backsaw is used primarily to cut

    A. complex curves in wood
    B. with the grain of wood
    C. across the grain of wood
    D. sheetrock

18. What should be put in old nail holes in walls before painting?

    A. Putty
    B. Caulk
    C. Cement
    D. Drywall dust

19. The tool shown above

    A. is a pipe cutter
    B. is a C clamp
    C. is a vise
    D. are calipers

GO ON TO THE NEXT PAGE.

20. The tool shown above is a

    A.   twist drill bit
    B.   reamer
    C.   countersink bit
    D.   punch

21. A rubber or wooden mallet is used with a chisel

    A.   to keep the chisel from slipping
    B.   to transfer more energy to the tip
    C.   to protect the worker's hands
    D.   to protect the chisel

22. Machine screws are used primarily in

    A.   pre-threaded holes in metal
    B.   attaching joists to the foundation
    C.   attaching saw blades to the handle
    D.   power drills

STOP!
IF YOU FINISH BEFORE THE TIME IS UP, YOU MAY
CHECK OVER YOUR WORK ON THIS PART ONLY.

PART 8

Mechanical Comprehension

Time: 19 Minutes—16 Questions

1. A boy kicks a football into the air. The football is moving most slowly

   A. just after it leaves the boy's foot
   B. at the height of its trajectory
   C. just before it hits the ground
   D. Not enough information is available.

2. 32 degrees Fahrenheit is equal to how many degrees Celsius?

   A. 212
   B. 100
   C. 64
   D. 0

3. Gear 1, which has 20 teeth, is turning gear 2, which has 30 teeth. If Gear 1 makes 6 revolutions, how many will Gear 2 make?

   A. 2
   B. 4
   C. 6
   D. 12

4. The ropes attached to the girder can support a maximum of 500 lbs. without snapping. What is the maximum weight that the girder can be before the ropes snap?

   A. 250 lbs.
   B. 500 lbs.
   C. 1000 lbs.
   D. 2000 lbs.

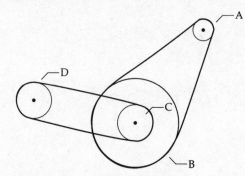

5. Which pulley turns the fastest?

   A. A
   B. B
   C. C
   D. D

6. The lever in the above picture provides a mechanical advantage of 3. What is the minimum amount the person must weigh in order to lift the boulder?

   A. 100 lbs.
   B. 200 lbs.
   C. 300 lbs.
   D. 600 lbs.

GO ON TO THE NEXT PAGE.

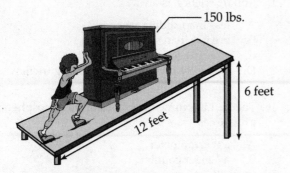

150 lbs.

6 feet

12 feet

7. How much force is needed to push the piano up the ramp?

A. 50 lbs.
B. 75 lbs.
C. 150 lbs.
D. 300 lbs.

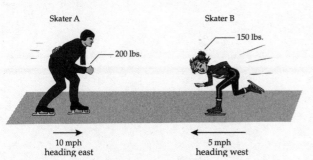

Skater A

Skater B

200 lbs.

150 lbs.

10 mph
heading east

5 mph
heading west

8. Skater A and B collide and stick together. After the collision, which of the following is true?

A. Both skaters stop at the point of impact.
B. The skaters will move to the west at a speed of less than 10 miles per hour.
C. The skaters will move to the east at a speed of greater than 10 miles per hour.
D. The skaters will move to the east at a speed of less than 5 miles per hour.

9. If all of the following objects are at the same temperature, which will feel the coldest?

A. A steel knife
B. A rubber tire
C. A wooden chair
D. A plastic fork

10. The speed of a falling object increases due to gravity at a rate of

A. 3.2 meters per second squared
B. 4.5 meters per second squared
C. 9.8 meters per second squared
D. 13.1 meters per second squared

11. If water is flowing into a lake at a rate of 120 gallons an hour and flowing out of the lake via another conduit at a rate of 3 gallons a minute, then the amount of water in the lake will

A. decrease 1 gallon per minute
B. increase 1 gallon per minute
C. decrease 60 gallons per minute
D. remain the same

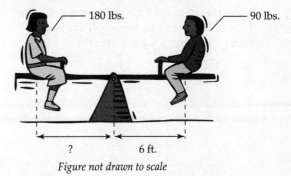

180 lbs.

90 lbs.

?

6 ft.

Figure not drawn to scale

12. At what distance from the fulcrum should the person on the left sit in order to perfectly balance the seesaw?

A. 2 feet
B. 3 feet
C. 6 feet
D. 12 feet

GO ON TO THE NEXT PAGE.

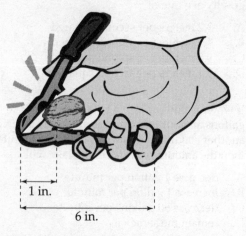

1 in.

6 in.

13. If the force required to crack the walnut is 60 lbs., how much force must be applied to the nutcracker to crack the walnut?

    A.   1 lbs.
    B.   5 lbs.
    C.   10 lbs.
    D.   30 lbs.

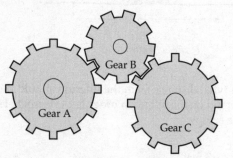

14. If gear A rotates counterclockwise, in which direction does gear C rotate?

    A.   Clockwise
    B.   Counterclockwise
    C.   Gear C does not rotate.
    D.   It is impossible for gear A to rotate counterclockwise.

15. Rolling friction is always

    A.   less than sliding friction
    B.   greater than sliding friction
    C.   equal to sliding friction
    D.   inversely proportional to sliding friction

16. The best instrument for measuring atmospheric pressure is

    A.   a thermometer
    B.   a Geiger counter
    C.   a Bourdon gauge
    D.   a barometer

STOP!
IF YOU FINISH BEFORE THE TIME IS UP, YOU MAY
CHECK OVER YOUR WORK ON THIS PART ONLY.

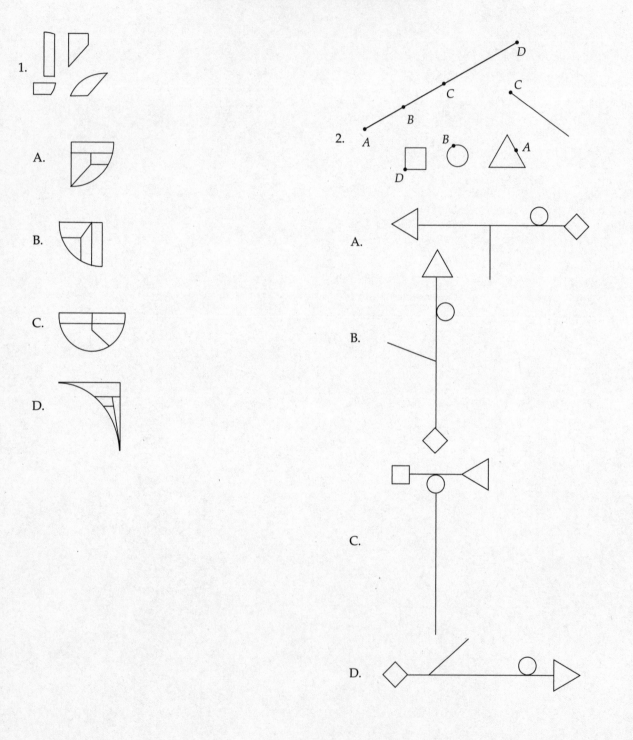

GO ON TO THE NEXT PAGE.

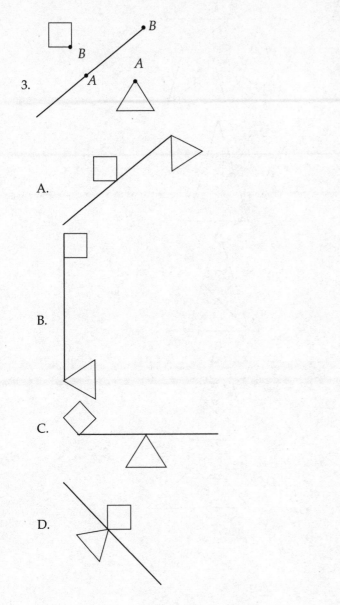

3.

A.

B.

C.

D.

4.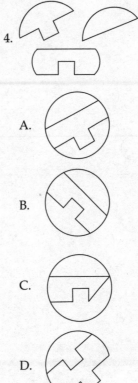

A.

B.

C.

D.

GO ON TO THE NEXT PAGE.

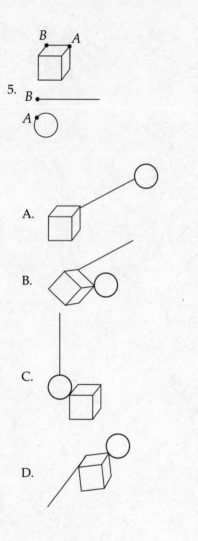

5.

A.

B.

C.

D.

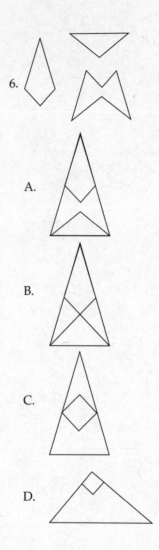

6.

A.

B.

C.

D.

GO ON TO THE NEXT PAGE.

7.

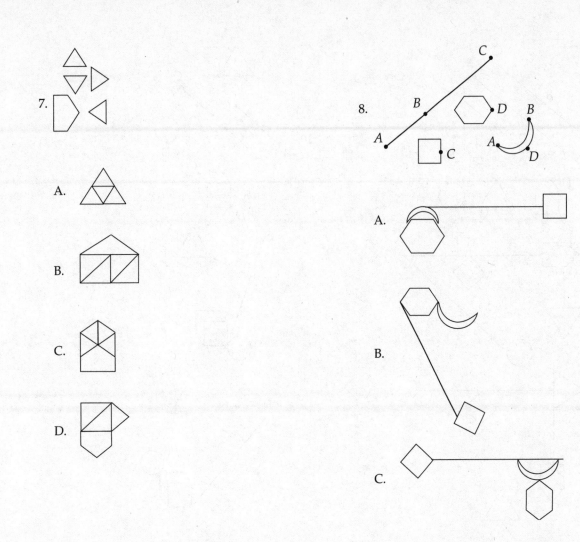

A.

B.

C.

D.

8.

A.

B.

C.

D.

GO ON TO THE NEXT PAGE.

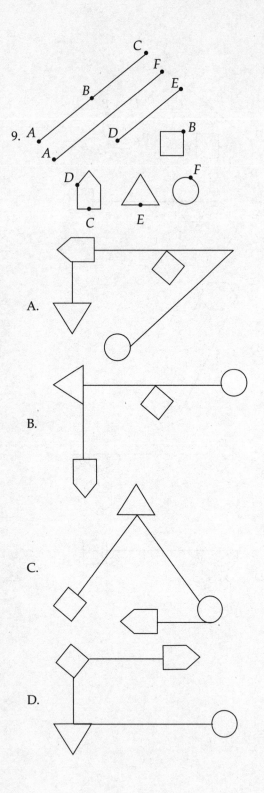

9.

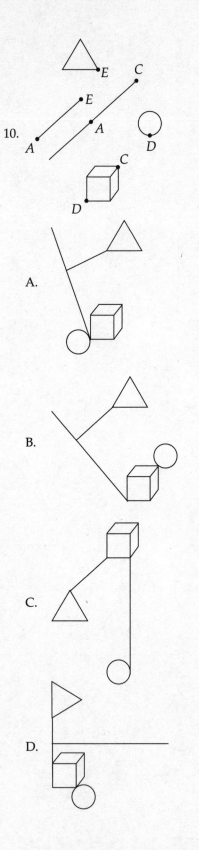

10.

A.

B.

C.

D.

11.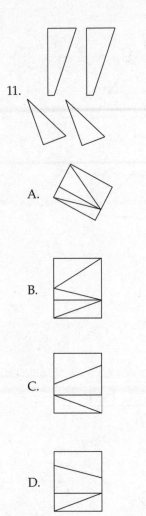

A.

B.

C.

D.

12.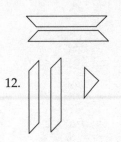

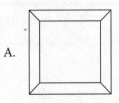

A.

B.

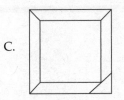

C.

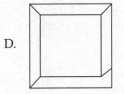

D.

GO ON TO THE NEXT PAGE.

13.

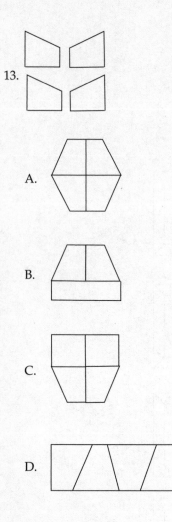

A.

B.

C.

D.

14.

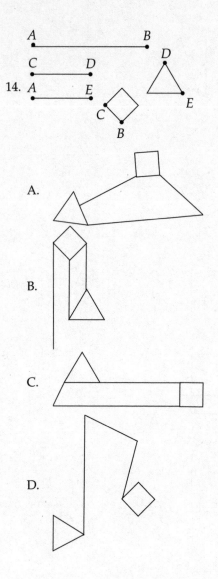

A.

B.

C.

D.

GO ON TO THE NEXT PAGE.

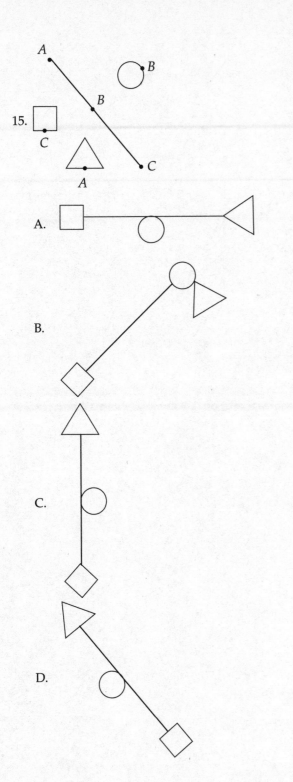

15.

A.

B.

C.

D.

16.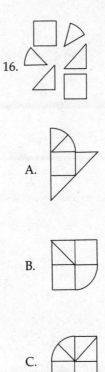

A.

B.

C.

D.

STOP!
IF YOU FINISH BEFORE THE TIME IS UP, YOU MAY
CHECK OVER YOUR WORK ON THIS PART ONLY.

Chapter 12
Practice Test 1:
Answers and
Explanations

PRACTICE TEST 1

CAT-ASVAB

ANSWERS AND EXPLANATIONS

Part 1—General Science

1. **C** The nervous system sends and receives information through electrical impulses.

2. **A** Chromosomes determine the genetic traits that offspring inherit from their parents.

3. **B** Producers make their own food. Plants are producers—they make their food through photosynthesis.

4. **D** Protons and neutrons both have a weight of approximately 1 atomic mass unit. By adding them together you get the mass of the atom. Electrons have practically no mass.

5. **A** Conduction occurs when heat travels from something hotter to something cooler.

6. **C** The Cenozoic Era started about 65 million years ago and continues today.

7. **B** Jupiter is the largest planet.

8. **D** The chromosomes line up at the middle of the cell during metaphase.

9. **C** Bryophytes are plants that do not possess stems or leaves.

10. **B** Deciduous forests have distinct seasons, lots of rain, trees that lose their leaves in the winter, and a wide variety of plant and animal life.

11. **A** The crust is a thin layer of rock that covers the Earth.

12. **C** A warm front occurs when warm air overtakes cooler air.

13. **D** A solar eclipse occurs when the Moon moves between the Sun and the Earth, blocking the Sun's light from the Earth.

14. **B** Pepsin is found in the stomach and is used to break down food.

15. **A** Type O is the universal donor.

16. **C** Rickets, a disease of the skeleton, is usually the result of a deficiency of vitamin D.

Part 2—Arithmetic Reasoning

1. **C** Plug the information into the formula for percent increases and decreases.

$$\text{Percent increase} = \frac{\text{difference}}{\text{original amount}}$$

$$.20 = \frac{x}{60}$$

$$12 = x$$

$$60 - 12 = 48$$

2. **A** 16 ounces = 1 pound, so Mrs. Abbott bought 3.5 lbs. of hamburger. 3.5 lbs. = $3.43, so you divide $3.43 by 3.5 to determine the cost per pound. It is $0.98.

3. **B** Use a Ratio Box to find the answer.

	Dogs	Cats	Total
	4	6	10
	× 10	× 10	× 10
	40	60	100

4. **A** Use Bite-Size Pieces to answer this one.

$$40 + 1.25x = 70$$

$$1.25x = 30$$

$$x = 24$$

5. **B** Use the formula $I = prt$

$$I = 100(.04)(10)$$

$$I = 40$$

The interest is 40. So the total in the account is 40 + 100 = 140.

6. **D** This is a proportion question. Match up the categories and solve for x.

$$\frac{1 \text{ scarf}}{2.5 \text{ hours}} = \frac{x \text{ scarves}}{17.5 \text{ hours}}$$

$$2.5x = 17.5$$

$$x = 7$$

7. **C** $7^2 + 4(7) - 6 = 49 + 28 - 6 = 71$

8. **C** Use Bite-Size Pieces to answer this one. First, find out how much he paid up front by multiplying 500 by .20. That gives you $100 for the initial payment. Then, multiply 60 by 8 to find the total for the 8 equal payments, which is 480. $100 + $480 = $580. $580 is $80 more than the original price of $500.

9. **D** $\sqrt{64} = 8$

10. **B** All you need to do for this problem is figure out Rob's discount. To do this, multiply 275 by 0.20. That gives you 55.

11. **C** The easiest way to solve this problem is to use the answer choices. Pick one and divide 120 by it. If it has a remainder of 1, you know it's the correct answer. The first two have no remainders when divided into 120. The fourth answer, 9, leaves you with a remainder of 3 when divided into 120. But $7\overline{)120}$ gives you 17 remainder 1, so that's your answer.

12. **A** First, figure out the percentage of the trip that he had his turn signal on. $\dfrac{32}{47}$ = .68 Then, subtract that from 100% to find how long he had his turn signal off. 100 − 68 = 32.

13. **B** $33 \times 0.8 = 26.4$

14. **D** $\dfrac{x}{4} = 24$

$x = 96$

15. **B** Use Bite-Size Pieces for this problem. Multiply $35 \times 8 = 280$. That is how much money Chris made from selling T-shirts. 355 − 280 = 75. So he made $75 from the hats. Each hat is $5 so divide 75 by 5. 75 ÷ 5 = 15.

16. **D** Line the equations up and subtract.

$$
\begin{array}{r}
12x^3 + 7x^2 - 9 \\
-\left(4x^3 + 2x^2 + 5\right) \\
\hline
8x^3 + 5x^2 - 14
\end{array}
$$

Part 3—Word Knowledge

1. **B** Accuse: To charge with a fault; to blame

2. **D** Unscrupulous: Without honor or morals

3. **C** Prominent: Noticeable

4. **A** Conclusive: Putting an end to any uncertainty or doubt; final

5. **B** Endure: To undergo (as a hardship)

6. **C** Overwhelm: To affect deeply in mind or emotion

7. **B** Abundant: Marked by great plenty (as of resources)

8. **A** Chagrin: A feeling of embarrassment caused by disappointment

9. **C** Anthology: A collection of literary pieces

10. **D** Dilute: To thin or weaken

11. **B** Wretched: Living in degradation and misery; miserable

12. **C** Precocious: Characterized by early development or maturity

13. **A** Utilize: To put to use

14. **D** Chastise: To punish

15. **A** Cynical: Distrustful of people's motives

16. **B** Feud: A bitter, prolonged quarrel

Part 4—Paragraph Comprehension

1. **A** The answer to this specific question lies in the last sentence, *"Franklin realized that this electricity could be guided to the ground by a metal wire or rod, thereby protecting houses...."*

2. **C** The passage never mentions dogs or hearing aids, so you don't know (A) or (B). The passage states that sound waves below 20 hertz cannot be heard by humans, but they can feel the vibration. So, (C) is correct.

3. **C** The lead words in this specific question are "the distant cannonade of a ship in distress." Once you find them in the passage, you can see from the context that they are describing the sound made by the explosion, (C).

4. **B** You have to read carefully to answer this one. The Augustan age was from 27 B.C. to 14 A.D., so you can eliminate (A). It was an autocracy, so you can eliminate (C). It brought about the *Pax Romana*, so you can eliminate (D).

5. **A** A person must be tested for blood type if they are going to receive red blood cells. Red blood cells are only found in whole transfusions, so the answer is (A).

6. **D** Choice (D) is the answer because the passage states that maple trees and corn do not need temperatures between 15 and 27 degrees centigrade for germination.

7. **A** The lead word is "antiseptics," and the passage is talking about how the use of them reduced the number of infections in hospitals. The passage never talks about milk, so (B) is out. Choice (C) really doesn't make sense in the context of the passage, and (D) is okay but not as good as (A).

8. **C** The lead words in the question are "Monarch butterfly." Find them in the passage and you see that the Monarch butterfly is an example of an organism that uses passive protection. The answer is (C).

9. **D** The best way to approach this type of question is step-by-step. First, determine if statement I is true or false. It's true, so eliminate any answer choice that doesn't include it. That gets rid of (B) and (C). You are left with (A) (I only) and (D) (I and III only). So you need to know if statement III is true. Since it is, the answer is (D).

10. **B** When answering an inference question, look for the answer that has the most support from the argument. Women are never mentioned, so (A) is out. Men not exposed to the chemical compound were never discussed, so (C) is out. Choice (D) is never mentioned, so that leaves (B).

11. **B** The archaeopteryx lived 150 million years ago, so it would be impossible for the scientists to study it in its native habitat because it's extinct. So (A) is out. The passage never mentions any modern descendants or old written records so (C) and (D) are out. That leaves (B).

Part 5—Mathematics Knowledge

1. **B** Plug in the values for x and y.

    $$3^2 + 4(3) - 3(3)(-4) + 2(-4)^2 = 9 + 12 + 36 + 32 = 89$$

2. **B** This problem is a little tricky. The easiest way to solve this one is to plug in numbers for the missing variables. For example, make $p = 5$ and $c = 10$ cents. That means that each piece of candy costs 2 cents. 10 pieces of candy will cost 20 cents. That is the target number. Now look at the answers. Plug the values for p and c into the answers and see which one will give you 20 cents. (B): $\dfrac{10(10)}{5} = 20$

3. **C** Start by drawing a rectangle with an area of 12. Assign lengths to the sides. It doesn't really matter what lengths you assign as long as the area is 12. For example, you can use 3 and 4. Then, double each of the lengths. The rectangle becomes 6 and 8. Find the area:

    $$\text{Area} = \text{length} \times \text{width} = 6 \times 8 = 48$$

4. **C** One inch equals 25 feet, so 2.5 inches equals 62.5 feet: $2.5 \times 25 = 62.5$.

5. **B** Plug in 12 for C and solve for F.

    $$12 = \frac{5}{9}(F - 32)$$
    $$12 = \frac{5}{9}F - 17.77$$
    $$29.77 = \frac{5}{9}F$$

    $$F = 53.6$$

6. **B** The easiest way to solve this one is to pick one of the answer choices and see if it works. For example, look at (B). If Roger pays \$20, then Adam pays \$10 and Vicky pays \$60. That adds up to \$90, which is the cost of the radio.

7. **C** Use the Pythagorean Theorem to find x.

    $$3^2 + 4^2 = x^2$$
    $$9 + 16 = x^2$$
    $$25 = x^2$$
    $$x = 5$$

8. **B**   This question involves similar triangles. The sides are proportional, so just set up the proportion and solve for the missing side.

$$\frac{25}{24} = \frac{13}{x}$$

$$25x = 312$$

$$x = 12\,\frac{12}{25}$$

9. **D**   The easiest way to solve this problem is to plug in numbers for the missing variables. Since the question asks you to figure out how old Marnie is in terms of d, start with d. Make $d = 8$. If $d = 8$, then Beth $= 10$ and Marnie $= 14$. Now look at the answer choices for the answer that will equal 14 when $d = 8$. That answer is (D), because $d + 6 = 8 + 6 = 14$.

10. **B**   The easiest way to solve this problem is to plug in a number for r. Make $r = 50$ cents. 50 cents, or 0.50, goes into \$5.00 10 times. Now find the answer choice that equals 10 when you plug 0.50 in for r. That answer is (B):

$$\frac{5}{.50} = 10$$

11. **B**   The easiest way to solve this problem is to use the answer choices. Pick an answer choice, subtract two from it, and see if the result is one-third of the original number. The correct choice is (B): $3 - 2 = 1$ and 1 is one-third of 3.

12. **D**   A hexagon is a six-sided figure. If you draw one it is easy to see that there would be 6 legs.

13. **D**   A right triangle by definition has a 90-degree angle. So the answer must have 90 degrees in it. That eliminates (A) and (B). All triangles have 180 degrees, so the other angle will be 65 degrees: $180 - 90 - 25 = 65$.

14. **C**   To find the area of a circle, use the formula Area $= \pi r^2$. The radius here is 3.5 (half the diameter), so Area $= \pi(3.5)^2 = 12.25\pi$.

15. **A**   First, expand the exponents: $2^3 = 8$ and $2^4 = 16$. The equation is now

$$11y + 8 = -5y + 16$$

$$16y = 8$$

$$y = 0.5$$

16. **C** Use Bite-Size Pieces to solve this problem. First, find the volume of Steve's pool:

Volume = length × width × height

$$9 \times 15 \times 10 = 1350$$

Next, find the volume of Jim's pool

$$12 \times 20 \times 12 = 2880$$

Then, subtract the volume of Steve's pool from the volume of Jim's pool:

$$2880 - 1350 = 1530$$

Part 6—Electronics Information

1. **D**
2. **A**
3. **D**
4. **C**
5. **A**
6. **A**
7. **D**
8. **A**

9. **A**
10. **B**
11. **B**
12. **C**
13. **D**
14. **D**
15. **C**
16. **A**

Part 7—Auto and Shop Information

1. **C**   The rotors are not found in the clutch system. The flywheel is connected to the engine and forms part of the connection system. The clutch plate is the friction plate that fits next to the flywheel. The drive shaft is the main shaft leaving the transmission.

2. **D**   You can eliminate (C) right away—the catalytic converter is located in the exhaust system. Before the fuel can be taken into the engine through the intake valves, it has to be mixed with air. The fuel pump moves fuel to the fuel injector, where it is siphoned out by the carburetor to be mixed with air.

3. **B**   The voltage regulator acts as a control to keep the voltage from the alternator from getting too high. With more voltage going into the rest of the car, the distributor will only take what it needs from the system. The increased voltage allowed to pass through the system would over-charge the battery.

4. **C**   For this question, it is probably best to look at the answer choices and determine what the effect of each of the answer choices would be on the car. Too much oil in the car might allow some of the oil to enter the combustion chamber and get burned away, but it wouldn't be re-sponsible for overheating the car. A rich fuel/air mix would cool the combustion temperature, but the cooling system would still be able to take the heat off the engine normally. A malfunc-tioning alternator would result in a dead battery and stall the car. However, if the water pump belt breaks, then the radiator cannot pull the heat out of the water fast enough to cool it to normal temperatures before it goes back into the engine, raising the temperature of the coolant and of the engine. The temperature would rise gradually and the car would begin to overheat.

5. **B**   Choice (C) looks like a good answer, but the diesel cycle only runs diesel engines (hence the name *diesel engine*). The gasoline cycle does not exist. It normally takes two full rotations of the crankshaft, or four strokes (two up and two down), to get just one power stroke.

6. **D**   The sudden drop in the pressure is the key. If the oil is too low, then the pressure would drop, but it would most likely be a gradual process and this would not explain the blue smoke. The head gasket is designed to keep the water, oil, and cylinders all separated from each other across the seam between the engine block and the engine head. If it blows, then water and oil can get into the cylinders and start to combust with the fuel, creating the tell-tale blue smoke.

7. **A**   Trace the problem through the car. If the water pump fails, then the coolant can't be circu-lated. This would cause the fluid in the engine to get very hot and not be able to cool down, overheating the engine.

8. **A**   This question is similar to question 1. You already evaluated that the rotor is part of the brakes and not the transmission. The stator, turbine, and pump make up the three main components in a torque converter that look like fans.

9.   **B**   Vapor lock is when fuel in the fuel line gets too hot and vaporizes into bubbles, thus preventing the fuel pump from pumping fuel to the carburetor and stalling the car. If the timing belt snaps or is harmed, the valves will not be able to open and close in sync with the piston movements. This will also stall the car. If a piston were to become lodged in one of the cylinders, the crankshaft would not be able to turn, stopping the engine. A worn clutch plate, however, will allow the engine to keep running but not transmit power to the wheels effectively.

10.   **A**   The timing belt has teeth like a gear so that the belt maintains the proper timing between the crankshaft and the valves and does not slip. Cams are smooth like an egg and push up on the rods leading to the rocker arm. The rocker arm is like a teeter-totter and has no use for teeth. The fan and alternator do not depend on exact timing like the valves. The fan belt has grooves that go along the length of the belt.

11.   **D**   Choice (A) looks good at first, but the piston rings are designed to expand to fit the cylinder. The vapors slipping past the piston would decrease power and be undesirable. Choice (D) is the answer. As pistons get heated from the explosions in the engine, the metal starts to expand. Pistons are cut to allow them to expand when they warm up. In fact, cars will not run efficiently until they have had a chance to "warm up" and the pistons expand.

12.   **D**   A reamer is used to enlarge existing holes, since the cutting parts on the bit are on the sides. Using the standard bit to enlarge a hole is not recommended, as the cutting edges are located at the tip of the bit and not the sides. A hacksaw does not cut corners and circles well. And an expansion bolt is used in masonry to allow a bolt to hold by expanding against the sides of the material.

13.   **B**   The teeth on a saw are bent slightly outward to allow the saw to move easily in the gap it cuts. The total width of the gap depends on the total width of the saw blades, known as the kerf. The set of the saw is the angle the teeth are bent to.

14.   **A**   This question requires that you distinguish between different types of wrenches. The pipe wrench has a moveable top jaw. The Allen wrench looks like a hexagonal rod. So you need to decide between the crescent wrench and the monkey wrench. The crescent wrench looks like a crescent, and the jaws open at an angle to the handle. The monkey wrench has jaws that open at an angle of about 90 degrees to the handle.

15.   **C**   The object shown is a plane. Planes are used for smoothing and flattening cut wood.

16.   **A**   The backsaw and the carpenters saw both consist of a handle and a blade. The hacksaw and coping saw both have blades that are stretched between the handle and an arm. The coping saw has a tall arm to allow the saw to cut farther into wood or metal. The hacksaw is a beefier saw designed for heavier use with a straight arm off of the handle.

17. **C** The stiff back on a backsaw gives it stability when cutting straight across the grain of wood.

18. **A** Choices (C) and (D) can be eliminated, because drywall dust will not stay in the hole and cement will not adhere to the drywall. Caulk is used to seal various joints to keep out water, such as in a shower or at the corners of walls and windows. Putty is a substance that is easy to spread over the hole and wipe away, leaving the hole filled. Eventually, the putty will harden in place.

19. **B** The device shown consists of a metal arm and a screw attached to one of its feet. There are no points that are used to measure, like on a caliper; no blades to cut into a pipe; and no way to mount the device to a bench, like on a vise.

20. **A** The bit has a twist down the shaft, so it's a twist bit.

21. **D** A metal hammer or mallet would damage the chisel, shortening the life of the tool. Using a rubber or wooden mallet reduces the damage.

22. **A** Machine screws work much like wood screws, except that wood screws can make their own threads when they are screwed into wood. Metals are too hard for the screw to make the threads, so machine screws can only be fastened into holes with threads already made.

Part 8—Mechanical Comprehension

1.	**B**	9.	**A**
2.	**A**	10.	**C**
3.	**B**	11.	**A**
4.	**B**	12.	**A**
5.	**A**	13.	**C**
6.	**B**	14.	**B**
7.	**B**	15.	**A**
8.	**B**	16.	**D**

Part 9—Assembling Objects

1. **A** The key feature here is that one of the shapes needs to be a quadrilateral, which in turn means none of its edges can be curved. Only (A) actually contains a quadrilateral.

2. **B** The short line must be connected to the midpoint of the larger line, leaving only (A) and (B) as possible answers. The difference here is that the circle must be between the triangle and the small line, which means (B) is the correct answer.

3. **C** The triangle needs to be connected at the midpoint and the square connected at the endpoint; (C) is the correct answer.

4. **B** The final shape needs to be a circle, so eliminate (D). The shape in the middle needs to have an indent on one side for the other shape to fit in. Choice (B) matches up with all of the correct shapes.

5. **B** The shapes connected to the cube need to be adjacent to each other and along the same edge. Only (B) can fit this description.

6. **A** The first thing to notice is that you should not have any squares, so you can eliminate (C) and (D). You should also have a total of three shapes, which eliminates (B), leaving (A) as the correct answer.

7. **C** You have a total of five shapes: four equilateral triangles and a pentagon. Choices (A) and (D) only have four shapes, so you can eliminate those. Choice (B) has a triangle instead of a pentagon, so (C) must be the correct answer.

8. **D** The two points of the crescent shape must both be connected to the line, which means only (C) and (D) can work. Choice (D) is the correct answer here because the square connected at the opposite end is connected by the side, as opposed to the corner, as it is in (C).

9. **A** The connection point on the triangle matches up with only one line, which means you should only have one line connected to the triangle and nothing else. The only choice that fits this is (A).

10. **B** The shapes connected to the cube must be on completely opposite corners of the cube: opposite side, opposite face, and opposite end. Only (B) shows the cube with the correct shapes connected in this fashion.

11. **D** You need a total of four shapes: two similar quadrilaterals and two similar triangles. Both (C) and (D) follow this. If you look carefully, the orientation is backwards in (C), which means (D) is the correct answer.

12. **C** There should be a total of five pieces, which narrows the choices down to (B) and (C). The triangle in (B) is too small, and, in addition, the rest of the shapes do not match up. The correct answer is (C).

13. **A** Rectangles are not a part of the original question, so only (A) or (D) could be correct. Since all of the shapes need to be similar, reflected images of one another, the correct answer must be (A). Not all of the shapes are similar in (D).

14. **C** Two lines must connect to the triangle, and two lines must connect to the square. Initially, (A) and (C) both are good possibilities, but closer examination reveals that the connecting points on the triangle need to be at the corners, not in the middle. This means the correct answer is (C).

15. **D** The square needs to be at one end of the line, and the triangle needs to be at the other end, with the circle tangent in the middle. The key here is to examine where the triangle and square connect to the line. Only (D) shows the correct configuration.

16. **C** The easiest way to approach this is to count the shapes; there are a total of six. Only (C) is composed of a total of six shapes.

Chapter 13
Practice Test 2
Student ASVAB

PART 1

General Science

Time: 11 Minutes—25 Questions

1. Which organism in the food chain is a primary consumer?

   A. Cow
   B. Tiger
   C. Human
   D. Shark

2. The mass extinction of many species, including all dinosaurs, occurred during the

   A. Precambrian Era
   B. Paleozoic Era
   C. Mesozoic Era
   D. Cenozoic Era

3. The reddish tint of soil in the southern United States is the result of

   A. humidity
   B. temperature
   C. convection
   D. oxidation

4. What do plants require for photosynthesis?

   A. Oxygen, water, and sunlight
   B. Carbon dioxide, water, and sunlight
   C. Water and soil
   D. Water, soil, and sunlight

5. Sperm are produced in the

   A. vas deferens
   B. ovaries
   C. seminiferous tubules
   D. urethra

6. A diploid cell possesses

   A. 46 chromosomes
   B. 92 chromosomes
   C. 23 chromosomes
   D. 16 chromosomes

7. When you walk on the beach you are in which marine biome?

   A. Aphotic zone
   B. Intertidal zone
   C. Neritic zone
   D. Oceanic zone

8. The atomic number for potassium is 19. Potassium always has

   A. 9 protons
   B. 9 electrons
   C. 19 electrons
   D. 19 protons

9. The three states of matter are

   A. liquid, metal, gas
   B. acid, solid, base
   C. solid, liquid, gas
   D. heat, sound, chemical

10. A blue object is reflecting

    A. blue light waves
    B. all light waves except blue
    C. blue and violet light waves
    D. red, orange, yellow, and green light waves

11. Smooth muscles are found

    A. in the heart
    B. in the stomach
    C. in the arm
    D. attached to bones

12. An organism in the mollusca phylum also belongs to the

    A. Monera kingdom
    B. Protista kingdom
    C. Plantae kingdom
    D. Animalia kingdom

GO ON TO THE NEXT PAGE.

13. The control center of a cell is located in the

    A. mitochondria
    B. nucleus
    C. ribosomes
    D. lysosomes

14. Cytokinesis occurs during

    A. prophase
    B. anaphase
    C. telophase
    D. metaphase

15. Igneous rock forms from

    A. cooling magma
    B. chemical reactions
    C. weathering
    D. oxidation

16. The ionosphere and exosphere are found in the

    A. troposphere
    B. thermosphere
    C. stratosphere
    D. mesosphere

17. Which of the following is a Jovian planet?

    A. Earth
    B. Mercury
    C. Venus
    D. Saturn

18. Energy that is found in a moving object is

    A. kinetic
    B. potential
    C. thermal
    D. nuclear

19. Which of the following is an element?

    A. Water
    B. Carbon dioxide
    C. Hydrogen
    D. Salt water

20. Which is an example of refraction?

    A. A light bulb shining
    B. A prism bending sunlight
    C. A mirror reflecting sunlight
    D. X-rays

21. Which subatomic particle has a charge of –1?

    A. Electron
    B. Neutron
    C. Proton
    D. Isotope

22. The brain is part of the

    A. autonomic nervous system
    B. somatic nervous system
    C. central nervous system
    D. peripheral nervous system

23. Two parents that are homozygous for the dominant trait brown eyes can have which type of offspring?

    A. Brown-eyed and non-brown-eyed
    B. Only brown-eyed
    C. Only non-brown-eyed
    D. Not enough information available

24. Which of the following is a characteristic of fungi?

    A. They are unicellular.
    B. They live off decomposing matter.
    C. They subsist by photosynthesis.
    D. They have stems and leaves.

25. Which biome is characterized by the heaviest rainfall on Earth?

    A. Tropical rain forest
    B. Deciduous forest
    C. Taiga
    D. Tundra

STOP!
IF YOU FINISH BEFORE THE TIME IS UP, YOU MAY
CHECK OVER YOUR WORK ON THIS PART ONLY.

PART 2

Arithmetic Reasoning

Time: 36 Minutes—30 Questions

1. 15 passengers agree to divide evenly the cost of renting a bus for a trip. If all but 7 of the passengers have paid their share, and a total of $177.60 has been collected, what is the total cost of renting the bus?

   A. $246.15
   B. $333.00
   C. $828.00
   D. $1,555.40

2. Lisa and Annette together weigh 222 pounds, and David weighs 168 pounds. What is the average weight of all three?

   A. 130
   B. 140
   C. 175
   D. 180

3. Gina drove for two hours at a rate of 55 miles per hour. She then drove for 3 hours at a rate of 60 miles per hour. How far did she travel?

   A. 180
   B. 240
   C. 290
   D. 300

4. A sack of marbles has 6 red marbles, 9 blue marbles, 2 green marbles, and 4 black marbles. If one marble is chosen from the sack at random, what is the probability that it will be a red marble?

   A. $\dfrac{4}{21}$

   B. $\dfrac{15}{21}$

   C. $\dfrac{6}{13}$

   D. $\dfrac{6}{21}$

5. Leasing a car costs $179 per month plus $0.06 per mile driven. If your monthly car budget is $500, what is the farthest that you can drive in one month (to the nearest mile) and remain within your budget?

   A. 5050
   B. 5240
   C. 5350
   D. 5450

6. Rita received a 90 in History, an 88 in Spanish, and an 85 in Biology. Suppose the classes have the following weights: History 2, Spanish 3, and Biology 4. What is Rita's average, rounded to the nearest tenth?

   A. 86.5
   B. 87.1
   C. 89.3
   D. 90.2

7. Mel bought a TV for $350. Three days later Jack bought the same TV at a 15% discount. How much more did Mel pay for the TV than Jack?

   A. $52.50
   B. $53.50
   C. $252.45
   D. $297.50

8. Kim is building a scale model of an airplane. Each inch represents 7 feet. If the real airplane is 115 feet long, approximately how long, in inches, is the model?

   A. 16.0 inches
   B. 16.5 inches
   C. 17.0 inches
   D. 17.5 inches

9. Dave bought 4 pounds 8 ounces of steak for $16.83. What is the cost of 1 pound of steak?

   A. $3.74
   B. $3.88
   C. $4.06
   D. $4.21

GO ON TO THE NEXT PAGE.

10. Max can build a chair in 2.5 days. Working at the same rate, how many chairs can he build in 55 days?

A. 21
B. 22
C. 23
D. 24

11. If $x = 9$, then $3x^2 - 7x + 4 =$

A. 156
B. 178
C. 182
D. 184

12. Farmer Andy expected to harvest 4300 bushels of corn this season. After a season of great weather, Andy harvests 4850 bushels of corn. Approximately what percentage of Andy's original harvest estimate did Andy actually harvest?

A. 89%
B. 113%
C. 119%
D. 150%

13. The cash register at Pet-A-Rama pet shop always starts with $100 in it every morning. On one day the following purchases were made: 2 dog collars at $8.89 each, 1 litter box at $12.50, 3 goldfish at $.79 each, 2 parakeets at $17.99 each, and 4 hamsters at $7.79 each. What was the total amount of money in the cash register at the end of the day?

A. $99.70
B. $100.00
C. $187.43
D. $199.79

14. What are the next three terms in the sequence: 1, 3, 7, 13 . . .?

A. 19, 21, 27
B. 21, 31, 43
C. 15, 17, 19
D. 21, 27, 31

15. In Mr. Kelley's social studies class, $\frac{2}{3}$ of the 36 students are Democrats, and the rest are Republicans. In Ms. Richey's social studies class, $\frac{3}{4}$ of the 28 students are Republicans, and the rest are Democrats. What are the total numbers of Democrats and Republicans in both classes?

A. 30 Democrats, 30 Republicans
B. 31 Democrats, 33 Republicans
C. 33 Democrats, 31 Republicans
D. 35 Democrats, 29 Republicans

16. $\sqrt{2}\sqrt{8} =$

A. 2
B. $2\sqrt{2}$
C. $4\sqrt{2}$
D. 4

17. A pet goat eats two pounds of goat food and one pound of grass each day. When the goat has eaten a total of fifteen pounds combined of goat food and grass, how many pounds of grass will it have eaten?

A. 2
B. 3
C. 5
D. 8

18. If $6x - 4 = 38$, then $x =$

A. 7
B. 10
C. 12
D. 14

19. A barrel is filled with 50 gallons of lemonade. If every person at a picnic drinks 1 pint of lemonade and the barrel is emptied, how many people are at the picnic?

A. 50
B. 200
C. 400
D. 500

GO ON TO THE NEXT PAGE.

20. The fraction $\frac{9}{72}$ is equal to what percentage?

   A. 9.0%
   B. 10.5%
   C. 12.5%
   D. 17%

21. What is the value of 5^3?

   A. 15
   B. 25
   C. 100
   D. 125

22. During one season, a professional basketball player tried 420 shots and made 294 of them. What percent of his shots did he make?

   A. 65%
   B. 70%
   C. 75%
   D. 80%

23. You are given $20 to buy ice cream for a party. If ice cream costs $3.20 per gallon, how many gallons of ice cream can you buy?

   A. 6.25
   B. 6.50
   C. 7.0
   D. 7.5

24. A backpack usually costs $35.00, but was reduced by 22% for a sale. What was the cost of the backpack on sale?

   A. $24.83
   B. $25.22
   C. $26.35
   D. $27.30

25. A bus travels 420 miles in 8 hours. What was the bus's average speed, in miles per hour?

   A. 50 mph
   B. 52.5 mph
   C. 55.5 mph
   D. 58.5 mph

26. If $3x + 5y = 15$ and $x - 2y = 10$, then $2x + 7y =$

   A. 5
   B. 10
   C. 15
   D. 25

27. If $-9m - 12 > 11 - 3m$, then

   A. $m < -\frac{23}{6}$

   B. $m > -\frac{23}{6}$

   C. $m > -\frac{23}{12}$

   D. $m < -\frac{1}{6}$

28. $12.46 \div 100 =$

   A. 1246
   B. 124.6
   C. 0.1246
   D. 1.246

29. $\frac{3}{5} + \frac{5}{6} =$

   A. $\frac{25}{30}$

   B. $1\frac{13}{30}$

   C. $2\frac{13}{30}$

   D. $\frac{23}{6}$

30. Three tankers each carry 10,000 tons of oil, and a fourth tanker carries 12,000 tons of oil. What is the average number of tons of oil carried by each of the four tankers?

   A. 10,000
   B. 10,050
   C. 10,500
   D. 11,500

STOP!
IF YOU FINISH BEFORE THE TIME IS UP, YOU MAY
CHECK OVER YOUR WORK ON THIS PART ONLY.

PART 3

Word Knowledge

Time: 11 Minutes—35 Questions

1. <u>Accidental</u> most nearly means

   A. purposeful
   B. unexpected
   C. taunting
   D. deliverable

2. <u>Refute</u> most nearly means

   A. discuss
   B. clarify
   C. disprove
   D. justify

3. <u>Revolution</u> most nearly means

   A. evolution
   B. overthrow
   C. cure
   D. elect

4. The candidate stressed the importance of having good <u>values</u>.

   A. beliefs
   B. finances
   C. defenses
   D. voters

5. <u>Poll</u> most nearly means

   A. rod
   B. exit
   C. report
   D. survey

6. <u>Conquer</u> most nearly means

   A. create
   B. devise
   C. defeat
   D. watch

7. <u>Disturb</u> most nearly means

   A. bother
   B. classify
   C. invent
   D. listen

8. Larry viewed his co-workers as <u>opponents</u> in the workplace.

   A. friends
   B. compatriots
   C. teammates
   D. enemies

9. <u>Adapt</u> most nearly means

   A. counter
   B. adjust
   C. tear
   D. exercise

10. <u>Awe</u> most nearly means

    A. wonder
    B. sickly
    C. implement
    D. boastful

11. <u>Colleague</u> most nearly means

    A. enemy
    B. predecessor
    C. co-worker
    D. soldier

12. Chris's statement about the movie was <u>misleading</u>.

    A. entertaining
    B. powerful
    C. glorifying
    D. deceptive

13. <u>Pledge</u> most nearly means

    A. commit
    B. clean
    C. taken
    D. coerce

GO ON TO THE NEXT PAGE.

14. <u>Resentment</u> most nearly means

   A. cooling
   B. affirmation
   C. respected
   D. hatred

15. <u>Sufficient</u> most nearly means

   A. choke
   B. limited
   C. enough
   D. excellent

16. The announcer was very <u>animated</u> in his description of the fight.

   A. drawn
   B. lively
   C. pessimistic
   D. terse

17. <u>Transparent</u> most nearly means

   A. opaque
   B. conductive
   C. clear
   D. difficult

18. <u>Graceful</u> most nearly means

   A. beautiful
   B. rude
   C. listless
   D. destructive

19. <u>Indignation</u> most nearly means

   A. independent
   B. aloof
   C. respect
   D. outrage

20. Pam's report on the current state of the economy was <u>insightful</u>.

   A. erroneous
   B. perceptive
   C. classic
   D. plagiarized

21. <u>Skeptical</u> most nearly means

   A. optimistic
   B. doubtful
   C. confident
   D. likely

22. <u>Reaction</u> most nearly means

   A. emotion
   B. explosion
   C. response
   D. therapy

23. <u>Validity</u> most nearly means

   A. truth
   B. candor
   C. search
   D. communicate

24. When Elliot lost his job, his life became full of <u>turmoil</u>.

   A. boredom
   B. commitments
   C. depression
   D. confusion

25. <u>Undermine</u> most nearly means

   A. strengthen
   B. found
   C. weaken
   D. trick

26. <u>Quarrel</u> most nearly means

   A. conflict
   B. fourth
   C. create
   D. declaration

27. <u>Potential</u> most nearly means

   A. possible
   B. knowledge
   C. opportunity
   D. encompass

28. The senator is a very <u>influential</u> person in Congress.

   A. respected
   B. amused
   C. mocked
   D. powerful

GO ON TO THE NEXT PAGE.

29. Infer most nearly means

    A. melt
    B. create
    C. conclude
    D. trap

30. Persuasive most nearly means

    A. beautiful
    B. convincing
    C. destructive
    D. encompassing

31. Precious most nearly means

    A. overpriced
    B. cherished
    C. lively
    D. diminished

32. Lisa thought the fight scene was irrelevant to the plot of the play.

    A. unimportant
    B. ambivalent
    C. crucial
    D. enlightening

33. Nostalgia most nearly means

    A. nasal
    B. royal
    C. longing
    D. tenuous

34. Impulse most nearly means

    A. charge
    B. stance
    C. urge
    D. effective

35. Hazardous most nearly means

    A. forceful
    B. onerous
    C. technical
    D. dangerous

STOP!
IF YOU FINISH BEFORE THE TIME IS UP, YOU MAY
CHECK OVER YOUR WORK ON THIS PART ONLY.

PART 4

Paragraph Comprehension

Time: 13 Minutes—15 Questions

1. In 1896 the United States Supreme Court in the case *Plessy v. Ferguson*, public schools and other institutions were legally segregated under the doctrine of "separate but equal." In 1954 the Supreme Court in the case *Brown v. Board of Education of Topeka*, unanimously reversed this decision and declared this policy unconstitutional. Chief Justice Earl Warren's decision stated that "separate educational facilities are inherently unequal" and ordered that all public schools desegregate.

   All of the following statements are true EXCEPT:

   A. Since 1954, segregating a public school is illegal.
   B. Before 1954, it was legal for schools to be segregated.
   C. The doctrine of "separate but equal" applied to segregated schools.
   D. Some of the members of the 1954 Supreme Court voted against reversing *Plessy v. Ferguson*.

2. Great artists are not normally confined by the "movements" that others may name for them. Rather, they transcend the conventional structure, working now in one style, then in another, and later in a third. Picasso's work, for example, can be categorized as a few different artistic movements—post-impressionist, surrealist, cubist—and other artists, too, work their way from one style to another. Indeed, artists are people and may decide to alter their style for no more complex a reason than that which makes most people want to "try something new" once in a while.

   The author mentions Picasso in order to

   A. describe an artist who didn't reflect numerous movements
   B. provide an example of an artist who exhibited many different artistic styles
   C. emphasize that not all artists were well regarded until after their deaths
   D. show how one artist can have a great influence on many other artists

3. During the Progressive Era in the United States (1900–1920), a group of journalists and writers known as muckrakers went about exposing all the nasty abuses of power and money that went on during the end of the nineteenth century. They stirred up public opinion and helped win public support for various social reforms.

   Which of the following is true about muckrakers?

   A. They blindly supported politicians.
   B. They committed abuses of power and money.
   C. They came about in the late twentieth century.
   D. They may have had something to do with some social reform.

4. The Boeing 747 is the largest passenger airplane currently in use. It takes about 10 months to build and is built in the largest building in the world. The cost of a 747 is well over $100 million.

   What can be inferred from the above passage?

   A. The 747 is the fastest commercial airplane built.
   B. It takes longer to build a 747 than any other airplane.
   C. There is no larger passenger plane than the 747.
   D. A 747 costs $140 million.

GO ON TO THE NEXT PAGE.

5. Neanderthals had different facial structures than Homo sapiens. They had virtually no forehead and lacked the jutting chin of Homo sapiens. Neanderthals had a substantial nose, thicker bones, and abnormally large teeth.

Which of the following statements is most likely true?

A. Neanderthals looked very similar facially to Homo sapiens.
B. Neanderthals had a different chin than Homo sapiens.
C. Neanderthals were generally taller than Homo sapiens.
D. Neanderthals had lighter bones than Homo sapiens.

6. Different chemical bonds naturally have different strengths. For instance, the bond between a carbon atom and an oxygen atom is stronger than the bond between two chlorine atoms. When a bond is relatively strong, we say its bond energy is high. Bond energy involves the amount of energy it takes to break a bond.

Which of the following can be inferred about chemical bonds?

A. They all have the same bond energy.
B. The bond between two chlorine atoms and the bond between a carbon and oxygen atom have different bond strengths.
C. The bond between a carbon atom and a chlorine atom has relatively high bond energy.
D. They have low bond energy when the bond is strong.

7. The digestive system of the cow is complex and interesting. Unlike humans, who have a simple stomach, the cow has a large four-chambered stomach. Cows eat plants, primarily grasses, which are only partly digested in one of the four chambers, called the rumen. The cow will then regurgitate, or bring back up, the partially digested plant fibers in a small mass called "cud." The cud is chewed further and swallowed again, this time into the second chamber, called the reticulum. It passes then to the third and fourth chambers until it is completely digested. It may sound unpleasant, but the cow is able to extract a maximum of nutrients from its food by digesting in this manner. The whole process may take more than three days.

The best title for this passage might be

A. "The Cow's Great Gift to Man: Milk"
B. "Digestive Systems and their Purposes"
C. "The Diet of the Cow"
D. "The Digestive System of the Cow"

8. Every substance "knows" how to be a solid, liquid, or gas, each of which is called a "state" or a "phase." Whether a substance is in one phase or another depends on temperature and pressure. Water, for instance, turns from solid to liquid or from liquid to solid at zero degrees Celsius and one atmosphere of pressure. It turns from liquid to gas or gas to liquid at one hundred degrees Celsius and one atmosphere of pressure.

Based on the above paragraph, what is true about water?

A. It does not change states.
B. Water freezes at zero degrees Fahrenheit.
C. When pressure equals two atmospheres, water boils at two hundred degrees Celsius.
D. Pressure has an influence on what state a substance is in.

GO ON TO THE NEXT PAGE.

9. This was our last watch fire of the year. Next week the other boys were to file back to their old places in the Sandtown High School, but I was to go up to the divide to teach my first country school in the Norwegian district. I was already homesick at the thought of quitting the boys with whom I had always played; of leaving the river, and going up into a windy plain that was all windmills and cornfields and big pastures; where there was nothing willful or unmanageable in the landscape, no new island, and no chance of unfamiliar birds—such as often followed the watercourses.

Why will the narrator remember this watch fire better than others?

A. It is the narrator's birthday.
B. The narrator is going away soon.
C. The narrator has just been born.
D. The narrator has recently gotten a new job.

10. A piece of rock, named rock number 84001, found in the Arctic, was discovered to be a piece of a meteor from Mars. When studied under a powerful microscope, scientists found what they thought were fossilized remains of microscopic Martian life forms. It turns out that the fossilized remains were mineral deposits and not Martian life.

What can be inferred from the above passage?

A. Remains from Mars can find their way to Earth.
B. There was microscopic life on Mars.
C. All meteors found on Earth are from Mars.
D. Most meteors found on Earth are found in the Arctic.

11. During the mid-nineteenth century, reformer Dorothea Lynde Dix, a former schoolteacher, carried on a one-person crusade to improve the treatment of the mentally ill. Her efforts were instrumental in the establishment of hospitals and asylums for the mentally ill.

Based on the information above, which of the following is most likely true?

A. Prior to the efforts of Dorothea Lynde Dix, there were relatively few hospitals or asylums for the mentally ill.
B. In the mid-nineteenth century there was a large swell of support to improve the treatment of the mentally ill.
C. There are currently relatively few hospitals and asylums for the treatment of the mentally ill.
D. Treatment of the mentally ill was a social priority at the beginning of the nineteenth century.

12. Making seat belt use mandatory will reduce automobile fatalities. State X has one of the lowest automobile fatality rates in the country, and law there requires seat belt use.

The paragraph means most nearly that

A. state X has low airline fatality rates as well
B. mandatory seat belt use does not work
C. seat belts lower insurance premiums
D. mandatory seat belt use will reduce automobile fatalities

GO ON TO THE NEXT PAGE.

Recent studies have confirmed what many people have suspected for years. Emotions can have an effect on your health. Research has shown that people with positive, upbeat attitudes are generally in better health than negative, pessimistic people. Stress, in particular, has been shown to be a factor in immune system functioning. People who are under stress for extended periods of time tend to have weaker immune systems than people who are not under stress. This may put them at risk for developing health problems or aggravate existing conditions.

Doctors have begun recommending support groups for patients with serious health problems such as cancer. Studies have shown that cancer patients who belong to support groups tend to live longer and feel better than patients who don't. Doctors are not sure why this is, but believe it may have something to do with the emotional support patients receive from each other. For many patients, support groups provide the only opportunity they have to share their feelings with others going through the same experiences.

While these new findings are certainly interesting, there is still a lot of work to be done. Researchers cannot explain why or how emotions affect the immune system. Nor can they explain why different emotions affect the immune system differently. Therefore, further research needs to be done to try and answer these perplexing questions.

13. What is the main point of the paragraph above?

A. Emotions such as unhappiness and loneliness can make you sick.
B. Cancer patients who attend group therapy live longer.
C. More research needs to be done to study the effects of emotions on health.
D. The immune system works independently of the rest of the body.

14. According to the passage, which of the following is NOT true of cancer patients who belong to support groups?

A. They live longer.
B. They learn more about cancer.
C. They feel better.
D. They receive emotional support.

15. Which of the following can be inferred from the passage?

A. If you are under a lot of stress, you will probably get cancer.
B. If you are positive and upbeat, you will never get sick.
C. Doctor's with cancer attend their own support groups.
D. There are still a lot of unanswered questions regarding emotions and their effects on health.

STOP!
IF YOU FINISH BEFORE THE TIME IS UP, YOU MAY
CHECK OVER YOUR WORK ON THIS PART ONLY.

PART 5

Mathematics Knowledge

Time: 24 Minutes—25 Questions

1. If $(7x)^2 = 441$, then $x =$

    A. 3
    B. 5
    C. 6
    D. 13

2. An architecture student built a scale model of a building. Each inch in the model represents 15 feet. If the building is 202 feet tall, approximately how high is the model?

    A. 12 inches
    B. $12\frac{1}{2}$ inches
    C. 13 inches
    D. $13\frac{1}{2}$ inches

3. A rectangle has a length of 7 inches and an area of 56 inches. What is its width?

    A. 49
    B. 21
    C. 8
    D. 7

4. There are 7 fruit stands on a road. Each fruit stand has x apples and y oranges. What is the total number of apples and oranges combined in all 7 fruit stands?

    A. $7xy$
    B. $\dfrac{7x}{y}$
    C. $7x + 7y$
    D. $7(x - y)$

5. The perimeter of a swimming pool is 70 feet. The pool's width is 5 feet less than its length. What is the length of the pool?

    A. 20
    B. 40
    C. 50
    D. 70

6. How many more sides does an octagon have than a quadrilateral?

    A. 4
    B. 8
    C. 10
    D. cannot be determined

7. $(x^2 + 6x + 3)(x + 3) =$

    A. $x^2 + 3x + 18x + 6$
    B. $x^3 + 6x^2 + 21x + 9$
    C. $x^3 + 9x^2 + 21x + 9$
    D. $x^2 + 18x + 6x + 18$

8. For what value of m does $2m + 4 = m^3$?

    A. 1
    B. 2
    C. 3
    D. 4

9. A circle has a radius of 4. What is the area? (Use 3.14 for π.)

    A. 12.14
    B. 25.12
    C. 50.24
    D. 200.96

10. If the area of a square is $64\pi^2$, what is the length of one side of the square?

    A. 8π
    B. 64π
    C. $8\pi^2$
    D. $64\pi^2$

11. What is the volume of a rectangular box with dimensions 2 by 3 by 4?

    A. 54
    B. 27
    C. 24
    D. 14

GO ON TO THE NEXT PAGE.

12. What is another way to write $2\sqrt{20}$?

    A. $2\sqrt{5}$

    B. $\sqrt{40}$

    C. $4\sqrt{5}$

    D. $4\sqrt{20}$

13. 25 percent of what number is equal to 10?

    A. 30
    B. 40
    C. 45
    D. 50

14. Which of these has 7 in the hundredths place?

    A. 2.0376
    B. 2.3067
    C. 2.7036
    D. 2.3706

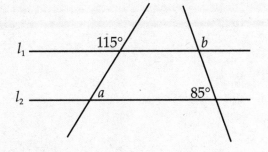

15. If l_1 is parallel to l_2, then $\angle a + \angle b =$

    A. 200
    B. 175
    C. 160
    D. 130

16. If $-9 \leq x < 7$, then x is

    A. less than 7 but more than –9
    B. less than 7 but more than or equal to –9
    C. more than or equal to 7 or less than –9
    D. more than –9 or more than 7

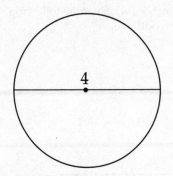

17. What is the circumference of the above circle? (Diameter = 4)

    A. 4π
    B. 6π
    C. 8π
    D. 16π

18. If $6x = 90$, then $x =$

    A. 12
    B. 13
    C. 15
    D. 18

19. Another way to write 3^3 is

    A. 9
    B. 18
    C. 24
    D. 27

20. A hexagon's sides are all 5 inches long. What is the perimeter of the hexagon?

    A. 25
    B. 30
    C. 35
    D. 40

21. Multiply: $2xy(4y - 5x^2)$

    A. $8xy^2 - 10x^3y$
    B. $8x^2y^2 - 10x^2y$
    C. $6xy^2 - 7x^3y$
    D. $8xy - 10xy$

GO ON TO THE NEXT PAGE.

22. If p is an odd integer, which of the following must also be an odd integer?

    A. $p + 1$

    B. $\dfrac{p}{2}$

    C. $p + 2$

    D. $2p$

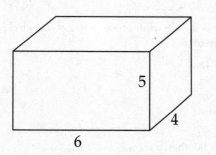

23. The surface area of the above rectangular box is

    A. 74
    B. 108
    C. 128
    D. 148

24. Solve: $-5x + 6 < 61$

    A. $x < 11$
    B. $x > 11$
    C. $x > -11$
    D. $x < -11$

25. A car drives south for 3 miles and stops. It then drives east for 4 miles and stops again. How far is the car from its original location?

    A. 7 miles
    B. 5 miles
    C. 4 miles
    D. 3 miles

STOP!
IF YOU FINISH BEFORE THE TIME IS UP, YOU MAY
CHECK OVER YOUR WORK ON THIS PART ONLY.

PART 6

Electronics Information

Time: 9 Minutes—20 Questions

1. Which of the following colors signify that a wire is grounded?

   A. Green
   B. Black
   C. Red
   D. Yellow

2. The current through a 100-ohm resistor is 0.5 A. What is the power rating of the resistor?

   A. 5 W
   B. 25 W
   C. 50 W
   D. 100 W

3. Opposition to current flow is known as

   A. capacitance
   B. resistance
   C. inductance
   D. conductance

4. Which of the following is the best conductor of electricity?

   A. Carbon
   B. Brass
   C. Silver
   D. Steel

5. Capacitance is measured in

   A. ohms
   B. amps
   C. watts
   D. farads

6. How much current will a 100-watt light bulb draw if it is plugged into a 120-volt socket?

   A. 0.25 A
   B. 0.5 A
   C. 0.8 A
   D. 1.0 A

7. Three wires protrude from

   A. a resistor
   B. a capacitor
   C. a diode
   D. a battery

8. Common household current is

   A. AC
   B. DC
   C. It varies according to time of year.
   D. It varies according to temperature.

9. A rheostat is a type of

   A. capacitor
   B. resistor
   C. transformer
   D. battery

10. What is the total resistance of a 6-ohm and a 16-ohm resistor in parallel?

    A. 2.67 ohms
    B. 4.5 ohms
    C. 10 ohms
    D. 20 ohms

11. The sum of the voltage drops around a circuit is equal to the source voltage. This is a statement of

    A. Ohm's Law
    B. Kirchhoff's Law
    C. Faraday's Law
    D. Edison's Law

12. Electrical energy, or charge, is measured in

    A. farads
    B. microfarads
    C. watts
    D. coulombs

GO ON TO THE NEXT PAGE.

13. Which household electric appliance uses the most current?

    A. A range
    B. A dishwasher
    C. A television
    D. A freezer

14. A newly soldered joint should be

    A. rough
    B. shiny and smooth
    C. balled up on the joint
    D. gray

15. Five lamps are connected in series. Each lamp requires 16 V and 0.1 amps. The total power used is

    A. 0.1 W
    B. 8 W
    C. 16 W
    D. 80 W

16. Which of the following appliances has the highest wattage?

    A. Clock
    B. Toaster
    C. Broiler
    D. Air conditioner

17. What is the efficiency of a transformer if it draws 600 W and delivers 300 W?

    A. 200%
    B. 100%
    C. 50%
    D. 25%

18. It's best to drive grounding rods using a

    A. power drill
    B. claw hammer
    C. ball peen hammer
    D. rotary hammer

19. The symbol above represents a

    A. diode
    B. transistor
    C. inductor
    D. capacitor

20. The symbol above represents a

    A. diode
    B. transistor
    C. inductor
    D. capacitor

STOP!
IF YOU FINISH BEFORE THE TIME IS UP, YOU MAY CHECK OVER YOUR WORK ON THIS PART ONLY.

PART 7

Auto and Shop Information

Time: 11 Minutes—25 Questions

1. If the first stroke on a four-stroke engine is the intake stroke, what is the second?

   A. Intake
   B. Power
   C. Exhaust
   D. Compression

2. A starter motor does not make any noise when the key is turned in the ignition, but the lights on the car work. The first thing that should be checked is

   A. the fuse box
   B. the battery charge
   C. the distributor
   D. the throttle valve

3. The device used to transfer power from the drive shaft to the rear axle is called the

   A. distributor
   B. differential
   C. master cylinder
   D. torque converter

4. The engine is overheating. One of the possible causes is

   A. not enough fluid in the radiator
   B. malfunctioning distributor
   C. lean air/fuel mixture
   D. vapor lock

5. A thick, black sludge is found in the tailpipe of the car. This is probably due to

   A. oil leaking into a cylinder
   B. rich fuel/air mixture
   C. condensation in the tail pipe
   D. a clogged exhaust manifold

6. The pinion gear is found on the

   A. braking system
   B. steering system
   C. transmission
   D. clutch

7. Condensation inside fuel tanks could lead to

   A. a sludge forming at the bottom of the gas tank
   B. potential for fire in the gas tank
   C. misfiring cylinders
   D. the vehicle stalling

8. An automatic transmission vehicle fails to accelerate as it should and does not shift smoothly. The problem is probably

   A. not enough transmission fluid
   B. jammed differential
   C. damaged wheel bearings
   D. improper timing

9. Spark plugs should be seated in the port with a torque wrench to prevent

   A. the piston from hitting the spark plug on the top of the stroke
   B. changing the timing of the distributor
   C. damaging the spark plug's body
   D. threading the engine block

10. The thermostat controls

    A. oil temperature in the engine
    B. water temperature in the manifold
    C. water temperature in the radiator
    D. the exhaust temperature

11. The engine seems to "run loud" in a car. The problem might be

    A. worn wheel bearings
    B. overextended piston rods
    C. a crack in the exhaust manifold
    D. too much oil

12. A high-pitched squeak comes from the wheels when stopping. The most likely problem is

    A. the master cylinder over-pressurized the lines
    B. the wheel bearings are damaged
    C. the brake shoes are worn
    D. the rims are rubbing on the wheel bearings

GO ON TO THE NEXT PAGE.

13. To oxidize unburned hydrocarbons, the catalytic converter uses

    A. special chemical-coated beads
    B. a burner
    C. a small oxygen tank
    D. positive exhaust ventilation

14. Calipers are used to

    A. clamp objects together
    B. pick objects up
    C. measure the outside diameter of a pipe
    D. remove stuck screws

15. Which of the following can be used when cutting an angle in a piece of wood stock?

    A. Jack plane
    B. C clamp
    C. Miter box
    D. Jointer plane

16. The tool pictured above is used to

    A. cut across the grain of wood
    B. cut sheet metal
    C. cut curves
    D. cut through nails embedded in wood

17. When tapping a hole for a screw, it is important to

    A. start with a center punch
    B. keep driving in until the threads are deep enough
    C. regularly back out the tap
    D. use a rubber mallet

18. Grinding wheels are used

    A. in place of a jack plane
    B. to sand wood
    C. to cut through sheet metal
    D. to remove metal burrs

19. The main constituents in concrete are

    A. cement and sand
    B. water and cement
    C. gravel, water, and cement
    D. sand, gravel, water, and cement

20. The cutting parts of a boring bit are found

    A. at the tips
    B. in the screw portion
    C. between the tips and the center
    D. in the main shaft

21. The screw length of a flathead screw is the length of the

    A. threaded portion only
    B. head, shanks and threaded portion
    C. the width of the head
    D. shank and the threaded portion

22. For optimum use, rivets should

    A. allow for the diameter of motion in the two sheets being joined
    B. be near a bolted connection
    C. be of the same material as the sheet metal being joined
    D. be hot during installation

23. The tool shown above is a(n)

    A. socket wrench
    B. box wrench
    C. open end wrench
    D. speed wrench

24. A chalk line is often used

    A. to measure the chalk content in concrete
    B. when dry lubricant is needed
    C. to mark a straight line between two points
    D. to write on wood

25. Which tool is used to determine when two objects are normal to each other?

    A. Miter box
    B. Level
    C. Calipers and rule
    D. Square

STOP!
IF YOU FINISH BEFORE THE TIME IS UP, YOU MAY CHECK OVER YOUR WORK ON THIS PART ONLY.

PART 8

Mechanical Comprehension

Time: 19 Minutes—25 Questions

1. 100 degrees Celsius is equal to how many degrees Fahrenheit?

   A. 0
   B. 32
   C. 100
   D. 212

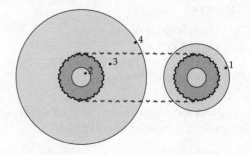

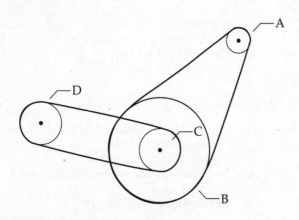

2. Which pulley turns the slowest?

   A. A
   B. B
   C. C
   D. D

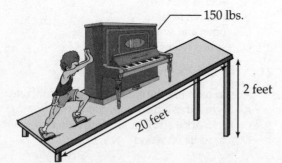

3. How much force is needed to push the piano up the ramp?

   A. 15 lbs.
   B. 50 lbs.
   C. 75 lbs.
   D. 150 lbs.

4. If the wheel above rotates, which of the dots will rotate at the slowest rate?

   A. 1
   B. 2
   C. 3
   D. All the dots will rotate at the same rate

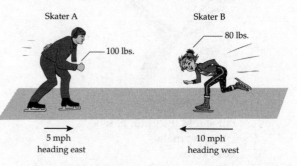

5. Skater A and B collide and stick together. After the collision, which of the following is true?

   A. Both skaters stop at the point of impact.
   B. The skaters will move to the west at a speed of less than 10 miles per hour.
   C. The skaters will move to the east at a speed of greater than 10 miles per hour.
   D. The skaters will move to the east at a speed of less than 10 miles per hour.

6. A ramp is an example of

   A. a lever
   B. a fulcrum
   C. a block and tackle
   D. an inclined plane

GO ON TO THE NEXT PAGE.

7. If all of the following objects are at the same temperature, which will feel the coldest?

A. A metal teakettle
B. A plastic bucket
C. A wool sweater
D. A blade of grass

8. If rock A weighing 2 lbs. and rock B weighing 3 lbs. are both dropped at the same time from a height of 100 m, which of the two will reach the ground first?

A. Rock A
B. Rock B
C. Both rocks will reach the ground at the same time.
D. Not enough information is available.

9. Gear A, which has a diameter of 4 feet, is turning gear B, which has a diameter of 1 foot. If gear A makes one revolution, how many revolutions does gear B make?

A. One revolution
B. Two revolutions
C. Four revolutions
D. Eight revolutions

10. If Mr. Thompson is pouring sand into a sandbox at a rate of 60 lbs. per minute and his daughter is removing sand from the sandbox at a rate of 1 lb. per second, then after two minutes the amount of sand in the sandbox will

A. have increased by 60 lbs.
B. have increased by 120 lbs.
C. have decreased by 60 lbs.
D. be exactly the same

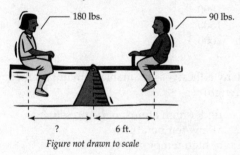

180 lbs.   90 lbs.

?   6 ft.

Figure not drawn to scale

11. Suppose that the person on the left is sitting three feet from the fulcrum on the side of the seesaw away from the person on the right. How heavy would the person on the left need to be in order to balance the seesaw?

A. 30 lbs.
B. 60 lbs.
C. 120 lbs.
D. 180 lbs.

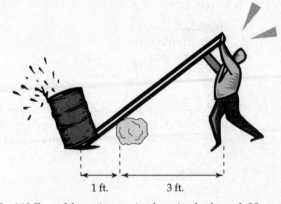

1 ft.   3 ft.

12. 160 lbs. of force is required to tip the barrel. How much force must the worker apply to the lever?

A. 20 lbs.
B. 40 lbs.
C. 60 lbs.
D. 80 lbs.

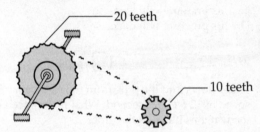

20 teeth

10 teeth

13. What is the theoretical mechanical advantage conferred by the gears of the bicycle?

A. $\frac{1}{2}$

B. 1

C. 2

D. 5

14. Which type of belt is least likely to stretch?

A. Leather
B. Rubber
C. Canvas
D. All three are equally likely to stretch.

GO ON TO THE NEXT PAGE.

15. Water condenses on pipes that

   A. contain hot water
   B. contain cold water
   C. contain steam
   D. are empty

16. The water pressure surrounding a submarine is 150 psi. A porthole on the submarine measures 10 square inches. What is the force on the porthole?

   A.   15 lbs.
   B.   150 lbs.
   C.   1500 lbs.
   D. 15,000 lbs.

17. If the temperature of a gas increases

   A. its charge will increase
   B. its charge will decrease
   C. its pressure will increase
   D. its pressure will decrease

18. Water flows into the pipe from the right at a speed of 12 feet per second. What is the speed of the water as it leaves the pipe?

   A. 2 feet per second
   B. 3 feet per second
   C. 8 feet per second
   D. 24 feet per second

19. If two pipes carry liquids moving at the same velocity, then the pipe with the least area will have the

   A. lowest flow rate
   B. highest flow rate
   C. the same flow rate as the other pipe
   D. highest mass

20. Which of the following is a substance commonly used to reduce friction?

   A. Gravel
   B. Sand
   C. Gasoline
   D. Oil

21. When shafts are not parallel, which type of gears should be used?

   A. Spur gears
   B. Bevel gears
   C. Helical gears
   D. Straight gears

22. Which of the following is a device designed to connect or disconnect driving and a driven member for the purpose of starting or stopping the driven part?

   A. A wheel
   B. An axle
   C. An engine
   D. A clutch

23. The device most commonly used to convey liquids against the force of gravity is the

   A. block and tackle
   B. clutch
   C. generator
   D. pump

24. One mile equals approximately how many meters?

   A.   500
   B. 1000
   C. 1500
   D. 2000

25. Many adhesives are unable to maintain their strength

   A. under high atmospheric pressure
   B. at low temperatures
   C. at high temperatures
   D. at room temperatures

STOP!
IF YOU FINISH BEFORE THE TIME IS UP, YOU MAY
CHECK OVER YOUR WORK ON THIS PART ONLY.

Chapter 14
Practice Test 2:
Answers and
Explanations

PRACTICE TEST 2
STUDENT ASVAB
ANSWERS AND EXPLANATIONS

Part 1—General Science

1. **A**   A primary consumer is an organism that lives off producers (plants) only.

2. **C**   Toward the end of the Mesozoic Era, a mass extinction of many species, including dinosaurs, occurred.

3. **D**   Oxidation occurs when metallic elements in rock combine with oxygen.

4. **B**   Carbon dioxide, water, and sunlight are all required for photosynthesis.

5. **C**   Sperm are produced in the seminiferous tubules, which merge into a large duct called the vas deferens.

6. **A**   Diploid cells contain 23 pairs of chromosomes, for a total of 46. Almost all human cells are diploid, except for sex cells.

7. **B**   The intertidal zone is located where the land and water meet.

8. **D**   The atomic number of an element is equivalent to the number of protons it has.

9. **C**   Matter has three states: solid, liquid, and gas.

10. **A**   A blue object reflects blue light waves only.

11. **B**   Smooth muscles are found in the stomach, cardiac muscles are found in the heart, and skeletal muscles are attached to bones.

12. **D**   Mollusks are technically animals.

13. **B**   The nucleus is called the control center of the cell.

14. **C**   Cytokinesis is the splitting of the cytoplasm.

15. **A**   When magma cools and solidifies it becomes igneous rock.

16. **B**   The thermosphere is divided into two regions, the ionosphere and the exosphere.

17. **D**   The Jovian planets are Jupiter, Saturn, Uranus, and Neptune.

18. **A**   Kinetic energy is energy found in a moving object.

19. **C** An element is a substance that cannot be broken down further by chemical means. Water, carbon dioxide, and salt water all can be broken down further; they are all made up of different elements.

20. **B** Refraction is the bending of light.

21. **A** Electrons have a charge of –1, protons have a charge of +1, and neutrons are neutral. Isotopes are not subatomic particles.

22. **C** The central nervous system consists of the brain and spinal cord.

23. **B** The two homozygous parents have a genotype of *BB*. They can only pass on *B* genes, never *b* genes, which they do not have. Therefore, their children will always have the genotype *BB* and always have brown eyes.

24. **B** Fungi are multicellular, but they do not have stems or leaves and do not carry on photosynthesis.

25. **A** Tropical rain forests get more rain than anywhere else on earth—hence the name.

Part 2—Arithmetic Reasoning

1. **B** Use Bite-Size Pieces to answer this problem. First, subtract the 7 people who haven't paid from the total number in the group: 15 − 7 = 8. That means that 8 people have paid. Divide the amount of money collected so far by 8: 177.60 ÷ 8 = 22.20. Each person is to pay $22.20. Multiply that by the 7 people who still need to pay: 22.20 × 7 = 155.40. That is the amount of money that still needs to be collected. Add that to the money already collected, and you have the answer: 177.60 + 155.40 = 333.00.

2. **A** Use the Average Pie to answer this question. Add David's weight to Lisa and Annette's combined weight to get the total. Put the total and the number of items in the set (3) into the Average Pie to find the average: 390 ÷ 3 = 130.

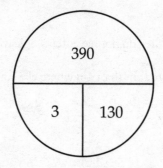

3. **C** Use Bite-Size Pieces to answer this problem. First, multiply 55 by 2: 55 × 2 = 110. That's how far Gina traveled in the first 2 hours. Then, multiply 60 by 3: 60 × 3 = 180. That's how far she traveled in the next 3 hours. Add the sums together: 110 + 180 = 290.

4. **D** To find the probability that a red marble will be chosen, add all the marbles in the sack together: 6 + 9 + 2 + 4 = 21. Then put the number of red marbles over the total: $\frac{6}{21}$. That's the probability that a red marble will be selected.

5. **C** Use Bite-Size Pieces for this problem. First, subtract the cost to lease the car from the monthly budget: 500 − 179 = 321. This is the amount of money you have to spend on mileage. Next, divide that by the cost per mile: 321 ÷ .06 = 5350.

6. **B** This is a weighted-average problem, so you need to weight the grades accordingly. Multiply each grade by the weight assigned to it: 90 × 2 = 180, 88 × 3 = 264, and 85 × 4 = 340. Add the products together and divide by the total number of weights: 784 ÷ 9 = 87.111.

7. **A** To find the answer, all you need to do is figure out what Jack's discount was. To find this, multiply 350 by 15%: 350 × 0.15 = 52.5.

8. **B** The real plane is 115 feet long and each inch of the model represents 7 feet. Divide 115 by 7 to find the length of the model: 115 ÷ 7 = 16.43 inches. The closest answer is (B).

9. **A**   1 pound = 16 ounces, so Dave bought 4.5 pounds of steak. Divide the total cost of the steak by 4.5 to find the cost per pound: 16.83 ÷ 4.5 = 3.74.

10. **B**   To answer a proportion question, match up the categories and solve for the missing item.

$$\frac{1 \text{ chair}}{2.5 \text{ days}} = \frac{x \text{ chairs}}{55 \text{ days}}$$

Then cross-multiply and solve.

$$2.5x = 55$$
$$x = 22$$

11. **D** $3(9)^2 - 7(9) + 4 =$
$3(81) - 63 + 4 =$
$243 - 63 + 4 = 184$

12. **B**   Divide the actual harvest by the estimated harvest: 4850 ÷ 4300 = 1.127, which rounds up to 113%.

13. **D**   Use Bite-Size Pieces for this problem. First, calculate the total cost for each type of item purchased: 2 × 8.89 = 17.78, 1 × 12.50 = 12.50, 3 × 0.79 = 2.37, 2 × 17.99 = 35.98, 4 × 7.79 = 31.16. Then, add up the products for the total amount of the day's purchases: 17.78 + 12.50 + 2.37 + 35.98 + 31.16 = 99.79. Add that total to the $100 that is already in the cash register: 100 + 99.79 = 199.79.

14. **B**   Subtract the second term from the first term (3 − 1 = 2) and the third term from the second term (7 − 3 = 4). The differences are 2 and 4. Subtract the fourth term from the third term (13 − 7 = 6). The difference is 6. The numbers in the sequence are increasing by multiples of two. So the fifth number will be 8 greater than the fourth number, the sixth 10 greater than the fifth, and the seventh 12 greater than the sixth.

15. **B**   Use Bite-Size Pieces to solve this problem. First, calculate the number of Democrats in Mr. Kelley's class: $36 \times \frac{2}{3} = 24$ Democrats. Therefore, there are 36 − 24 = 12 Republicans. Next, calculate the number of Republicans in Ms. Richey's class: $28 \times \frac{3}{4} = 21$ Republicans. That leaves 28 − 21 = 7 Democrats. Add the number of Democrats from each classroom and the number of Republicans from each classroom. Democrats: 24 + 7 = 31. Republicans: 12 + 21 = 33.

16. **D** $\sqrt{2}\,\sqrt{8} = \sqrt{16} = 4$

17. **C** Make a Ratio Box for this problem and fill in everything you know.

Grass	Food	Total
1	2	3
		15

What multiplied by 3 gives you 15? 5 does, so fill it in.

Grass	Food	Total
1	2	3
× 5	× 5	× 5
5	10	15

From the table you can see that when the goat has eaten 15 pounds of food, 5 pounds is grass and 10 pounds is goat food.

18. **A** $6x - 4 = 38$

$6x = 42$

$x = 7$

19. **C** Figure out how many pints there are in the 50-gallon barrel. There are 8 pints in a gallon. Multiply 50 gallons by 8 pints: $50 \times 8 = 400$ pints.

20. **C** Start by reducing this fraction into something a little easier to work with: $\frac{9}{72} \times \frac{9}{9} = \frac{1}{8}$. Recall that a fraction bar implies division. So divide 1 by 8: $1 \div 8 = 0.125$, or 12.5%.

21. **D** $5^3 = 5 \times 5 \times 5 = 125$

22. **B** Divide the number made by the number attempted: $294 \div 420 = 0.7$, or 70%.

23. **A** Divide 20.00 by 3.20: $20 \div 3.20 = 6.25$.

24. **D** 22% of $35.00 is $7.70: $0.22 \times 35 = 7.7$. Subtract that from the regular cost: $35.00 - 7.70 = 27.30$.

25. **B** Distance = rate × time

$420 = 8 \times$ rate

rate = 52.5

26. **A** Subtract $x - 2y = 10$ from $3x + 5y = 15$.

$$\begin{array}{r} 3x + 5y - 15 \\ -(x - 2y + 10) \\ \hline 2x + 7y = 5 \end{array}$$

27. **A** $-9m - 12 > 11 - 3m$. To solve this one, you need to isolate the variable. Add $3m$ to both sides. This gives you: $-6m - 12 > 11$. Next, add 12 to both sides and you get: $-6m > 23$. Finally, divide both sides by -6. Remember, since this is an inequality and not an equal sign, you need to flip the sign around since you're dividing by a negative number. This gives you the answer: $m < -\dfrac{23}{6}$.

28. **C** When dividing by a multiple of ten, move the decimal point to the left one space for each 0. Since you are dividing by 100, which has two 0s, move the decimal to the left two spaces.

29. **B** Use the Bow Tie. Multiply the denominators to find a common factor: $5 \times 6 = 30$. Then cross-multiply to find the new numerators: $3 \times 6 = 18$ and $5 \times 5 = 25$. Then add

$$\frac{18}{30} + \frac{25}{30} = \frac{43}{30} = 1\frac{13}{30}$$

30. **C** Add the weights of the four tankers to find the total: $10{,}000 + 10{,}000 + 10{,}000 + 12{,}000 = 42{,}000$. The number of items is 4. So divide by 4 to find the average: $42{,}000 \div 4 = 10{,}500$.

Part 3—Word Knowledge

1. **B**   Accidental: Happening by chance or unexpectedly

2. **C**   Refute: To disprove

3. **B**   Revolution: A political overthrow

4. **A**   Values: Beliefs of a person or social group

5. **D**   Poll: To obtain and analyze information or opinions from people; a survey of people's opinions

6. **C**   Conquer: To defeat an opponent

7. **A**   Disturb: To interfere with

8. **D**   Opponent: One who takes an opposite position

9. **B**   Adapt: To adjust or make usable

10. **A**   Awe: An emotion combining fear and wonder

11. **C**   Colleague: A co-worker

12. **D**   Misleading: Deceptive

13. **A**   Pledge: To make a binding commitment to do or give or refrain from something

14. **D**   Resentment: Deep hatred

15. **C**   Sufficient: Enough

16. **B**   Animated: Filled with life, activity, vigor, or spirit

17. **C**   Transparent: Clear; see-through

18. **A**   Graceful: Characterized by beauty of movement, style, form, etc.

19. **D**   Indignation: Moral outrage

20. **B**   Insightful: Exhibiting clear and deep perception

21. **B**   Skeptical: Doubtful; disbelieving

22. **C**   Reaction: The act or process or an instance of responding; a response

23. **A**   Validity: Truth; correctness

24. **D**   Turmoil: A state or condition of extreme confusion, agitation, or commotion

25. **C** Undermine: To remove support from; to weaken

26. **A** Quarrel: A verbal conflict between antagonists

27. **A** Potential: Possible

28. **D** Influential: Having influence or power

29. **C** Infer: To conclude or figure out

30. **B** Persuasive: Able to move people to act or believe

31. **B** Precious: Highly esteemed or cherished

32. **A** Irrelevant: Having no connection to a subject

33. **C** Nostalgia: Longing for familiar things or persons, or for a period of time or an occurrence that has past

34. **C** Impulse: Force or urge

35. **D** Hazardous: Involving risk or danger

Part 4—Paragraph Comprehension

1. **D** This is an EXCEPT question, so you're looking for the answer that is not stated in the passage. Choice (D) is the answer because the court voted unanimously.

2. **B** Choices (A) and (B) are saying the opposite of each other, so one of them is probably the correct answer. By referring back to the passage, you can see that Picasso was an example of an artist who demonstrated many artistic styles in his work. Hence, the answer is (B).

3. **D** Politicians are never mentioned in the passage, so get rid of (A). They exposed abuses of power and money, so get rid of (B). They came about in the beginning of the 20th century, so get rid of (C). That leaves you with (D).

4. **C** Look for a paraphrase of the passage. Choice (C) paraphrases the first sentence, so it's the answer.

5. **B** The passage says that Neanderthals had different facial structures than Homo sapiens so eliminate (A). Choice (C) is never mentioned, and (D) is the opposite of what the passage says, so the answer is (B).

6. **B** Since it's an inference question, look for a paraphrase of the passage. The best answer is (B).

7. **D** This is a main idea question in disguise. The main idea of the passage is not milk or the diet of the cow, so eliminate (A) and (C). Choice (B) is too general, so the answer is (D).

8. **D** Choice (A) isn't true, so cross it off. Water freezes at zero degrees Celsius, not Fahrenheit, so cross off (B), and the passage never mentions (C), so the answer is (D).

9. **B** The passage states that the author is leaving home next week.

10. **A** Choice (A) can be inferred from the passage because remains from Mars must be able to find their way to Earth if a meteor from Mars was found in the Arctic. The passage doesn't say (B) or (D), and (C) is extreme.

11. **A** The passage states "Her efforts were instrumental in the establishment of hospitals and asylums for the mentally ill." This supports (A).

12. **D** Choices (A) and (C) are never mentioned, and (B) is the opposite. So, the answer is (D).

13. **C** Choices (A) and (B) are mentioned in the passage, but are not the main point. Choice (D) is never stated. Choice (C) is a nice paraphrase of the last sentence, which is the main point.

14. **B** Use the lead words "cancer patients" to guide you to the answer. Cross off answers that are mentioned in the passage, and that leaves you with (B).

15. **D** Look for the sentence that paraphrases the question. Choices (A) and (C) are never stated, and (B) is extreme. Choice (D) is a paraphrase of the main point.

Part 5—Mathematics Knowledge

1. **A**   The easiest way to solve this problem is to Plug In the Answers. If you plug in 3 (A) for x you get: $[7(3)]^2 = [21]^2 = 441$.

2. **D**   The scale is 1 inch = 15 feet. Divide 202 by 15 to find the height of the scale model: $202 \div 15 = 13$ remainder 7, or 13.4. That's approximately $13\frac{1}{2}$ inches.

3. **C**   If the area is 56 inches and the length is 7 inches, then you can use the area formula to find the width.

    $$\text{Area} = \text{length} \times \text{width}$$
    $$56 = 7w$$
    $$w = 8$$

4. **C**   Use Plugging In to solve this problem. Say each fruit stand has 5 apples and 4 oranges. That's 9 pieces of fruit at each stand. Then we multiply that number by 7, since there are seven stands, for a total of 63 pieces of fruit. So 63 is the target number. Now you need to plug in 4 and 5 into the answer choices to find the target number. When you plug in those numbers, only (C) works: $7(5) + 7(4) = 35 + 28 = 63$.

5. **A**   Perimeter is found by adding the lengths of all sides. The best way to find the length of the pool is to plug in numbers from the answer choices. If you plug in (A), 20, then you get: length = 20 and width = 15.

    $$20 + 20 + 15 + 15 = 70$$

6. **A**   An octagon has 8 sides, and a quadrilateral has 4. The difference is 4.

7. **C**   Multiply each term in $x^2 + 6x + 3$ by x, then multiply each term by 3.

    $$x(x^2 + 6x + 3) = x^3 + 6x^2 + 3x, \text{ and } 3(x^2 + 6x + 3) = 3x^2 + 18x + 9.$$

    Then add the results together.

    $$x^3 + 6x^2 + 3x + 3x^2 + 18x + 9 = x^3 + 9x^2 + 21x + 9$$

8. **B**   Plug In the Answers to find the one that works. If you plug in (B), which is 2, then you get

    $$2(2) + 4 = 2^3$$
    $$4 + 4 = 8$$

9. **C**   Area $= \pi r^2$, so in this problem, area $= 16\pi$. The problem tells you that $\pi = 3.14$, so $16 \times 3.14 = 50.24$. Or you can Ballpark to find the answer.

10. **A**   The area of a square is side^2, or side $\times$ side, so you have $\sqrt{64\pi^2} = 8\pi$.

11. **C** Volume = length × width × height. So for this problem, volume = 2 × 3 × 4 = 24.

12. **C** Two factors of 20 are 4 and 5. Four has a square root, 2, which can be pulled out. So you get

$$2\sqrt{20} = 2\sqrt{4 \times 5} = 2\sqrt{2 \times 2 \times 5} = 2 \times 2\sqrt{5} = 4\sqrt{5}$$

13. **B** $25\% = \dfrac{1}{4}$. So ask yourself: $\dfrac{1}{4}$ of what number equals 10? Try plugging in the answer choices. When you try (B), you have $\dfrac{1}{4}$ of forty, 10, so you've found the answer.

14. **D** Recall that the order after the decimal point is: tenths, hundredths, thousandths.

15. **C** Remember Fred's Theorem. $\angle a = 65$ and $\angle b = 95$, so $a + b = 160$.

16. **B** $x < 7$ means that x is less than 7, and $-9 \leq x$ means that x is greater than or equal to -9.

17. **A** Circumference = $2\pi r$, or π diameter. Since the diameter is 4, the answer is 4π.

18. **C** Solve for x by dividing both sides of the equation by 6: $x = 15$.

19. **D** $3^3 = 3 \times 3 \times 3 = 27$

20. **B** A hexagon has six sides, and the perimeter is the sum of the lengths of all the sides, so: $6 \times 5 = 30$.

21. **A** Multiply $2xy$ by both of the terms inside the parentheses. Remember that when multiplying exponents, you add them together and that any variable by itself without an exponent is the same as that variable with an exponent of 1 ($y = y^1$). So $2xy \times 4y = 8xy^2$ and $2xy \times 5x^2 = 10x^3y$. The answer is (A).

22. **C** Use Plugging In on this one. Choose any odd integer and plug it into the answer choices. Try using 3. If you plug 3 into the answer choices, the only answer that is also an odd integer is (C): $3 + 2 = 5$.

23. **D** Find the area of each side of the box and add the areas together: front = 30, back = 30, top = 24, bottom = 24, side = 20, side = 20. 30 + 30 + 24 + 24 + 20 + 20 = 148.

24. **C** Remember, you must always flip the inequality when multiplying or dividing by a negative number.

$$-5x + 6 < 61$$
$$-5x < 55$$
$$x > -11$$

25.   **B**   Draw a picture of the car's route. Then sketch a line from the end point to the starting point. That is the distance you are trying to find. Your sketch should look something like this.

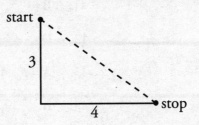

Does this look familiar? It should—it's a right triangle. Use the Pythagorean Theorem to find the distance.

$$3^2 + 4^2 = x^2$$
$$9 + 16 = x^2$$
$$25 = x^2$$
$$x = 5$$

Part 6—Electronics Information

1. **A**
2. **B**
3. **B**
4. **C**
5. **D**
6. **C**
7. **C**
8. **A**
9. **B**
10. **B**
11. **B**
12. **D**
13. **A**
14. **B**
15. **B**
16. **D**
17. **C**
18. **D**
19. **A**
20. **B**

Part 7—Auto and Shop Information

1. **D** After the air and fuel is taken into the cylinders, the valves close, and the piston returns to the top of the cylinder. This is the compression stroke. Next is the power stroke, during which the spark plug ignites the fuel/air mixture. Then the exhaust valve opens, and the piston returns to the top of the cylinder to expel the exhaust gases.

2. **A** When looking for problems in the vehicle, it is important to start from the source and work back toward the malfunctioning component. This allows you to identify big-picture problems that could be cheaper to fix. The lights on the car work, but not the starter. That means that the battery works. Following the power from the working battery, the next problem could be a blown fuse in the fuse box. After that, the connection of the electrical cables leading to the starter should be checked. If you still can't find the problem at this point, then the starter itself is probably at fault.

3. **B** The distributor controls the timing and distribution of electricity to the spark plugs. The master cylinder is in the braking system. The torque converter works like a clutch in an automatic transmission. The differential gear is a grouping of gears that connects the driveshaft to the rear axles.

4. **A** Choice (D) would cause the engine to stall. Choice (B) would cause the engine to stall out or to sputter and misfire. A lean fuel/air mix would actually cool the engine a bit, as it reduces the combustion temperature. But if there is not enough coolant in the cooling system, then the coolant will not be able to cool significantly before it reenters the engine block to take up more heat.

5. **A** A thick black sludge normally forms in the tail pipe due to something burning and depositing in the exhaust system. Choice (B) is incorrect because unburned fuel usually evaporates and leaves the vehicle. Choice (D) is wrong because a clogged exhaust system would not allow anything to pass out of the system. Choice (C) is wrong because, though water can mix with built-up carbon deposits and accumulate in the exhaust system, its sludge is normally thin and runny. Oil, however, is heavy and, when burned, does not always exit the exhaust system, leaving a thick black sludge.

6. **B** The pinion is used in conjunction with the rack gear to turn the wheels.

7. **A** If you have ever seen an oil slick on water, you have seen that the water tends to sink and the oil moves to the surface of the water. This is true in a gas tank as well. The water moves to the bottom of the tank, where it mixes with the impurities that settle out of the gas. This typically causes sludge to form at the bottom of the tank. As for (B), the only way to start a fire in the gas tank is to put it near a heat source or spark. And water in the cylinders still allows the fuel to burn and the cylinder to go through its power stroke, though the combustion will not be as complete.

8. **A** Choices (B) and (C) both deal with problems that would occur farther down the drive train. Improper timing prevents the cylinders from firing in the right sequence and would affect the smoothness of the engine. But, because automatic transmissions use a torque converter, if there is not enough fluid, the pump will not be able to turn the turbine properly.

9. **D** The torque wrench allows the user to know how much force is being applied to the bolt. This prevents the tool from overtightening and potentially from stripping the threads.

10. **B** The thermostat opens when the water in the manifold reaches a certain temperature and then closes again to allow the water into the radiator to cool. The water in the radiator can't get back into the engine without the thermostat opening, but its opening is based only on coolant temperatures in the manifold.

11. **C** Choice (A) can be discarded because the wheels are not part of the engine. One of the purposes of the exhaust system is to help quiet the car. If there is a crack in the manifold before the gases can go through the exhaust system, then the car will "run loud." Too much oil will generally quiet the vehicle.

12. **C** Since the sound only comes when stopping, the sounds are probably coming from the brakes. Damaged wheel bearings would make noise whether the vehicle is stopping or just cruising down the road.

13. **A** The oxidation process in the catalytic converter is entirely chemical. The chemical coating on the beads works to push ahead the oxidation process without burning the gases.

14. **C** Calipers are strictly a measuring device and should not be used for anything else.

15. **C** A miter box is used to hold the saw's blade in line while cutting angles. Planes are used to shape wood surfaces. A C clamp just holds objects together.

16. **C** The first step is to identify the picture as a coping saw. The coping saw has a thin blade to allow it to flex and cut curves and corners in wood.

17. **C** If a tap is not taken completely out of the hole while the threads are being made, the shavings will clog in the end of the tap and jam the tap in the hole. The tap should be taken out of the hole every 5 turns to clean off the shavings.

18. **D** Grinding wheels are not used to remove large pieces of material; they are designed to remove small pieces of metals or to smooth or polish a surface. The jack plane is used on wood, not metal.

19. **D** To make concrete, you need all of these components mixed wet and allowed to dry.

20. **C** A boring bit uses a different method from that of standard bits. The boring bit uses a threaded part to draw it into a piece of stock. Two points then scribe a circle that is to be drilled. The material is then removed from within this circle by the cutting blades located between the center and the tips.

21. **D** The length of a screw is the distance that it will sink into a piece of wood. So if the head is a standard round head, the length is the shank and threaded portion only, since the head will stick up above the surface of the wood. If the head is a countersink head, then the length of the screw is the full length of the fastener including the head. The question does not tell you that the screw is a countersink head, so assume it's a standard.

22. **C** Rivets should fit snugly into the rivet holes, but the materials *must* be the same. If they are not the same, then chemical reactions can take place at the interface between the two metals and the joint will be very weak.

23. **B** Since the end of the wrench is closed, this must be a box wrench.

24. **C** Chalk lines are ropes covered in chalk that are stretched between two points and laid on the ground. The line is then snapped upward, and some of the chalk falls off, leaving a temporary line of chalk between the two points. As for (A), there is no chalk in concrete. And a pencil, not a chalk line, is the best thing for writing on wood.

25. **D** "Normal" means at a right angle. The tool to use in this case is a square. A level only allows the user to see if something is horizontal or vertical and is therefore not the best tool for the job.

Part 8—Mechanical Comprehension

1. **D**
2. **B**
3. **A**
4. **D**
5. **D**
6. **D**
7. **A**
8. **D**
9. **C**
10. **D**
11. **C**
12. **B**
13. **C**
14. **B**
15. **A**
16. **C**
17. **C**
18. **B**
19. **A**
20. **D**
21. **B**
22. **D**
23. **D**
24. **C**
25. **C**

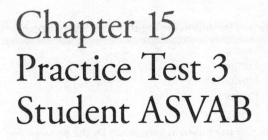

Chapter 15
Practice Test 3
Student ASVAB

PART 1

General Science

Time: 11 Minutes—25 Questions

1. The atomic number for magnesium is 12. Magnesium always has

    A. 12 protons
    B. 12 electrons
    C. 12 neutrons
    D. 12 molecules

2. The lungs are part of the

    A. skeletal system
    B. vascular system
    C. respiratory system
    D. immune system

3. Which of the following organisms is a producer?

    A. Lions
    B. Fungi
    C. Humans
    D. Plants

4. Which of the following are made by the process of meiosis?

    A. Zygotes
    B. Sex cells
    C. Chromosomes
    D. Nuclei

5. What type of muscles are found in the heart?

    A. Cardiac
    B. Smooth
    C. Rough
    D. Skeletal

6. Which of the following is a universal recipient of a blood donation?

    A. Type A
    B. Type B
    C. Type AB
    D. Type O

7. Ova are produced in the

    A. ovaries
    B. uterus
    C. Fallopian tubes
    D. vas deferens

8. The largest planet in the solar system is

    A. Neptune
    B. Earth
    C. Jupiter
    D. Mercury

9. Parent A has a genotype *bb* for a certain trait, and Parent B has a genotype *Bb* for the same trait. Which of the following represents the list of possible genotypes of these parents' offspring?

    A. *Bb bb bb bb*
    B. *Bb Bb bb bb*
    C. *BB BB Bb Bb*
    D. *BB BB BB BB*

10. Cell fragments that are involved in blood clotting are called

    A. plasma
    B. red blood cells
    C. white blood cells
    D. platelets

11. Which of the following is NOT part of the nervous system?

    A. Peripheral
    B. Lymphatic
    C. Somatic
    D. Autonomic

12. This biome is found south of the tundra in the northern hemisphere and is populated by evergreen trees and bears, wolves, elk, beavers, and moose.

    A. Biome 2
    B. Biome 3
    C. Biome 4
    D. Biome 5

GO ON TO THE NEXT PAGE.

13. The earliest geologic time period is the

    A. Paleozoic Era
    B. Cenozoic Era
    C. Precambrian Era
    D. Mesozoic Era

14. Which of the following is the study of the interactions between living things and their environments?

    A. Geology
    B. Ecology
    C. Biology
    D. Meteorology

15. Which of the following is NOT a biome into which the ocean is divided?

    A. Neritic Zone
    B. Intertidal Zone
    C. Tundra Zone
    D. Oceanic Zone

16. The layer of atmosphere that is closest to Earth is the

    A. Stratosphere
    B. Mesosphere
    C. Thermosphere
    D. Troposphere

17. Which of the following correctly lists the layers of the Sun from innermost to outermost?

    A. Core, atmosphere, inner zones
    B. Core, inner zones, atmosphere
    C. Inner zones, core, atmosphere
    D. Atmosphere, core, inner zone

18. A lunar eclipse occurs when the

    A. Sun blocks the Moon
    B. Moon blocks the Sun's light
    C. Earth blocks the Sun's light
    D. Moon moves behind the Sun

19. The bronchus, larynx, epiglottis, and pharynx are parts of the

    A. digestive system
    B. excretory system
    C. circulatory system
    D. respiratory system

20. A deficiency in which of the following vitamins can result in scurvy?

    A. A
    B. B_1
    C. C
    D. D

21. Which layer of Earth's atmosphere is farthest from the core of the Earth?

    A. Troposphere
    B. Stratosphere
    C. Mesosphere
    D. Thermosphere

22. A hot air balloon is controlled by heating and cooling the air in the balloon. This process is called

    A. convection
    B. conduction
    C. radiation
    D. magnetism

23. Which geologic time period spanned the greatest number of years?

    A. Precambrian Era
    B. Paleozoic Era
    C. Mesozoic Era
    D. Cenozoic Era

24. Which term refers to the rate at which work is done?

    A. Momentum
    B. Power
    C. Speed
    D. Velocity

25. Which of the following pH levels indicates the strongest acid?

    A. 2
    B. 4
    C. 8
    D. 13

STOP!
IF YOU FINISH BEFORE THE TIME IS UP, YOU MAY
CHECK OVER YOUR WORK ON THIS PART ONLY.

PART 2

Arithmetic Reasoning

Time: 36 Minutes—30 Questions

1. If $x = 6$, then $x^2 + 7x - 5 =$

   A. -11
   B. -1
   C. 73
   D. 83

2. Tristan purchased three model helicopters for $7.85 each, two model airplanes for $14.25 each, and two bottles of model glue for $3.50 each. If Tristan gave the cashier a $100 bill, how much change did he receive?

   A. $40.95
   B. $48.80
   C. $74.40
   D. $125.60

3. What is the difference between $9x^2 + 14x - 28$ and $2x^2 - 12x + 43$?

   A. $7x^2 - 2x - 15$
   B. $7x^2 + 26x - 71$
   C. $11x^2 - 2x - 71$
   D. $11x^2 + 26x - 15$

4. A jar has 20 red jellybeans, 14 green jellybeans, 12 orange jellybeans, and 7 yellow jellybeans. If one jellybean is chosen at random, what is the probability that it will be a green jellybean?

   A. $\dfrac{14}{53}$

   B. $\dfrac{14}{39}$

   C. $\dfrac{12}{53}$

   D. $\dfrac{20}{33}$

5. Which of the following lists all of the single digit prime numbers?

   A. 1, 2, 3, 5, 7, 9
   B. 2, 3, 5, 7, 9
   C. 1, 2, 3, 5, 7
   D. 2, 3, 5, 7

6. Northridge High School has 570 students, of whom 30% are seniors. How many students are not seniors?

   A. 171
   B. 399
   C. 741
   D. 969

7. $5x^3y^4(3x^4y) =$

   A. $8x^{12}y^4$
   B. $8x^7y^5$
   C. $15x^{12}y^4$
   D. $15x^7y^5$

8. Joe can run 3 miles in 17 minutes. At the same rate, how long will it take him to run 12 miles?

   A. 17 minutes
   B. 34 minutes
   C. 51 minutes
   D. 68 minutes

9. What are the next four terms in the sequence 1, 4, 9, 16....

   A. 25, 36, 49, 64
   B. 24, 29, 36, 44
   C. 1, 4, 9, 16
   D. 2, 8, 18, 32

10. If $5x - 7 = 33$, then $x =$

   A. 3.3
   B. 5.2
   C. 6.6
   D. 8

GO ON TO THE NEXT PAGE.

11. $\dfrac{4}{7} + \dfrac{3}{8} =$

    A. $\dfrac{7}{15}$

    B. $\dfrac{1}{15}$

    C. $\dfrac{11}{56}$

    D. $\dfrac{53}{56}$

12. A pair of boots that usually sells for $95.00 was discounted by 25%. What was the sale price of the pair of boots?

    A. $70
    B. $71.25
    C. $118.75
    D. $120

13. At a certain gas station, a gallon of gas costs $2.85. If Bob has $30, how many full gallons of gas can he put in his car?

    A. 10
    B. 10.52
    C. 11
    D. 12

14. All residents in the town of Parker drive either red cars or blue cars. If the ratio of red cars to blue cars owned by residents of Parker is 5 : 7 and there are 264 cars in the town, how many red cars and blue cars are there?

    A. 110 red, 264 blue
    B. 154 red, 264 blue
    C. 110 red, 154 blue
    D. 110 red, 110 blue

15. Krissi is selling sets of earrings for $10 and necklaces for $12. If she sold 17 sets of earrings and collected $194, how many necklaces did she sell?

    A. 2
    B. 4
    C. 6
    D. 8

16. If $x = -4$, then $x^2 + 4x - 12 =$

    A. -44
    B. -12
    C. 12
    D. 20

17. On a road trip, John and Sunni drove a combined distance of 310 miles, and Jose drove 140 miles. What is the average distance they each drove?

    A. 150
    B. 225
    C. 260
    D. 390

18. $\sqrt{5}\sqrt{20} =$

    A. 2
    B. 4
    C. 7
    D. 10

19. Jessica rode her bike for 4 hours at an average speed of 20 miles per hour. After a brief rest, she continued riding for an additional two hours at an average speed of 18 miles per hour. What was the total distance she traveled?

    A. 19
    B. 36
    C. 80
    D. 116

20. Which of the following fractions is equal to 88.89%?

    A. $\dfrac{7}{8}$

    B. $\dfrac{7}{9}$

    C. $\dfrac{8}{9}$

    D. $\dfrac{9}{10}$

21. If $x = 7$, what is the value of 7^4?

    A. 28
    B. 49
    C. 343
    D. 2401

GO ON TO THE NEXT PAGE.

22. Miguel purchased a computer on sale for $650. Several days later, Ana bought the same computer for $800. What percent discount did Miguel receive when he purchased his computer on sale?

    A. 18.75%
    B. 23%
    C. 81.25%
    D. 123%

23. A major league baseball player had an on-base percentage of .350. If he was at bat 460 times in the season, how many times did he get on base?

    A. 161
    B. 299
    C. 460
    D. 1314

24. $\sqrt{144} =$

    A. 11
    B. 12
    C. 13
    D. 14

25. If $6x = 72$, what is the value of x?

    A. 6
    B. 12
    C. 66
    D. 78

26. Amanda purchases a pair of shoes that regularly sell for $90 and gives the cashier a coupon valid for a 15% discount. What is the final amount she pays for the shoes?

    A. $13.50
    B. $15
    C. $76.50
    D. $103.50

27. Louis ran the first 5 miles of a marathon with his sweatshirt and sweatpants on and the next 5 miles without the sweatshirt. He ran the remaining 16.1 miles without either the sweatshirt or sweatpants. For approximately what percentage of the entire trip did he wear the sweatshirt and sweatpants?

    A. 19%
    B. 38%
    C. 57%
    D. 61%

28. A drawer of socks has 10 blue pairs, 6 white pairs, 7 black pairs, and 4 black pairs of socks. If one pair is pulled from the drawer at random, what is the probability that it will be a black pair of socks?

    A. $\dfrac{4}{27}$

    B. $\dfrac{6}{27}$

    C. $\dfrac{7}{27}$

    D. $\dfrac{10}{27}$

29. $37.8456 \times 100 =$

    A. 0.378456
    B. 3.78456
    C. 378.456
    D. 3784.56

30. If $4a + 7b = 20$ and $2a + 3b = 12$, then $6a + 10b =$

    A. 8
    B. 16
    C. 32
    D. 48

STOP!
IF YOU FINISH BEFORE THE TIME IS UP, YOU MAY
CHECK OVER YOUR WORK ON THIS PART ONLY.

PART 3

Word Knowledge

Time: 11 Minutes—35 Questions

1. The teacher's role was <u>didactic</u> in nature.

   A. instructive
   B. therapeutic
   C. deceptive
   D. supportive

2. <u>Pictorial</u> most nearly means

   A. ideal
   B. illustrated
   C. changing
   D. verbal

3. The last-ditch effort had an <u>inconsequential</u> impact on the outcome of the game.

   A. significant
   B. fundamental
   C. final
   D. trivial

4. <u>Callous</u> most nearly means

   A. rude
   B. indifferent
   C. loving
   D. concerned

5. <u>Incoherent</u> most nearly means

   A. understandable
   B. unintelligible
   C. educated
   D. incapable

6. <u>Dubious</u> most nearly means

   A. doubtful
   B. creative
   C. insensitive
   D. certain

7. To <u>indict</u> most nearly means

   A. to judge
   B. to defend
   C. to sentence
   D. to accuse

8. The couple had an emotional <u>quarrel</u>.

   A. affair
   B. conversation
   C. argument
   D. ceremony

9. <u>Laudatory</u> most nearly means

   A. praiseworthy
   B. brave
   C. disruptive
   D. risky

10. To <u>vend</u> most nearly means

    A. to sell
    B. to forgo
    C. to sell
    D. to create

11. The woman <u>pledged</u> her loyalty to her friend.

    A. decreased
    B. included
    C. denied
    D. committed

12. The elderly couple was <u>nostalgic</u> as they talked about their youth.

    A. overpowering
    B. wistful
    C. emotional
    D. sad

13. <u>Stupor</u> most nearly means

    A. inertia
    B. activity
    C. eloquence
    D. unintelligent

GO ON TO THE NEXT PAGE.

14. To <u>rile</u> most nearly means

 A. to ruminate
 B. to love
 C. to irritate
 D. to strand

15. To <u>pilfer</u> most nearly means

 A. to steal
 B. to waste
 C. to build
 D. to prevent

16. <u>Narcissistic</u> most nearly means

 A. scornful
 B. vain
 C. fascinating
 D. tardy

17. The <u>headstrong</u> child was very unwilling to cooperate.

 A. delusional
 B. angry
 C. docile
 D. stubborn

18. To <u>cultivate</u> most nearly means

 A. to create
 B. to develop
 C. to help
 D. to challenge

19. <u>Morose</u> most nearly means

 A. gloomy
 B. upbeat
 C. scared
 D. worried

20. <u>Belligerent</u> most nearly means

 A. cooperative
 B. continuous
 C. argumentative
 D. exhausted

21. The soldier cleaned his weapon in <u>meticulous</u> fashion.

 A. precise
 B. slow
 C. predictable
 D. quick

22. <u>Transient</u> most nearly means

 A. poor
 B. contradictory
 C. changing
 D. temporary

23. <u>Novel</u> most nearly means

 A. verbal
 B. new
 C. strange
 D. short

24. <u>Diligent</u> most nearly means

 A. hardworking
 B. persistent
 C. dilatory
 D. precious

25. The teacher's <u>ambiguous</u> answer left the students confused.

 A. vague
 B. complicated
 C. detailed
 D. sarcastic

26. <u>Therapeutic</u> most nearly means

 A. preventative
 B. disruptive
 C. damaging
 D. curative

27. The employee was <u>inundated</u> with work.

 A. disillusioned
 B. overwhelmed
 C. appreciated
 D. depressed

28. The revolution left the country in <u>turmoil</u>.

 A. peace
 B. anarchy
 C. commotion
 D. clarity

GO ON TO THE NEXT PAGE.

29. <u>Devious</u> most nearly means

    A. deceptive
    B. mean
    C. vain
    D. genuine

30. The witness <u>embellished</u> his story.

    A. recounted
    B. changed
    C. enhanced
    D. improved

31. To <u>mar</u> most nearly means

    A. ruin
    B. deface
    C. help
    D. wed

32. <u>Despair</u> most nearly means

    A. hopelessness
    B. sadness
    C. grief
    D. depression

33. <u>Credible</u> most nearly means

    A. unbelievable
    B. difficult
    C. trustworthy
    D. obvious

34. <u>Inscrutable</u> most nearly means

    A. visible
    B. understandable
    C. believable
    D. mysterious

35. <u>Astute</u> most nearly means

    A. clever
    B. studious
    C. intelligent
    D. obvious

STOP!
IF YOU FINISH BEFORE THE TIME IS UP, YOU MAY
CHECK OVER YOUR WORK ON THIS PART ONLY.

PART 4

Paragraph Comprehension

Time: 13 Minutes—15 Questions

1. Inside the metal container surrounding a microwave, a microwave generator called a magnetron converts electricity into high-powered radio waves. These waves blast into the food compartment through a channel called a wave guide. The microwaves bounce all around off the reflective walls of the compartment and penetrate through food, making the food molecules vibrate more quickly. As a result, the temperature of the food increases.

   Based on the information above, which of the following is most likely true?

   A. The metal container serves only a cosmetic purpose.
   B. The faster molecules vibrate, the hotter they become.
   C. The microwave generator converts radio waves to electricity.
   D. Microwaves can also cool food.

2. Michelangelo Buonarroti, one of the most revered artists of all time, was born in Caprese, Italy, in 1475. The son of a government administrator, Michelangelo began studying art at the age of 13 when he became an artist's apprentice. His earliest major work was the *Pieta*, a sculpture depicting the body of Christ in the Virgin Mary's lap. Due to the acclaim he received from this work, he was commissioned to carve a statue of the biblical character David. Later in life he was commissioned to paint the ceiling of the Sistine Chapel—the most sacred space in the entire Vatican. Michelangelo continued to create art until he died at the age of 88.

   Which of the following can be inferred about Michelangelo?

   A. Michelangelo created art for 75 years.
   B. Michelangelo was the only artist to paint the Sistine Chapel.
   C. Michelangelo was commissioned to paint the Sistine Chapel as a result of the acclaim he received for the *Pieta*.
   D. No art that Michelangelo created before the *Pieta* was good.

3. Russian psychologist Ivan Pavlov is known primarily for his work in classical conditioning, even though his interest in the topic came about almost by accident. During an experiment intended to study animal digestion, he discovered the basics of what we now call classical conditioning. Every time he rang a bell to alert the dogs to their food being available, they started to salivate. Eventually, he could ring the bell without presenting the food, and the dogs would still salivate. This idea of using stimuli to influence behavioral reactions has had wide-reaching impact, especially in education.

   Based on the information above, which of the following did Pavlov discover?

   A. Double pneumonia
   B. Gastric function
   C. Animal digestion
   D. Classical conditioning

4. Historical archaeology is a division of archaeology that studies cultures that have left numerous written records, specifically those that are not related to literature or politics. The study of these records gives insight into the day-to-day lives of individuals who died long ago.

   Based on the information in the passage, which of the following would be of most interest to a historical archaeologist?

   A. Ancient excavation sites
   B. Books found in a tomb
   C. Old jewelry
   D. Antique weapons

GO ON TO THE NEXT PAGE.

5. Cranes can be found on every continent except South America and Antarctica. Their habitats are directly impacted by the warming and cooling of the Earth's atmosphere. Additionally, crane populations are negatively impacted when their marshy habitats are drained to make way for human settlements.

Based on the information above, which of the following is most likely true?

A. Crane populations decrease in areas where human populations increase.
B. Crane populations increase when the climate gets warmer.
C. Crane populations decrease when the climate gets warmer.
D. Cranes have never lived on South America or Antarctica.

6. Dance innovator Martha Graham trained her body to move in revolutionary ways. "Life today is nervous, sharp, and zigzag," she said. "It often steps in midair. That is what I aim for in my dances." She insists she never started out to be a rebel. It was only that the emotions she had to express could not be projected through any of the traditional methods of dance, so she had to create her own.

Which of the following statements are true?

I.   Graham's style of dance was different from those of her contemporaries.
II. Graham earned a living as a dancer.
III. Graham lived during the 20th century.

A. I only
B. I and II only
C. II and III only
D. I, II, and III

7. The California Pepper Tree is so adaptable that one of the first trees planted in 1830, originally in a row of ten trees next to the Mission San Luis Rey, still stands today. The second-oldest surviving tree is at another mission and is much larger than the first.

What can be inferred from the paragraph above?

A. The oldest surviving California Pepper Tree was planted in 1830.
B. The biggest California Pepper Tree was planted in 1830.
C. The second biggest California Pepper Tree was planted in 1830.
D. The first California Pepper Tree was planted in 1830.

8. An air mass is a very large body of air—usually at least 1,600 kilometers across and several kilometers thick—that forms when a portion of the lower atmosphere moves slowly or rests over a relatively flat surface. Two air masses of different temperatures are separated by a front, a very narrow zone of transition between the two masses. A warm front usually brings warm temperatures with it, while a cold front triggers a drop in temperature.

According to the passage, all of the following could be true EXCEPT:

A. An air mass can be less than 1,500 kilometers across.
B. An air mass is formed when part of the upper atmosphere moves slowly.
C. Fronts can trigger changes in temperature.
D. Fronts do not form over mountainous terrain.

GO ON TO THE NEXT PAGE.

9. Ghirardelli Square in San Francisco is a particularly striking example of an historic building that had fallen into disrepair and was rehabilitated instead of being destroyed. The square was the original home of the Ghirardelli family's chocolate factory and was one of a series of buildings that were retained and refurbished after World War II. Even the Ghirardelli sign was preserved, and it has since become a symbol of San Francisco's identity.

Based on the paragraph above, which of the following is true about Ghirardelli Square?

A. It was built before World War I.
B. It was located in San Diego.
C. It was demolished.
D. It was built before World War II.

10. Many millions of years ago, the rock from which the Grand Canyon is formed was a relatively flat plateau with 10,000 more feet of rock than it has today. While it used to be that fourteen layers of rock were visible, today there are only nine layers exposed. The additional layers of rock material were worn away by water erosion from rivers. Further contributing to the canyon's formation has been water erosion from rain and snow, changes in temperature, and damage from chunks of rock that break off and roll down the sides of cliffs.

Which of the following is NOT listed as a contributing factor to the formation of the Grand Canyon?

A. Volcanic activity
B. Water erosion
C. Friction
D. Temperature changes

11. Lowell Observatory was established by Percival Lowell in 1894 in Flagstaff, Arizona. The desert environment and high altitude—7,000 feet—in Flagstaff provided clear, dry air that was ideal for observing Mars. Lowell's initial study of the planet focused on dark patches and lines he saw on the surface of the planet. He believed these markings were actually canals built by some kind of intelligent life-forms. He never confirmed this theory, though, and this work ultimately fell by the wayside.

The best title for this passage might be

A. Astronomy Then & Now
B. Mars—Does Alien Life Exist?
C. The Early Days of the Lowell Observatory
D. Vacation in Flagstaff

12. It can be difficult and sometimes dangerous to cross freely across Canada due to a number of landforms, like rivers and lakes, that create natural barriers. Early European explorers sought access to the interior and west of Canada for many purposes, including trade and religious missions. As these settlers became more familiar with the rivers and lakes, they began to understand how to navigate them more safely. Ultimately, the waterways aided the settlers in their attempts to colonize Canada.

What can be inferred from the above passage?

A. Canada has many natural resources.
B. Canada was settled by Europeans.
C. European settlers navigated Canadian waterways easily.
D. Europeans were searching for gold when they ventured toward the Canadian west.

GO ON TO THE NEXT PAGE.

13. Before the agricultural development of the Midwest and West of the United States, massive migrations of Rocky Mountain locusts (Melanoplus spretus) frequently caused terrible damage to local economies. The worst of these migrations occurred in 1875, and the severity of the damage is indicated by a revision of the original state constitution of Nebraska to include policies to deal with such economic problems. In Missouri alone, damage to crops and land was estimated to exceed 15 million dollars, never mind the fact that many settlers went hungry due to lack of food availability.

The author mentions Nebraska and Missouri in order to

A. indicate that they were impacted by locusts
B. show the severity of the impact of locusts
C. argue that the Midwest was impacted
D. prove that many people died from the locusts

14. For many years, scientists believed that craters on the Moon were created by volcanic activity, as were those on Earth. However, scientists now believe that craters on the Moon cannot be explained in the same way that craters on Earth can be explained. This is due to two major differences between the craters on the Moon and those on Earth: shape and size.

Which of the following is true about Moon craters?

A. They were created by volcanoes.
B. They are all of consistent shape and size.
C. They are different from those on Earth.
D. They were created by meteors.

15. The steel industry had a direct and significant impact on the railroad industry. Early railway rails were made of iron, but those rails were not strong enough to support heavy trains traveling at high rates of speed. Steel, however, was at least ten times stronger and could last twenty times longer than iron. However, steel was much more expensive than iron and was typically only used to create small items like tools.

Which of the following statements is most likely true?

A. Trains could go faster on steel rails.
B. Iron is as expensive today as it was in the 19th century.
C. Railroad executives would have used steel for rails if it was less expensive.
D. Steel was used to create eating utensils.

STOP!
IF YOU FINISH BEFORE THE TIME IS UP, YOU MAY
CHECK OVER YOUR WORK ON THIS PART ONLY.

PART 5

Mathematics Knowledge

Time: 24 Minutes—25 Questions

1. An isosceles triangle has one angle of 40 degrees. How big are the other two angles?

    A. 140 degrees and 140 degrees
    B. 40 degrees and 40 degrees
    C. 40 degrees and 70 degrees
    D. 40 degrees and 100 degrees

2. Laura buys an octagon-shaped mirror to hang in her bathroom. If she puts a bracket at each corner of the mirror, how many brackets does she need?

    A. 8
    B. 7
    C. 6
    D. 5

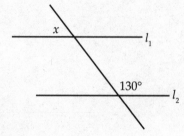

3. If lines 1 and 2 are parallel, what is the degree measure of $\angle x$?

    A. 30
    B. 45
    C. 50
    D. 130

4. If $12 > x + 5$, which of the following expresses the entire range of possible values for x?

    A. $x < 7$
    B. $x \le 4$
    C. $x \le 3$
    D. $x = -7$

5. Twice the sum of the number of degrees in a triangle and the number of degrees in a rectangle is

    A. 360
    B. 480
    C. 720
    D. 1080

6. A highway merge sign has 3 equal sides of length 9. What is its perimeter?

    A. 6
    B. 12
    C. 27
    D. 30

7. What is the product of $(x + 4)$ and $(x - 6)$?

    A. $x^2 + 10x - 24$
    B. $x^2 + 2x + 12$
    C. $x^2 - 10x - 12$
    D. $x^2 - 2x - 24$

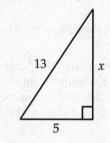

8. What is the length of x?

    A. 3
    B. 4
    C. 6
    D. 12

GO ON TO THE NEXT PAGE.

9. What is the value of $x^2 + 2x - 4xy + 2y^2$ if $x = 5$ and $y = -2$?

    A. −10
    B. 24
    C. 67
    D. 83

10. If the lengths of the sides of a rectangular field with an area of 48 square feet are halved, what is the new area of the pen in square feet?

    A. 12
    B. 24
    C. 96
    D. 192

11. If m movie tickets cost d dollars, then how much will 5 movie tickets cost?

    A. $5dm$ dollars

    B. $\dfrac{dm}{5}$ dollars

    C. $\dfrac{5d}{m}$ dollars

    D. $\dfrac{5m}{d}$ dollars

12. For what value of a does $3a^2 + 8 = 14a$?

    A. 3
    B. 4
    C. 5
    D. 6

13. The perimeter of a corral is 80 feet. The length of the corral is 4 feet longer than its width. What is the width of the corral?

    A. 18
    B. 20
    C. 22
    D. 24

14. The volume of a rectangular box with length 5 and width 7 is 280. What is the height of the rectangular box?

    A. 5
    B. 6
    C. 7
    D. 8

15. If n is an even integer, which of the following must also be an even integer?

    A. $\dfrac{n+2}{2}$

    B. $\dfrac{n+2}{4}$

    C. $n + 1$

    D. $5n$

16. Brendan runs east for 6 miles and then runs south for 8 miles. How far is Brendan from his starting point, in miles?

    A. 6
    B. 8
    C. 10
    D. 12

17. A circle has a diameter of 20. What is its area?

    A. 10π
    B. 20π
    C. 40π
    D. 100π

18. 30 is what percent of 200?

    A. 10
    B. 15
    C. 20
    D. 30

19. Colleen is five years older than Paige and three years younger than Scott. If Paige is p years old, how old is Scott, in terms of p?

    A. $2p - 7$
    B. $p + 6$
    C. $p + 8$
    D. $p + 10$

20. Three less than a certain number is one-fourth of that number. What is the number?

    A. 3
    B. 4
    C. 5
    D. 6

GO ON TO THE NEXT PAGE.

21. An engineer is studying a scale drawing of a building. Each inch on the drawing represents 12 feet. If the height of the building on the drawing is 8 inches, how high will the building be, in feet?

    A. 8
    B. 12
    C. 48
    D. 96

22. Which of the following values has a 4 in the thousandths place?

    A. 5.024
    B. 5.042
    C. 5.402
    D. 5.420

23. If $7y = 91$, then $y =$

    A. 7
    B. 9
    C. 11
    D. 13

24. Another way to write $3\sqrt{40}$ is

    A. $3\sqrt{10}$
    B. $6\sqrt{10}$
    C. $\sqrt{120}$
    D. $6\sqrt{40}$

25. What is another way to write 2^5?

    A. 32
    B. 25
    C. 16
    D. 10

STOP!
IF YOU FINISH BEFORE THE TIME IS UP, YOU MAY CHECK OVER YOUR WORK ON THIS PART ONLY.

PART 6

Electronics Information

Time: 9 Minutes—20 Questions

1. The flow of charges is called

   A. current
   B. voltage
   C. ohms
   D. load

2. To determine the total resistance in a series

   A. multiply the inverse of the resistance of each resistor
   B. multiply the resistance of each resistor
   C. add the inverse of the resistance of each resistor
   D. add the resistance of each resistor

3. Each of the following is an insulator EXCEPT

   A. Porcelain
   B. Oil
   C. Glass
   D. Silver

4. How much current will a 90-watt light bulb draw if it is plugged into a 120-volt socket?

   A. 0.25 A
   B. 0.5 A
   C. 0.75 A
   D. 1.0 A

5. An ohmmeter would be used to measure

   A. power
   B. current
   C. resistance
   D. voltage

6. The symbol above represents a

   A. resistor
   B. capacitor
   C. transformer
   D. inductor

7. Capacitance is measured in

   A. ohms
   B. farads
   C. amps
   D. watts

8. The portion of the circuit that is at the lowest voltage is the

   A. ground
   B. AC voltage source
   C. DC voltage source
   D. resistor

9. To find the total resistance in a parallel circuit

   A. multiply the inverse of the resistance of each resistor
   B. multiply the resistance of each resistor
   C. add the inverse of the resistance of each resistor
   D. add the resistance of each resistor

10. Which of the following describes an application of a transistor:

    A. amplify sound
    B. mitigate sound
    C. increase voltage
    D. transform AC current into DC current

11. The symbol above represents a

    A. resistor
    B. capacitor
    C. transformer
    D. inductor

GO ON TO THE NEXT PAGE.

12. Opposite poles of magnets will

    A. do nothing
    B. provide AC current
    C. attract each other
    D. repel each other

13. The most common device in almost any circuit is a(n)

    A. resistor
    B. capacitor
    C. ground
    D. inductor

14. Which of the following forces current to flow in a circuit similar to the way gravity forces water to flow in a river?

    A. Resistance
    B. Voltage
    C. Amperage
    D. Power

15. The voltage difference in between the two sides of a device is called the

    A. potential energy
    B. power
    C. voltage drop
    D. amplitude

16. Six strands of holiday lights are strung together in a series. Each strand requires 120 V and 15 amps. The total power used is

    A. 6 W
    B. 8 W
    C. 10 W
    D. 12 W

17. Which of the following tools is best to use when driving a grounding rod into the earth?

    A. Axe
    B. Pliers
    C. Rubber mallet
    D. Hammer

18. Which of the following household electrical appliances uses the least current?

    A. Blender
    B. Vacuum
    C. Surround sound system
    D. Television

19. What is the total resistance of an 8-ohm and a 16-ohm resistor in parallel?

    A. $\dfrac{1}{16}$

    B. $\dfrac{3}{16}$

    C. $\dfrac{1}{8}$

    D. $\dfrac{1}{4}$

20. Which of the following colors signifies that a wire is positive, or "hot"?

    A. Red
    B. Yellow
    C. Blue
    D. Green

STOP!
IF YOU FINISH BEFORE THE TIME IS UP, YOU MAY
CHECK OVER YOUR WORK ON THIS PART ONLY.

PART 7

Auto and Shop Information

Time: 11 Minutes—25 Questions

1. A car's front wheels are connected to a steering bar that is attached to the

    A. axle
    B. tie rod
    C. rack
    D. pinion

2. A vehicle's temperature gauge indicates that the car is overheating. The first thing that should be checked is

    A. the fuse box
    B. the battery charge
    C. radiator coolant level
    D. transmission fluid level

3. An engine cranks when the key is turned in the ignition, but the car fails to start. All of the following should be checked EXCEPT:

    A. fuel level
    B. catalytic converter
    C. spark plugs & wires
    D. battery charge

4. The flywheel is part of the

    A. cooling system
    B. drive train
    C. manual transmission
    D. electrical system

5. A car doesn't steer straight and pulls to one side. The most likely action that needs to be taken is

    A. an oil change
    B. a wheel alignment
    C. cooling system flush
    D. replace the brakes

6. If a clutch seems to be slipping, the first part to be checked is the

    A. camshaft
    B. water pump
    C. flywheel
    D. radiator

7. If the second stroke on a four-stroke engine is compression, what is the third?

    A. Intake
    B. Power
    C. Exhaust
    D. Compression

8. The power windows suddenly stop working. The first thing to check is

    A. battery charge
    B. window switch function
    C. fuse box
    D. alternator function

9. The brake pedal sinks slowly to the floorboard while sitting at a stoplight. The first thing to check is

    A. master cylinder function
    B. brake fluid level
    C. rotor thickness
    D. transmission fluid level

10. The oil you put into the car is part of which system?

    A. ignition system
    B. cooling system
    C. exhaust system
    D. electrical

11. A scraper removes little chips of wood when its handle is struck by

    A. a mallet
    B. a hand
    C. a hammer
    D. another scraper

12. Which of the following is NOT a part of a hammer?

    A. Head
    B. Heel
    C. Neck
    D. Face

GO ON TO THE NEXT PAGE.

13. The distance that the teeth of a saw are bent from the edge of the saw blade is called what part of the saw?

   A. Kerf
   B. Rip
   C. Crosscut
   D. Set

14. Which of the following tools is used to shape material after it has been cut?

   A. Chisel
   B. Pipe cutter
   C. Shears
   D. Coping Saw

15. When using a grinder, the part to be ground should always be in contact with what part of the wheel?

   A. Upper
   B. Lower
   C. Inner
   D. Outer

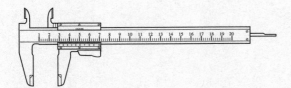

16. The tool shown above is a

   A. Flathead screwdriver
   B. Carpenter's hammer
   C. Hacksaw
   D. Slide caliper

17. In some situations, it is advisable to make a small indentation in metal to allow the drill bit to drill in the right place. This indentation can be made with a

   A. punch
   B. drill bit
   C. hammer
   D. reamer

18. When accuracy in small measurements is important, it is best to use a

   A. Carpenter's Level
   B. Slide Caliper
   C. Vernier Caliper
   D. Micrometer

19. The tool shown above is a(n)

   A. Allen wrench
   B. box wrench
   C. open-ended wrench
   D. socket wrench

20. The cutting edges on a reamer are located

   A. on the drill
   B. on the end of the drill bit
   C. on the outside edge of the drill bit body
   D. a reamer doesn't have cutting edges

21. Which of the following requires a tool to be connected to a voltage source and that the tool come in contact with a metal object?

   A. Bracing
   B. Arc welding
   C. Boring
   D. Welding

22. The most common type of drill bit is a

   A. boring tool
   B. countersink bit
   C. reamer bit
   D. twist drill bit

23. The part of a saw that contains the teeth is the

   A. blade
   B. handle
   C. toe
   D. heel

GO ON TO THE NEXT PAGE.

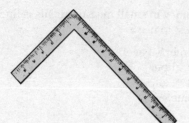

24. The tool shown above is a

   A. carpenter's square
   B. carpenter's level
   C. T Square
   D. micrometer

25. Which of the following is NOT a part of a screwdriver?

   A. Blade
   B. Shank
   C. Socket
   D. Handle

STOP!
IF YOU FINISH BEFORE THE TIME IS UP, YOU MAY
CHECK OVER YOUR WORK ON THIS PART ONLY.

PART 8

Mechanical Comprehension

Time: 19 Minutes—25 Questions

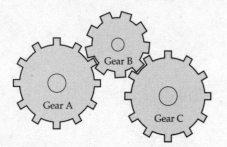

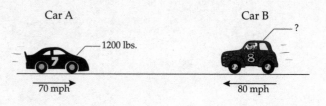

Car A   1200 lbs.   Car B   ?

70 mph   80 mph

1. If gear B rotates clockwise, in which direction do gears A and C rotate, respectively?

   A. Clockwise, clockwise
   B. Clockwise, counterclockwise
   C. Counterclockwise, counterclockwise
   D. Counterclockwise, clockwise

2. If a bodybuilder lifts a 300-pound weight 3 feet in the air, how much work is he doing?

   A. 100 ft-lbs
   B. 300 ft-lbs
   C. 900 ft-lbs
   D. 1000 ft-lbs

3. The volume of a liquid that passes through a cross section of a pipe in a certain amount of time is called the

   A. flow rate
   B. momentum
   C. force
   D. speed

4. If the volume of a gas increases, its pressure will

   A. increase, then decrease
   B. decrease
   C. increase
   D. remain the same

5. The water pressure on a glass bottom boat is 100psi. The area of the glass is 350 square inches. What is the force on the pothole?

   A. 3.5 pounds
   B. 350 pounds
   C. 35,000 pounds
   D. The water exerts no pressure on the glass.

6. How much must Car B weigh in order for both cars to come to a complete stop when they collide?

   A. 10,000 lbs.
   B. 10,500 lbs.
   C. 11,000 lbs.
   D. 11,500 lbs.

7. How will the speed at which a point near the outside of a wheel rotate compared to the speed at which a point near the inside of the wheel?

   A. The point near the outside will rotate faster.
   B. The point near the inside will rotate faster.
   C. The two points will rotate at the same rate.
   D. The speeds of the two points are unrelated.

8. If a propulsion gear with 30 teeth is paired with a gear with 6 teeth, what is the mechanical advantage this pairing can provide?

   A. $\dfrac{1}{5}$

   B. $\dfrac{1}{6}$

   C. $\dfrac{5}{6}$

   D. $\dfrac{6}{5}$

GO ON TO THE NEXT PAGE.

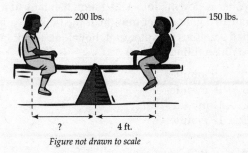

Figure not drawn to scale

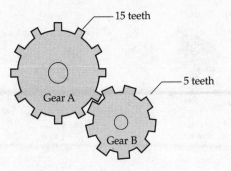

9. How far away from the fulcrum should the person on the left sit in order for the seesaw to balance perfectly?

   A. 3 feet
   B. 3.5 feet
   C. 4 feet
   D. 4.5 feet

10. The part of a lever that will never move is the

    A. mechanical advantage
    B. force
    C. load
    D. fulcrum

11. Gear A, which has a diameter of 6 feet, is turning Gear B, which has a diameter of 2 feet. If Gear A makes one revolution, how many revolutions does Gear B make?

    A. 1
    B. 2
    C. 3
    D. 4

12. The person jumps off the boat at a speed of 6 feet per second. After he jumps, the boat

    A. will move right at a speed of about 3 feet per second
    B. will move right at a speed of about 5 feet per second
    C. will move left at a speed of about 3 feet per second
    D. will move left at a speed of about 5 feet per second

13. How many times will Gear B turn if Gear A turns 3 times?

    A. 3
    B. 6
    C. 9
    D. 12

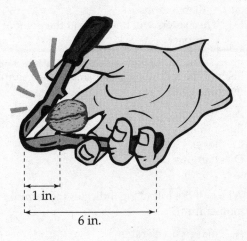

14. If the force required to crack the walnut is 120 pounds, how much force must be applied to the nutcracker to crack the walnut?

    A. 5 lbs.
    B. 10 lbs.
    C. 15 lbs.
    D. 20 lbs.

GO ON TO THE NEXT PAGE.

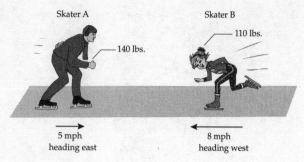

Skater A   Skater B

140 lbs.   110 lbs.

5 mph   8 mph
heading east heading west

15. Skater A and B will collide and stick together. After the collision which of the following will happen?

A. The skaters will move to the left at less than 8 mph.
B. The skaters will move to the right at more than 8 mph.
C. The skaters will move to the right at less than 8 mph.
D. The skaters will both stop at the point of impact.

16. Each of the following is an example of a simple machine EXCEPT:

A. wedge
B. pulley
C. lever
D. hammer

17. Which of the following indicates the formula for momentum?

A. mass × acceleration
B. force × velocity
C. mass × veolcity
D. force × distance

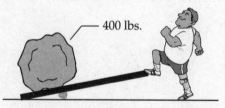

400 lbs.

18. The 400-pound rock in the figure above is sitting on a steel lever that provides a mechanical advantage of 2.5. How heavy must the person be in order to successfully lift the rock?

A. 140 lbs.
B. 160 lbs.
C. 180 lbs.
D. 200 lbs.

19. Water is flowing into a 30-gallon fish tank at a rate of 3 gallons per minute. If the tank already had 3 gallons of water in it, how long will it take to finish filling the tank?

A. 9 minutes
B. 10 minutes
C. 11 minutes
D. 12 minutes

20. The multiplication of force is called

A. force
B. force squared
C. power
D. mechanical advantage

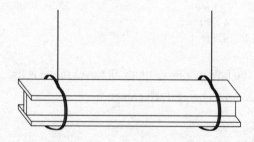

21. The ropes attached to the girder above can each support a maximum of 350 pounds without snapping. What is the maximum possible weight of the girder that the ropes can support?

A. 0 lbs.
B. 100 lbs.
C. 350 lbs.
D. 700 lbs.

22. Often, the mechanical advantage conferred by a gear is

A. 0
B. 1
C. less than 1
D. greater than 1

23. One mile is approximately how many yards?

A. 440
B. 880
C. 1760
D. 2200

GO ON TO THE NEXT PAGE.

25. 50 degrees Fahrenheit is equal to how many degrees Celsius?

    A. 10
    B. 11
    C. 12
    D. 13

24. Which point on the bicycle wheel above will move the most slowly?

    A. Point 1
    B. Point 2
    C. Point 3
    D. They will all move at the same rate.

STOP!
IF YOU FINISH BEFORE THE TIME IS UP, YOU MAY
CHECK OVER YOUR WORK ON THIS PART ONLY.

Chapter 16
Practice Test 3:
Answers and
Explanations

PRACTICE TEST 3
STUDENT ASVAB
ANSWERS AND EXPLANATIONS

Part 1—General Science

1. **A**   The atomic number always indicates the number of protons in an atom of an element. Therefore, since the atomic number for magnesium is 12, an atom of magnesium will have 12 protons.

2. **C**   The lungs are part of the respiratory system.

3. **D**   Plants are always the first level of a food chain because they provide fuel for consumers.

4. **B**   Meiosis is the process by which sex cells are made. Meiosis occurs only in sex organs called gonads: testes in males, ovaries in females.

5. **A**   The only kind of muscle in the heart is cardiac muscle, and the heart is the only part of the body that has cardiac muscle. It is the cardiac muscles you feel when your heart is pounding.

6. **C**   Blood Type AB is known as a universal recipient because it won't react negatively to any new type of blood introduced to it during a blood transfusion.

7. **A**   Ova, or egg cells, are produced in the female gonads, or ovaries.

8. **C**   Jupiter, one of the four Jovian planets, is the largest planet in the solar system.

9. **B**   Draw yourself a Punnett Square that looks like this.

	b	*b*
B	*Bb*	*Bb*
b	*bb*	*bb*

Next look at answers and eliminate (A), (C), and (D) because they do not match.

10. **D**   The cell fragments that are involved in blood clotting are called platelets.

11. **B**   The somatic and autonomic nervous systems are part of the peripheral nervous system—those are all part of the nervous system, so eliminate them. Choice (B), the lymphatic system, has nothing to do with the nervous system.

12. **A**   Biome 2 is the Taiga, which is found a little south of the tundra, is known for its conifer (evergreen) trees, and long, severe winters. Animals of the Taiga include bears, wolves, elk, beavers, deer, squirrels, rabbits, and moose.

13. **C** There are four geologic time periods, also called eras. In order from earliest to latest, they are Precambrian, Paleozoic, Mesozoic, and Cenozoic, which is the era in which we live today.

14. **B** Ecology is the study of the interactions between living things and their environments. Geology is the study of the origin, history, and structure of the Earth. Biology is the study of life and living things, including their structure, function, growth, evolution, distribution, identification, and taxonomy. Meteorology is the study of the Earth's atmosphere, including the atmospheric conditions that cause weather.

15. **C** The ocean is divided into three Marine Biomes. Biome 1 is the Intertidal Zone; Biome 2 is the Neritic Zone; Biome 3 is the Oceanic Zone. The Tundra is not one of the marine biomes.

16. **D** There are four primary layers of the atmosphere. From closest to the ground to farthest away, they are the Troposphere, Stratosphere, Mesosphere, Thermosphere.

17. **B** The core is the center of the Sun. Surrounding the core are the inner zones, which include the radiative zone and the convective zone. The outermost layer of the Sun is the atmosphere.

18. **C** A lunar eclipse occurs when the Earth moves between the Sun and the Moon, blocking the sunlight and casting a shadow over the Moon.

19. **D** The bronchus, larynx, epiglottis, and pharynx are parts of the respiratory system.

20. **C** A deficiency of Vitamin C can result in scurvy. Vitamin C can be found in citrus fruit, tomatoes, vegetables, and strawberries.

21. **D** There are four primary layers of the atmosphere. From closest to the ground to farthest away, they are the Troposphere, Stratosphere, Mesosphere, Thermosphere.

22. **A** Convection occurs when a gas or liquid changes density due to higher heat. As the air inside a hot air balloon is heated, it expands, causing it to rise.

23. **A** The Precambrian Era spanned 4.6 million years, more than the other three eras combined.

24. **B** The rate at which work is done is called power. It is measured in watts. The formula for power is $power = \dfrac{work}{time}$.

25. **A** The pH scale ranges from 0 to 14. Anything below 7 is an acid—the smaller the number, the stronger the acid. A substance with a pH of 7 is considered neutral. Any substance with a pH greater than 7 is a base—the higher the number, the stronger the base.

Part 2—Arithmetic Reasoning

1. **C** Plug in 6 for every x in the equation: $6^2 + 7(6) - 5 = 73$.

2. **A** First, figure out the cost of Tristan's entire bill: $(3 \times \$7.85) + (2 \times \$14.25) + (2 \times \$3.50) = \$59.05$. Then, subtract that from the $100 bill he had: $\$100 - \$59.05 = \$40.95$.

3. **B** Subtract like terms: $9x^2 - 2x^2 = 7x^2$. Eliminate (C) and (D). When subtracting the next two terms, be careful: $14x - (-12x) = 14x + 12x = 26x$. Eliminate (A).

4. **A** Probability is always a representation of the number of things that satisfy what you're looking for out of the total number of things available. There are 14 green jellybeans, so that goes on top. Then, add the others together: $20 + 14 + 12 + 7 = 53$. That goes on the bottom: $\frac{14}{53}$.

5. **D** A prime number is a number that is divisible only by itself and 1. Eliminate (A) and (B) because 9 is not prime. One is not considered prime, so eliminate (C).

6. **B** Multiply the total number of students by 30% to find the number of seniors: $570 \times \left(\frac{30}{100}\right) = 171$. Subtract that value from the total number of students to find the number of non-seniors: $570 - 171 = 399$.

7. **D** Multiply the integers first: $5 \times 3 = 15$. Eliminate (A) and (B). Then add the exponents in each term: $3 + 4 = 7$. Eliminate (C).

8. **D** Set up a proportion: $\frac{3}{17} = \frac{12}{x}$. Cross-multiply and solve: $3x = 204$. Divide both sides by 3 and $x = 68$.

9. **A** The four terms in the sequence are all perfect squares: $1^2 = 1$, $2^2 = 4$, $3^2 = 9$, $4^2 = 16$. Continue the pattern: $5^2 = 25$, $6^2 = 36$, $7^2 = 49$, $8^2 = 64$.

10. **D** Start by adding 7 to both sides: $5x = 40$. Then divide by 5 to isolate the variable: $x = 8$.

11. **D** Use the bowtie method to convert the fractions into common denominators: $4 \times 8 = 32$, $7 \times 3 = 21$. $\frac{32 + 21}{7 \times 8} = \frac{53}{56}$.

12. **B** Calculate the discount: $\$90 \times .25 = \$22.5$. Subtract the discount from the original price of the boots: $\$90 - \$22.5 = \$71.25$.

13. **A** Start by dividing the money available by the cost per gallon: $\frac{\$30}{\$2.85} = 10.52$ *gallons*. Be sure to read carefully: the question asks how many *full* gallons of gas that Bob can put in his car. That means he can get 10 full gallons.

14. **C** Create a Ratio Box to keep your work organized.

Red	Blue	Total
5	7	12
		264

Next, determine that the multiplier is 22 by dividing 264 by 12.

Red	Blue	Total
5	7	12
22	22	22
110	154	264

Remember to read the question carefully: it's asking how many red cars (110) and blue cars (154) are in Parker.

15. **A** Write an equation using the information given: $10(17) + 12x = 194$. Solve for x to find that $x = 2$. $170 + 12x = 194$. Subtract 170 from both sides: $12x = 24$. Divide both sides by 12 to find that $x = 2$.

16. **B** Plug in -4 for every x in the equation: $(-4)^2 + 4(-4) - 12 = 16 - 16 - 12 = -12$.

17. **A** To find the average, add the total distance traveled and divide by the number of drivers: $\frac{310 + 140}{3} = \frac{450}{3} = 150$.

18. **D** Square roots that are being multiplied can be put under the same square root sign: $\sqrt{5}\sqrt{20} = \sqrt{5 \times 20} = \sqrt{100} = 10$.

19. **D** Multiply the time by the average to get the total distance for each segment of her trip: $4 \times 20 = 80$, $2 \times 18 = 36$. Add these two values together: $80 + 36 = 116$.

20. **C** Divide each fraction—only one gives the correct decimal value.

21. **D** Multiply $7 \times 7 \times 7 \times 7 = 2401$.

22. **A** To find the percent discount, use the percent change formula: $\frac{difference}{original} \times 100$. Difference = $800 - 650 = 150$. Put that over the starting price and calculate: $\frac{150}{800} \times 100$ and find that the amount of the discount was 18.75%.

23. **A** Multiply the number of times the player was at bat by his on-base percentage: $460 \times .35 = 161$.

24. **B** What number times itself turns into 144? 12.

25. **B** Divide both sides by 6 to isolate the variable and determine that $x = 12$.

26. **C** First, calculate the amount of the discount: $90 × .15 = 13.50$. Be careful—that doesn't answer the question. Next, subtract the discount from the original cost of the boots: $90 − 13.50 = 76.50.

27. **A** The question indicates that he wore the sweatshirt and sweatpants for the first 5 miles out of the entire 26.1-mile race ($5 + 5 + 16.1 = 26.1$). Divide 5 by 26.1 to find the percentage of time he wore both the sweatshirt and sweatpants: $\frac{5}{26.1} \approx 19\%$.

28. **C** Probability is a representation of what satisfies the requirements divided by the total number of possible results. In this case, there are 7 black pairs, which goes in the numerator. Add all of the pairs together to find there are 27 pairs: $\frac{7}{27}$.

29. **D** Multiply the values, or move the decimal two places to the right: 3784.56.

30. **C** Stack and add

$$
\begin{array}{r}
4a + 7b = 20 \\
+\ 2a + 3b = 12 \\
\hline
6a + 10b = 32
\end{array}
$$

Part 3—Word Knowledge

1. **A** Didactic: Instructive in nature

2. **B** Pictorial: Illustrated in pictures

3. **D** Inconsequential: Of little importance

4. **B** Callous: Insensitive; indifferent; unsympathetic

5. **B** Incoherent: Not capable of being understood

6. **A** Dubious: Doubtful; questionable

7. **D** Indict: To formally accuse

8. **C** Quarrel: An angry disagreement

9. **A** Laudatory: Worth of praise or recognition

10. **A** Vend: To sell

11. **D** Pledge: A sincere promise

12. **B** Nostalgic: Feeling a sentimental yearning of a former time, place, or situation

13. **A** Stupor: Mental slowness, apathy

14. **C** Rile: To irritate

15. **A** Pilfer: To steal, especially in small quantities

16. **B** Narcissistic: Having an unreasonable fascination with oneself; vain

17. **D** Headstrong: Stubborn; determine to get one's own way

18. **B** Cultivate: To produce or improve

19. **A** Morose: Gloomy; ill-humored

20. **C** Belligerent: Aggressive; argumentative; tending toward war

21. **A** Meticulous: Taking extreme care; paying attention to fine details

22. **D** Transient: Short-lived; not lasting a long time

23. **B** Novel: New; original

24. **B** Diligent: Putting forth constant effort

25. **A** Ambiguous: Open to more than one meaning

26. **D** Therapeutic: Intended to heal

27. **B** Inundated: Flooded; overwhelmed

28. **C** Turmoil: State of significant commotion or confusion

29. **A** Devious: Indirect; not straightforward

30. **C** Embellished: Made beautiful with ornaments; enhanced with fictitious additions

31. **B** Mar: To damage or make less attractive

32. **A** Despair: Loss of hope

33. **C** Credible: Believable

34. **D** Inscrutable: Unable to be investigated or understood

35. **A** Astute: Clever; cunning; discerning

Part 4—Paragraph Comprehension

1. **B** The metal container mentioned in the passage is never described in terms of its purpose, so eliminate (A). The passage does clearly state that the "microwaves bounce all around...making the food molecules vibrate more quickly. As a result, the temperature of the food increases." This directly supports (B). Choice (C) is a reversal of what is stated in the passage. Choice (D) is not at all supported, since the passage never discusses the process of cooling food.

2. **A** The passage indicates that Michelangelo began studying art at the age of 13 and continued to create art until his death at the age of 88. Subtract 13 from 88, and you find that he created art for 75 years. The passage never says that Michelangelo was the *only* artist who painted the Sistine Chapel, so eliminate (B). While the passage mentions that Michelangelo was commissioned to create a statue of David as a result of the acclaim he received for the *Pieta*, it does not say the same for the Sistine Chapel, so eliminate (C). Choice (D) is also extreme and not supported by the passage: it never says that *no* art created before the *Pieta* was good.

3. **D** Double pneumonia is never mentioned in the passage, so eliminate (A). "Gastric function" is another way of saying "digestion," but that's not what Pavlov discovered, rather that's what he was studying. Eliminate (B) and (C). The passage states that he discovered the basics of what is now called classical conditioning, so (D) is the correct answer.

4. **B** The passage indicates that historical archaeologists are interested in written records. Choices (A), (C), and (D) do not reference written artifacts, so they can be eliminated. The only answer that does indicate a written document is (B).

5. **A** The passages tells you that crane populations are "negatively impacted" when "marshy habitats are drained to make way to human settlements." This directly supports (A), because "negatively impacted" means the population would decrease. There is no indication of *how* crane populations are impacted with changes in the temperature of the atmosphere, so neither (B) nor (C) can be proven. Choice (D) is an extreme interpretation of the first sentence of the paragraph: Cranes do not currently live on either continent, but we can't prove that they never have.

6. **A** Be careful not to let any potential outside knowledge influence your decision. Statements II and III are true about Graham, but the passage does not mention either fact. The only statement that is supported by the passage is statement I, so (A) is the correct answer.

7. **A** Always make sure to read extremely carefully and compare answer choices. The passage states that the second-oldest surviving tree is located at another mission. The only other tree mentioned in the passage is one of the ones planted in 1830 at Mission San Luis Rey. Combining these two statements supports (A). You don't know anything about the size of the trees, so eliminate (B) and (C). You also don't know that the tree in question was the first tree to be planted, so eliminate (D).

8.   **B**   Pay attention to the "EXCEPT" and remember to eliminate answers that *are* true and choose the answer that is *not* true. The passage states that an air mass is *usually* at least 1,600 kilometers across, but doesn't say they can't be smaller; therefore, (A) could be true. The passage also states that a front is formed when a portion of the *lower* atmosphere moves slowly, which is the opposite of what (B) says; therefore, (B) can't be true. The passage further supports (C) by indicating that warm fronts bring warm temperatures and cold front bring colder temperatures. The passage also supports (D) by saying that fronts form over relatively flat surfaces—not mountainous terrain. Since (A), (C), and (D) are true, eliminate them and select (B).

9.   **D**   Remember to read the passage and answers carefully and go back to the passage for proof. The passages says that Ghirardelli Square was rehabilitated after World War II, after it had fallen into disrepair. So that means it must have been built before World War II, supporting (D). While it could have been built before World War I, there is no proof in the passage to back this up, so eliminate (A). The passage also says it was located in San Francisco, not San Diego, so eliminate (B). The fact that it was rehabilitated is exactly the opposite of (C), which should be eliminated.

10. **A**   Pay attention to the "NOT" in the question, and remember to choose the answer that does not match the passage. Choices (B) and (D) are all listed explicitly in the passage. Choice (C) is also mentioned implicitly—friction is caused when rocks break off and roll down the sides of cliffs.

11. **C**   Choice (A) is too broad, as the passage only discusses one small aspect of astronomy. Choice (B) is too narrow—it only covers one point mentioned in the passage. Choice (C) matches the content of the passage. Choice (D) sounds good because it mentions Flagstaff, which was mentioned in the passage, but the passage doesn't have anything to do with vacation.

12. **B**   Choice (A) is appealing because it's very close to what the passage says. But, the passage says that Canada has landforms that create natural barriers, not that it has many natural resources. Choice (B) is provable because the passage says that "European explorers sought access" and that "these settlers became familiar." Choice (C) is the opposite of what is said in the passage. Choice (D) is not provable—searching for gold is never mentioned in the passage.

13. **B**   On purpose questions, pay particular attention to the verbs in the answers. Choices (C) and (D) are too strong—the passage doesn't argue or prove anything. Choice (A) is close—the states were, in fact, impacted. But that doesn't answer the question, which is *why* the states were mentioned. There were included in the passage to show how significantly the Midwest and West were impacted by the locusts.

14. **C**   Choice (A) is a direct opposite of what is said in the passage. Choices (B) and (D) are not discussed in the passage at all. This leaves (C), which is directly supported by the second sentence of the paragraph.

15. **D**   The passage says that iron rails could not support heavy trains traveling fast, but it didn't give any indication about whether trains could go faster overall on iron or steel rails, so eliminate (A). The passage doesn't give any information about the cost of iron today, so the comparison in (B) can't be supported. While it might make sense that railroad executives would have opted to use steel rails if they had been less expensive, that's predicting the future, which is not provable—eliminate (C). The passage does say that steel was used to create small tools, and eating utensils could definitely be considered small tools. Choice (D), therefore, is the most likely to be true.

Part 5—Mathematics Knowledge

1. **D** An isosceles triangle has two equal sides and two equal angles. So, if one of the angles is 40, the other two angles must add up to 140 degrees. If the other two angles were equal, they would each be 70 degrees—but that's not in the answers. So, instead look at the answers and eliminate any that don't add to 140 degrees. This allows you to eliminate (A), (B), and (C).

2. **A** An octagon is a shape that has 8 sides and 8 corners. If Laura puts a bracket at each corner, she will need 8 brackets.

3. **C** When parallel lines are intersected by another line, three things happen: 1) you get big angles and small angles; 2) all the big angles are equal and all the small angles are equal; 3) any small angle plus any big angle will always equal 180 degrees. The given angle of 130° is a big angle and x is a small angle, so: $130 + x = 180$. Solve to find that $x = 50$.

4. **A** Subtract 5 from both sides to find that $7 > x$, which is the same as (A).

5. **D** Translate the question into math: "twice the sum" means "2 times something added together," which looks like this: 2(+   ). The two things being added together are the number of degrees in a triangle (180) and the number of degrees in a rectangle (360). So the final mathematical expression would be: 2(180 + 360). That becomes 2(540) = 1080.

6. **C** Multiply $3 \times 9 = 27$ to find the perimeter of the three-sided shape.

7. **D** Using FOIL, start by multiplying the first value in each expression: $x \times x = x^2$. All the answers have x^2, so no answers can be eliminated just yet. Then multiply the outsides: $x(-6) + (x)(4) = -2x$. Look at the answers to find that (A), (B), and (C) can all be eliminated.

8. **D** Remember the Pythagorean triples? They're in play here: 5-12-13. If you don't have the Pythagorean triples memorized, use the Pythagorean Theorem to solve: $5^2 + x^2 = 13^2$. Solve to find that $x = 12$.

9. **C** Plug in the values presented into the expression: $5^2 + 2(5) + 4(5)(-2) + 2(-2)^2$. Solve to find that this expression is equal to 67.

10. **A** Draw a rectangle and label it with sides that would yield an area of 48 square feet. Any of these values could work: 1×48, 2×24, 3×16, 4×12, 6×8. Let's say you used 6×8. The question says the sides have to be "halved," meaning cut in half. Now, the sides are 3 and 4. The new area is $3 \times 4 = 12$.

11. **C** Plug in values for the variables. Try $m = 10$ and $d = 20$. That means that 10 tickets cost \$20. At that rate, 5 tickets will cost \$10. That's your target. Then plug in 10 and 20 for the variables in the answers and find the answer choice that matches \$10. Choice (A) gives you $5(10)20 = 1000$, which doesn't match, so get rid of it. Choice (B) gives you $\frac{20 \times 10}{5} = 40$, which also doesn't match, so eliminate it. Choice (C) is $\frac{5 \times 20}{10} = 10$, so keep it. But remember to check all four answers. Choice (D) is $\frac{5 \times 10}{20} = 2.5$, which isn't 10, so eliminate it.

12. **B** The easiest way to tackle this question is to Plug In the Answers. Start with either (B) or (C), since they're in the middle. Choice (B) gives you $3(4)^2 + 8 = 14(4)$, or $3(16) + 8 = 14(4)$. 56 does equal 56, so (B) is the right answer.

13. **A** This is another question that you should attack by Plugging In the Answers. The answers represent the width, and the question says the length is 4 feet longer. So, start with (B) again. If the width is 20, then the length is 24. If you add all the sides together, you get $2(20) + 2(24) = 88$. That's more than the perimeter indicated in the question, so eliminate (B) and everything larger; the answer is (A).

14. **D** Use the formula $v = lwh$. Plug in the values given in the question and solve: $280 = 5(7)h$. Solve to find that $\frac{280}{35} = 8$, (D).

15. **D** The words "must also be" indicate that you'll likely need to plug in more than once. So plug in an even integer (try $n = 10$) into each answer choice. Choice (A) gives you $\frac{10 + 2}{2} = 6$, which is even, so keep it. Choice (B) gives you $\frac{10 + 2}{4} = 3$, which is odd, so eliminate it. Choice (C) becomes $10 + 1 = 11$, which is odd, so get rid of it. Choice (D) is $5(10) = 50$, which is even, so keep it. Now, plug in another even integer: try $n = 12$. Choice (A) becomes $\frac{12 + 2}{2} = 7$. That's odd, so eliminate it; the answer is (D).

16. **C** Draw a coordinate plane. Starting at the origin, or Brendan's starting point, go to the right (east) 6 units and then down (south) 8 units. Draw a point there and then draw a straight line from that point to the origin. Then draw a line from the point back up to the x-axis. You now have a right triangle with one leg of 6 and one leg of 8. Using the Pythagorean Theorem, you can solve for the hypotenuse: $6^2 + 8^2 = c^2$, $100 = c^2$, $10 = c$.

17. **D** The diameter of a circle is twice the radius, so if the diameter is 20, then the radius is 10. Use the formula for area of a circle to solve: $A = \pi r^2$. $A = \pi 10^2 = 100\pi$

18. **B** Translate from English to math: $30 = \left(\frac{x}{100}\right) \times 200$, or $2x = 30$. Divide both sides by 2 and find that $x = 15$.

19. **C** Remember to plug in any time the question has variables. Start with a value for Paige's age: $p = 10$. Colleen is five years older than Paige, or 15, and Colleen is also three years younger than Scott. That means Scott is 18. That's your target. Now plug $p = 10$ into the answers to find the one that equals 18. Choice (A) becomes $2(10) = 20$ which doesn't match—get rid of it. Choice (B) becomes $10 + 6 = 16$, which also doesn't match—get rid of it. Choice (C) becomes $10 + 8 = 18$, which does match. Remember to check (D): $10 + 10 = 20$, which doesn't match, so get rid of it.

20. **B** Translate from English into math: $x - 3 = \left(\dfrac{1}{4}\right)x$. Then Plug In the Answers, starting with (B) or (C). Since (B) is 4, it will be easier to work with than 5, since it's easier to find $\dfrac{1}{4}$ of 4 than $\dfrac{1}{4}$ of 5. So, using 4: $4 - 3 = \left(\dfrac{1}{4}\right)4$, or $1 = 1$. That's a true statement, so (B) is the answer.

21. **D** Use a proportion to solve. 1 inch = 12 feet, so set up the proportion like this: $\left(\dfrac{1\ inch}{12\ feet}\right) = \left(\dfrac{8\ inches}{x\ feet}\right)$. Cross-multiply to get $x = 96$.

22. **A** The thousandths place is the second one to the right of the decimal. Choice (A) is the only answer that has a 4 in the second place to the right of the decimal.

23. **D** Divide both sides of the equation by 7 to find that $\dfrac{91}{7} = 13$.

24. **B** Simplify $\sqrt{40}$ by asking yourself "What factors of 40 are perfect squares?" 4 is, and $\sqrt{4} = 2$. So bring the 2 to the outside of the expression and leave the remaining 10 inside ($40 = 4 \times 10$): $2 \times 3\sqrt{10}$. This turns into $6\sqrt{10}$.

25. **A** Write this out if you need to: $2^5 = 2 \times 2 \times 2 \times 2 \times 2 = 32$.

Part 6—Electronics Information

1.	**A**	11.	**B**
2.	**D**	12.	**C**
3.	**D**	13.	**A**
4.	**C**	14.	**B**
5.	**C**	15.	**B**
6.	**D**	16.	**B**
7.	**B**	17.	**C**
8.	**A**	18.	**D**
9.	**C**	19.	**B**
10.	**A**	20.	**A**

Part 7—Auto and Shop Information

1.	A	14.	A
2.	C	15.	B
3.	D	16.	D
4.	B	17.	A
5.	B	18.	D
6.	C	19.	A
7.	A	20.	C
8.	B	21.	B
9.	A	22.	D
10.	B	23.	A
11.	A	24.	A
12.	B	25.	C
13.	D		

Part 8—Mechanical Comprehension

1.	C	14.	D
2.	C	15.	A
3.	A	16.	D
4.	B	17.	C
5.	C	18.	B
6.	B	19.	A
7.	C	20.	D
8.	A	21.	D
9.	A	22.	C
10.	D	23.	C
11.	C	24.	D
12.	C	25.	A
13.	C		

NOTES

NOTES

NOTES

International Offices Listing

China (Beijing)
1501 Building A,
Disanji Creative Zone,
No.66 West Section of North 4th Ring Road Beijing
Tel: +86-10-62684481/2/3
Email: tprkor01@chol.com
Website: www.tprbeijing.com

China (Shanghai)
1010 Kaixuan Road
Building B, 5/F
Changning District, Shanghai, China 200052
Sara Beattie, Owner: Email: sbeattie@sarabeattie.com
Tel: +86-21-5108-2798
Fax: +86-21-6386-1039
Website: www.princetonreviewshanghai.com

Hong Kong
5th Floor, Yardley Commercial Building
1-6 Connaught Road West, Sheung Wan, Hong Kong
(MTR Exit C)
Sara Beattie, Owner: Email: sbeattie@sarabeattie.com
Tel: +852-2507-9380
Fax: +852-2827-4630
Website: www.princetonreviewhk.com

India (Mumbai)
Score Plus Academy
Office No.15, Fifth Floor
Manek Mahal 90
Veer Nariman Road
Next to Hotel Ambassador
Churchgate, Mumbai 400020
Maharashtra, India
Ritu Kalwani: Email: director@score-plus.com
Tel: + 91 22 22846801 / 39 / 41
Website: www.score-plus.com

India (New Delhi)
South Extension
K-16, Upper Ground Floor
South Extension Part–1,
New Delhi-110049
Aradhana Mahna: aradhana@manyagroup.com
Monisha Banerjee: monisha@manyagroup.com
Ruchi Tomar: ruchi.tomar@manyagroup.com
Rishi Josan: Rishi.josan@manyagroup.com
Vishal Goswamy: vishal.goswamy@manyagroup.com
Tel: +91-11-64501603/ 4, +91-11-65028379
Website: www.manyagroup.com

Lebanon
463 Bliss Street
AlFarra Building - 2nd floor
Ras Beirut
Beirut, Lebanon
Hassan Coudsi: Email: hassan.coudsi@review.com
Tel: +961-1-367-688
Website: www.princetonreviewlebanon.com

Korea
945-25 Young Shin Building
25 Daechi-Dong, Kangnam-gu
Seoul, Korea 135-280
Yong-Hoon Lee: Email: TPRKor01@chollian.net
In-Woo Kim: Email: iwkim@tpr.co.kr
Tel: + 82-2-554-7762
Fax: +82-2-453-9466
Website: www.tpr.co.kr

Kuwait
ScorePlus Learning Center
Salmiyah Block 3, Street 2 Building 14
Post Box: 559, Zip 1306, Safat, Kuwait
Email: infokuwait@score-plus.com
Tel: +965-25-75-48-02 / 8
Fax: +965-25-75-46-02
Website: www.scorepluseducation.com

Malaysia
Sara Beattie MDC Sdn Bhd
Suites 18E & 18F
18th Floor
Gurney Tower, Persiaran Gurney
Penang, Malaysia
Email: tprkl.my@sarabeattie.com
Sara Beattie, Owner: Email: sbeattie@sarabeattie.com
Tel: +604-2104 333
Fax: +604-2104 330
Website: www.princetonreviewKL.com

Mexico
TPR México
Guanajuato No. 242 Piso 1 Interior 1
Col. Roma Norte
México D.F., C.P.06700
registro@princetonreviewmexico.com
Tel: +52-55-5255-4495
+52-55-5255-4440
+52-55-5255-4442
Website: www.princetonreviewmexico.com

Qatar
Score Plus
Office No: 1A, Al Kuwari (Damas)
Building near Merweb Hotel, Al Saad
Post Box: 2408, Doha, Qatar
Email: infoqatar@score-plus.com
Tel: +974 44 36 8580, +974 526 5032
Fax: +974 44 13 1995
Website: www.scorepluseducation.com

Taiwan
The Princeton Review Taiwan
2F, 169 Zhong Xiao East Road, Section 4
Taipei, Taiwan 10690
Lisa Bartle (Owner): lbartle@princetonreview.com.tw
Tel: +886-2-2751-1293
Fax: +886-2-2776-3201
Website: www.PrincetonReview.com.tw

Thailand
The Princeton Review Thailand
Sathorn Nakorn Tower, 28th floor
100 North Sathorn Road
Bangkok, Thailand 10500
Thavida Bijayendrayodhin (Chairman)
Email: thavida@princetonreviewthailand.com
Mitsara Bijayendrayodhin (Managing Director)
Email: mitsara@princetonreviewthailand.com
Tel: +662-636-6770
Fax: +662-636-6776
Website: www.princetonreviewthailand.com

Turkey
Yeni Sülün Sokak No. 28
Levent, Istanbul, 34330, Turkey
Nuri Ozgur: nuri@tprturkey.com
Rona Ozgur: rona@tprturkey.com
Iren Ozgur: iren@tprturkey.com
Tel: +90-212-324-4747
Fax: +90-212-324-3347
Website: www.tprturkey.com

UAE
Emirates Score Plus
Office No: 506, Fifth Floor
Sultan Business Center
Near Lamcy Plaza, 21 Oud Metha Road
Post Box: 44098, Dubai
United Arab Emirates
Hukumat Kalwani: skoreplus@gmail.com
Ritu Kalwani: director@score-plus.com
Email: info@score-plus.com
Tel: +971-4-334-0004
Fax: +971-4-334-0222
Website: www.princetonreviewuae.com

Our International Partners

The Princeton Review also runs courses with a variety of
partners in Africa, Asia, Europe, and South America.

Georgia
LEAF American-Georgian Education Center
www.leaf.ge

Mongolia
English Academy of Mongolia
www.nyescm.org

Nigeria
The Know Place
www.knowplace.com.ng

Panama
Academia Interamericana de Panama
http://aip.edu.pa/

Switzerland
Institut Le Rosey
http://www.rosey.ch/

All other inquiries, please email us at
internationalsupport@review.com